GLOBAL PERSPECTIVES ON HEALTH CARE

Eugene B. Gallagher, Editor
University of Kentucky

Janardan Subedi, Editor
Miami University (Ohio)

Prentice Hall, Englewood Cliffs, New Jersey 07632

Library of Congress Cataloging-in-Publication Data
Global perspectives on health care / Eugene B. Gallagher and Janardan
    Subedi, editors.
        p.   cm.
    Includes bibliographical references and index.
    ISBN 0-13-315078-X (paper)
    1. Social medicine.   2. Medical policy.   I. Gallagher, Eugene B.
II. Subedi, Janardan.
    RA418.G53   1995
362.1—dc20
                                            94-35679
                                            CIP

Acquisitions Editor: Nancy Roberts
Production Editor: Alison Gnerre
Copy Editor: Pam Price
Cover Design: DeLuca Design
Buyer: Mary Ann Gloriande
Editorial Assistant: Pat Naturale

© 1995 by Prentice-Hall, Inc.
A Simon & Schuster Company
Englewood Cliffs, NJ 07632

Printed in the United States of America
10 9 8 7 6 5 4 3 2 1

ISBN   0-13-315078-X

Prentice-Hall International (UK) Limited, London
Prentice-Hall of Australia Pty. Limited, Sydney
Prentice-Hall Canada Inc., Toronto
Prentice-Hall Hispanoamericana, S.A., Mexico
Prentice-Hall of India Private Limited, New Delhi
Prentice-Hall of Japan, Inc., Tokyo
Simon & Schuster Asia Pte. Ltd., Singapore
Editora Prentice-Hall do Brasil, Ltda., Rio de Janeiro

Contents

chapter 1

chapter 2

chapter 15

RATIONING MEDICAL RESOURCES: FROM ADVOCACY TO ALLOCATION IN BRITISH AND AMERICAN NURSES, 244

Donna V. Stevenson, Richard M. Levinson, and Nancy J. Thompson

chapter 16

MAJOR ORIENTATIONS IN JAPANESE HEALTH CARE, 255

T. Neal Garland

chapter 17

SOCIETY AND INDIGENOUS HEALTH CARE: THE CASES OF NEPAL AND ALASKA, 268

Janardan Subedi, Nancy Andes, and Sree Subedi

chapter 18

A COMPARISON OF NURSE ASSISTANTS IN NURSING HOMES IN THE UNITED STATES AND WARD ASSISTANTS FOR THE ELDERLY IN GHANA, 277

Dorothy J. Blackmon, Lawrence A. Kannae, and T. Neal Garland

chapter 19

INTERNATIONAL DEPENDENCY AND HEALTH: A COMPARATIVE CASE STUDY OF CUBA AND THE DOMINICAN REPUBLIC, 292

Annette M. Schwabe

PART VI   GLOBAL THEMES   311

chapter 20

RISK EVALUATION OF MEDICAL TECHNOLOGY IN GLOBAL POPULATION CONTROL, 312

Ingar Palmlund

chapter 21

About the Contributors

James G. Anderson is professor of sociology, Purdue University, West Lafayette, Indiana.

Nancy Andes is associate professor, University of Alaska, Anchorage.

Dorothy J. Blackmon is affiliated with the Department of Sociology, University of Akron, Akron, Ohio. Her areas of specialization are urban sociology and gerontology.

Nancy Halsted Bryant formerly served as Director of Nursing, Aga Khan University, Karachi, Pakistan. Her current research interest is the role of women in nursing in Islamic societies.

Joan Ferrante is associate professor, Department of Sociology, Northern Kentucky University, Highland Heights, Kentucky.

Eugene B. Gallagher is professor of medical sociology in the Departments of Behavioral Science and Sociology, University of Kentucky, Lexington, Kentucky.

T. Neal Garland is professor of sociology, University of Akron, Akron, Ohio, specializing in medical sociology and sociology of the family.

Ofra Greenberg is an affiliate lecturer, Open University, Israel.

Frederic W. Hafferty is professor, Department of Behavioral Sciences, University of Minnesota, Duluth, Minnesota.

Melissa Penn Jameson is resource specialist, Center for Global Education, Cuernavaca, Morelos, Mexico.

Ezekiel Kalipeni is visiting assistant professor of geography and coordinator of the African Studies Program, Colgate University, Hamilton, New York.

Lawrence A. Kannae is instructor in sociology, Department of Sociology, University of Akron, Akron, Ohio.

Ande Kidanemariam is a lecturer, Department of Sociology, University of Kentucky, Lexington, Kentucky.

Anuradha Kumar is currently affiliated with the Special Programme of Research, Development, and Research Training in Human Reproduction, World Health Organization, Geneva, Switzerland.

Richard M. Levinson is associate professor, Division of Behavioral Sciences and Health Education, Emory University School of Public Health, Atlanta, Georgia.

Irina V. McKeehan is adjunct professor of sociology, European Division (Germany), University of Maryland and President, Inter-PR., Nyack, New York.

Renee Oscarson is a doctoral candidate in child development and family studies, Purdue University, West Lafayette, Indiana.

Ingar Palmlund is associate professor, Department of Technology and Social Change, Linkoping University, and research associate, Department of International Health Care Research, Karolinska Institutet, Sweden.

Annette M. Schwabe is a doctoral candidate, Department of Sociology, Kent State University, Kent, Ohio.

Kodjo A. Senah is a lecturer, Department of Sociology, University of Ghana, Legon-Accra, Ghana.

Margaret Sherrard Sherraden is assistant professor, Department of Social Work and research associate, Center for Public Policy, University of Missouri, St. Louis, Missouri.

Judith T. Shuval is Louis and Pearl Rose Professor of Medical Sociology, Hebrew University of Jerusalem, Israel.

James V. Spickard is assistant professor of sociology, Department of Sociology and Anthropology, University of Redlands, Redlands, California.

Donna V. Stevenson is research nurse, Grady Memorial Hospital, Atlanta, Georgia.

Sree Subedi is assistant professor of sociology, Miami University at Hamilton, Ohio.

Janardan Subedi is assistant professor, Department of Sociology and Anthropology, Miami University, Oxford, Ohio.

Nancy J. Thompson is assistant professor of behavioral sciences and epidemiology, Emory University School of Public Health, Atlanta, Georgia.

Yan Yu is a doctoral candidate in sociology, Purdue University, West Lafayette, Indiana.

Introduction

Eugene B. Gallagher
Janardan Subedi

Scientific medicine is turning into a global institution, widely practiced and widely sought in remote locales as well as in the metropolises of the world. As it diffuses and envelopes the globe, it is at the same time transforming human perceptions and values concerning illness, health, and life itself. Besides being a valued modality for coping with disease and disability, scientific medicine is a symbol of modern aspirations, displacing traditional attitudes of passive resignation. Beyond its symbolic meanings, scientific medicine is also a complex institution—a network of linked professional roles, organizational forms, financial outlays, resource flows, and accretions of biomedical knowledge and practical technology. In industrialized societies and developing societies alike, it must compete, and sometimes compromise, with older doctrines and entrenched techniques. Occasionally, in developing countries, it moves into a virtual vacuum and quickly establishes its hegemony as the only avenue back to health for those in illness.

The foregoing considerations strongly suggest that the social sciences should be useful for understanding medicine and health care. Disease always has a sociocultural and an environmental context; thus, for example, the infantile diarrhea that is prevalent in developing societies is strongly associated with poverty as a sociocultural fact and with contaminated drinking water as a daily environmental reality. In the treatment of illness, the patient's own understanding and participation are often an essential part of the treatment. This is as true in mass public health campaigns as it is in individualized clinical medicine—and as much for chronic illness as for acute illness.

Textbooks of scientific medicine and manuals of treatment give the tacit impression that medicine simply applies itself. (Since Dr. Albert Sabin made a live-virus vaccine for polio in 1960, that takes care of polio, doesn't it?) But the history of medicine is one thing, and the real-world delivery of health care is another. Medicine does not apply itself separately from the social, cultural, economic, and environmental forces that bear upon the patient. Further, whatever the high esteem in which the doctor stands, he or she is far from being a god-like, omnipotent figure. Even in medically bounteous milieux, doctors must learn to cope with varied social expectations, material conditions, and environmental constraints.

To suppose that medicine simply applies itself, via an automatic, transparent implementation of bioscientific knowledge, is a vast oversimplification of what goes on in medicine. Many things must be brought to bear upon the patient's illness and distress—the doctor's understanding and treatment resources; the scientific and technological base of modern medicine; reliable, accessible medical-recordkeeping; the hospitals, clinical laboratories, clinics, village dispensaries, and other settings of health care. All of these must transpire, in the right balance and timing, for effective care to occur.

Medical sociologists, anthropologists, geographers, public health experts, health policy analysts, and other social scientists are formulating concepts and research approaches for studying medicine practically, in its sociocultural contexts and connections. The growing focus on health and health care is a dynamic frontier in the contemporary social sciences as the trend of publications, professional meetings, organizational development, and academic instruction all indicate. This book grows out of that ferment. As the reader will see, it dips into, and draws forth from, a range of social sciences in order to compose a distinctive, timely picture of health care in a global framework.

In gathering manuscripts for *Global Perspectives on Health Care* and its contrasting companion book (*Culture, Medicine, and Illness: Transcultural Perspectives*, edited by Jan Subedi and Eugene B. Gallagher, also published by Prentice-Hall), we worked through many channels—academic conferences, professional societies, newsletters, and journals, as well as personal contacts. We decided to cast our net broadly in order to obtain fresh manuscripts from active investigators who may at present be relatively unknown. We also sought the somewhat more predictable contributions coming from seasoned investigators who have been engaged in international and cross-cultural studies for many years. We also hoped that our net would stretch to investigators in Third-World countries who are doing good work under difficult conditions. We were not disappointed in this hope.

We also decided on a broad approach in regard to range of content. In an evocative rather than definitive casting of topics, we told potential contributors that the following were of interest:

- gender and ethnic differentials in health status and medical care
- social factors in the production of disease
- planning and implementation of national primary health care programs
- health services in rural and metropolitan areas
- health status and medical care of refugee and migrant populations
- medical care under conditions of societal dislocation
- health professionals in the social structure of developing countries
- health professional education
- international migration of health professionals
- economic barriers to the delivery of health services
- social and cultural factors in the diagnosis and treatment of disease and disability
- diffusion of health care technology

The response to our search for manuscripts was rapid and handsome. It suggested that this book and its companion have come at a timely moment for social science and international health. We received many excellent submissions, on relevant topics that we would not have thought of ourselves, from many scholars both inside and outside the U.S. and concerning health care in both developing and industrialized countries.

We had originally intended to publish a single book. However, looking at the solid merit and the rich patterning of the many manuscripts submitted to us, we decided to publish two books. Both books would be deeply, and equally, suffused with international substance and outlook. However, this book (Gallagher and Subedi, editors) would deal primarily with **health care**; in contrast, the Subedi-Gallagher book would deal primarily with **health behavior**.

Health care is at the center of *Global Perspectives on Health Care*. We intend **health care** to be an all-embracing term. It includes what doctors do (sometimes denominated as "medical care") as well as what nurses, herbalists, and folk healers do—and, at a broader remove, the work of health policymakers and biomedical scientists. It includes professional and lay care directed at people in good health as well as care directed to people who are ill. It is not confined to decisive, biomedically proved interventions but includes other responses that are intended to diagnose or assess health/illness status, to tend to the sick, to manage illness, to prevent it, to assist with disabilities, to pursue rehabilitation goals—and, not least, to establish or organize the frameworks of resources and personnel within which these diverse elements of care can be coordinated and delivered.

THE SECTIONS OF THIS BOOK

As an analytic structure for viewing the contents of this book, we have organized the text into six parts: Part I, Culture and Biomedicine; Part II, Ethnomedicine; Part III, Sociopolitical and Regional Dimensions; Part IV, Societal Dislocation; Part V, Comparative Studies; and Part VI, Global Themes. These groupings reflect theoretical emphases and concepts that are used by other researchers and scholars in the social sciences. They have special pertinence to the study of health care.

Next we will give the reader a critical preview of the chapters in the six sections.

Part I. Culture and Biomedicine

Culture has been variously characterized as a "comprehensive design for living," "the human system of symbols, values, ideas, and beliefs," and "a way of life, cues for action, and logic for reasoning for the members of a cultural community." We find particularly keen the idea that a particular culture is, to any member of the community that it embraces, as difficult to describe and to analyze as the water in a goldfish bowl would be for the goldfish who swims about in it. Culture is in us and all around us. If anything was made to be taken for granted, it is culture. Our social expectations, everyday routines, and modes of expression partake deeply of it; if forced to, we can bring to consciousness and articulation some knowledge of these basics of our lives, but it is not easy.

What people in a community do when confronted with bodily discomforts, pain, disease, and disabilities is very much a matter of their culturally shaped beliefs. At the forefront are their beliefs about the nature and causes of, and remedies for, pathology; why it is I rather than you (or we rather than they) who have fallen ill; why now rather than then; and especially what the authority, rationale, logic, and vindication for our beliefs may be. Culture tells us more than this, however. It also evaluates the intersection of the illness with the ill person characterized by his status in the community, gender, age category, vocation, lifestyle, vulnerability to illness, and suitability for various kinds of alleviation and remedy. Culture also tells us who and what to turn to for diagnosis and treatment, and it regulates our hopes and anticipations regarding the relief of our distress.

The foregoing statements are a highly compressed idealization of health beliefs and practices as the product of culture. The implication that there is a single such set of beliefs and practices prevalent within a given community may have been true at one time, but it no longer holds for the increasingly multifarious, pluralistic global community. In actual fact, there are various differentiated domains of health belief and practice that within modern communities stand in relations of competition, coexistence, complementarity, and dominance. Among these domains is scientific medicine.

"Biomedicine," or so-called "scientific," "modern," "Western" or "cosmopolitan" medicine, is a relatively coherent belief system that has grown up within the past 150 years and has spread outward from Europe into many non-European nations and cultures. The five chapters in Part I look at the place of scientific medicine in several cultures. These chapters provide fresh material for inspection and debate by social scientists seeking to understand the place of medicine in society. The questions and issues they pose have to do with whether scientific medicine considered solely as a belief system changes exclusively by the accretion of new knowledge and technology, or whether, inserted into non-Western cultures, its scientific tenets concerning basic mechanisms of pathology are altered at a deeper level.

Equally important are questions of how the scientific knowledge embodied in scientific medicine is expressed and implemented. For example, if there were an oversupply of doctors or physicians in a given society, could they, by themselves, do all the medical work, patient care, and operation of medical apparatus and technology that are currently carried out by other health workers? How important is access for all members of society to medical care based upon scientific medicine? If it is deemed to be a high priority, then what obstacles hinder universal access, and how can they be reduced? How can scientific medicine be rescued from its own excesses and pathologies—its brusqueness, its rationalized hyperefficiency, its frequent failure to incorporate the "patient's point of view"? These questions pass over the actual knowledge base of scientific medicine but go the heart of its implementation—the cultural matrix of understandings and priorities concern the provision and receipt of modern medical care.

Anuradha Kumar's chapter, "Gender and Health: Theoretical Versus Practical Accessibility of Health Care for Women in North India," rises fresh from her field research in rural Rajastan. From her intimate knowledge of the lived experiences of village women, she finds that although there may be no "theoretical" objection to the appropriateness for women of scientific medicine as given at a Primary Health Centre, there are tremendous practical obstacles. The steady burden of daily responsibility for household, children, husband, and other relatives, plus the *purdah* proprieties governing the movement of females through public space, even to relieve serious health problems—these, coupled with prevalent poverty, are the daily reality of the women. From her observations, Kumar has no difficulty demonstrating the effects—in the main, adverse effects—of culture on the life of the women.

"Japan's Health Care System: Western and East Asian Influences," by James G. Anderson, Renee Oscarson, and Yan Yu, is an important contribution to the continuing effort of Western social scientists to understand Japan. How can Japanese people be so "Western," so highly organized, and so fast-track in electronic and computer technology and yet still read, write, and speak *Japanese*? Why does Japan continue to be an enigmatic culture of dutiful deference and circumspect patience in interpersonal relationships? Anderson and colleagues explore this in the health care ambience. They show how the cultural context influences the role of the patient and the role of the doctor in Japan. They also argue that the cultural shaping of the provider roles allows the provider to be at once both "scientific" and "personal." Japanese doctors are trained in, and practice, scientific medicine but they do so in a style that addresses many needs that patients have for personal recognition and affiliation. Reading between the lines of Chapter 2 also makes one wonder whether the sheer residential stability of Japanese families, and of providers in their practice sites, is not in itself a factor that promotes solidarity between patients and their doctors.

Nancy H. Bryant's chapter, "Progress and Constraints of Nursing and Nursing Education in Islamic Societies," reviews the history and present status of nursing in the Middle East. She makes it clear that the nursing profession faces obstacles there. From her position as a nurse educator at Aga Khan University in Karachi, Pakistan, she is well situated to take up the topic. The obstacles do not come from cultural resistance to Western medicine as a belief system, nor do they stem from the division of labor in medicine and medical care. Most people who think about it do believe that nurses are a necessary and valuable component of health professional manpower. The sticking point is something like, "Yes, nurses are important but I do not want my daughter to become one."

This sentiment, felt and voiced in thousands of Middle Eastern families, becomes a conservative bulwark against the training of nurses, and against the organization and progress of nursing as a profession. The sentiment, at once protective and restrictive regarding the participation of women in society, is of course far from unknown in Western nations; it was in fact common 100 years ago but much less so nowadays. Bryant's observations concerning women as providers of health care echo Kumar's views regarding women as recipients of health care. In both cases, a deeper understanding of the cultural constraints can yield insights concerning points of leverage for helping women to improve their situation and gain new opportunities.

Sree Subedi and Janardan Subedi portray biomedicine as a powerful social institution in a poor developing country in their chapter, "Dominance and Elitism: The Modern Health Care System in Nepal." Despite its social power, however, its impact is restricted to the urban, educated elite of Nepal—those able to afford its services, which are available mainly in the private section. They show how the modern health care system in Nepal rests upon the interlocking of the medical profession, hospitals, pharmaceutical companies, and the nation's one medical school. The picture they paint is unflinchingly honest in its depiction of professional greed, incompetence, and corruption. The majority of Nepalis—poor, rural, uneducated—get very little benefit from modern medicine. One can only hope that sooner or later a stronger spirit of public service will animate the government and the medical profession in policies and practice concerning medicine.

Eugene B. Gallagher's chapter, "Culture and Technology in Health Care, as Exemplified in Gulf Arab Medicine," examines dominant characteristics of Arab culture in their bearing upon the giving and receiving of medical care. It draws upon his ethnographic work in three Gulf Arab societies and his teaching experience in their medical schools, to construct a picture of current medical care there. He finds that Gulf Arab medicine is highly technology-dependent and asks how this affects the doctor-patient relationship.

Part II. Ethnomedicine

In all societies, some indeterminate portion of the total of health care delivered lies outside the realm of biomedicine. This "nonscientific" portion actually spans a wider array of theories, schools of thought, techniques, and practitioners than does scientific medicine. There is no settled system of terminology for designating the complexity and variety of phenomena to be found in the nonscientific zone. Among the terms commonly used are: ethnomedicine, traditional medicine, complementary medicine, popular medicine, folk medicine, and alternative medicine. This lexicon, however, is not simply different words for exactly the same thing; instead, they move in somewhat different, though partially overlapping directions.

Folk medicine and popular medicine point to remedies and treatments that are in the prescientific vernacular of many societies. They include the prevailing "granny cures," the potions, ointments, and nostrums based on locally available plant, animal, and mineral substances—the superstitious practices and the magical rites found in many parts of the world. Frequently called folk medicine, the theoretically sophisticated Hippocratic humoral doctrine—that illness and healing depend on the balance of hot/cold and wet/dry elements and that the microcosm of the body must for health be in equilibrium with the macrocosm of the environment—has widespread application in Latin America, Asia, Mediterranean societies, and elsewhere.

Alternative medicine is a term that has come into vogue within the past two decades. Depending on one's point of view, alternative medicine is a good thing or a bad thing. To scientific medical orthodoxy, alternative medicine connotes humbug, fraud, charlatanism, and quackery; it is an object of derision. Short of condemnation, however, alternative medicine can be used as a neutral term to designate theories and techniques that, though not traditional, lie outside the realm of science and that seek cures and healing which go beyond the established biomedical provenance. In a different mode, alternative medicine stands as a critique of the shortcomings of contemporary medical practice. Chiropractic, with its heavy reliance upon manual technique, is sometimes regarded as a form of alternative medicine—a form that achieves its results by establishing a healing tactile bond between professional and patient. However, other alternative practitioners are even more focused upon touch and massage than are chiropractors. Holistic medicine and complementary medicine are yet other related terms used to designate a wide array of contemporary techniques and theories outside scientific medicine. Alternative, complementary, and holistic medicine are strongest in modern societies that already possess substantial resources for the delivery of biomedical services; they often flourish in the shadow of biomedicine.

We use the somewhat technical, academic term "ethnomedicine" to designate this section. We use it to mean roughly the same thing as conveyed by the terms traditional and folk medicine. Those terms, however, have the connotation of something static and hallowed. This connotation is misleading because new meanings and techniques do accrue in this realm. For example, the phenomenon of AIDS in Africa, known as the "slim disease" (i.e. wasting) there, has led many traditional healers to compound new potions and salves, not part of their inherited armamentarium, to deal with it.

In this section, Ofra Greenberg's chapter, "The Case of Hannah Azulai, Illustrating the Confluence of Western and Folk Medicine in an Israeli Immigrant Community," pays particular attention to the role of the patient's relatives when the patient consults a non-scientific healer—in the case she describes, religious healers. It is a well-known, sometimes lamented fact that Western biomedicine has little imagination concerning the potentially constructive role of family members, and that in hospitals the family is frequently regarded as being "in the way," interfering with the accomplishment of proper, efficient care and treatment of the patient. Reciprocally, the patient's family relinquishes, sometimes with relief, full responsibility for dealing with the patient. In contrast, the family is more closely and continuously involved in the patient's dealing with traditional healers, as the case of Hannah Azulai clearly shows.

Greenberg's study was conducted in Israel, a modern welfare state with no history of strong colonial dominion, even though it was for many years under British occupation. Kodjo A. Senah's chapter, "Ethnomedicine in the Context of Health Care Delivery in Ghana," stands in striking contrast. Senah's theme is the competitive, somewhat precarious position of traditional healing in Ghana vis-à-vis biomedicine. During British colonial administration, traditional healing was politically and ideologically suppressed as a backward and vestigial remnant of primitive society. Today, although Ghana has been independent for many years and respects its African heritage, traditional healers do not enjoy official favor. Programs of systematic research into indigenous medicine, a mainstay of Ghanaian ethnomedicine, have had only episodic support.

Part III. Sociopolitical and Regional Dimensions

Health care intersects with politics at many points. One such point is the formal legitimation of medical/healing activities. Practitioners of the medical arts are more likely to be given, and be required to have, official sanction than cobblers or secretaries because of the gravity of health/illness issues for individuals and society as a whole. Medical doctors, nurses, and dentists, as representatives of scientific medicine, are the practitioner categories most likely to be licensed. Other categories may or may not be licensed; unlicensed practitioners may in fact be quite numerous and play an important part in the total health care delivery apparatus. In a related fashion, government may play an important part in evaluating the adequacy of institutions for training health professionals and the safety/efficacy of various treatment modalities, especially medicines.

Another point of connection between government and health care can be seen in publicly funded medicine. In some societies, publicly funded medicine constitutes virtually the whole of health care; that is, the central and/or provincial government employs the practitioners and provides the hospitals, equipment, and medicines for treatment. It should be understood that what is referred to here as "publicly funded medicine" not only includes, but also extends well beyond, the traditional domain of public health. The latter has traditionally been concerned with the prevention of infectious diseases, sanitary provision and, more recently, the distribution of vaccines and the health education of the public, especially in maternal/child health. Government appropriation pays for virtually everything in public health, but in many countries it also pays for most of clinical medicine, in which individual practitioners treat individual patients for identified pathologies (i.e., not in a preventive mode).

The United States goes very far in the opposite direction, by giving great scope to "market medicine." Although almost half of medical care in the United States is paid for by government at local, state, and national levels, government is in the position of paying many private practitioners, community hospitals, and for-profit providers who offer their services on a relatively free market.

Developing countries present their own special version of publicly funded health care systems. Usually there is a strong bias toward hospital-based rather than clinic- or office-based medical care. There is also a strong metropolitan bias that leads to a severe shortage of health care in rural areas. Many developing countries have a low standard of living and a relatively modest annual per capita expenditure on health care of all varieties. Discrimination against rural regions, which are, as a rule, also the more impoverished part of the nation, has the effect of accentuating the already extreme inequalities within the population in access to essential resources in living.

The extremes of maldistribution and inequality found in developing countries fall within a rubric that can be called "the political geography of health." The phenomenon of unequal access is also a convenient basis for reminding ourselves of the obvious yet overlooked point that health care depends for its delivery not only upon highly specialized resources but also upon a general infrastructure of transportation, communication, adequate living standards, political stability, and population literacy. Some of the requirements and predisposing assets for health care are tangible, such as good roads for the movement of patients and practitioners, refrigeration for perishable drugs, and sterile conditions in hospitals and clinics; others are relatively intangible, such as population literacy and community attitudes that see good health as a nonaccidental, relatively achievable public asset (in other words, not a matter of fate or chance).

It is against this backdrop that the three chapters in Part III assume their significance.

Margaret S. Sherraden's chapter, "Development of Health Policy and Services for Rural Mexico," focuses upon health service in rural Mexico. In an historical vein she shows that the democratic goals of the Mexican constitution concerning health care for the rural peasantry have been slow in achieving realization. Nevertheless, cumulative progress has been made in episodic jolts, especially within the past fifteen years. A large majority of Mexican villages now have at least minimal health services, and the growing disparity between city and countryside has been diminished. Mexican incrementalism offers a policy alternative in Latin America to models found in Cuba, Costa Rica, and Chile.

Ande Kidanemariam's chapter, "Health and Development in the Third World: The Political Economy of Infant Mortality in Brazil," is a study in political economy applied to health care. He begins with the empirical observation that Brazil's infant mortality rate is "too high" for the country's general level of industrial development. To account for the discrepancy, he turns to world system/dependency conceptions and state/society relationships, showing that the benefits of industrialization in Brazil have been highly concentrated among a small urban upper and upper-middle class. The ruling party in Brazil has subscribed to a "trickle-down" theory of economic development that, in practice, means the perpetuation of privilege and oligarchy, with dire consequences for the welfare of the majority. Infant mortality is a particularly sensitive indicator of poverty and lack of access to health services; it was for that reason chosen by the author for focused analysis.

Ezekiel Kalipeni's chapter, "Demographic and Spatial Aspects of the Health Care Delivery System in Malawi," adopts an explicit geographic/spatial perspective in looking at health care in Malawi. He shows that health care in Malawi has been, and remains, in a precarious position, reflected in high rates of infant mortality, maternal mortality, AIDS, and tuberculosis. Part of the problem lies in rigid, overly centralized policy formulation and implementation; Kalipeni believes that a more decentralized approach, in line with the WHO's "Health for All by the Year 2000," will be more fruitful for the rural majority of the population.

Part IV. Societal Dislocation

The systematic study of health care as a differentiated social structure or subsystem, as well as a dynamic process in society, goes back not more than forty or fifty years. This field of study emerged within the social sciences as the object of its scrutiny—the health care system—became a more important part of society, consuming more resources, yielding more benefits, and responding to rising public concerns about health and expectations of benefit. Attention has been drawn to how society supports a rapidly evolving, resource-consuming health care system much more than to how the health care system responds to changes in society.

Indeed, in the social study of health care, an assumption has implicitly prevailed that society remains static while health care progresses under the pressure of biomedical innovation and the broadening of access to previously unserved groups. Or if not viewed as absolutely static, society in its relevance for health care is viewed as unfolding in predictable modes that lie within the comfortable habitude of social scientists. These modes include industrialization, urbanization, the gradual spread of education and literacy, in short, the interrelated, orderly changes encapsulated in the ideas of societal progress and modernization.

Upheaving, violent, precipitous changes are more difficult for social scientists to accommodate within their conceptual armamentarium. However, precisely because of the mounting social importance of health care, it is important that we attend to it here. Under the rubric of "societal dislocation," we examine how health care is valued, organized, and delivered in disrupted, catastrophic circumstances such as war, societal collapse, environmental disaster, and massive population uprooting.

Irina V. McKeehan's chapter, "Planning of National Primary Health Care and Prevention Programs: The First Health Insurance Law of Russia, 1991–93" belongs to the early wave of reports on health care in Russia following the political collapse of the Soviet Union in 1991. Her account shows that the new Russian government intends, in the face of radical politico-economic *perestroika*, to maintain the earlier concept of health care as a basic human right. But instead of the earlier panoply of direct government services, health care will be rendered under the auspices of employment-based health insurance. Physicians and most other health professionals no longer will be civil servants of the Ministry of Health; instead, they will be self-employed or they will function as the employees of organizations that contract with insurance plans. None of these ambitious designs is achieving rapid or smooth implementation: McKeehan makes it clear that this is a difficult transition for the public, the health professions, and the government.

Israel's approach and record in bringing modern health care to a continuing influx of immigrants form the crux of Judith T. Shuval's chapter, "Migrants, Refugees, and Health: Some Policy Implications of Israel's Experience." She discusses the difficulties of communication across the cultural gaps that typically separate Israel's health professionals from the recipient populations. She argues that Israel's experience may contain valuable lessons for other nations that will serve as host countries for a mounting tide of persons worldwide who are migrating from economic privation, ethnic strife, and political upheaval.

The final chapter in this section, "Postwar Health Care in Rural El Salvador: Healing the Wounds of War," deals with the most severe dislocations in health care. In this chapter, James V. Spickard and Melissa P. Jameson study the aftermath of the brutal and devastating twelve-year civil war in El Salvador. There health care was, far from being a fundamental right or a purchasable service, a weapon of war. The central government and the military, attempting to weaken the resistance forces in the countryside, systematically prevented health personnel and medicines from slipping through the porous boundaries of guerilla insurrection. Their analysis suggests patterns that will no doubt come to light as more information becomes available concerning current civil strife in Afghanistan, Angola, Peru, Somalia, and the former Yugoslavia.

Part V. Comparative Studies

The comparative study of health care delivery and health care systems is an emerging subfield for investigators in the social sciences of health. There is no single methodological or conceptual approach, nor even one central question motivating this new subfield, but it is nevertheless a natural and necessary development in the study of health care. One common line of comparison is suggested by current efforts in many countries toward cost-containment in health care. In this vein, a comparative thrust might well address the question: per unit of input (whether monetary or real, such as an hour of physician time), which of two or more countries has the greater output (as measured in services performed, or in ultimate results such as national life-expectancy)?

Other fruitful kinds of comparison can focus on the similarities and differences in the implementation of specific technologies across nations. Dental care, treatment for chronic renal failure, and treatment for AIDS, to take three examples, all involve a relatively finite set of diagnostic and treatment techniques, yet they vary in their organization and delivery in different societies, depending partly on the economics of treatment, professional styles, and other factors. Another critical realm of comparison concerns the relationship of modern medicine, conceived as a relatively self-contained entity, to the premodern and contemporary "alternative" forms of health care that are found in virtually every society.

Much of value can be gleaned from such investigations. On the scientific level, they can lead to deeper understanding of the "comparative anatomy" of society. In the study of health policy, they can lead to fresh approaches in the design of health administration and organization, in ways of improving the delivery of services, and in methods of conceptualizing and measuring resource inputs into, and result outputs from, health care systems.

In Part V, we present six studies that represent widely varied grapplings with comparative issues.

Frederic W. Hafferty's chapter, "Medicine as a Profession: Lessons from Some Cross-National Case Studies," enlarges the scope of work on medicine as a profession that began in the United States in the 1970s. His chapter draws upon fifteen national case studies. He also introduces and refines the notion of secular dynamics in the relation of the medical profession to society (especially the political domain). Thus he traces out phases of medical ascendance, maintenance, and decline and relates them to changes in the political and social fabric in the nations under examination.

The chapter by Donna V. Stevenson, Richard M. Levinson, and Nancy J. Thompson, "Rationing Medical Resources: From Advocacy to Allocation in British and American Nurses," takes up the issue of "advocacy versus allocation," which refers to two divergent stances of health care providers (the physician especially). Should the provider ignore expense and advocate the use of all possible resources on behalf of the patient—or should the provider be content to work within a system of allocation or rationing that, at a higher level of control, channels and limits resources for individual patients? These investigators found, contrary to their expectations, that American nurses were generally more favorable toward rationing than British nurses.

T. Neal Garland's chapter, "Major Orientations in Japanese Health Care," reaches conclusions surprising to those of us who think of Japanese society as being homogeneous and conformist by comparison with American society. In his study of Japanese health care, he finds the opposite to be true. Although modern medicine has come to be the predominant means of health care in Japan, so-called *kanpo* medicine, derived from traditional Chinese medicine, remains viable and widespread. Moreover, everything else acquired by Japan from other cultures, both modern medicine and *kanpo*, have been substantially altered as they have become integrated into Japanese culture.

Janardan Subedi, Nancy Andes, and Sree Subedi deal with two strongly contrasting societies—Nepal and Alaska—in their chapter, "Society and Indigenous Health Care: The Cases of Nepal and Alaska." Despite their geographic differences, both societies have many remote rural areas and both have flourishing systems of indigenous health care that coexist with modern medicine. The provision of health care in Alaska is affected to a marked degree by social organizational factors pertaining to the Alaska state government and the U.S. Federal Bureau of Indian Affairs. Public health outreach and government policy are less marked in Nepal; traditional medical cultures are still predominant in many outlying communities.

Dorothy J. Blackmon, Lawrence A. Kannae, and T. Neal Garland have written a chapter that compares health workers in Ghana and the United States in their attitudes toward elderly patients. "A Comparison of Nurse Assistants in Nursing Homes in the United States and Ward Assistants for the Elderly in Ghana" bases itself on the premise, implicit in modernization theory, that less modernized societies such as Ghana accord higher status to the elderly and that health workers in this type of environment would have more positive attitudes toward the elderly than in more modernized societies such as the United States. Their data failed to support this premise. Their study is similar to Garland's study of Japan and Stevenson (et al.'s) study of Great Britain, which demonstrates that comparative health studies can serve as a way of testing presumptions that we hold concerning macrosocial characteristics of societies.

The final chapter in this section is Annette M. Schwabe's comparison of health care in two sharply differing Caribbean societies, the Dominican Republic and Cuba. The chapter she has written, "International Dependency and Health: A Comparative Case Study of Cuba and the Dominican Republic," is couched in dependency theory. She looks at the positions of the Dominican Republic and Cuba in the world system of political economy. She finds that access to health care resources, and health outcomes, have become increasingly stratified in the Dominican Republic. In contrast, by avoiding entanglement and dependency in the world system, Cuba has developed a health care system with broad-based access to care and more evenly distributed health outcomes. While still maintaining a high degree of equity, the Cuban system has, however, been sorely strained by the ending of its bilateral reciprocity with the former Soviet Union.

Part VI. Global Themes

Each of the chapters discussed thus far occupies a specific geographic niche in the study of international health care care—it deals with a country or region that one could point to on the globe and say, "Here it is." The final two chapters are, in contrast, "global," in that they have a worldwide systemic compass, not localizable to particular nations or regions. Hence, the designation, "Global Themes," for Part VI, the last section of this book.

Ingar Palmlund's chapter, "Risk Evaluation of Medical Technology in Global Population Control," looks at diverging views between the industrialized world and the developing world concerning population growth and contraception. She shows that the current international tensions have earlier analogues within the internal dynamics of national states, where some population groups—the socially prestigious and dominant strata—were encouraged in high fertility and other, socially inferior groups were discouraged or inhibited. She also looks at contraceptives as a profitable export item for pharmaceutical companies in industrialized countries. Last, she raises questions concerning "contraceptive ethics." Her ethical focus is not on religious/moral scruples about contraception but rather on the exposure of female contraceptors in developing countries to unknown long-term medical risks.

The final chapter by Eugene B. Gallagher and Joan Ferrante, "Toward an Analysis of Medicalization in the Global Context," looks toward looming issues in health care that will engage international health researchers in coming decades. Problems of access to health care—an important aspect of equity and social justice—are a mounting concern in both industrialized and developing countries. The capabilities of biomedicine are constantly being enhanced by medical research, which in turn stimulates public expectations for treatment, and challenges professional providers and government planners to broaden access. However, between biomedical discovery and its application lie complex processes—publicizing, informing, influencing, setting priorities—directed toward practicing professionals, current and future patients, and the public at large. These processes, loosely termed "medicalization," are much affected by the fabric and values of a particular society and its ways of allocating health care. Most research on medicalization has occurred in industrialized societies with technologically advanced systems of health care. This chapter delineates the basic process of medicalization as it has unfolded in the industrialized societies and sets forth its interrelated components: social inclusion, biomedical transcendence, and health absolutism. The paths that medicalization will take in developing societies, and the ways in which they will intertwine with traditional/folk/indigenous medicine, are topics ripe for exploration by the social sciences of medicine.

PART I

CULTURE AND BIOMEDICINE

Gender and Health: Theoretical Versus Practical Accessibility of Health Care for Women in North India

Anuradha Kumar

INTRODUCTION

That differences in the health of men and women exist in the developing world is well known. Several comprehensive papers detailing the problems are available (Jacobson 1993; Koblinsky et al. 1993; Germaine and Antrobus 1989). Governments and international health agencies, often under pressure from women's health advocacy groups, are responding to the cry to focus energies on the critical and unique health needs of women. Nonetheless, much more needs to be accomplished. The statistics are grim, indeed: at least one million women will die of reproductive causes this year, and more than 100 million will contract serious illnesses (Jacobson 1991). In Southern Asia alone, the maternal mortality ratio is 570/100,000 live births as opposed to 26 in developed countries (Ross et al. 1992). Data on morbidity, particularly reproductive morbidity, is difficult to obtain in developing countries and the incidence of maternal morbidity is largely unknown. Pregnancy-related illnesses range from mild to severe, short- and long-term, and are often difficult to identify (Senanayake 1991). Complications arising from pregnancy are numerous and include hypertension, pre-eclampsia, ectopic pregnancy, postpartum and postabortion infections, obstructed labor, uterine prolapse, and vaginal fistula. Reproductive morbidity also includes disease not necessarily related to pregnancy, such as sexually transmitted disease, reproductive tract infections, reproductive cancers, and AIDS. It has been estimated that the global burden of disease, which is a statistic that combines loss of life from premature death and loss of healthy life from disability, for sexually transmitted disease (excluding HIV infection) is 15.2 million life-years lost globally and 3.2 million life-years lost in India alone (World Bank 1993).

While access to care is an important part of the health picture, accessibility figures can be misleading. In India, for example, it is estimated that 75 percent of the population has access to health care and yet only 17 percent of children under 12 months are immunized against measles and 58 percent against DPT (World Bank 1990). In Tamil Nadu, a recent study of two communities shows a contraceptive prevalence rate of 27 percent, "despite their having physical access to health facilities and an expressed desire to limit family size" (Ravindran 1993: 32). It appears that there is a gap between the availability/accessibility of health services and their actual use.

This paper focuses on the reasons women are unable to make use of health care that is theoretically "accessible" to them. This is, of course, only one issue among the many that fall under the broad category of women's health but it is a significant one. Until strategies are developed to clear the path for women to seek health care, no amount of community outreach or research will alleviate the suffering experienced by so many.

Many of the reasons that keep women from seeking care stem from cultural roots that are deeply entrenched in the life of the community. Gender ideology and gender-based behavior are some of the cultural beliefs and practices that influence health behavior. An understanding of the daily lives of women will be helpful in understanding why health facilities are not used and in addressing those problems appropriately.

The aim of this paper is to describe how the sociocultural conceptualization of gender in a rural setting, as expressed in the lived experiences of women, impacts on women's health. Data from field research conducted by the author in rural North India is presented. The central thesis is that, despite the fact that a Primary Health Center (PHC) exists in this town, few women make use of the facility for their own health needs because social definitions of womanhood prevent them from doing so. It is, therefore, critical to understand what those definitions are and how they impinge upon health behavior. In addition to these considerations, attention to the economic and time constraints most women experience must be kept at the fore.

Naturally, the reasons women give in this community cannot be said to apply to all women in India, and certainly not to all women in the developing world. Still, the analysis of a particular case will highlight the sorts of constraints women face and, it is hoped, spur others to consider barriers to health care in a different light. This work also attempts to build on previous research of this nature in other communities so as to provide health workers, planners, and policy makers with a series of pictures of women's lives around the world (Browner 1989; Lane and Meleis 1991; Khattab 1992).

In this paper I will begin by describing the geographic setting and methods used in the research, then move on to a description of gender relations in the community and how they impact on women's ability to seek health care. Finally, the chapter provides a brief case history—an account is provided of the steps one woman in the community took to seek care for a reproductive tract infection.

SETTING AND METHODOLOGY

The women described in this study live in a town called Shaktipur (a pseudonym) in the northern state of Rajasthan, India. Shaktipur town is the seat of the *tehsil*, or subdistrict, within Jaipur district. Jaipur district is the most populous district in Rajasthan with 4,719,257 persons (1991 provisional population totals). There are 151 villages within the *tehsil*, according to the 1981 census, having a total population of 104,342. The town of Shaktipur had a population of 7,502 in 1981. Latest figures from the Indian Institute for Health Management Research indicate a population of approximately 9,100 in 1990.

The 1981 Census of India refers to Shaktipur as a village, though in terms of population, it is a large village. By virtue of its being the *tehsil* seat, Shaktipur is somewhat urbanized. It is electrified, there is a paved road leading to it, buses connect it to the city of Jaipur (50 km away) and other locales, and it has a Primary Health Center (PHC) and secondary schools. In terms of modern conveniences, Shaktipur is far ahead of surrounding villages, and it is for these reasons and its larger population that it is referred to as a town in this paper. Still, it should be pointed out that Shaktipur is largely a rural, agricultural area. Beyond the paved road leading to the bus stand is a network of dirt paths, concrete homes stand next to mud houses, and a short distance off lie the fields. The majority of residents are involved in cultivation either as land owners or as agricultural laborers. The people of Shaktipur make a distinction between their "village" life and the city life of Jaipur. They travel to Jaipur for particular services that they feel are of superior quality there than in Shaktipur or are simply unavailable in Shaktipur. While travelling to Jaipur is relatively easy and some men commute regularly to their jobs there, people generally only go for a specific purpose, not just to visit. Thus, in no way can Shaktipur be considered to be an extension of Jaipur or the nearer, rapidly expanding town of Sanganer, nor can it be called urban in the way that Jaipur is. Shaktipur is a community at a crossroads, moving towards urbanization but still rooted in rural life ways. The term "town" refers to its intermediate status of not quite a city but not exactly a "typical" village.

Rajasthan has many different regional dialects, the one spoken in the Shaktipur area is Marwari, a dialect of Hindi, and the people here are referred to as Marwaris. The landscape is flat, dry, and dusty, though not as arid as the desert regions of Jasailmer, Sikar, or Bikaner. Trees and shrubs are wiry and tough. Crops include chickpeas, mustard, mung dal (lentil), wheat, corn, millet, buckwheat, and sesame. Goats, cows, and sheep are kept for their milk, while camels and oxen are kept for their labor.

Rajasthan is considered one of the less "developed" states in the union. The literacy rate for the state is 38.8 percent overall and 20.8 percent for women, the lowest in the country (Bose 1991). The sex ratio is 913 as compared to the already low national figure of 929. The infant mortality rate in 1989 was 96/1,000 births and 103/1,000 births in rural areas. Finally, the decennial growth rate for 1981–1991 was 28.1 percent which is 4.6 percent higher than that of the nation as a whole. Rajasthan, like its northern neighbors, is an example of the malaise that has come over Indian development efforts. It is among the "Hindi-belt" states that, for various reasons, have not responded to development programs as the indicators above show. Particularly striking in this statistical scenario are the low literacy rates for women and the low sex ratio. Andhra Pradesh, Bihar, Madhya Pradesh, Orissa, Rajasthan, and Uttar Pradesh, states which make up 51 percent of India's total population, account for 59 percent of its illiterate population (Bose 1991).

It was in this larger setting that fieldwork in Shaktipur town was conducted. The research project was divided into three phases, the total project lasting nine months (September 1991–May 1992).[1]

The first phase consisted of a door-to-door household survey of 210 homes, with information gathered on a total of 1,523 people. The survey consisted of questions about household composition, income, ownership of various consumer goods, occupation, educational status, caste, and religion. In this purposive sample of households, an attempt was made to get as heterogenous a study population as possible. Ultimately, there were 29 different caste groups represented, three religious traditions, a mix of economic classes and neighborhoods within the town.

In the second phase, 65 currently married women of reproductive age (15–45) with children and with various levels of educational attainment were selected from the 210 households for a more structured survey. From the 65, information was collected on 50 women. The interview questions elicited reproductive histories, opinions about contraception, use of the PHC, reasons for going to the PHC, use of non-allopathic healers, immunization status of children, ideas about family size and sex composition, ideas about marriage arrangements, and future plans for children. The responses were often a catalyst for extended conversations about these and other topics. Interviews ranged from 30 to 90 minutes in length and most were tape recorded. In addition, data on time use was also gathered by spending one day in selected respondents' homes and recording their activities.

In the third phase, multiple interviews were conducted with 23 out of the 50 women. These were open-ended conversations, with plenty of opportunity for dialogue on the immediate topics of the research project and also about other matters.

Participant observation was also a key methodology. The daily workings of an extended family—weddings, birth ceremonies, funeral feasts, schooling, and the health center—were all events or areas observed. People of all ages and both sexes provided information, though not all were formally interviewed.

WOMANHOOD IN SHAKTIPUR

Women in Rajasthan in general and Shaktipur in particular observe *ghungat*, or veiling, which includes not only the actual covering of the face and body with a veil, but also a whole host of restrictions placed on women's speech, mobility, their relationships with others, and their expression of emotions.[2]

The restrictions associated with *ghungat* on the familial level apply only to married women when they are living in their affinal home, or *sussral*. In Rajasthan, where the effective age at marriage can be as early as 15, this means that for most of her life a woman must live within the confines of *ghungat*. In those instances where a girl is not married by the age of 15 or 16, restrictions are often placed on her mobility, though she need not cover her head and face until she is married. When a woman visits her natal home, or *pihar*, she does not need to adhere to *ghungat* restrictions with her brothers, cousins, or father. This one of many characteristics that separates daughters and daughters-in-law.

The distinction between a woman's *sussral* and her *pihar* is strictly maintained throughout her life. Her behavior and others' expectations of her behavior are dependent on whether she is in her *sussral* or her *pihar*. At all times and in front of everyone, a woman must cover her head, if not her face, in her *sussral*. In fact, one of the reasons women gave for maintaining *ghungat* is so that others can identify a woman as married or not, if she is a daughter or daughter-in-law of the family, and act accordingly towards her.

Ghungat is practiced by women towards men outside of their *sussral*, and with male family members who are older than the woman's husband. The reference point for determining how a woman ought to behave towards a man is her husband, not the woman herself. The relationship between any particular man and the woman's husband determines whether she should sit in front of him, how much of her head and face she should cover, where she should sit in relation to him, and if she can speak to him. For example, a woman sitting with her sister-in-law with only her head covered would quickly pull her *sari* or *ordni* (scarf) over her face if her older brother-in-law came into the room. If a male relative younger than her husband came in, she would not need to cover her face fully. The restrictions placed on a married woman are strictly enforced in the first years of her married life. As the years go by and she bears children, the restrictions are eased, though the distinction between a woman's *sussral* and *pihar* is never completely forgotten.

The restrictions of *ghungat* also include patterns of speech. Inside the home, a woman should not speak in front of men older than her husband, i.e., the same men that she would avoid appearing before or only appear before in full *ghungat*. In public, the restriction applies to all men, regardless of their relationship to her husband. In fact, a woman will not even speak to her husband in public. She will only communicate with men with whom she must talk in order to get her work done, that is, shop owners or vegetable vendors. In these situations, she will speak in a low tone and, if at all possible, will ask someone else to speak for her, such as a child or other companion. The essential point is that a woman's voice should be heard as seldom as possible, and certainly not in front of strangers.

Women's ability to move about in public is also regulated. Regardless of caste affiliation, the preference is for women to stay inside as much as possible and to go outside only when their bodies, heads, and part of their face are covered. It is a common sight to see women lifting the veil just enough to see the path ahead of them. Rarely do women leave the house alone. The daily chores of fetching water, gathering fodder, and walking back and forth to the fields are done in pairs or groups. In fact, this is one of the few moments when women have the opportunity to talk to each other. Often, a woman will be accompanied by a young niece or nephew as security. If possible, women will send their children or neighbors to do their errands for them rather than going to the market themselves. Men are often responsible for purchasing the food that is to prepared by women.

It is extremely important to note that *ghungat* and its associated behaviors are not simply about men versus women, dominator against subordinate, but about proper behavior in a social world where the rank and position of a person and kin group depends on it. *Ghungat* cannot and has not been eliminated because men as well as women have a stake in its continuation. The importance of *ghungat* lies in two related and deeply significant concepts in the social lives of Shaktipur residents: *izzat* and *sharam*, that is, honor and shame.

Both men and women have *izzat*, though the paths to achieving it are different. *Izzat* is held by individuals, families, and the *jati* as a whole.[3] The behavior of specific individuals directly contributes to the standing of larger social groupings. Those of high *jati* and/or economic standing in the community may have *izzat* stemming from the position of their family. Ascribed characteristics such as *jati*, age, gender, and wealth are only the building blocks of *izzat*; correct moral behavior can build on the foundation of ascribed status or tear it down.

To summarize a rather complex ideological process, *izzat* is a quality that is built and maintained by the display of specific behaviors: spirituality, control, and acceptance. *Sharam* is that quality that people who find themselves in a dependent position (women, young sons, younger brothers) must have in order to keep their own and their kin group's *izzat*. *Sharam* implies a modesty of demeanor as well as appearance. A young boy should feel shy in front of his elders and a young bride should feel *sharam* to such an extent that she wishes to hide her body and herself behind a veil.

Reasons for connecting the female body with shame are many and relate to ideas of cleanliness, the necessity of maintaining a "pure" patrilineage, and fear of uncontrolled sexuality. The literature on purity and pollution ideology is extensive and I will not delve into it here (see Dumont 1970; Wadley 1975; Srinivas 1989). A few specific examples are provided of reproductive processes that point to the interaction between the body, ideas about cleanliness, and social practices that manage the body.

Menstruation and childbirth are both bodily events that result in further restrictions being placed on women. This is primarily due to the powerful meaning ascribed to blood as a particularly "dirty" substance (Srinivas 1989). A menstruating Hindu or Jain woman (only a minority of Shaktipur residents were Muslim) cannot enter a temple, a kitchen, or touch a water source for 3–5 days. Women from Jain families may even sleep on a separate mattress, away from their husbands for the initial days of bleeding. Women who have just given birth are confined indoors for a period ranging from one to two months. In addition, their home is considered unclean and must be washed before visitors will enter. A series of cleansing baths must be administered to the woman, usually by her mother-in-law, to recapture her prechildbirth state of cleanliness. Anything touched by a woman during this period of confinement is considered unclean, whether it be another person, an animal, a tool, or anything else.

In terms of sexuality, it should be remembered that *ghungat* rules are only activated once a woman is perceived to be a sexual being, that is, upon marriage. Covering the body with a cloth has dual implications in this community: one is that an exposed female body is automatically sexually enticing, and the other is the belief that sexual desire is very difficult to control. Therefore, covering the female body is an effective solution to maintaining rules about sexuality that call for sexual relations only between a married couple.

Acceptance is a quality that builds *izzat* for men and women, but especially for women. Acceptance, in this context, is not a sign of weakness, but an indication of self-knowledge. Those in positions of power must learn to accept the responsibilities that come with these positions, and those in dependent positions must also accept their state. A woman's ability to withstand physical and emotional pain is valued, and she is more honorable because of her ability to accept what fate has given her. It is felt that intolerance breeds unhappiness and this should be avoided in a setting where the harmonious functioning of the extended family is very important.

In sum, *ghungat* is a practice that confers honor on both men and women. It is a visual expression of the acceptance of the power differential between men and women, an act of deference by women for the patricentered social order. It also confirms the control men and the patrilineage have over women, and it is not entirely voluntary. Newly married women are told when to practice *ghungat* and are scolded if they do not. They are also encouraged to be shy and hide themselves from strangers.

ECONOMIC CONSTRAINTS ON WOMEN

Measuring the financial resources of an individual, or, even, of a household in this area is very difficult. Some households depend solely on farming, others on wage income, and others still on a combination of the two. Depending on a person's occupation and the circumstances of the work agreement, a worker may not be paid in cash but in kind. Since a significant proportion of the population is engaged in farming, either as landowners or laborers, income data is unreliable. Farm laborers are often paid by a share of the crop. On the other hand, relying solely on land holdings is also inaccurate since some of the population has moved away from agriculture. In addition, study participants were not always certain of, or did not wish to reveal, their exact cash income.

Instead of using income as measure of household earnings, two surrogate variables were used. The first comes from a checklist of what are considered luxury items in the community, such as a radio, a bicycle, a sewing machine, or electricity. Out of 209 households surveyed, 55 percent did not have any such items, 34.4 percent had one or two, and 10.5 percent had more than two. Looking specifically at women of reproductive age, 48.7 percent lived in a household that had no consumer goods, 36.3 percent had one or two, and 15 percent had more than two goods in their home.

Further analysis of the economic situation, using a variable that combined ownership of consumer goods and land holdings, revealed that 34.8 percent of households lived in the lowest economic category; that is, they do not own any land nor do they have the resources to purchase consumer goods. Slightly more, or 40.1 percent, were in a middle category, and 25.1 percent were in the high economic bracket; that is, they were landowners and/or able to purchase goods. The percentages were similar for women of reproductive age.

These figures should be interpreted considering what the overall standard of living for the town is, rather than as class categories. While there is variation in economic resources within Shaktipur, in general, the majority of the population does not enjoy a high standard of living. All residents get water from standing pipes or wells, not every home has electricity, and yet owning a radio is not necessarily a sign of wealth. What is notable about these figures is the high percentage of households that have nothing, not a radio nor electricity nor land. They also point to the fact that residents have little disposable income, either because they do not participate fully in the cash economy or because they are, simply, poor.

The place of women within this rather grim economic scenario is difficult to locate due to the confusion over what constitutes employment. The results of a national survey done in 1987 state that 90 percent of all women engaged in economically productive work are "casual" workers whose wages are generally one-half or less than men's (Government of India, 1987). There are roughly three categories of labor women perform. First, there are a few women who work strictly for wages, such as teachers and seamstresses. Out of the 339 women aged 15–45 in the study sample, only four were actually engaged in this type of work and all of them were estranged from their husbands or widowed. Second, there are women who work in the traditional occupations of their *jati*, sometimes performing the same tasks as their husbands. These women, such as sweepers, domestic servants, and washerwomen, are sometimes paid in kind while their husbands may receive cash payment. Their "earnings" may or may not be reported to an interviewer. In the Shaktipur sample, in only twenty-four homes can it be said with certainty that women were engaged in the traditional occupations of their *jati*.

The third category includes women who are engaged in work that is also traditionally done in their *jati* but they are not paid. This work is usually complementary to their husband's and the final product of both their labor may be a saleable product. This work is considered to be a part of a woman's domestic responsibilities, despite the fact that it is also economically productive labor. For example, in the potter *jati*, women are responsible for locating clay and fuel for the blaze created to fire the pots. They are also responsible for bringing it all back to the home. Men throw the pots and are primarily responsible for the firing, though the entire family may participate in this labor-intensive endeavor. Finally, the marketing of the pots is usually done by the man or another relative able to sit in the market, such as a brother or parent. Other examples of occupations that fall into this category are farm laborers, where men's and women's tasks are clearly established; gem cutters; and jewelry makers. Certainly, women are contributing significantly to the economic life of the family, but they are not paid for their efforts. The majority of women in the study sample belonged in this third category.

The control of resources is another part of this economic picture. Whatever profits are made from the collective effort of the family is kept by the elder men of the household and redistributed into the home. Even earnings that a woman has from her independent labor is often turned over to the head of the household, usually a man. Ideally, the household head is aware of the needs of the women and children in the home and provides for them as necessary. If a special need arises, his wife or mother may make a request for financial aid. This request, however, can be refused. Women do not own land in Shaktipur and cannot inherit it, for social rather than legal reasons. Some women are able to save a few rupees occasionally and may have a small nest egg for emergencies. In general, however, the only monetary resource at a woman's disposal is her jewelry, which is usually given to her at the time of marriage. Unfortunately, it is not easy to convert jewelry into cash, nor is it considered desirable. In essence, women in Shaktipur have little access to economic resources, monetary or otherwise.

TIME CONSTRAINTS: WOMEN'S RESPONSIBILITIES

In this section, observational data on women's daily activities are described. There is, of course, variation in the kinds of tasks women perform depending on the economic standing of the household and the occupation of the family. Nonetheless, there are tasks that are exclusively done by women; not surprisingly, these revolve around the domestic arena.

Typically, a woman's day begins early with the collection of water. As mentioned above, residents of Shaktipur use standing pipes or wells. Water is a serious concern in this desert area and the job of obtaining it and ensuring that a sufficient quantity is available is a critical one. Water from the standing pipes comes for 20–30 minutes a day, its source being a river approximately 15 kilometers away from Shaktipur. The cleanliness of this water is dubious: in rural India as a whole, only 50 percent of the population had access to safe drinking water in 1985 (Ross et al. 1992). As the hot, dry summer months approach, less water is available and the difficulties involved in getting it become pronounced. The standing pipes dry up and practically every conversation, at some point, turns to the topic of water. Even during cooler months, women must bear the load of transporting the water to their homes. In the hotter months, as different wells dry up, women are forced to go farther and farther for even small quantities of water. The chore of fetching water is one part of the responsibility, the other is managing the water to maximize use. Allocating water for bathing, cooking, and drinking is left to women.

In addition to obtaining water, women are responsible for cleaning the home, which usually entails sweeping the floor every morning and washing clothes and kitchen utensils. Precious water is not used for these tasks; most residents use the nearby lake for washing clothes and ash for polishing kitchen utensils. Other domestic tasks include cooking meals, getting fodder for the animals, locating fuel for stoves, and providing child care. In an extended family, the wives of brothers share cooking chores and childcare is often shared by several members of the family, though mothers are ultimately held responsible. Getting fodder, fuel, and washing clothes is a significant time commitment. Childcare involves not only making sure children are fed, bathed, and clothed, but also that they are attending school, completing their homework, and monitoring their health.

In addition to these domestic tasks, many women, particularly those belonging to poorer households, are also engaged in other types of labor. For example, women work in the fields, run small stalls in the market, take in sewing, and spin cotton thread.

Women are also responsible for taking care of visitors; that is, providing them with food or drink and ensuring that they are comfortable. Hospitality is highly valued in this community, as well as in India in general, and households are judged by how well guests are treated. Generosity is a reflection of the wealth of the home and of the kindness of its inhabitants. It is important for men, women, and the family as a whole to be able to share its wealth with others. In a community where reciprocal exchange relationships are valued, caring for guests takes on increased significance.

It is also important to point out other activities women are involved in that contribute to the social life of the family and to its social standing in the town. Women pay social calls on neighbors and friends when a birth has occurred, or if there is a wedding in the home, or if a family member has died. Men are also involved in these social activities, but separately from women. Women console other women, women share joys with other women, and women share other women's work. By participating in and organizing social events, women help to maintain social networks that have been in place for generations. The women who do this, those who have married into the town, are strangers to the majority of people they encounter. Yet this service to the patriline is part of their responsibility as wives and daughters-in-law.

From the above general description of women's work, it is clear that women contribute in important ways to the social and economic life of a family. The interdependency between men and women should also be noted. While it is true that women and children are primarily financially dependent on men, men are socially dependent on women. Women manage the home, look after children—the hope of the family and lineage—and maintain social alliances.

STEPS TO HEALTH CARE

The social practices and ideologies described above impose serious restrictions on women's use of the Primary Health Center. Woman rarely visit the PHC for their own health needs. Usually, they come seeking care for their children, and, even then, they rarely come alone. More often, children are brought to the clinic by one their grandparents. This is not surprising, given the restrictions placed on women's movements in public and the sharing of childcare responsibilities. Most of the women mentioned that, while they were usually the ones who noticed health problems in their children, they could not immediately act on this. Instead, they had to consult with their husbands and/or their in-laws. The child was only taken to the clinic if the authority figures in the family agreed. This was true even for immunizations, and could partially explain the low immunization figures mentioned earlier. While children have people other than their mothers who are interested in their well-being, women are not always so fortunate.

There are several steps a married woman goes through if she is unwell. A case study of a Shaktipur woman will be provided after outlining the basic steps most women follow when handling an illness. The first of these is that a woman tries to tolerate whatever discomfort she may have and deny that it is a problem. If the symptoms disappear, as they sometimes do in the case of sexually transmitted disease, she believes she has done the right thing by not seeking care and by tolerating the discomfort. If the symptoms persist, she may tell her husband or mother-in-law. If they are sympathetic, she may seek treatment at a non-allopathic healer; for example, an herbalist or Ayurvedic practitioner. She may also go to one of the medical offices set up by nurses and pharmacists from the PHC in their spare time. These practitioners operate clinics out of their homes at times when the PHC is closed or they are off-duty. They tend to charge high fees and prescribe drugs freely. While the quality of their services is dubious, at least they are open at night and are known to the community. The physicians that serve in the PHC and most of the nursing staff are not from the region, much less the village. If, however, her *sussral* strictly follows *ghungat*, the woman who is unwell may not be able to go to these healers alone; she must wait until someone can accompany her. This may never happen. Of the sixty-five women in the subsample, only one reported going to the PHC for a personal health concern.

Assuming that a sick woman has made it to the PHC, accompanied by either her husband or other relative, she is likely to encounter barriers even here. The PHC, like other parts of the Indian health services, is stretched to the limit in many ways: personnel, equipment and supplies, and resources. There are long lines to see providers and the time spent on diagnosis is brief. Patients are seldom physically examined. Instead, questions are posed and a diagnosis made based on verbal accounting of symptoms. The physician-client relationship is characterized by a significant imbalance of power, with the more educated physician often making decisions for poorer, less educated clients. This sort of relationship is not at all specific to the rural setting, as verbatim dialogue of physician-client interaction in an urban clinic illustrates (Gupta 1993).

For several of the months that I lived in the village, no doctor was regularly present in the PHC. Furthermore, the doctors that are generally posted here are men and this poses a significant barrier in a community where gender segregation is the ideal. Most of the women and some of the men I spoke with mentioned their hesitancy in going to the PHC and being "looked at" by the male doctor. This was especially true if a woman was suffering from a reproductive tract infection. This is not surprising in a social setting that demands women actively cover their bodies from the gaze of strangers. Thus, even when a woman arrives at the PHC after negotiating the obstacles in her home life, she may be met with a poorly staffed PHC containing few supplies and no female physician.

If she manages to be seen by the health provider, a woman faces yet another problem: lack of financial resources to fill the prescription for treatment. It is well known throughout India that health practitioners over-prescribe for their patients. In general, the privately owned pharmacy that is located adjacent to, or in the same compound as, the PHC, profits from this over-prescription, giving a portion of their profits to the prescribing physician. This often results in a total prescription costing Rs. 50–150 (equals U.S. $1.50–$4.50) for the patient. Most of the "padding" is in the form of harmless vitamins and minerals, which may be beneficial for the sick patient but are not vital. The vast majority of the patients cannot distinguish which is the curative medicine and which is not. Therefore, they are forced to buy it all or make arbitrary guesses as to what to purchase. Needless to say, this is a great financial hardship on most families, and especially on women who have little financial resources of their own.

Another potential barrier to using health services is the time spent waiting to be seen. Women who bear the responsibility of the household cannot afford to spend half a day waiting to be seen by a health provider. Unfortunately, this is exactly what is expected of them; women's time and work is undervalued.

Some women do manage to sneak out of their home and go to the PHC on their own. But they are risking a great deal: their social position and that of their family's. In choosing between physical health and social status, bodily concerns are not always given priority. This is not surprising in a community where social standing is extremely important and women believe they should be able to tolerate great discomfort. The combination of these social forces keeps women from seeking care even when it is relatively easily available. The following case study will illustrate some of the issues mentioned above.

Lata

Lata, age 33, is married to a local reporter for a Jaipur newspaper who is part of the Pareek *jati*. Pareeks in Shaktipur are known to be more educated than other *jatis* and hold occupations that require literacy. Lata was married at the age of 13 and came to live in her *sussral* after failing her ninth-class exams. She is the only girl in a family of three boys. Lata is the mother of six children: five girls and one boy. The boy is the second child. Neither her *sussral* nor her *pihar* is wealthy, nor are they poor. In Lata's *sussral*, her father-in-law makes all the decisions. Even now, her husband gives all his income to his father, who budgets the expenses. Lata is the only daughter-in-law, since her husband is an only child.

Lata has more formal schooling than most women in Shaktipur, but she has never been employed outside the home. As a married woman, Lata observes strict *ghungat*. She will not speak in front of her father-in-law and even feels uncomfortable sitting in the same general area as him. During her first years of marriage, she covered her face in front of her mother-in-law. Lata told me that a central problem in the home was that her husband had not been financially successful, and only landed his present job recently. In contrast, her father-in-law had been prosperous and was respected in the community. Thus, Lata's husband was unable to assert his own authority in the home, and everyone deferred to his father. Virtually every detail of family life, from the children's shoes to farming to the number of children Lata bore, is under the authority of Lata's father-in-law.

Soon after I arrived in Shaktipur, I met Lata. Though I spoke to Lata frequently, I rarely taped our conversations since they were never formal interviews. It was not until later in my stay in Shaktipur that I realized Lata's experiences were shared by many other women and were an important aspect of women's health behavior. By then, we had a close friendship and taping conversations would have been awkward. I did take notes on our conversations and have reconstructed some dialogue.

The residents of Shaktipur are not taken aback by health workers coming into the home, and I was often mistaken for one. On one of my initial visits with Lata, she described symptoms that appeared to me to be caused by a urinary tract infection. I urged her to go to the PHC and seek treatment. I eventually came to know Lata's daughter and the whole family quite well. Several months later, Lata's daughter came to me looking quite troubled. She informed me that her mother was in acute pain and seemed very ill. I asked what was being done about this, but was told that Lata's husband had not made any decisions about it and his father was away. I went to Lata's home and found her crying from the pain.

> AK: Why didn't you go to the PHC earlier? Lata: There was no woman doctor at the PHC. AK: And now? Lata: I can't go alone. He (husband) said he would take me when he got back from his newspaper rounds. AK: When will he be back? Lata: In 30 minutes.

So, I waited with her. An hour later, with Lata still in terrible pain, her daughter and I went to look for her husband. I found him sitting in a tea stall with his friends. We told him of Lata's condition and his daughter asked if she should take Lata to a small clinic on the outskirts of Jaipur where a female doctor practices, or if he would. He replied that she should go with her mother.

In the end, the three of us went by bus to a small clinic where Lata was examined, a diagnosis of a urinary tract infection was made, and a prescription written. The prescription included vitamins, analgesics, and antibiotics totalling Rs. 80. The doctor charged Rs. 15 for the visit and Rs. 10 (equals U.S. $.30) for a urine test. The total bill, including roundtrip bus fare, cost Rs. 120 (equals U.S. $3.60). Lata did not have this much cash and so I read the prescription and eliminated items, such as vitamin C, that I felt were not critical. This money was not given to her by her husband or father-in-law, but saved by her over a period of months. This one trip to a health care facility wiped out months of saving. The total time, including travel time, was 4–5 hours. This is a significant time commitment for a mother of six to make. Fortunately, all of Lata's children were school age and she did not worry about being away for a few hours.

This is only one example out of a study population of 727 women. The prevalence of reproductive tract infections in rural India is unknown, but a recent study in rural Maharashtra found that 92 percent of 650 women examined suffered from at least one gynecological disease (Wasserheit 1989; Bang 1989). Reproductive tract infections are obviously a serious problem in rural India, particularly in communities where women have limited ability to seek treatment independently.

CONCLUSION

By describing the social and economic circumstances of women in a rural Indian community, this study has shown how difficult it is for these women to seek care at a PHC which is nominally accessible to them. Thus it bears out "theoretical versus practical accessibility" referred to in the title. A combination of factors keeps women in Shaktipur from actively seeking health care: *ghungat*, ideological beliefs, poor living conditions, and time constraints. Social practices that restrict women's movement, speech, and interactions with others also prevent them from going to the PHC. Furthermore, beliefs that encourage women to be tolerant of pain, physical or emotional, prevent them from voicing fear or concern about health problems. Beliefs surrounding the body and the need to separate certain men from certain women also engender *sharam* (shyness, embarrassment, modesty) among women about submitting to an examination, verbal or physical, from a male doctor.

In addition to the above social constraints, poverty is a significant deterrent to seeking care. In general, women do not have control over financial resources and are economically dependent on the head of the household. This means that any expenditure must be approved by the household head. If he is indifferent to the woman's illness, then she has little recourse. Women are nervous and afraid to ask for money and will often wait until the situation is desperate. Preventive care is unheard of, and even curative care usually takes place only when the disease is significantly advanced.

A woman's workload also does not permit her to seek care. Because women are expected to do all household tasks and childcare, they have little time for self-care. This is compounded by the fact that waiting time in clinics is long.

All of these factors came into play in the case study described. Though she was aware she was having problems with her health, Lata did not attempt to seek treatment until months later. This was because she did not want to go to the male doctor at the PHC and could not go alone to a clinic outside of Shaktipur. By the time she sought treatment, she was in extreme pain and in danger of serious pelvic infection. Despite this, Lata was fortunate to have a daughter old enough to be concerned about her and able to accompany her to another clinic. She was also lucky not to have young children that would have demanded her constant attention.

In light of these social conditions, several steps can be taken to improve the health status of rural Indian women. These include:

- Establishing mobile clinics that go to neighborhoods in a town so that women do not have to travel alone to the PHC. It should be noted that this study did not include women who live in more remote areas of Rajasthan and for whom travelling to the PHC is very difficult.

- Recruiting women to be posted in rural clinics, perhaps by providing salary incentives. Not only do women hesitate in going to a male doctor, but their husbands and family members object as well.

- Reduce lax prescribing patterns and corruption among pharmacists and clinic staff.

- Train local non-allopathic healers to recognize common, easily treatable diseases and to advise clients where to go for care. With training, these healers may also be able to provide basic care for clients themselves in addition to their established healing practices.

- Educate children in secondary schools about basic health needs and encourage them to accompany their mother to clinics, if necessary. Children are a mother's closest ally, often communicating their mother's needs to the larger family and also helping her to address problems.
- Encourage health workers specifically to ask women about their own health concerns, even if they have come to the clinic for another reason.

These suggestions may sound idealistic, and they are, but in a health care system that is falling short of providing adequate care, experimentation is necessary. Some of the suggestions, such as recruiting female doctors and reducing corruption, are remarkably obvious but difficult to do. There are complex political reasons why such steps have not been taken. Nonetheless, it needs to be stated and reiterated that corruption exists, that people are aware of it, and that it must be stopped.

This account has shown how social and economic constraints prevent women from using health facilities that are theoretically available and accessible to them. The problems women in Shaktipur face are by no means unique, and yet little has been done to address them. The first step in changing the current health situation is to understand the social context of women's lives. If women's health status is to improve, then programs must operate in harmony within that context. Asking women to defy their circumstances may just be asking too much.

NOTES

[1] Support for this research was provided by the Fulbright Fellowship Program (IIE), the Andrew W. Mellon Foundation and Flora Hewlett Foundation Research Residencies Grant, and Sigma Xi.
[2] *Ghungat* is the local, Marwari term for veiling. *Purdah* is the usual term used in the literature on veiling in South Asia.
[3] In Shaktipur, and throughout North India, *jati* or *jat* are the terms used to denote caste. Caste is a European word. *Jati* is a post-Vedic, local system of classification whereas the four castes (*varnas*) described in most texts are of Vedic origin. The only one of the Vedic categories recognized by Shaktipur residents is *brahmin*. Local *jatis* include Pareek, Soni, and Nai, for example. In this text, the local *jati* name is used.

REFERENCES

BANG, RANI, and A. BANG. 1989. "Commentary on a Community-based Approach to Reproductive Health Care." *International Journal of Gynecology and Obstetrics* Suppl. 3:125–29.
BOSE, ASHISH. 1991. *Demographic Diversity in India 1991 Census, State and District Level Data. A Reference Book*. Delhi: B.R. Publishing Corporation.
BROWNER, CAROLE H. 1989. "Women, Household and Health in Latin America." *Social Science and Medicine* 28 (5):461–73.
DUMONT, LOUIS. 1970. *Homo Hierarchicus: An Essay on the Caste System*. Chicago: University of Chicago Press.
GERMAINE, ADRIENNE, and PEGGY ANTROBUS. 1989. "New Partners in Reproductive Care." *Populi* 16:4.
GOVERNMENT OF INDIA. 1987. *Report on the Quinquennial Survey on Employment and Unemployment, Survey Result: All-India*. National Sample Survey Organization, 1987, Thirty-Eighth Round, No. 341, Department of Statistics, Ministry of Home Affairs, New Delhi, pp. 337–38.
GUPTA, JYOTSNA A. 1993. (May) " 'People Like You Never Agree to Get It': An Indian Family Planning Clinic." *Reproductive Health Matters* (1):39–43.
JACOBSON, JODI L. 1991. "Women's Reproductive Health: The Silent Emergency." *Worldwatch Paper* 102: Washington D.C.: Worldwatch Institute.

———. 1993. "Women's Health: The Price of Poverty." Pp. 3–31 in *The Health of Women: A Global Perspective*, edited by Marge Koblinsky, Judith Timyan, and Jill Gay. Boulder, CO: Westview Press.

KHATTAB, HIND A. S. 1992. *The Silent Endurance: Social Conditions of Women's Reproductive Health in Rural Egypt*. Cairo, Egypt: UNICEF and The Population Council.

KOBLINSKY, MARGE, JUDITH TIMYAN, and JILL GAY. 1993. *The Health of Women: A Global Perspective*. Boulder, CO: Westview Press.

LANE, SANDRA D., and AFAF I. MELEIS. 1991. "Roles, Work, Health Perceptions and Health Resources of Women: A Study in an Egyptian Delta Hamlet." *Social Science and Medicine* 33 (10):1197–1208.

RAVINDRAN, SUNDARI T. K. 1993. (May) "Women and the Politics of Population and Development in India." *Reproductive Health Matters* (1):26–38.

ROSS, JOHN A. et al. 1992. *Family Planning and Child Survival Programs as Assessed in 1991*. New York: The Population Council.

SENANAYAKE, PRAMILLA. 1991. "Women's Reproductive Health—Challenges for the 1990s." *Advances in Contraception* 7:129–36.

SRINIVAS, M. N. 1989. *The Cohesive Role of Sanskritization and Other Essays*. Delhi: Oxford University Press.

WEDLEY, SUSAN. 1975. *Shakti: Power in the Conceptual Structure of Karimpur Religion*. Chicago: University of Chicago Press.

WASSERHEIT, JUDITH N. 1989. "The Significance and Scope of Reproductive Tract Infections among Third World Women." *International Journal of Gynecology and Obstetrics* Suppl. 3:145–68.

WORLD BANK. 1990. *Social Indicators of Development, 1990*. Baltimore: The Johns Hopkins University Press.

———. 1993. *World Development Report, 1993: Investing in Health*. New York: Oxford University Press.

CHAPTER 2

Japan's Health Care System: Western and East Asian Influences

James G. Anderson

Renee Oscarson

Yan Yu

INTRODUCTION

Systems of medicine and health care evolve according to their unique cultural context.[1] Concepts of health, illness, and disease etiology arise from this cultural context. Thus, medical practice can only be understood by examining cultural beliefs that determine diagnostic and therapeutic techniques and the roles of patients and providers (Lock 1980; Payer 1988). Even when indigenous systems of health care are overlaid with Western medicine, major modifications are made to adapt Western practices to the cultural values of the society into which they are introduced (Anderson 1992; Sidel and Sidel 1973).

Since early times, people in East Asia have understood themselves mainly in relation to their physical and social environment rather than as individuals. This is evident in Japan's holistic approach to medical care and to health care in general. Western medicine emphasizes specific symptoms that lead to a differential diagnosis and therapeutic interventions that alleviate the symptoms. Holistic approaches look instead to man's environment in order to maintain a harmonious balance that promotes health. Instead of identifying specific symptoms of a disease or illness, practitioners consider social, psychological, environmental, and genetic factors that make a patient vulnerable to illness. Such factors need to be adjusted to reduce the patient's vulnerability in the future (Dubos 1968).

In this paper we describe the cultural background of Japan and East Asian medicine in order to demonstrate adaptations of Western medicine to this unique cultural context. By focusing on the way that medical practices and beliefs are shaped by the interaction of culture and technology, it is possible to gain insight into the variety of ways that societies deal with the universal problems of disease and illness. Japan provides an important setting for such a study. Since it has had over one hundred years of experience with Western medicine, we can study how a traditional medical system and a Western medical system have adapted to one another. After briefly describing cultural beliefs and social practices related to health and illness, we discuss how this cultural context influences the sick role of patients and professional medical practice, the treatment of the mentally ill, and the aged in contemporary Japan

CULTURAL ASPECTS OF HEALTH CARE

The influence of *Shinto*, the native religion of Japan, on East Asian and Western medicine is evident in modern Japanese social practices. A brief overview of social practices and cultural beliefs in modern Japan provides insight into attitudes and expectations regarding health and medical care. The Japanese believe that the maintenance of health is a *duty*. This is accomplished mainly by proper diet, rest, and exercise, as well as by being in harmony with one's family and society. Lack of balance and harmony results in disease. Consequently, starting at the age of four, children are trained to develop an inner calm and stability. The expression of anger and strong emotions is discouraged. In Japan this is termed *seishin jotai*, or mental state (Lock 1980).

Culturally, Japan can be described as having a highly developed sense of group consciousness, together with strong feelings of responsibility for members of the group. The group can encompass diverse entities such as the family, village, neighborhood, office, or factory work unit. The family is the foremost group to which allegiance is required and the family in turn has traditionally looked after its members (Lock 1980).

Dependency is valued and encouraged in Japan; group duties and obligations take precedence over individual aspirations. Children are taught that failure and irresponsibility will reflect upon their family. Sickness in a child indicates failure on the part of the child's mother, whereas sickness in an adult indicates his or her failure to be aware of environmental factors or to maintain good social relations with others (DeVos 1973).

Furthermore, the close mother-child relationship creates a need to be nurtured. Individuals are assured of support and care if they are hardworking, responsible, and submissive to their family and work group. If they become ill, it is acceptable to become highly dependent on their group. Illness thus becomes a means of reinforcing interdependency and group solidarity (Caudill 1962; Doi 1973; Lock 1980).

Japanese are trained to be sensitive to their bodily functions and, consequently, commonly report numerous subjective symptoms to the doctor (Lock 1980). In East Asian medicine, there is great importance given to *hara*, or the abdominal region (Lock 1980). This concept has been blurred with that of the anatomical stomach, resulting in an elevated concern over the stomach's proper functioning and in the frequent reports of problems and diseases such as cancers of the stomach (Lock 1980). The concern for *hara* is evident in many common expressions: "*hara* is big" meaning "to be generous"; "*hara* is decided" meaning "to make up one's mind"; and "an honest man in his *hara*" meaning "an honest man at heart." Also, the practice of *harakiri* or suicide means, literally, the art of cutting the belly to demonstrate the depth and sincerity of one's feelings and emotions (Lock 1980). The psychological and symbolical significance of *hara* in East Asian medicine has been transferred to the modern concept of the anatomical stomach.

Ancient Shinto beliefs of spiritual purity have also been translated into purity of body and the surroundings in the socialization process. Illness has become a state that is considered polluting, so therapy based on Shinto beliefs was designed to purge and expel the pollution. Sweating baths, for instance, are believed to let dirt come out from inside the body (Lock 1980). Excessive concern of the Japanese people about body odor probably also has its origins here. Moreover, the Japanese people differentiate between relatives and members of their group considered to be "inside, safe, and clean" and outsiders considered to be "dirty and potentially dangerous" (Douglas 1966).

THE DOCTOR-PATIENT RELATIONSHIP

Many characteristics of contemporary private practitioners in Japan had their origin in the Edo period (1603–1867). Doctors were classified as craftsmen, third from the top in a four-caste system. At the same time, they were prohibited from receiving earned payment for their work; they had to accept gratuities from their patients instead. This custom of accepting gifts from patients persists to the present time (Fuse 1979).

While the status of private practitioners has improved, they are still referred to as town doctors (*Machi-isha*). Largely, they are neighborhood family doctors who treat patients and dispense medicine. Many have their offices in their homes and are often assisted by their wives, who act as receptionists and pharmacists. They advertise in the yellow pages of the telephone book, in the newspapers, and on billboards. While they do not enjoy the same status as doctors who practice in large hospitals and university medical centers, they are trusted because of their relationship to the families in their neighborhood (Ohnuki-Tierney 1984).

Medical specialization is not as well established in Japan as in Western countries and general practice is encouraged. However, many private practitioners list more than one specialty, even though they are not certified in these areas. Because of the emphasis on the stomach and on abdominal illnesses described earlier, there are many physicians and clinics that specialize in the stomach (*icho-ka*), a recognized specialty in Japan similar to gastroenterology in the West (Ohnuki-Tierney 1984).

In contrast to the United States, seeking medical care in Japan does not begin with making an appointment. Clinics and outpatient departments of hospitals typically do not use appointment systems, nor do they require referral. Patients go to the clinics and wait. However, because of recent dissatisfaction, some out-patient departments have attempted to decrease waiting time by using appointments (Powell and Anesaki 1990).

As in the United States, many prospective patients consider recommendations from family members and friends in the selection of a physician or a medical facility. "Introductions" are used and may serve to strengthen the perceived emotional bond between doctor and patient. Japanese behaviors and expectations are affiliative or interdependent rather than independent. The Japanese language includes terms to describe people who are connected and people who are not connected with oneself; i.e., insiders and outsiders (Caudill 1976b; Doi 1973). The Japanese custom of distributing name cards is a method of introduction that facilitates a connection between oneself and an outside person. The name card is representative of personal involvement. Ohnuki-Tierney (1984) gives examples of cases where name cards were attached to the first page of patients' medical records. The name card is likely to be from an "introducer" of high social standing, whether it be a former physician, a friend or relative, or it may be the card of the patient him/herself.

Because the Japanese emphasize reciprocity in their relationships, an introduction may be enhanced with the offer of a small gift (Powell and Anesaki 1990). Through the introduction and gift giving, patients and families choose their doctors. Also, they attempt to establish a personal bond between themselves and the doctors. Once the doctor is entrusted with responsibility for the patient, he is expected to care for the psychological and social needs as well as provide necessary medical care. Ohnuki-Tierney (1984) reports that doctors tolerate or even encourage special foods brought in for the hospitalized patient (*sashiire*), visiting (*mimai*) and patient care by family members, and the provision of professional attendants (*tsukisoi*) in order to accommodate nonmedical patient needs.

Gift giving to people to whom one feels indebted is customary in Japan, especially at certain times of the year. This practice not only expresses thanks, but it is also a way of requesting special attention from the physician. Lock (1980) found, however, that this custom is declining. The relationship between the patient and Western-trained physicians is becoming more utilitarian. Patients are beginning to view doctors as rendering a service for which they are paid.

Also, in referring a patient to another doctor, the referring doctor's name card is frequently transferred to the second doctor, usually a specialist. This indicates personal involvement with the patient. The second doctor may call the referring doctor to appraise him of the patient's progress and may invite him to visit a hospitalized patient (Ohnuki-Tierney 1984).

The doctor-patient relationship has been described as one of trust (Powell and Anesaki 1990) and complete dependence of the patient on the physician (Munakata 1986). The dependence or trust results in a relationship that is hierarchical and nonverbal (Haug et al., 1991). Doi (1973) described Japanese interpersonal relationships as based on the concept of *amae*, the feelings and dependence that an infant normally feels toward his/her mother. According to Doi (1973), *amae* continues into adult relationships. It is frequently exhibited in a patient's relationship with his or her physicians (Munakata 1986). That is, physicians assume total responsibility for their patients, who depend on them in the same way that children rely on their mothers.

Moreover, because the Japanese culture prohibits the exposure of one's "real self" (*honne*), it is difficult for Japanese patients to discuss their true feelings with a physician. Rather, transactions between patients and their families and physicians take place through symbolic presentations of self through the use of nonverbal communications (Caudill and Doi 1963).

One important result of this pattern of indirectness is that Japanese patients who are terminally ill are usually not told their true diagnosis. Instead, patients with lung cancer are frequently told they have pneumonia; those with stomach cancer are told they have an ulcer. However, one member of the family is told the true diagnosis. Thus, the family is expected to aid the physician in encouraging the patient to cooperate with treatment and to keep fighting the disease.

Again, proper role behavior dictates that the patient be emotionally and physically dependent on the physician. It is not appropriate for the physician to place part of the burden on the patient by informing him or her of the fatal diagnosis. In addition, the family is responsible for keeping the patient from "giving up," as well as providing much of the physical care that is needed. By keeping the true diagnosis from the patient, the family is better able to perform its proper role according to this conception. Further, patients frequently pretend that they don't know their true diagnosis in order to protect family members and the doctor from feeling that they failed (Long and Long 1982).

Since the Japanese are socialized to be sensitive to their body functions, they generally report many subjective symptoms and body states to their doctor. They also classify themselves by type, such as "easily tired" (*tskareyasui*), "of allergic disposition" (*allerugi taishitsu*), or "of nervous temperament" (*shinkeishitsusha*), for example (Lock 1980).

In close Japanese relationships, people learn to guess (*sassuru*) or understand another's feelings without words (Munakata 1986). Thus, Japanese patients and their families often assess their prognoses based on nonverbal communication. Because doctors take responsibility for the psychological as well as physical well-being of their patients, they often "protect" patients by disguising or evading their diagnoses (Ohnuki-Tierney 1984). The disguise of a diagnosis also serves to maintain an illusion that a physician has complete responsibility for, or control over, a patient's health status.

In Japan, illness of a family member is of concern to the entire family. Furthermore, women play a critical role in assuming responsibility for the person who is ill. It is not uncommon for a woman to serve as a surrogate for the patient. A mother may represent her daughter and a wife may represent her husband. The surrogate explains the symptoms to the doctor, obtains the prescription, and makes sure that the doctor's orders are carried out. The patient does not have to be physically present as long as the doctor has seen the patient in the past and is familiar with the patient's problem (Ohnuki-Tierney 1984).

SOCIOCULTURAL ASPECTS OF HOSPITALIZATION

The impacts of historical and cultural factors can also be seen in the structure and operation of Japan's clinics and hospitals. Although modern, government-funded research hospitals in Japan are similar in physical appearance to top medical centers in the United States (Ohnuki-Tierney 1984), the structure and services provided by medical facilities reflect their history. Patient beds are located in clinic facilities, as well as in hospitals. Japan's bed-to-population ratio is among the highest in the world (Powell and Anesaki 1990). The law distinguishes between clinics and hospitals based on number of beds and length of "hospitalization." Japanese clinics differ from offices of U.S. physicians primarily in that clinics may have up to 19 inpatient beds and that clinic physicians do not have admitting privileges in hospitals, which have 20 or more beds (Iglehart 1988a,b; Ikegami 1991). The Medical Service Law of 1948 stipulated that patients may not stay in clinic beds for more than 48 hours (Powell and Anesaki 1990), although the law is not strictly enforced.

Japanese clinics are also unique in that they are often family owned and operated. Of over 79,000 medical clinics that existed in 1986, over 90 percent were owned and operated by physicians (Iglehart 1988a,b). Many physicians have offices in their homes, with family members frequently serving as health care professionals or in administrative roles (Ohnuki-Tierney 1984).

Because clinic physicians do not have hospital privileges, they relinquish care of patients who need to be hospitalized. Due to the widespread belief that the quality of care is better in a hospital outpatient department than in a clinic, patients who have been referred to a hospital often do not return to clinics (Ikegami 1991). Thus, clinic physicians are encouraged to postpone hospitalization for continuity of patient care and to maintain their own livelihoods. Rather than give up care of patients, many clinic physicians who provide inpatient services choose to expand their facilities and range of services. That is, they develop what are legally designated as hospitals. Thus, the predominance of small hospitals is related to the importance of primary care physicians in small, neighborhood facilities and is the result of competition for patients.

In choosing a hospital, patients gather extensive information from friends, relatives, and especially family members. Proximity is important since family members continue to provide much of the patients' care even after they are hospitalized. Despite the perceived dependence of the patients on physicians, the process of entry into the medical system and the care during hospitalization allows a patient to maintain his/her own individual and or social identity. As discussed earlier, a personal introduction to the doctor is very important, especially in the case of hospitalization. These introductions by a referring physician, a relative, or an influential friend may be accompanied by a substantial gift of cash or goods. The process of gift giving during "introduction" establishes a sense of reciprocity (Haug et al. 1991) and emphasizes the patient's role in choosing a physician. These practices are designed to establish personal social relations with the doctor. This assures personal attention to the patient. Once hospitalized, a patient is able to choose clothing rather than wear hospital gowns and to receive care and meals from family members. Thus, patient care is not completely transferred to a physician or hospital.

Because the size of the nursing staff is often inadequate, it is frequently necessary for family members to provide care or to hire a private nurse to assure basic care (Powell and Anesaki 1990). Care is often provided by a *tsukisoi*, a round-the-clock attendant who is hired to help meet a patient's physical needs. The attendant, usually hired by the family, is a middle-aged or older woman who does not have household responsibilities. This attendant takes care of the patient's bodily needs and functions, prepares meals, and receives visitors for the patient (Caudill 1961). Visitation (*mimai*) is a cultural tradition and visitors bring gifts for the patient, usually food. This custom persists despite the fact that it interferes with the emphasis on peace and quiet (*ansei*). Family members also stay with patients and provide relief for the attendants (Ohnuki-Tierney 1984). Care provided by the family allows a patient to maintain or strengthen kinship ties during hospitalization and enables hospitals to operate with fewer expenses.

The law requires that employee health insurance cover most inpatient and outpatient treatments, including medication, surgery, and hospital services (Hashimoto 1984). In most hospitals, families may be reimbursed for payment to an attendant if the physician indicates the need for one. However, some hospitals are certified as providing complete care; in such cases, families are prohibited from hiring an attendant. Although families get around this regulation by hiring attendants who pose as family members, families will not receive insurance reimbursement for this care. Thus, some families pay out-of-pocket to provide adequate care (Ohnuki-Tierney 1984). Through formal introductions, patient care by family members or a professional attendant, visitation, and gift giving, the family creates the optimal conditions for successful treatment and recovery and prevents the patient from being overwhelmed by an impersonal institution. Moreover, the doctor is expected to treat the patient as a human being who is embedded in a network of family and social relationships (Ohnuki-Tierney 1984).

LENGTH OF HOSPITALIZATION

The average length of hospital stay in Japan, approximately five times as long as the average U.S. hospital stay, is the longest in the world (Ohnuki-Tierney 1984; Powell and Anesaki 1990). In part, Japanese hospitalizations are longer because hospitals are not divided into acute and chronic care facilities (Powell and Anesaki 1990). That is, much "nursing home care" is provided in Japanese hospitals. It has also been argued that Japanese hospitals provide poor care, resulting in slow recovery and longer stays (Okuyama 1976, cited in Ohnuki-Tierney 1984). Nevertheless, a large influence on length of hospitalization is the culture in which Japanese hospitals exist.

Disorders that are recognized or legitimized as illness vary from society to society. Ohnuki-Tierney (1984) notes that the Japanese recognize more conditions to be "illnesses" than are recognized in biomedicine as "diseases." Furthermore, in Japan, a major treatment for most illnesses is "peace and quiet" or *ansei*. The emphasis on *ansei*, together with an attitude that the sick should be "pampered," contribute to lengthier hospital stays. In addition, the dependency (*amae*) exhibited in interpersonal relationships elicits *amayaskasu*, a caretaking response (Caudill 1962; Doi 1973; Lebra 1976). The sense of obligation for providing care (*amayakasu*) conflicts with the concept of promoting rehabilitation, particularly with the elderly (Kiefer 1987). In addition, the hospital physician assumes complete responsibility for patient care in the hospital, as well as follow-up after discharge (Powell and Anesaki 1990). It is more convenient for patients to remain hospitalized until they are no longer in need of care. Therefore, cultural perceptions of treatment and caregiving contribute to a prolongation of the sick role.

Financial influences also contribute to long hospital stays. Because hospitals are financed through a point-fee system without reimbursement limits and because patient stays cost hospitals less at the end of a stay when less care is required, patients may remain hospitalized longer than is medically necessary (Powell and Anesaki 1990). Also, due to the considerable amount of in-hospital care provided by family members, lengthy hospitalizations are more financially feasible in Japan than in the U.S.

Furthermore, families may be better off financially if patients remain in the hospital instead of being discharged. Because families have primary responsibility for the sick and elderly, home care and community services are underdeveloped (Munakata 1986). Thus, it may be both expensive and inconvenient to provide home care for recovering patients. In contrast, most hospital expenses are covered by the government or by private health insurance. Therefore, patients have financial incentives to remain hospitalized.

PSYCHIATRIC DIAGNOSIS AND CARE

Psychiatric diagnosis and care in Japan are deeply rooted in Japanese cultural and social traditions. First of all, the experience of mental illness tends to be limited to the individual or within one's immediate family. Individuals are expected to assume responsibility for their own health. Consequently, those who suffer from a mental illness or alcohol or drug dependence are expected to exercise self-control. The family is expected by the society to care for patients with mental illness, which is believed to be a private matter not requiring professional treatment (Munakata 1986). Families unable to care for mentally ill members are socially criticized and experience feelings of guilt.

Since the Japanese consider mental illness hereditary, the family of the mentally ill person is stigmatized (Tseng 1975). Marriage to someone who has been mentally ill or to a blood relative of a mentally ill person is strongly opposed. In order to avoid this, a search is usually conducted into the mental health background of a prospective marriage partner (Lock 1980). Also, patients and their families are reluctant to talk about their family relations with doctors for fear that the social standing of the family will be affected. The family attempts to hide the fact that there is a mental patient in the family (Munakata 1986). Moreover, because of stigma, much greater use is made of medications and hospitalization than of psychotherapeutic methods for patients with psychiatric problems (Reynolds 1987).

Under Japan's Mental Health Act, families are required to assume heavy responsibilities and authority over the mentally ill. Mental hospitals and other public facilities are normally used as substitutes only when families are unable to continue the care, although quality of family care for the mentally ill is questionable (Munakata 1986). Lin and others (1978) have identified a process that families go through before institutionalizing a mentally ill or handicapped member. If the family's initial attempts fail to eliminate the abnormal behavior, they next turn to trusted outsiders in their community for help. In the third phase, outside religious healers, herbalists, and physicians are asked to treat the ill person. If treatment fails to eliminate the abnormal behavior, the patient is labeled mentally ill by the practitioners and community members who have been consulted. At this point the family frequently accepts the fact that the member is mentally ill and has him or her admitted to a distant mental hospital. This process frequently takes several years. As a result of this strong sense of family obligation to provide care for their mentally ill members, the ratio of mental hospital beds to population in Japan is much lower than in other countries (Munakata 1984).

As discussed earlier, Japanese patients and their families try to form emotional ties with their doctors. Doctors are thus made to feel as if they belong to the same family and that they are responsible entirely for the diagnosis and care of the patients. As a result, doctors feel a sense of guilt if they cannot fulfill all of the expectations of the patient and family. Thus, doctors avoid explaining anything about the patient unless they are certain. They also frequently disguise a diagnosis of mental illness as neurasthenia, a malfunction of the autonomous nervous system, or a psychosomatic disorder. In doing so, they attempt to protect patients and their families from a sense of powerlessness and hopelessness that would result from the knowledge of the chronic nature of the illness (Munakata 1986).

Moreover, diagnosis and treatment of mental illness are a social process. Japanese society cultivates self-responsibility for the occurrence of illness. Consequently, psychotherapy in Japan relies heavily upon techniques of introspection. During intake interviews, patients are required to give precise descriptions of self and symptoms. Many Japanese patients tend to be overly focused upon themselves, a condition that appears to result from their early dependency in social relations (*amae*). Also, many patients have problems in dealing with authority figures. Consequently, most therapy attempts to use introspection to alter this self-focus and to restructure patients' relationships to authority figures (Reynolds 1987; Tatara 1982).

JAPANESE CULTURE AND CARE FOR THE ELDERLY

Traditionally, as dictated by the culture, the Japanese family has been the main provider of care for their elders who cannot care for themselves (Freed 1990; Kuroda et al. 1992; Martin 1988, 1991). But the presumed responsibility of the family in caring for the elderly has recently proven ineffective and difficult for both the caregivers and the elderly (Freed 1990; Kiefer 1987; Kuroda et al. 1992; Maeda 1983; Martin 1988, 1991). Numerous studies have pointed to the serious problems that confront the public in fulfilling this task (Freed 1990).

The Japanese have traditionally cared for the elderly at home. Only the destitute resort to residential care (Freed 1990; Martin 1988). In this fashion, institutionalization of one's elders symbolizes the family's inability to fulfill their role obligations and this is condemned by the culture. Dependence is fostered and little effort is made to rehabilitate the frail and impaired elderly. If necessary, the elderly are placed in hospitals instead of nursing homes for lengthy periods. A study by Kuroda et al. (1992) shows that many elders stay in hospitals for reasons other than needing medical treatment, such as being a woman, living alone, or not having their own home.

Another characteristic of Japanese culture is that it indirectly encourages passive helplessness rather than rehabilitation (Kiefer 1987). Rehabilitation of the bedridden violates deeply held cultural norms for expressing and gratifying dependence needs (Caudill 1962; Doi 1973; Kiefer 1987; Lebra 1976). In contrast to the Western emphasis on individual autonomy, the Japanese caretaker (*amayakasu*) takes care of all of the patient's needs, while the patient assumes a passive role (*amae*). This may reflect Asian medicine's emphasis on the relationship between the sick person and his/her environment (Kiefer 1987). It also reflects early socialization practices in the family (Doi 1973). Patients who are bedridden are often perceived to be in a permanent condition. Most stroke patients are simply cared for and do not receive rehabilitation. The Japanese introduced Western medicine and nursing homes without introducing the idea of rehabilitation. Only about 4.4 percent of Japanese nursing home patients are offered rehabilitation services (Kiefer 1987).

Many families who cannot escape from the responsibilities of caring for their elderly, especially those that are fragile and who cannot care for themselves, are in a state of ambivalence and conflict as a result of traditional expectations (Freed 1990). To make matters worse, residential care in nursing homes and homes for the aged is frowned upon by the Japanese. Families face criticism from the society and from relatives if they put their elderly in nursing homes (Freed 1990; Kuroda et al. 1992). Although the Japanese government tries to encourage children to support their elderly parents by giving tax rebates, recent studies have shown that families feel trapped in doing so.

Modern Japanese value self-realization over self-sacrifice and put the obligation for one's children before responsibility toward one's aging parents (Freed 1990). Women (spouses of elderly persons, daughters, and daughters-in-law) traditionally have made up the majority of caretakers. More and more women are obtaining higher education and are seeking a career outside the household. As a result, the ratio of elderly persons to housewives will increase from 42/100 in 1985 to 123/100 in the year 2025 (Freed 1990; Martin 1991). At the same time, many young people are leaving the rural areas for big cities where housing is congested, leaving families less capable of caring for elderly persons (Freed 1990).

Attitudes toward the aged are beginning to be more like those in the Western industrial countries. Filial piety is no longer as strong among the Japanese (Freed 1990; Ogawa and Retherford 1993). A study of suicide in Japan showed that elderly people living in three-generation households are more likely to commit suicide than are those who live alone (Martin 1988). Since World War II, the proportion of elderly people expecting to depend on their children in old age decreased from 50 percent to 25 percent in 1970 (Martin 1988). As a result, more Japanese elders plan to leave their property to the child who will take care of them instead of to the eldest son, as has been traditional (Tsuya and Martin 1992).

Traditional practices alone will not suffice as the basis for care of the expanding aged population. As more and more Japanese families find it difficult to care for their elderly at home and the government finds it too costly for hospitals to provide care for them, growth of residential facilities such as nursing homes is expected (Martin 1991). Home care and community care, such as visiting home makers, respite care centers, and day nursing homes or adult day care, are important complementary care services that will make home care possible and will be needed to prevent lengthy hospital stays (Martin 1991; Sonoda 1988). The current trend in Japan is that more and more elders expect to live apart from their children. Therefore, independence in advanced age becomes an important issue. Such independence of the impaired and the frail elderly can only be facilitated through rehabilitation programs designed for the aged. The Japanese government expects to put 28 percent of the bedridden elderly into geriatric rehabilitation centers and to drastically reduce hospital use (Martin 1991; Sonoda 1988). However, the traditional power of the Japan Medical Association and the unwillingness of physicians to delegate authority to the other helping professions may make it difficult to implement this policy. Nursing homes, home care, and day care require well-trained nurses and allied health personnel. The supply of such personnel, however, depends upon professional recognition and the delegation of a certain degree of autonomy (Kiefer 1987).

CONCLUSION

This paper has provided a description of the social and cultural factors that have been instrumental in shaping the health care system of modern Japan. In the hundred years since Western medicine was introduced into Japan, it has been shaped and adapted to fit into the cultural context of East Asian medicine. In this way medicine is congruent with the needs of Japanese patients. The hypothesis that traditional medicine in a society will become obsolete or peripheral after the introduction of Western medicine is not borne out in the case of Japan (Kleinman 1978). Instead, this examination supports Lieban's (1973) observation that human groups adapt to their environment by combining biological and cultural resources.

Japanese society, which is based on a dense network of interpersonal relations, has adapted Western medicine in ways that limit the impersonal aspects of biomedicine. They have managed to involve the entire social group in the healing process, unlike many Western nations (Ohnuki-Tierney 1984). Moreover, the existence of a pluralistic medical system that offers a variety of approaches to disease and illness is highly functional. It has the potential to meet many of the needs of patients with chronic diseases or with psychological needs that are not met by Western medicine.

Japan's experience with Western medicine has important implications for developing countries. In countries undergoing rapid social change, Western medicine must be integrated into existing cultural beliefs and practices.

Finally, Japanese medicine provides a number of important concepts that help to shed light on the strengths and weaknesses of Western medicine. Traditional Japanese medicine emphasized preventive over therapeutic medicine. Second, it considered man's adaptation to his/her environment as critical in preserving health. Third, it recognized the primary effects of social behavior on health. According to this view, responsibility for health and healing do not only reside with medical practitioners. Rather, the individual, the family, and the community at large are significant participants in health care (Lock 1980).

NOTE

[1] We wish to acknowledge the assistance of Marilyn M. Anderson, Alan P. Farkas, and Ashok Pillai in the preparation of this paper. An earlier version of the paper was presented at the meeting of the Midwest Sociological Society, Chicago, IL, April 7-10, 1993.

REFERENCES

ANDERSON, JAMES G. 1992. "Health Care in the People's Republic of China: A Blend of Traditional and Modern." *Central Issues in Anthropology* 10:67-75.

BOWERS, JOHN Z. 1970. *Western Medical Pioneers in Feudal Japan*. Baltimore: Johns Hopkins University Press.

CAUDILL, WILLIAM. 1961. "Around-the-Clock Patient Care in Japanese Psychiatric Hospitals: The Role of the Tsukisoi." *American Sociological Review* 26 (2):204-14.

CAUDILL, WILLIAM. 1962. "Patterns of Emotion in Modern Japan." Pp. 115-31 in *Japanese Culture*, edited by R.J. Smith and R.K. Beardsley. Chicago: Aldine.

CAUDILL, WILLIAM. 1976a. "Everyday Health and Illness in Japan and America." Pp. 159-77 in *Asian Medical Systems*, edited by Charles Leslie. Berkeley, CA: University of California Press.

CAUDILL, WILLIAM. 1976b. "Social Change and Cultural Continuity in Modern Japan." Pp. 18-44 in *Responses to Change*, edited by George DeVos. New York: Van Nostrand.

CAUDILL, WILLIAM, and TAKEO DOI. 1963. "Interrelations of Psychiatry, Culture and Emotion in Japan." Pp. 374-421 in *Man's Image in Medicine and Anthropology*, edited by Iago Galdston. New York: International University Press.

DEVOS, GEORGE A. 1973. *Socialization for Achievement: Essays on the Cultural Psychology of the Japanese*. Berkeley, CA: University of California Press.

DOI, TAKEO. 1973. *The Anatomy of Dependence*. New York: Harper and Row.

DOUGLAS, MARY. 1966. *Purity and Danger: An Analysis of the Concepts of Pollution and Taboo*. New York: Pantheon Books.

DUBOS, RENE. 1968. *Man, Medicine, and Environment*. New York: Praeger.

FREED, ANNE O. 1990. "How Japanese Families Cope with Fragile Elderly." *Journal of Gerontological Social Work* 15 (1/2):39-56.

FUSE, SHOICHI. 1979. *A History of Medical Doctors in Japan*. Tokyo: Chuo Koronsha.

GOTO, K. 1988. "Health Care in Japan." *Minnesota Medicine* 72:339-42.

HAGLAND, M.M., J. JOHNSON, and H.J. ANDERSON. 1991. "Looking Abroad for Changes to the U.S. Health Care System." *Hospitals* 65 (10):30-35.

HASHIMOTO, M. 1984. "Health Services in Japan." Pp. 335-70 in *Comparative Health Care Systems*, edited by Marshall W. Raffel. University Park, PA: Pennsylvania State University Press.

HAUG, MARIE R., HIROKO AKIYAMA, GEORGEANNA TRYBAN, KYOICHI SONODA, and MAY WYKLE. 1991. "Self Care: Japan and the U.S. Compared." *Social Science and Medicine* 33 (9):1011-22.

IGLEHART, JOHN K. 1988a. "Japan's Medical Care System." *New England Journal of Medicine* 319:807-12.

IGLEHART, JOHN K. 1988b. "Japan's Medical Care System—Part Two. *New England Journal of Medicine* 319:1166-72.

IKEGAMI, NAOKI. 1980. "Growth of Psychiatric Beds in Japan." *Social Science and Medicine* 14A:561-70.

IKEGAMI, NAOKI, and SETH B. GOLDSMITH. 1982. "The Japanese Health Services: An Overview." *Journal of Ambulatory Care Management* September:78-86.

IKEGAMI, NAOKI. 1991. "Japanese Health Care: Low Cost through Regulated Fees." *Health Affairs* 10 (3):87-109.

KIEFER, CHRISTIE W. 1987. "Care of the Aged in Japan." Pp. 89-109 in *Health, Illness, and Medical Care in Japan: Cultural and Social Dimensions*, edited by Edward Norbeck and Margaret Lock. Honolulu: University of Hawaii Press.

KLEINMAN, ARTHUR M. 1978. "International Health Care Planning from an Ethnomedical Perspective: Critique and Recommendations for Change." *Medical Anthropology* 2:71-74.

KOYANO, WATARU, HIROSHI SHIBATA, KATSUHARU NAKAZATO, HIROSHI HAGA, YASUO SUYAMA, and TOSHIHISA MATSUSAKI. 1988. "Prevalence of Disability in Instrumental Activities of Daily Living among Elderly Japanese." *Journal of Gerontology: Social Sciences* 43 (2):41-45.

KURODA, KENJI, KOZO TATARA, TOSHIO TAKATORIGE, LIN ZHAO, and FUMJAKI SHINSHO. 1992. "Factors Related to Long-Term Stay in Hospitals by Elderly People in a Japanese City." *Age and Aging* 21:321-27.

LEBRA, T. 1976. *Japanese Patterns of Behavior.* Honolulu: University of Hawaii Press.

LIEBAN, RICHARD W. 1973. "Medical Anthropology." Pp. 1031-72 in *Handbook of Social and Cultural Anthropology,* edited by John Joseph Honigmann. Chicago: Rand McNally.

LIN, T. et al. 1978. "Ethnicity and Pattern of Help-Seeking." *Journal of Culture, Medicine and Psychiatry* 2:3-13.

LOCK, MARGARET M. 1980. *East Asian Medicine in Urban Japan: Varieties of Medical Experiences.* Berkeley: University of California Press.

LOCK, MARGARET M. 1985. "Impact of the Chinese Medical Model on Japan or, How the Younger Brother Comes of Age." *Social Science and Medicine* 21 (8):945-50.

LONG, SUSAN ORPETT. 1987. "Health Care Providers: Technology, Policy, and Professional Dominance." Pp. 66-88 in *Health, Illness, and Medical Care in Japan,* edited by Edward Norbeck and Margaret Lock. Honolulu: University of Hawaii Press.

LONG, SUSAN O., and BRUCE LONG. 1982. "Curable Cancers and Fatal Ulcers." *Social Science and Medicine* 16:2101-08.

MAEDA, DAISAKU. 1983. "Family Care in Japan," *The Gerontologist* 23 (6):579-83.

MARTIN, LINDA G. 1988. "The Aging of Asia." *Journal of Gerontology: Social Sciences* 43 (4):99-113.

MARTIN, LINDA G. 1991. "Population Aging Policies in East Asia and the United States." *Science* 251:527-31.

MUNAKATA, T. 1984. *Sociology of Mental Health Care.* Tokyo: Koubundo.

MUNAKATA, T. 1986. "Socio-Cultural Factors of Japanese Attitudes Toward Mental Illness and Mental Health Care Delivery System." Pp. 69-96 in *Proceedings from the Workshop on Modernization of East-Asian Medicine,* edited by D.Y.H. Wu and Kyoichi Sonoda. Honolulu, Jan 7-19, 1986.

NORBECK, EDWARD, and MARGARET M. LOCK, eds. 1987. *Health, Illness and Medical Care in Japan.* Honolulu: University of Hawaii Press.

OGAWA, NAOHIRO, and ROBERT D. RETHERFORD. 1993. "Care of the Elderly in Japan: Changing Norms and Expectations." *Journal of Marriage and the Family* 55:585-97.

OHNUKI-TIERNEY, EMIKO. 1984. *Illness and Culture in Contemporary Japan.* Cambridge University Press.

PAYER, LYNN. 1988. *Medicine and Culture.* New York: Henry Holt and Co.

POWELL, M., and M. ANESAKI. 1990. *Health Care in Japan.* London and New York: Routledge.

REYNOLDS, DAVID K. 1987. "Japanese Models of Psychotherapy." Pp. 110-29 in *Health, Illness, and Medical Care in Japan,* edited by Edward Norbeck and Margaret Lock. Honolulu: University of Hawaii Press.

SIDEL, VICTOR W., and RUTH SIDEL. 1973. *Serve the People: Observations on Medicine in the People's Republic of China.* New York: Josiah Macy, Jr. Foundation.

SONODA, KYOICHI. 1988. *Health and Illness in Changing Japanese Society.* Tokyo: University of Tokyo Press.

STESLICKE, WILLIAM E. 1987. "The Japanese State of Health: A Political-Economic Perspective." Pp. 24-65 in *Health, Illness, and Medical Care in Japan,* edited by Edward Norbeck and Margaret Lock. Honolulu: The University of Hawaii Press.

TATARA, M. 1982. "Psychoanalytic Psychotherapy in Japan." *Journal of the American Academy of Psychoanalysis* 10:225-39.

TSENG, WEN-SHING. 1975. "Traditional and Modern Psychiatric Care in Taiwan." Pp. 177-94 in *Medicine in Chinese Cultures: Comparative Studies of Health Care in Chinese and Other Societies,* edited by Arthur Kleinman. Washington, DC: U.S.DHEW, PHS, DHEW Publ. No. (NIH)75-653.

TSUYA, NORIKO O., and LINDA G. MARTIN, 1992. "Living Arrangements of Elderly Japanese and Attitudes Toward Inheritance." *Journal of Gerontology: Social Sciences* 47 (2):45-54.

CHAPTER 3

Progress and Constraints of Nursing and Nursing Education in Islamic Societies

Nancy Halsted Bryant

INTRODUCTION

This chapter represents a review of the literature about the history and status of nursing and nursing education in selected Islamic countries, starting with Egypt and travelling across the Middle East to the Asian subcontinent. The countries included are Egypt, Turkey, Lebanon, Syria, Jordan, Iraq, Iran, the Arabian Gulf countries, Pakistan, and India.

The choice of nations was based on several factors. Except for India, they are all in the Eastern Mediterranean Region (EMR) of the World Health Organization (WHO) and have a majority population that is Islamic. In addition, most of them are interconnected and enjoy reasonably good relations through trade, travel, and migration of workers. Certain marked variations are also present among these countries: the vast wealth of the oil-rich Gulf Region as compared with low income countries such as Pakistan and India; the varied roles and positions of women within each society; the status and image of nursing as part of the country's health care system; the effects of a secular versus an Islamic form of legal system; and the results of external influences/forces upon the government and the life of the population.

Finding published information about nursing in these countries also became a determining factor in the choice of countries, as well as my own experience of over seven years as a nurse educator and school of nursing administrator in Karachi, Pakistan. Two books by Ruth Woodsmall, *Women In the Changing Islamic System* (1936) and *Women and the New East* (1960), played an important part in choosing the countries to be included in this study, and provided the basic information about how modern nursing started in each country.

Other books that contained accounts of the early histories of medicine and nursing were also helpful, as were those written about women in Islam. The latter has become a popular topic, with numerous books written by Middle Eastern women since the late 1970s and early 1980s. Journal articles pertinent to the subject of this paper are not plentiful, but some can be found to cover the important issues related to nursing in a specific country or region.

A chronological framework has been used in presenting the changes that have taken place in nursing in Islamic countries. In several instances, individual countries are discussed in detail.

The first section deals briefly with the early history of nursing, which includes the pre-Christian period up to the time of Florence Nightingale and the beginning of modern nursing. Information about the role of women in nursing in early Islam is scarce. Also included is a short discussion on the customs and traditions of Islamic women.

The second section of the chapter extends from about 1900 to 1930. Little information about women in nursing is available during this period because the role of women in Islamic societies was mainly within the home. Woodsmall (1936), however, describes the early educational opportunities and career choices available to women living behind the veil or in purdah. She points out the changes that began to take place gradually in many Middle Eastern countries after World War I.

The next period of change, 1930 to 1960, again reported by Woodsmall (1960), offers insights into the wide variation in the roles of Islamic women between countries and between rural and urban areas within countries. The part played by government efforts to develop health care systems and the role of external funding agencies are noted as important to the progress of nursing and nursing education during this period.

The last period, 1960 to the present, does not have a comprehensive study similar to Woodsmall's other two, but depends largely on journal articles about the status of nursing, reports of nursing education projects, and personal communication with individuals who have worked in these Islamic countries. In addition, books written about women in Islam provide valuable material about the current roles of women which is helpful in explaining the present status and image of nursing.

The conclusion attempts briefly to examine the major factors influencing the progress and development of nursing education revealed by this literature review.

EARLY HISTORY OF NURSING

In order to measure the progress of nursing in the Middle East and other Islamic societies, it is helpful to review the early history of medicine and nursing. Both professions had their early beginnings in this same geographic region before shifting westward into Europe and beyond.

In ancient Egypt, physicians had developed treatments for numerous illnesses, and had established public hygiene and sanitation to a remarkable scale. Nutting and Dock (1935) state [although] "There is no mention to be found of nurses, yet it seems unreasonable to suppose that a nation which had brought medicine, pharmacy, and sanitation to so orderly and systematic a state should not have had a nursing class; or that women should not have taken an active share in good works" (pp. 53–54).

A concise summary of the contributions of Arabian medicine and the most important physicians of the time is found in Jamieson, Sewall, and Suhrie (1966). They state: "To this Islamic interest in learning, medicine owes a great deal. Physiology and hygiene were studied and an extensive materia medica developed. Although Moslem belief in the uncleanliness of the dead forbade dissection, surgeons practiced and learned to use hyoscyamus, cannabis indica, and opium as anesthetics. . . ." "With advancing knowledge of medicine, great hospitals were built and those of Bagdad and Cordova became famous. We hear of women working in them, but instruction seems not to have gone beyond bedmaking" (pp. 89–90).

From ancient times, women have assumed the role of nursing the sick, whether it was within the family, during epidemics or casualties from the battlefields. Since the history of modern nursing has evolved from the work of women in the early Christian church, it is necessary to briefly examine the role of these women and note how it has changed over time.

Deaconesses were the earliest orders of women workers in the Church, and the ones especially concerned with nursing. The deaconesses are generally considered to be the first "visiting nurses," since their responsibilities included distribution of food and medicines, caring for the sick in their homes and in the prisons, as well as performing their clerical duties. Phoebe (60 A.D.), a friend of St. Paul, was the first deaconess. She had a high social standing and wealth of her own. The order of deaconesses spread over Asia Minor into Syria and throughout Italy into Spain, Gaul, and Ireland. It was especially active in the Eastern church, where Olympia, the young widow of the Roman prefect of Constantinople, organized and guided the work of forty deaconesses.

The order of deaconesses died out early in Rome because the Western church (Rome) opposed the role they played in conducting churchly functions. "The female diaconate lasted in the East as an institution until the eight century, but Schafer says that from the end of the fourth it steadily declined in importance. It was deprived of its clerical character by the decrees passed by the Gallic councils of the fifth and sixth century" (Nutting and Dock 1935, p. 114).

This action seems to be an early example of power and status being taken from women who were performing "nursing" and charity roles. The church leaders did not want them on an equal footing with the clergy, and resented their ordination and their freedom of mobility and lifestyle. The women workers of the church (who at that time did not perform nursing duties) who were tolerated and brought into the formal structure were widows and virgins. These women became nuns, joined orders, and lived in convents under the rule of male clergy.

Another group of women who distinguished themselves in the field of nursing were noble Roman matrons. "These were women of wealth, intelligence and social leadership who, having been converted to Christianity, founded hospitals and convents and worked for the good of others" (Dolan 1978, p. 45). The best known of these matrons were St. Helena (250–330 A.D.), Empress Flacilla (346?–395 A.D.), St. Marcella (340?–420 A.D.), St. Fabiola (390 A.D.), and St. Paula (347–404 A.D.).

During the early medieval period three famous hospitals were built outside monastery walls and they are still in existence today. They are: the Hotel Dieu in Lyons, established in 542, where nursing was carried out mainly by repentant women and by widows called sisters and male nurses called brothers; the Hotel Dieu in Paris, founded in 650, where the nursing staff was composed of Augustine sisters; and the Santo Spirito Hospital in Rome, founded in 717 to take care mainly of the sick rather than also serving as an almshouse (Dolan 1978). The pattern of nursing that developed during the Middle Ages continued well into the 19th century. This is the situation that largely prevailed when Florence Nightingale took up the torch in the mid-1800s.

Although very little information is recorded in Western books about the early role of Islamic women in nursing, several publications from the East include reports of nursing activities carried out by females during the time of the Prophet Mohammed. Shaikh and Abbasi (1981) report that women nursed the wounded soldiers and provided water and food to needy persons. One woman, Umme Atiya, claims that she participated in seven battles along with the Holy Prophet where she prepared food and attended the sick and wounded. The authors give the names of many other Muslim women who at that time carried out similar duties on the battlefields and helped establish tent hospitals.

An interesting account by Hussein (1981), about the "First Nurse In Islam," Rufida, was published in the *Bulletin of Islamic Medicine* as part of the Proceedings of The First International Conference on Islamic Medicine in January, 1981. Rufida learned healing and nursing skills from her father, Saad al-Aslamy, who was a prominent healer in Yethreb, Arabia. Hussein (1981) claims that she started the first nursing school in Islam when she organized a team of Muslim women and young girls to train and teach them the art of nursing the wounded and sick. Rufida continued her work in the development and improvement of nursing even after the battles were over and until her death. According to Hussein (1981), "She laid down the first code of Nursing Rules and ethics in the world. This was 14 centuries ago and she is still a symbol of noble deeds and self-denial. Twelve centuries later came Florence Nightingale who followed her footsteps" (pp. 261–62).

After these early reports, however, there are few recordings of progress in nursing among Muslim women until Western missionaries reintroduced these activities in the 1880s.

WOMEN OF ISLAM: THEIR CUSTOMS AND TRADITIONS

More than almost any other group of women, those of the Islamic faith are bound by customs and traditions that have changed little from the time of the Prophet. In fact, several modern authors would argue that because of conservative interpretations of the Quran by succeeding clerics, many rules and regulations restraining the activities of women have been added over the centuries (Beck 1980; Reeves 1989; and Engineer 1987).

In examining some of the customs and traditions related to women in Islamic countries, it is not surprising that professions such as nursing and midwifery have had to overcome many obstacles in order to progress and develop.

Minai (1981) discusses traditions and transition in the Middle East, tells of the effects of national liberation and women's liberation on the customs of veiling, purdah, and the harem. Little by little, since the days of Ataturk in the early 1920s, prominent, wealthy women have led the way in demanding the rights for women guaranteed in the Quran. Initially, they helped secure educational opportunities for girls, especially through secondary school and then for university admission. She also notes, however: "Because the harem mentality has remained an important part of the code of honor, education has invariably thrown Muslim women in conflict with their traditional culture. School opened their eyes to wider horizons and prepared them to take active roles in their society, while home restricted their freedom in order to guard their reputation and marriageability" (p. 129).

The natural progression for all women in Islam after education is marriage and family. It is against the established norm to consider working and supporting oneself. Although some women in Middle Eastern countries do prepare themselves for a profession and do hold jobs outside the home, it is still done by only a small proportion of the population, who are mostly urban, and usually within the traditional context of marriage and children. Conditions for most Muslim women do not differ greatly today from the 1930s when Woodsmall (1936) reported: "Eastern society as a whole, not only the Islamic system, has assigned to women a position of economic dependence as regards their earning a livelihood. The Eastern man has always assumed the responsibility for the support of all the women in his family, and guarded this responsibility as a matter of personal honour and pride. Hence, the idea of having a woman earn her own living has been considered a direct reflection on the husband or father or brother, whoever may be responsible for her support. . . . A woman under the established social order of the East, therefore, has never been regarded as an independent member of society, but always as a part of a home group" (pp. 239–40).

Minai (1981) and other authors note the contradictions existing in this situation when from 50 to 70 percent of rural workers in agriculture are women, most of whom receive no wages for their arduous work.

The custom of women being responsible for the care of the children and the smooth running of the household, with little help from male family members, also impacts on the ability to choose and pursue a career. Recent years have seen the disintegration of the extended family, with its built-in babysitters, in many Eastern cities. For example, there are Turkish women whose grandmothers combined careers with marriage, but this caused no difficulty in the old days, when the extended family lived together and maids were easily available. The career woman did not have to redefine her domestic role then. For all practical purposes, she simply relegated it to a surrogate. Today, with more than 70 percent of the families reduced to nuclear size in Turkey's metropolitan areas, the professional woman is the first to assume the double burden (Minai 1981).

EDUCATION AND CAREERS FOR WOMEN (1900–1930)

A good summary of educational opportunities and career choices for Muslim women before 1930 can be found in *Women in the Changing Islamic System* (1936) by Ruth Woodsmall. In 1929, she completed a year of travel/study, sponsored by the Rockefeller Foundation, observing signs of change in the lives of women in the Muslim world. Her travels took her from Egypt across the Near East into India. Her study focused on the changes in education, economic roles, health, family, religions and social roles for women in these numerous and varied countries of the Middle East and South Asia.

Woodsmall was familiar with her topic and much of the area she reports on, having worked as the regional director of the YWCA in Istanbul, Turkey for nine years and having made previous trips to Syria, Egypt, Palestine and Trans Jordan. As she points out in the introduction of her book, the changes that took place in the Middle East and India after World War I were far reaching and irreversible.

Woodsmall (1936) makes the following observations about the status of Muslim women's education and their opportunities for a professional career in 1930:

> Throughout the Near East, the Middle East and India, the one profession which has long been accepted for women is teaching. Certainly from Egypt to India marriage and teaching have been, and still are, the only unquestioned avenues for a woman's activity. The Moslem world, because of the veil, has afforded special opportunities for women in the teaching profession, since girls could not be taught by a man except perhaps chanting of the Koran might be carried on under the direction of an elderly sheikh. (p. 241)
>
> The majority of Moslem girls who are preparing to teach is from the middle class—in Iraq, Syria, Palestine and Egypt. Economic necessity is for them the determining factor. For the increasing number of girls who face the need to earn their own livelihood and share in the support of the family, teaching is the logical and practically the only possible choice as long as the veil persists. . . . teaching, especially in some countries, for example Egypt and Palestine, has gained a certain social prestige because of the Government promotion of girls' education. Foreign scholarships and good salaries give the teaching profession for women a definite status, which sets up a strong counter force to social traditions. (p. 243)
>
> The entrance of trained Moslem women into the teaching profession in India has lagged behind that of Christians and Hindus. This is a natural result of the retarded educational development of Moslem girls as a whole which as we have shown is largely due to purdah. An outstanding Moslem woman teacher who remains in strict purdah in the Punjab, illustrates the fact that one can be a teacher and not necessarily break with social tradition. The need for women teachers in India is greater than in any other country because of the rigidity of the purdah system, which makes it impossible to have men teachers in girls' schools. The recognition of this need and the special promotion of education for Moslem girls at the present time will lead to a steady increase in the number of Moslem women teachers. (pp. 243–44)
>
> Indian women have unusual opportunities for the higher educational posts, as principals and inspectresses, since social tradition debars men from any positions in girls' schools. The very lack of social equality in the East thus has been the major factor in promoting professional equality. (p. 244)

Indian married women have a distinct natural advantage over single women in professional life due to the fact that under existing social conditions, it is easier for a married woman to carry on an independent career. In some socially conservative communities, especially in rural areas, an unmarried professional woman does not have an established social status. Here the married woman is practically essential. Marriage is therefore considered in India an advantage for earning a living, if it can be carried on without a sacrifice of essential home duties. (pp. 243–44)

In Iran also married women keep steadily at work and merely take off a little time when the babies are born. Servants are easily found, and the wet-nurse, an honest institution among wealthy people, is always available, so that the outside life of a married teacher has not made reconstruction of her life necessary. (p. 245)

Egypt and Palestine, in contrast to India and Iran, have restricted the employment of married women teachers, but exceptions have been made for head-mistresses of unusual qualifications. . . . Syria, on the other hand, recognizes the desirability of having married teachers. In Aleppo if a man and wife both teach, the Government arranges to allocate them to the same place. (p. 245)

The progress in the field of teaching during the last decade is the forerunner of the general advance of Moslem women toward economic independence. (p. 247)

The above observations are important since they explain how women in Eastern countries became teachers as the first and only acceptable job outside the home. The development of teaching as a professionally acceptable position for women helped nursing in two ways. First, it provided the opportunity for girls to receive an education, without which they would not be prepared for any professional job, and second, once women were allowed to enter one profession, the opportunity to choose others was bound to follow. This is exactly what happened, but not at the same speed in each country.

Woodsmall (1936) points out that because the institution of purdah prevented Muslim women from receiving medical care from men, there was an urgent need for women doctors and nurses in the East. "It has been possible in India even for Moslem women who were still veiled to take up medical service because of the zenana (women's) hospitals which strictly observe purdah. Even so, only a few Indian Moslem women have entered the medical profession and an even smaller number in other Eastern countries where zenana hospitals are not in operation" (p. 247). The public attitude toward the medical profession at that time was not adverse, but the persistence of the veil blocked the way for most females.

The attitude toward nursing and midwifery, in contrast, was distinctly prejudicial. It was the social stigma against these professions throughout the East, that made the promotion of nursing as a career for well-educated Muslim girls a challenge. Woodsmall (1936) reported slow but definite progress through the collective influence of Christian hospitals, government health programs, and the private efforts of Eastern leaders.

To summarize, "In India there are fewer trained Moslem nurses and midwives than Moslem doctors. The number of Moslem women in Iran in both careers in 1929 was under thirty. Iraq at that time had one Moslem trained nurse (an orphan brought up in a government hospital) and no Moslem midwives. A special course for nurses opened in the government hospitals in 1933 has attracted a few Moslem girls of lower middle class. Since the first Moslem midwife finished the course in 1924 in Palestine, a few new trained midwives are added each year. Four Moslem nurses represented the total for Palestine in 1930. Trans Jordan shows a zero as to Moslem women in medicine and health service. Syria has probably fifty trained Moslem midwives and half a dozen Moslem nurses, but Moslem girls of the better class have not yet entered any of the health services. In contrast with the rest of the Moslem East, and also the rest of Egypt, Cairo has a fair number of Moslem midwives and nurses, mostly employed in government service and well paid. The salary may be the reason why Moslem girls of a slightly better class in Egypt than in other countries have been attracted to these two professions" (Woodsmall 1936, p. 249).

It appears that teaching, medicine, nursing, and midwifery make up the professions which were at that time available for Moslem women in the Islamic world, as these were considered the only professions distinctly requiring women and the only ones possible within the limits of the veil.

THE 1950S

In Woodsmall's second book, *Women and the Near East* (1960), she examines further changes that have occurred in the role of Muslim women in Middle Eastern and South Asian countries. There is a wealth of material in this book covering the education, health, economic, political, legal, and social status of women in six countries of the area. Of interest here is the information concerning health careers for women, with particular reference to nursing, as a comparison to her previous study (1929–30), and as a reference point for further comparisons about Muslim women in nursing today. In order to understand the changing role of women and the position of nursing within this geographic area, it is helpful to consider several countries individually.

Turkey

By the mid-1950s, the growth of education for females in Turkey had accelerated greatly since the 1920s in both government and foreign schools. At the same time that women's education was expanding, the health care system was adding hospitals, health centers, maternity and child care homes, and educational institutions for training health professionals. In December, 1955 there were only 7,070 doctors—700 women and 6,370 men—861 practicing dentists, 1,248 pharmacists, 1,983 practicing midwives, and 1,521 nurses (30,000 were needed) for a population of over 24 million. Since the first group of six women students graduated from the University of Istanbul Medical Faculty in 1927, there has been a steady increase of women in the medical profession (Woodsmall 1960).

It was the increase of health professional schools and universities that permitted this expansion of the number of health professionals. By 1960, the Midwifery School in Istanbul University was 40 years old and had graduated over 1,500 midwives who worked in the health centers throughout Turkey. The Red Crescent School of Nursing, begun in 1925, was the only Turkish school until 1945, when the Government opened seven schools. More schools were opened by the late 1950s, including a postgraduate course of nine months to prepare nurses for positions as instructors, heads of hospitals, and public health nurses. In 1960 a new College of Nursing opened with Turkish nurses educated at Teachers College, Columbia University (U.S.) serving as faculty members.

Woodsmall (1960 p. 19) found that "In the past ten years the status of nursing has changed materially. Before that time, social attitudes were changing slowly. . . . The fact that there were, in 1957, about 1,600 Moslem graduate nurses, a major increase in ten years, indicates the change in the attitude of both the public and the parents. In Istanbul, Ankara, and Izmir, nursing is now accepted as a profession, and increasingly in the interior, as nurses studying in Ankara and Istanbul return to their homes."

She also states: "Several progressive steps in government policy have had helpful effects in upgrading nursing and changing the public attitude: (1) the recognition of nurses as government employees, not menial workers, which came with the new regime (1927); (2) grading nurses' schools as equal to lycees (1942); (3) the opening of a large number of new schools all over Turkey (after 1945); (4) the adoption of a Nursing Law which recognized nursing as a profession (1954). These steps have definitely advanced the position of nurses" (pp. 19–20).

Woodsmall concludes that progress made in introducing women to teaching, health, and other professions in Turkey can probably be attributed to the change in the legal code from the Islamic Shariah Law to the Swiss Code during the government of Ataturk and to the lifting of the veil.

Iran

Just as the lifting of the veil in Turkey permitted the rapid expansion of education for girls, so the abolishment of the Chaddur by Riza Shah further promoted education for girls in Iran. Even before this act, however, girls' education had been recognized as a national necessity and an increase in the number of girls in primary and secondary schools, as well as certain liberal trends in the curriculum, such as physical education, had taken place. This came after many years of promotion of education for girls by mission schools and by the establishment of schools by female Iranian educators.

Woodsmall (1960) also points out that "The lack of trained women personnel was the major problem to be solved in the promotion of health service for women and children. In 1949 the estimated total number of nurses in the nurses training schools in Iran, less than ten in number at that time, was 360 for a population of approximately eighteen million. The mission hospitals, American and British, had on their staffs Iranian nurses they had trained themselves. Many other hospitals did not have a single nurse, only poorly trained men workers, mostly uneducated, many of them illiterate. Aside from the 360 trained nurses, there were no trained women health workers" (p. 58).

Woodsmall (1960) continues with her description of nursing in Iran up to 1956. ". . . the schools before 1949—all except one, perhaps—were below full nursing standards. Since 1949, new schools have been developed. The number as of September 1956 was thirteen. An interesting change in the nursing situation is the fact that before Riza Shah there were practically no Moslem nurses. For example, the Church Missionary Society Hospital in Shiraz in 1947 had only two Moslem nurses, and in 1955–56, twenty-five. The number of Moslem applicants is growing. Well-educated young Moslem women are now choosing nursing as their career" (p. 61).

It is important to note, as Woodsmall does, that the gains in the numbers and opportunities for woman in economic life in Iran were mostly within the educated middle- and upper levels of society and this is in the three professions of medicine, teaching, and nursing. Women in the lower-middle and lower class were as yet an unrealized potential in Iran. Women in rural life (who constitute the great majority of the population) have always been an economic asset, since they carry more than half of burden of agriculture, but are unrecognized for their contribution. This situation is similar to that in most developing countries.

Pakistan

Most recorders of the event would agree with Woodsmall (1960), that "The partition of India and Pakistan, with its aftermath of tragedy and terror, confusion and lawlessness in the uprooting of seven million people, had tremendous impact on women of all classes in Pakistan. For the women of the masses, victims in the wholesale evacuation of Moslems from India, the Partition meant a violent disruption of their lives, often personal danger, and utter helplessness. For the women of the educated upper class, whether themselves also refugees from India or those who were already established in Pakistan, as in Lahore, partition meant a sudden unparalleled opportunity to meet tragic human need and serve their new nation" (p. 101).

The Pakistan Nursing Council's (1992) recent book states: "Mohtarma Fatima Jinnah, mother of the nation; Begum Raana Liaquat Ali Khan wife of the then Prime Minister, and Lieutenant Colonel S.M.K. Mallick former Inspector General of Civil Hospitals Punjab, urged the women folk to come out of the threshold of their homes and take care of their sick and injured refugee brothers. In a surprising move, the women reciprocated with enthusiasm. The social and cultural taboos and mores, which had long inhibited Muslim women from joining the ranks of this profession, were found crumbled. The young and middle aged women of Punjab, particularly from Lahore, flocked to the emergency hospitals and refugee camps" (p. 16).

Thus began the nursing profession in Pakistan in 1947–48. But once the euphoria of freedom was over and the sociocultural dictates were restored, the profession again suffered from the previous views society held about nursing and from the lack of education among Muslim women (Pakistan Nursing Council 1992, pp. 17–18).

Education of girls could not progress, however, before women teachers were prepared. "The need for women teachers in primary and secondary schools is crucial because of purdah. In the primary schools a large proportion of the teachers must be women, since men teachers are not acceptable for girls beyond the third class. In the secondary schools the effect of the shortage of women teachers is shown by the fact that the low proportion of girls in secondary schools is in direct ratio to the lack of women teachers" (Woodsmall 1960, p. 106).

Over the years, this situation has improved somewhat, but the high rate of population growth has outstripped the number of schools and teachers available for both boys and girls. Even in 1993, the literacy rate in Pakistan was not much different from that found by the Population Census of 1981, namely, 27 percent for boys and 16 percent for girls (World Bank Country Study 1989, p. 39). In some rural areas, the literacy rate for girls was found to be below one percent and in some villages, none of the girls attend school. Compared to the time of Partition, however, by the late 1950s a remarkable growth in higher education for women had occurred. It was because of this growth that women in Pakistan were educationally prepared to enter various professions such as teaching, medicine, law, and nursing.

Woodsmall (1960) records that "In the first decade [after Partition], 1947–1957, the Government took the following constructive measures to promote the training of nurses and nursing services: Forty-four girls were sent to the United Kingdom (1947) for training; three training centers were started in 1950—Dacca, Lahore and Karachi—by the Central Government; each admitting forty students; the Pakistan Nursing Council was organized (1949) to establish standards of training for nurses, midwives, and health visitors; the nursing school at the Dacca Medical College set up a three-year program to improve teaching and practice facilities, which was carried out with the help of WHO technical assistance (personnel and fellowships) and of UNICEF (teaching equipment and supplies). A nursing advisor was assigned in 1954 at the Government's request by the WHO to the Directorate, to improve the all-Pakistan facilities for nurses training; and a postgraduate College of Nursing was started by the Government in cooperation with the ICA by giving a small well-qualified group further training adequate for the teaching of nursing in training schools. The College offers a one-year course in teaching and administration to nurses and midwives" (p. 113).

The number of registered nurses almost tripled in six years from 370 in 1948 to 1,076 in 1954, including 106 males. But at the same time there were about 6,000 doctors in Pakistan, whereas the ratio of nurses to doctors should be about four to one. The number of nurses employed in government hospitals in 1956 was far below the number needed. Most hospitals in rural areas had no nursing staff.

As in other Eastern countries, recruiting young Muslim women into nursing has always been a difficult task. Miss K. Hardeman, first Principal of the Post Graduate College of Nursing in Karachi, pointed out in 1956 that its low status in public opinion "makes it difficult to secure well-educated Muslim girls of good family for training. Nursing stands low in the students' choice of careers and often meets with strong family opposition, if a girl decides to enter training. . . . The basic reasons for the continuing low status of nursing were summed up by Miss Hardeman as follows: The unfavorable attitude of the doctors, adverse living conditions in hospitals, the unregulated working hours, the lack of the full official status of a 'gazetted' officer (an upper grade) and lack of appreciation in the community, as well as a lack of professional and legal protection, because the existing law is not enforced. . . . The Pakistan Nursing Council was established in 1947 as was a Council for each Province, but lack of central guidance prevents effective registration of nurses" (Woodsmall 1960, pp. 114–15).

1960 TO PRESENT

Many changes have taken place with regard to nursing in Middle Eastern and South Asian countries since the early 1960s. Progress and constraints will be discussed mainly by individual countries. The Gulf States present a different picture of development regarding the needs, recruitment, and progress of nursing than do the other Middle East countries, and they will be discussed separately.

Egypt

The World Health Organization Statistics Annual (1988) indicates that there were 12,458 nurses in Egypt in 1985, with 4,834 working in urban areas and 7,624 working in rural areas (p. 60). The Egyptian government's policy to staff rural health centers can be credited for this large number of nurses/midwives in rural areas. This is not the case for most other countries in this region, which have great difficulty in recruiting young women to work in rural areas—often stationed alone, with low pay and poor living and working conditions (Middle East 1988). In addition, Egypt appears to have a preponderant ratio of nurses to doctors—1 to 0.8—which is also unusual for Eastern countries (WHO Annual 1988, p. 60).

Although Egypt is educating large numbers of nurses annually in its high school, technical institute, and university programs, many of the nurses are seeking employment outside the country. Egyptian nurses can be found working in many of the oil-rich Gulf States, where they receive higher wages and better working conditions. Even though the Egyptian Nurses Syndicate is working to raise salaries, obtain better work conditions and increase the number of nursing students, many graduates are still leaving the country (Middle East 1988).

In Egypt, as well as other Middle Eastern countries, most graduates from degree programs immediately become teachers in schools of nursing or go into nursing service administration positions. With only limited clinical experience, they are not adequately prepared for these leadership roles. Clinical nursing, as a clinical specialist, is not even considered as a career path option by nurses with advanced degrees. Avoidance of clinical nursing is part of the problem related to the continued low status and menial image of nursing. This situation is not helped by the low wages paid to nurses in government hospitals. Although teaching and administrative positions do not pay very well, they do allow nurses to take on consulting work with international agencies such as WHO, Project Hope, etc.

Another concern for the Ministry of Health is that nurses do not work in the health system very long. Many leave after marriage and those prepared at university level continue to seek work in the Gulf States. The outward migration of the most experienced nurses has left the schools of nursing with mostly junior faculty doing the teaching. These events, plus the inability of the junior faculty to conduct mature research, can lead to lowering the quality of the degree programs.

In addition, Egypt, like many other neighboring countries, has no licensing requirement for registering R.N.s. Presently, Project Hope is working with senior Egyptian nursing officials to develop standards of practice that could be implemented countrywide.

Jordan

The nursing profession in Jordan has come a long way since Woodsmall reported that the number of women in the various health services was practically nil in the late 1920s. According to the WHO Annual (1988), there were 2,596 nursing/midwifery personnel in 1984, making a rate of 9.9 nurses per 10,000 population. But Abu Gharbieh and Suliman (1992) paint a discouraging picture of the current status of nursing in Jordan. The authors see the main problem as failure of Jordanian nurses to negotiate a role consistent with their education.

They claim that although "the University of Jordan's nursing programme resembles baccalaureate programmes in the U.S. to a certain extent" . . . the curriculum is really a "combination diploma nursing/medical sciences programme established by physicians and British diploma nurses in 1973" (p. 150). For example, despite the availability of Jordanian nurses trained at the doctoral level, a physician was dean of the nursing program until 1983 and physicians continue to represent nursing on national committees and councils.

In addition, although students are taught that nurses are autonomous individuals with a unique body of knowledge, and should develop collegial relationships with physicians, students realize that physicians and some nursing service administrators are unfamiliar with these views of nursing. Instead, they expect that nurses will "know their place" and get on with their tasks of carrying out physicians' orders and housekeeping duties.

Another problem facing the development of professional nursing in Jordan (and many of the countries in this study), "is that there are few clinical nurse experts capable of putting theory into practice and demonstrating the negotiation process. Although faculty members are well-prepared theoretically, they lack training and experience in clinical nursing. Lacking confidence and credibility, faculty avoid the clinical setting, and clinical instruction is left to teaching assistants who tend to be less likely and less capable role models" (Abu Gharbieh and Suliman, 1992, p. 150).

The authors also point out that "The early socialization experience of Jordanian women may also interfere with socialization into nursing because of the incongruity between traditional roles of women in Jordanian society—wife, mother, daughter—and some of the roles ascribed to the professional nurse" (p. 151). They also wonder if a woman who is dependent upon, and subordinate to, male family members, with little chance to communicate with unrelated males, can be expected to initiate change, exercise independent judgement, and develop collegial relationships with primarily male physicians.

Another factor that affects the quality of graduates is the nursing program's inability to recruit students with such characteristics as academic ability, positive attitudes toward nursing, and adequate English language skills, rather than taking those students assigned to the nursing faculty because they did not make their first choice. Abu Gharbieh and Suliman (1992) state that it is time for the profession to: begin recruiting students with high academic ability; develop a consensus about nurse roles; develop a curriculum that fits the Jordanian culture and health problems; and increase physician and public awareness of nurses' knowledge and training.

Iraq

Picking up where Woodsmall left off, Boyle (1989) provides a concise history of nursing in Iraq since the early 1960s. At that time both the policies of the government and the aspirations of nursing coincided in the desire to advance professional nursing through opportunities in higher education. Nurses as well as other professionals were sent to Great Britain and the United States for further studies, returning with masters degrees and certificates of advanced training. As a result, a major advance for the profession occurred when a baccalaureate program in nursing was begun in 1963 and a master's program in 1986 at the College of Nursing at the University of Baghdad.

The July 17, 1968 Revolution brought Saddam Hussein to power and a new era of national development began. Nursing benefitted from the increased construction of health facilities and the emphasis on education, especially for women.

As Boyle (1989) points out, the Free Education Law of 1975 "promoted access to education for both men and women, thus providing an opportunity for women to attain a basic education with admission to the universities and, later, entitlement to financial support for advanced education abroad. Many women entered the nursing profession who otherwise might have been denied a university education. Small numbers were given government-financed scholarships that allowed them opportunities to advance their education abroad" (p. 169).

As expected, the Iran-Iraq War had profound effects on the nursing profession in Iraq. Boyle (1989) reports that because the services of many health professionals were required for the war effort, a course in Military Nursing is required for all nursing students in the senior year of the baccalaureate program. Since the majority of nurses engaged in active military service in Iraq are males, by "1988 it was reported that 75 percent of the baccalaureate students admitted to the nursing program were males who join the military services on graduation. Such a policy leaves only 25 percent of the graduates (female) available to fill leadership positions in the domestic health care system. The consequences are a shortage of professional nurses and dilution of the impact of professional nursing care" (p. 169).

In keeping with the male-controlled workplace, Boyle (1989) comments that although all faculty members at the College of Nursing are women, the "Dean of the College is a male and a nonnurse, and he, rather than a nurse represents nursing in the larger university and outside community. . . . Within areas of health policy making and program planning, nurses do not hold positions that allow them to exert influence over decision making that affects nursing or patient care. In fact, it is difficult to obtain information on nursing or about what nurses do in a professional capacity. In the Official Abstract of Statistics, published in 1985, there is no specific category identifying nurses or nursing under information about 'medical personnel' " (p. 170). However, statistics from the WHO Annual (1988), indicate that Iraq reported 9,442 physicians and 9,931 nurses in 1987.

Boyle (1989) reports that a severe setback for nursing occurred in August 1988, when the Minister of Education met with the faculty of the College of Nursing to inform them that the College would be closed. (The degree programs were considered too expensive and financial resources were needed to rebuild the country at the end of the Iran-Iraq War.) This action eliminated the only baccalaureate and master's degree programs in the country, thus effectively placing future nurses out of the mainstream of university education and blocking preparation of nurses for leadership roles. Since that time, Iraq has been involved in yet another war. Thus far we do not know the effects of the 1990 war on the nursing profession.

Persian Gulf Countries

An excellent review of the nursing situation in the Persian Gulf countries by Meleis and Hassan (1980) focuses on the main issues that contribute to the nursing shortage in this region. The Gulf countries with similar geographic, social, and economic characteristics included in their study are Saudi Arabia, Kuwait, Qatar, Bahrain, United Arab Emirates, and Oman.

Because of their oil resources, these countries are extremely rich economically, but poor in human resources. "Despite the fact that their governments are spending substantial amounts of money on health, education and public works, they are suffering a severe shortage of nurses" (Meleis and Hassan, 1980). The authors also point out that further problems occur because almost all nurses practicing in this region come from other countries, namely, Egypt, India, Pakistan, Philippines, Korea, United Kingdom, and the United States.

Formal nursing education did not begin until the 1960s, "when most of the Persian Gulf countries achieved their independence and began to expand their educational institutions . . . giving nursing a high priority. The number of programs vary, as do their educational requirements—from diploma to junior college to senior college preparation—but each Gulf area country has at least one diploma school, and Iraq and Saudi Arabia each have two or more diploma schools and one baccalaureate program. All admit students to the diploma school after six to nine years of schooling (the norm is nine years). Schools are still relatively few in number, however, and recruitment of faculty is a major problem" (Meleis and Hassan 1980, p. 239).

As in other Islamic countries, very few women in this wealthy region want to become nurses. Therefore, the schools of nursing in the Persian Gulf countries are filled mostly from waiting lists of foreign students, especially Palestinians, Jordanians, and Egyptians. This was a problem in 1980 when Meleis and Hassan conducted their study and it is still a problem today, more than thirty years after the first schools were opened.

Meleis and Hassan explain that education for women has greatly improved and the governments are continuing to expand opportunities in higher education and professional training. In order to address the problems arising from the diversity of nursing education programs in the area, as well as the crisis in health care in general and in nursing in particular, the Gulf area governments established a consortium for health care. The Secretariat for Health, composed of the ministers of health of each country or their representatives, met in 1967 with the directors of all the nursing programs in the region.

Meleis and Hassan feel that certain conditions must exist in order to address the problems causing the continued nursing shortage in the Gulf area. First, control of nursing must be given back to nurses, in collaboration with other members of the health team and other educators; second, nursing education should be under the jurisdiction of the ministries of education and the universities in collaboration with the ministries of health; and third, within the near future, more faculty should be recruited from abroad through a system of sister institutions, while at the same time, postbasic scholarships to study abroad should be awarded to encourage better-qualified young women to enter nursing.

In addition, Meleis and Hassan (1980) suggested that a nursing consortium be formed that would "consider what type of educational programs would benefit the region most and on what model their implementation should be based" (p. 243). They also recommended that the consortium: collaborate in a limited number of nursing programs that could be easily attended by nurses within the Gulf region; establish a unified program of education that would improve the status of nursing; and recruit qualified faculty, administrators, and clinical specialists from abroad with appropriate rewards that would outweigh the difficulties of adjusting to life in a society quite different from their own.

Several articles published since 1980 document progress in the development of nursing service and education in the Arabian Gulf countries and are discussed below.

Bahrain and United Arab Emirates

When the Ministry of Health of Bahrain was seeking to further develop their local health manpower, they turned to the American University of Beirut (AUB), Lebanon for assistance. This prestigious institution has provided higher education opportunities for young men and women throughout the Arab world for over 100 years. It has been especially successful in promoting health professions education for both Muslin and Christian young women. Kronfel and Athique (1986) state that AUB "established the College of Health Sciences in the State of Bahrain and designed and programmed its curricula and managed that institution on behalf of the Ministry of Health for the first four years (1976–1980)" (p. 5).

Kronfel and Affara (1982) describe the nursing educational program developed by AUB in Bahrain that is designed to address the need to prepare competent, well-trained general nurses, while at the same time providing for some nurses to meet university degree requirements so they may advance into leadership positions.

The purpose of their paper was to "propose a comprehensive system for nursing education within a unifying curricular framework and to suggest a career ladder which integrates the academic and professional dimensions of nursing. It is hoped that such a system will be regarded by the prospective recruits and those already in nursing as one that allows them to enjoy strong continuing education opportunities and to achieve a greater degree of career mobility. Furthermore, as the Arabian Gulf society places a high value on educational achievement, such an approach will help to put nursing into the mainstream of higher education in this region" (Kronfel and Affara 1982, pp. 90–91).

The nursing education model proposed for the Bahrain health system by Kronfel and Affara (1982) is interesting and deserves consideration in light of comments made by Meleis and Hassan regarding the need to develop a program that would be suitable for the Gulf region.

The model has three distinct levels: (1) High School, (2) Associate Degree, and (3) Bachelor. The High School nurse is the product of three years of education and training after nine years of general education. The authors explain that "The 'High School' nurses are expected to function under supervision as supporting nursing staff. There is no doubt that this level is very much needed in view of the shortage of nursing manpower and the level of general education in the Region, and will continue to be for many years to come and possibly for generations. Therefore it becomes essential to design a curriculum that assures a quality output yet with well-defined possibilities of future advancement. . . . Screening procedures are introduced to minimize the concerns often expressed about joining nursing at an early age. At the end of their training, these nurses practice under the supervision of nurses trained to at least an Associate degree level, or continue into the Associate degree program if they meet the entrance requirements" (p. 93).

"The Associate degree in the nursing program is intended to prepare fully competent nurses who are able to assume full responsibilities for patient care within health care facilities. The entry level to this program includes the graduates of the high school level as well as secondary school leavers from the general education streams (12 years of schooling)" (pp. 93–94).

The Bachelor degree level also has two sources of intake: the secondary school student who meets the university entrance requirements, and the students who enter from the Associate degree level, although the course of studies is shorter for the latter category. The authors feel strongly that this kind of career ladder is essential to encourage young women to enter nursing and to be prepared to adapt appropriately to the rapid social changes and the increasing responsibilities of the expanding health services in Bahrain and the Gulf.

The above educational program was implemented in 1982 and has continued successfully to the present. Several nurses from the area have gone abroad for master's and doctoral studies and returned to teach in the schools and serve in the Ministry of Education and Health. The number of student recruits remains somewhat small, and although classes are mostly comprised of other Arab students, there has also been an increase in the number of Bahrainian nationals entering the programs.

Again in 1982, the American University of Beirut was approached by the health ministry of the United Arab Emirates to help establish a College of Health Sciences for the education and training of nursing and allied health personnel. "After a detailed study, the AUB team submitted a feasibility report on the Development of Health Manpower in the U.A.E." (Kronfel and Athique, 1986, p. 5). The authors recommended a three-step career structure similar to the one developed in Bahrain. By 1986, the first phase of the plan, that of the Secondary School Nurse had been implemented. Since then, the Associate Degree and Bachelor in Nursing Degree programs have been established.

Kuwait

Kuwait is another Gulf country that has attempted to seek solutions to its expanding health manpower needs, especially its nursing shortage. Over the past two decades it has arranged to share its oil wealth among its citizens, restructured its health care system to provide free health care to the entire population on an equal basis, and greatly enlarged its educational system to provide free education from kindergarten through graduate school for qualified citizens.

When Meleis (1979) surveyed the nursing situation in the late 1970s, the population of Kuwait was slightly more than a million people, with over half being non-Kuwaitis (immigrants and workers from Palestine, Jordan, Egypt, and other countries), and 60 percent of the population being under the age of 20 years.

With an increase in the number of hospitals from four to eleven during the 1970s, the need for more nurses was urgent. Meleis (1979) describes the history of nursing in this way: "Nursing education in Kuwait began in 1962, under the direct planning and supervision of the Ministry of Public Health (MOPH). Realizing the need for preparing nurses in Kuwait, the MOPH undertook the difficult task of recruiting Kuwaiti women to nursing education. Nursing education appropriately modeled its admission requirements after teachers' education and other vocational education. To be admitted to the School of Nursing, girls had to have finished eight years of schooling. Students were educated for three academic years, at the completion of which the graduates received a diploma in nursing. A year of specialization would qualify them as specialists and give them the opportunity to compete for admission to a B.S. programme in nursing in universities of Egypt, admission being contingent on passing special examinations in English, chemistry and physics. The graduates enjoyed government appointments at the fifth rank (while others with the same education were a rank lower), and were granted other monetary rewards for entering nursing" (p. 107).

Meleis (1979) reports that nursing education has increased over the years, with seven Kuwaitis and six non-Kuwaitis graduating in 1965 to an anticipated 120 students graduating with a general diploma in nursing and 140 in areas of specialization in 1980. Progress in recruiting Kuwaiti women into nursing has been slow. The government has tried numerous tactics, only some of which have been successful. The problems centered on the difficulty in recruiting expatriate faculty, the low image held by the public about nursing, and the disadvantage, until recently, of not having a university-based program to attract better qualified students.

A more recent article by Dalayon (1990) describes the current progress and constraints in nursing in Kuwait. She states that obtaining the required number of health professionals to service the health care system is a continuing problem. Dependence upon foreign labor remains a problem, as it does in most other areas of highly technical activity. "In the distribution of workers under the Ministry of Public Health, Kuwaitis are 68 percent of the number of administrators, but only 21 percent of physicians, 34 percent of dentists, 16 percent of pharmacists, 8 percent of nurses, and 30 percent of other professional and technical workers" (Dalayon 1990, pp. 129–130).

In order to address the need for more nurses and also to prepare nursing leaders, a baccalaureate nursing program was opened in Kuwait University in 1982. Unfortunately, it has had the highest attrition rate among the five allied health programs offered. Dalayon (1990) states: "Career-minded young women turn to medicine, law, or engineering in the face of the prevailing poor image of what nurses are and can do" (p. 132). She feels that more needs to be done by nurses themselves and the Kuwait Nurses Association in providing accurate, updated information to the media in order to change the public's negative perceptions about professional nursing.

Additional challenges to nursing, noted by Dalayon, are found in the traditional roles of the nurse, such as carrying out orders of the physicians; being blamed for what goes wrong and not defending oneself; having to constantly guard one's personal status; lack of administrative channels to manage grievances; the tendency for nurses to scapegoat each other; and the stress related to facing language and cultural diversities in the work setting.

Dalayon (1990) concludes that nursing is still a young profession in Kuwait and has yet to develop the management expertise needed to organize its efforts. "For the present, nurses' own divisions are nursing's worst enemy. To gather the power to professionalize their roles and public image, Kuwaitis and non-Kuwaitis, Arabs and non-Arabs—all nurses must unite around their common interests. With a strong, actively involved membership, the Kuwait Nursing Association could be the catalyst which enables nurses to cope with the challenges and opportunities of coming decades" (p. 134).

India

In comparison to other countries in this survey, India has accomplished a great deal in developing nursing since independence. Mehra (1989) summarized some of the accomplishments as follows: the Indian Nursing Council Act, for establishing standards of training and certification, was passed in December, 1947; a BSc (Hons) nursing course was developed, which integrated public health and psychosocial concepts to enable graduates to work in the hospital as well as in the community; and, in 1959, an MSc Nursing program began to prepare clinical nurses, specialists, educators, and administrators. She also reports: "Since then nearly 30 universities throughout India have established BSc nursing programmes. By the early '80s four programmes led to a Master's in nursing, and some nurses had even begun working toward a PhD in India itself" (p. 121).

Although India has over 170,000 registered nurse-midwives, the population in 1985 was over 700 million, resulting in the nurse/10,000 population ratio of only 2.2. The well-known Bhore report of 1946 recommended an increase in nurses to meet a ratio of one nurse for every 500 people, stating that "sickness and mortality in the country can be halved by the employment of properly trained nurses, health visitors and midwives in sufficient numbers; although the doctors should be increased fourfold, a corresponding increase in nurse and health visitors should be a hundred times and midwives twenty times" (Mehra 1989, p. 121).

Instead, during the '60s and '70s, India overemphasized medical education and the resulting production of all kinds of doctors has, according to Mehra (1989), unbalanced the health team and has resulted in a paucity of funds for nurses and nursing development. Mehra feels strongly that the future of nursing in India, on the threshold of the 21st century, seems bleak if nurses do not receive adequate recognition, gain control over a separate nursing budget, or learn to communicate their capabilities to medical colleagues and the public.

A sociological study of nurses was conducted by Suryamani (1989) on a group of 150 nurses working in King George Hospital in the State of Andhra

Pradesh, India. The results that interest us deal with the nurses' religious and family background, their socioeconomic status, and the image of nurses as perceived by their parents, husbands, and colleagues.

Of the 150 respondents, Suryamani found that 54 percent were Christian, 43 percent were Hindus, and 3 percent were Muslims. She points out that "This pattern not only agrees with the findings of the earlier studies but also confirms the all-India pattern. . . . According to the above-mentioned All India Survey of Nurses, 65 percent of the nurses were Christian, 30 percent of the nurses were Hindus, 2.5 percent were Muslims and the rest of the religious communities constituted 2.5 percent" (p. 61).

Suryamani's study also revealed that 64 percent of the nurses had from 5-15 years of work experience; 80.7 percent were married and living with their husbands; and that the nurses' husbands were better educated and earned more money than their fathers, which means that they had experienced an upward mobility in terms of their class position.

When the nurse respondents were asked to rank their status position in relation to doctors, hospital administrators, health visitors, social workers, etc., 80 percent ranked themselves second in the hospital hierarchy after the doctors, while only 12 percent ranked themselves in third place, after doctors and administrators.

In relation to family attitudes toward nursing, Suryamani found that most parents (62.7 percent) had been in favor of their daughters joining the nursing profession and 68.7 percent still had a quite favorable attitude toward nursing. Husbands were found to have a most favorable attitude (45.5 percent), favorable (29.8 percent), and only 16.5 percent an unfavorable attitude toward nursing.

Pakistan

Compared to many other countries in this survey, Pakistan has made substantial progress in certain aspects of nursing. The governance of nursing at the federal level is the responsibility of the Pakistan Nursing Council, an autonomous body created by an official Act of the Government. The council is responsible for the establishment of a uniform system of training for nurses, midwives, and health visitors. The Nursing Council provides rules and regulations for all diploma nursing schools as well a standardized curriculum, which has recently been revised. The council's president is, by tradition, the Director General of Health, a physician, but one senior nurse serves as Nursing Advisor to the Ministry of Health.

At the provincial level, nursing is regulated through Nursing Examination Boards. Each board is charged by the council with the responsibility of regulating the registration of nurses, midwives, and health visitors, and of setting and conducting the licensing examinations.

Pakistan has also had a professional organization for nurses since the time of Partition. Although the Nursing Federation was active in the beginning, it was dormant for many years and has just recently been meeting regularly to discuss the many issues of nurses.

The Ministry of Health of Pakistan is well aware of the problems that the nursing profession faces. A major factor is the severe shortage of female health personnel, which prevents the government from providing adequate Maternal and Child Health (MCH) services and care at the community level throughout the country. The effects of this shortage are especially serious in rural areas where women and children's health status is unacceptably low.

Efforts to recruit females into the health care system are hindered by the general low level of education for girls and the cultural resistance to women becoming nurses. (Secondary school enrollment for females was 13 percent in 1985/86 [World Bank Country Study 1989, p. xvii]). This situation is made worse by low salaries and inadequate arrangements to motivate, support, and protect female health workers in the health services.

The Government of Pakistan has specifically addressed these problems in its current National Health Policy (NHP). Women's health has an important place in the NHP because of the vital role women play in the development of the social sectors. The NHP has also recognized that one longstanding problem in MCH is the "culturally accepted neglect of women and children" (Ministry of Health and Social Welfare 1990, p. 19). The issue of women's health cannot be adequately addressed, however, without including plans for increasing the number of nurses, midwives, lady health visitors (LHV), and female village health workers.

The ratio of working personnel to population is 1/3,699 for physicians and 1/12,120 for nurses. Pakistan has about four physicians for every one nurse, which is high for a developing country, and the reverse ratio compared to Western countries, where there are four nurses for each doctor. The WHO Annual (1988) shows a total of 20,285 registered nurses and 34,850 registered physicians. However, the number of nurses actually working in the country is estimated by the Ministry of Health at only 6,000 to 8,000. The remainder are inactive, working in other countries (especially the Middle East and Gulf States), or have emigrated (Chappy et al, 1988).

Preparing the additional number of nurses, lady health visitors, health technicians, and midwives that the government feels are necessary—500 per year in each category—will be an extremely difficult task.

There is no doubt that nursing and nursing education in Pakistan have progressed since the late 1950s. Progress, however, has been slow, for the same reasons given for lack of progress in other countries in this survey. "Despite the social welfare orientation of the Islamic faith, nursing is seen in Pakistan as a menial occupation and therefore unsuitable as a field of study for the daughters of middle- and upper-class Muslim families. Young women who enter nursing are rarely aware of the possibility of becoming leaders. Nursing is not seen as a professional career with a future. Moreover, because of the cultural demand for marriage and a family, the concept of a career as a choice for women is viewed as unacceptable" (Harnar et al., 1992).

The Pakistan Nursing Council (1992) does report growth and improvement, noting that the country now has seventy general nursing schools (three of which are for male nurses), seventy midwifery schools, and seven public health schools that prepare lady health visitors. The Pakistan Armed Forces Nursing Service has been in existence since 1952 and operates thirteen schools of nursing. Armed Forces nurses are given the rank of Lieutenant in the army on completion of the program and can rise to the rank of Brigadier. Civilian nursing positions in government hospitals have taken many years of work by dedicated leaders to secure reasonable salaries in graded posts with improved working conditions. Opportunities for promotion are still limited and require completion of specific diploma courses offered in limited numbers at the four nursing colleges.

One major factor that held back nursing education in Pakistan was the outdated curriculum that remained unchanged for about twenty years. Only in 1992 was a new curriculum introduced. Implementing it will require substantial efforts in upgrading teachers and training facilities.

Additionally, a severe lack of qualified nursing faculty has hindered the growth of new schools and programs of higher education in nursing. This situation limited the growth of leaders in nursing who are on par with other nursing leaders from the region as well as in other parts of the developing world.

The Aga Khan University Medical Center—A Brief Case Report on an Innovative Program in Nursing Education.   The Aga Khan University Medical Center (AKUMC) is attempting to address the nursing problems of Pakistan by defining new roles for nursing, developing curricula to prepare nurses for those roles, and creating work settings in which their roles can be made operational.

The AKU School of Nursing (AKUSON) opened in 1980 with the express purpose of developing a quality program that would help raise the standards and the status of nursing in Pakistan. His Highness the Aga Khan, religious leader of the Ismaili Muslim community, has vigorously supported nursing as a suitable career for young women.

When the school opened, all national teachers were registered nurses and midwives and had Diplomas in Teaching and Ward Management from the College of Nursing in Karachi. The first teachers were supplemented by several expatriate faculty who stayed several years and were then replaced by others. A grant from the Canadian International Development Agency (CIDA) to the Aga Khan University and McMaster University, Canada, allowed seven Pakistani faculty members to attend McMaster University to obtain their Bachelor of Science in Nursing (BScN) degrees.

Since then, scholarships from the Aga Khan Foundation in Geneva, the Norwegian Agency for Development, and CIDA have enabled young faculty members and community health nurse supervisors to obtain master's degrees in the United States, Canada, and the Philippines. Thus far, eight have returned to the institution with master's degrees in programs of community health, medical/surgical nursing, or nursing education. Currently, four nurses are studying for their master's degrees in pediatrics, psychiatric, and administrative nursing. Young nursing faculty members with master's degrees are gradually replacing the expatriate faculty in the degree program and have assumed leadership roles in the diploma program.

The shortage of nurses in Pakistan, mentioned previously, presented AKUSON with the challenge of graduating sufficient nurses to staff the University Hospital, which opened in 1985, and to provide community health nurses for the university's primary health care centers. Graduating 100 nurses per year was accepted by the school's administration as a primary goal. Additional goals were to work in community health and to work toward upgrading the level of nursing by starting the first post-diploma BScN course in the country.

Over the past thirteen years, AKUSON's admissions committee (and office) and a full time recruitment officer carried out an extensive recruitment program in order to reach its goals. Admissions in the diploma program increased from 35 to 113 students per year with retention rates averaging about 78 percent. Factors that contribute to the high drop-out rate in some cases were issues related to the role of women, arranged marriages, lack of professional employment opportunities, and other traditional constraints. A major success was the graduation of 93 RNs in the Class of 1990. The number of students recruited from the rural areas outside Karachi and the northern provinces has also increased.

Preparing Leaders

Access to higher nursing education in Pakistan is extremely limited. Financial and material resources for nursing education are scarce. Therefore, the level and type of education needed to prepare nurses for leadership positions is generally unavailable. Just a few years ago there were only two or three Pakistani nurses with master's degrees in the entire country. Nurses with bachelor's degrees were also rare and until 1990, all were educated abroad. In 1988 a two-year post-RN Bachelor of Science in Nursing (BScN) program was started at the Aga Khan University, the first of its kind in Pakistan. With grants from CIDA, the Overseas Development Administration of the UK, and the Aga Khan Foundation, the program graduated its first class of 15 students in 1990. Since then 50 have received their degrees. Enrollment figures have risen gradually in each succeeding class with students recruited from the government and private sector as well as from AKUMC.

A major component of both nursing programs has been the community health nursing courses which are taught in all three years of the diploma program and as a required subject in the degree program. Students in the BScN course may also choose a senior elective in community health nursing. Until recently, AKUSON was the only school in Pakistan preparing nurses in community health.

The position and role of the community health nurse has risen from the need for nurses to take a leading role in the field sites of the Community Health Sciences Department of the Medical College at AKU. These have developed over a period of years since 1985 to provide not only much needed health care for the people of the squatter settlements in Karachi, but also to give an opportunity for community-based field experiences to both medical and nursing students. The number of these centers has increased to seven in urban Karachi, and one in a rural location.

Community Health Nurses assist the Field Directors in the management of the centers and supervise and evaluate other workers, provide assistance and are even in charge at many primary care health centers. They carry out home visits and health education; assist in the collection, aggregation, and analysis of data and research; and in general provide supportive supervision to community health workers. They also provide role models for nursing and medical students and act as preceptors for students during their field experiences (Walani et al., 1991).

In Pakistan, where a nurse is thought of as someone who takes care of the sick in hospitals, and where nurses are very scarce in the country as a whole, the concept of a nurse working with communities in urban and rural health centers is very new and in many ways not culturally acceptable to parents of young women. It took courage for the first nurse/midwives to volunteer for this new position. But the number has gradually increased until the Community Health Sciences Department cannot appoint all who apply.

CONCLUSIONS

A theme that runs through the literature about nursing in Islamic countries is how difficult it is to recruit Muslim girls/women into nursing and then to retain them in the profession.

Starting from the studies of Woodsmall in the late 1920s and mid-1950s, and extending to the more recent articles by Meleis and Hassan (1980), Boyle (1989), Dalayon (1990), and Abu Gharbieh and Suliman (1992), the reasons given are similar and recurring: low status and image of nursing; low pay; poor working conditions; and cultural and traditional constraints. Looking back in history, these are many of the same reasons why women did not enter nursing in Western countries fifty or seventy-five years ago.

In reviewing the literature about nursing in Islamic countries, one can identify a number of contributing factors that seem to have a marked influence on the development of nursing. I have selected the following four to discuss briefly.

Status of Women

Culture and traditions in each society determine the scope of women's activities. Women and girls belonging to very conservative Islamic families will be less likely to receive higher education, work outside the home, or make independent decisions. Most rural Muslim women and some urban women are still living in such families. This does not mean that they are powerless within their own homes. In fact, they usually have complete responsibility for the operation of the household and for the care of the children. But they are not the group from which we can expect to recruit most future nurses.

As society changes, however, with modernization and urbanization, girls tend to receive more education, are exposed to employment opportunities, and may influence other family members to agree to their joining a profession. The need for additional family income also plays a role in accepting a value (i.e., working women) that was previously unacceptable.

As shown by Woodsmall (1936), once the profession of teaching is accepted as appropriate for women, then other professions become acceptable. Within the context of accepting any profession, however, is the dominant consideration that all females marry and bear children. The single professional woman, who previously made up a large part of the teaching and nursing professions in the West, is not an acceptable alternative in Muslim society. As Minai (1981) points out, in pursuing a profession in an Islamic society, women must be prepared to have the responsibilities of family and children as well as performing on the job.

Status and Image of Nursing

The greatest factor affecting the progress of nursing is its generally low image and status in many countries. This has been mentioned again and again by each author who discussed issues relating to women and nursing. A Middle East Conference on Images of Nursing held in Jordan in 1990 concluded that: "Nursing's image problems are global not regional . . . after reviewing 40 papers covering the various aspects of the nursing profession and its development in the Arab world" (Jordan 1990, p. 323).

From the time of Florence Nightingale and her efforts to establish nursing as a profession—up to present times—it has been an uphill battle to raise both the image and the status of nursing. To a large extent, nursing has achieved professional status in the West. But, as most of the reviewed literature indicates, nursing still suffers from a low image and is not held in high esteem in many Islamic cultures. As Meleis (1979) pointed out, the caring and nurturing aspects of nursing are highly appreciated and congruent with Islamic values, but, the interacting with male physicians and patients, and working night and evening shifts are still not accepted by most members of society. This paradox presents a major constraint in the development of nursing within Islamic countries.

Several authors (Meleis and Hassan 1980; Dalayon 1990; Abu Gharbieh and Suliman 1992; and Pizurki et al. 1987) dealt with another issue that greatly affects the status and image of nursing, namely, control. It is felt that unless nurses, rather than physicians, gain control over their profession, nursing will continue to be viewed as a paraprofession and will not attract the bright, committed females who are seeking careers.

It is worth mentioning one factor—demand for services—that helps immensely to raise the image and status of nursing. In each of the countries reviewed in this paper, the need for nurses far exceeded the numbers available. This situation was true in the 1920s and is still true in the 1990s. Whether it be the demands of war, the advances in medical technology, or reform of health services, the requirements for more and better educated nurses are recognized and being acted on by many countries.

National and Political Environment

The countries included in this paper are similar in that they each have a large Islamic population. But, as described by Hirschfeld (1987), they also differ from each other in many ways, especially in forms of government—ranging from monarchies to democratically elected parliaments—and in how these governments affect or control the role of women within society.

Countries that follow strict Islamic laws (Shariah) and require women to be covered or veiled, provide a very different environment for educating young women and promoting career choices than countries that have a secular judicial system or a combination of both. For example, Saudi Arabia and Iran are governed by Islamic laws, Turkey and India by secular systems, and Pakistan has a combination of both.

The judicial system and other issues work to promote or discourage the development of nursing at the governmental level. National and provincial leaders can publicly support nursing as have the presidents and prime ministers in

Pakistan. In addition, recognition of the need for nurses and other female health workers within the country's health care system can result in the upgrading of nursing positions and providing career mobility to high levels in government. Along with this action is the need to continue to improve the quality and quantity of general and higher education for all girls and women, thus preparing them for leadership positions.

In order to carry out the above suggestions, however, a financial commitment is required in the national and provincial budgets. Gulf Region countries have the financial ability to further develop nursing, but have thus far not convinced their female citizens to choose this profession. Other countries have strongly promoted nursing and midwifery—Turkey and Egypt—but because of financial constraints and society's conservative views about women in the workforce, their efforts have been only moderately successful. Still other countries, such as Iraq and Pakistan, have made sporadic efforts in various five-year-plans to develop midwifery and nursing schools and upgrade government positions, but they do not always follow through with financial commitments.

The good intentions of many government officials, however, are often hampered or cancelled by political unrest, sudden changes in government leadership, and wars. Examples of these situations are present in countries such as Pakistan, Iran, Iraq, Lebanon, and Kuwait. Overall, an unstable or uninterested national and political environment can greatly affect the long-term goals of promoting and developing the nursing profession within a country.

External Influences

Several authors noted the assistance received from international agencies, foreign governments, and religious organizations in many of the Islamic countries. Many of these efforts were a general involvement in health care and women's education, but often the help given was specific to the development of nursing. Early recorded efforts were Florence Nightingale's work in Turkey, and her suggestions for sanitary reforms in India (Solomon 1990; Hays 1989); and the development of hospitals and nursing/midwifery programs by North American and European missionaries (Woodsmall 1936 and 1960) in almost all the countries reviewed.

Woodsmall listed the many mission societies, country aid programs, and international foundation scholarships that specifically focused first, on developing modern nursing programs and later, on improving the level of nursing education and practice.

To say that these organizations and agencies were successful is an understatement. There is no doubt that the nursing profession in each country has been greatly helped by outside assistance. But this assistance has also brought its own set of problems. The influence of Western ideas and nursing theories into a relatively underdeveloped nursing profession has in many cases caused conflict and discord with traditional values and customs. Some of these conflicts have not been resolved, but several authors (Kronfel and Affara 1982; Kronfel and Athique 1986; Meleis and Hassan 1980; and Abu Gharbieh and Suliman 1992) have initiated or suggested changes in nursing education programs that propose a better fit with the prevailing cultures and lifestyles of modern Muslim societies.

As mentioned earlier, other events have had major influences upon nursing in Eastern countries. First are the advances in medical science and second are the effects of war. In reference to the first, it is no longer possible for nursing to continue as a dependent, submissive profession when new medical technology demands professionals who are intelligent, well educated, committed, and able to make independent decisions. Many doctors in Eastern countries receive training abroad and return home with the ability to carry out highly sophisticated techniques in modern medicine. They are expecting nurses who can work with them in these efforts. The conflict arises, however, when nurses are expected to perform with new skills, but act within the old cultural norms (Abu Gharbieh and Suliman 1992).

The second event that greatly affects each country, and especially its nursing personnel, is war. We learn from the Pakistan Nursing Council (1992) about the results of the War of Independence on the nursing profession in that country and from Boyle (1989) about the tragedy for nursing resulting from the Iraq-Iran War. From Kuwait comes the report of trying to restart the university nursing program with almost no foreign faculty left in the country after the 1990 Gulf War (R. Gannon, personal communication, February 1993).

Primary Health Care

One theme that is missing in most of the nursing literature from this region is the role of the nurse in Primary Health Care (PHC). Since the time of the international meeting in Alma Ata, where Health For All By The Year 2000 became a goal embraced by member nations of WHO, there has been an effort to define and expand the role of nurses in PHC. The current literature shows, however, how discussions of the problems and constraints of nursing are still focused on nurses working mainly in hospitals.

The requirements for nurses to function effectively in the primary health care team have been neglected in nursing education, practice, and legislation. The work described by Hamar et al. (1992) and Walani et al. (1991) in Pakistan and at the Aga Khan University are examples of preliminary efforts to address a country's need for more PHC workers and a university's attempts to develop prototype PHC centers and to educate and train nurses and doctors to work in them.

These programs, as well as those in India and a few other countries in the region, are struggling to put into practice the recommendations made by the report, WHO Expert Committee on Education and Training of Nurse Teachers and Managers with Special Regard to Primary Health Care (1984). It is recognized that unless nurses, who comprise the largest group of health professionals worldwide, are educated and permitted to take on major responsibilities in the development and implementation of PHC, many countries will fail to attain their health care goals by the year 2000 or beyond. This is an especially important consideration for countries in the Middle East and South Asia, where the role of the community health nurse seems in conflict with the cultures and traditions associated with the role of women.

REFERENCES

ABU GHARBIEH, PATRICIA, and WAFIKA SULIMAN. 1992. "Changing the Image of Nursing in Jordan through Effective Role Negotiation." *International Nursing Review* 39:(5), 144, 149–52.
BECK, LOIS. 1980. "The Religious Lives of Muslim Women." Pp. 27–60 in *Women in Contemporary Muslim Societies*, edited by Jane I. Smith. Cranbury, NJ: Associated University Presses.

BOYLE, JOYCEEN S. 1989. "Professional Nursing in Iraq." *Image: Journal of Nursing Scholarship* 21:(3), 168-71.

CHAPPY, EDWARD, NANCY BRYANT, RUTH HARNAR, PATRICIA SCOTT, and WINNIFRED WARKINTON. 1988. *Pakistan Nursing Strategy*. Karachi, Pakistan: Aga Khan University, Unpublished.

DALAYON, ANNIE. 1990. "Nursing in Kuwait: Problems and Prospects." *Nursing Management* 21:(9), 129-34.

DOLAN, JOSEPHINE A. 1978. *Nursing in Society: A Historical Perspective* (14th ed.). Philadelphia: W. B. Saunders.

ENGINEER, ASGHAR A. 1987. *Status of Women in Islam*. Karachi, Pakistan: Ajanta Publications.

HARNAR, RUTH, YASMIN AMARSI, PAULA HERBERG, and GRACE MILLER. 1992. "Health and Nursing Services in Pakistan: Problems and Challenges for Nurse Leaders." *Nursing Administration Quarterly* 16:(2), 52-59.

HAYS, JUDITH C. 1989. "Florence Nightingale and the India Sanitary Reforms." *Public Health Nursing* 6:(3), 152-54.

HIRSCHFELD, MIRIAM J. 1987. "The World Health Organization's Regions of the Eastern Mediterranean and Europe: Aging of the Population and Nursing Care." *Journal of Advanced Nursing* 12:(2), 151-58.

HUSSEIN, SUAD. 1981. "Rufida Al-Asalmia: First Nurse in Islam." Proceedings of the First International Conference on Islamic Medicine. *Bulletin of Islamic Medicine* 1:(2), 261-62.

JAMIESON, ELIZABETH M., MARY F. SEWALL, and ELEANOR B. SUHRIE. 1966. *Trends in Nursing History: Their Social, International and Ethical Relationships* (6th ed.). Philadelphia: W. B. Saunders.

"Jordan: First Conference on Images of Nursing." 1990. *International Nursing Review* 37:(5), 323.

KRONFEL, NABIL M., and MAROUF M. ATHIQUE. 1986. "Nursing Education in the United Arab Emirates." *International Journal of Nursing Studies* 23:(1), 1-10.

KRONFEL, NABIL M., and FADWA A. AFFARA. 1982. "Nursing Education in the Arabian Gulf: The Bahrain Model." *International Journal of Nursing Studies* 19:(2), 89-98.

MEHRA, PREM. 1989. "The Outlook for Nursing in India." *International Nursing Review* 36:(4), 121-22.

MELEIS, AFAF I., and SOAD H. HASSAN. 1980. "Oil Rich, Nurse Poor: The Nursing Crisis in the Persian Gulf." *Nursing Outlook*, April, 238-43.

MELEIS, AFAF I. 1979. "International Issues in Nursing Education: The Case of Kuwait." *International Nursing Review* 26:(4), 107-10.

"Middle East: The Nurse Flight." 1988. *International Nursing Review* 35:(2), 32.

MINAI, NAILA. 1981. *Women in Islam*. New York: Seaview Books.

Ministry of Health and Social Welfare (Health Division). 1990. *National Health Policy*. Islamabad: Government of Pakistan.

NUTTING, M. ADELAIDE, and LAVINIA L. DOCK. 1935. *A History of Nursing*, Vol. 1. New York: G. P. Putnam's Sons.

Pakistan Nursing Council. 1992. *The History of Nursing in Pakistan*. Islamabad: Pakistan Nursing Council.

REEVES, MINOU. 1989. *Female Warriors of Allah: Women and the Islamic Revolution*. New York: E. P. Dutton.

SHAIKH, N. M., and S. M. MADNI ABBASI. 1981. *Women in Muslim Society*. Karachi: International Islamic Publishers.

SOLOMON, JACQUELINE. 1990. "From Florence Nightingale to Critical Care Nursing: A Visit to Istanbul." *Focus on Critical Care* 17:(5), 370-73.

SURYAMANI, ESWARA. 1989. *The Organization and the Semi-Professional: A Sociological Study of Nurses*. New Delhi: Jainsons.

WALANI, SALIMAH, GHAZALA KABANI, LAILA GULZAR, RUTH HARNAR, and NANCY BRYANT. 1991. "Policy Linked Recruitment and Job Opportunities for Female Health Personnel in Pakistan." Presented at the American Public Health Assoc. Annual Meeting, November 10-14th.

WOODSMALL, RUTH F. 1936. *Women in the Changing Islamic System*. New York: The Round Table Press.

WOODSMALL, RUTH F. 1960. *Women in the New East*. Washington, D.C.: The Middle East Institute.

World Bank Country Study. 1989. *Women in Pakistan: An Economic and Social Strategy*. Washington, D.C.: The World Bank.

World Health Organization Statistics Annual. 1988. *The Health Professions in the 1980's: A Statistical Update*. Geneva: World Health Organization, pp. 43-70.

CHAPTER 4

Dominance and Elitism: The Modern Health Care System in Nepal

Sree Subedi

Janardan Subedi

INTRODUCTION

Modern (Western) medicine has only come to much of the developing world in the last couple of decades. Moreover, where modern medicine has entered the third world, it has not so much displaced older, more traditional forms of health care as it has taken its place alongside them. Nepal offers a very clear example of this medical pluralism, where modern and nonmodern (i.e., folk and traditional) forms of health care exist side by side, and people utilize them.

It would be a mistake, however, to view these different systems of health care as equals. Medicine is clearly implicated in the class structure of Nepal. Since its introduction, planned expansion, and growth, the modern health care system has become the dominant medical system enjoying elite status, privileges, and sponsorship from the government and other bureaucracies. As an entrepreneurial enterprise, modern health care essentially remains an expensive, urban based, curative oriented, technology dependent, specialized, and bureaucratic institution catering to a limited clientele.

The objective of this discussion is to show that, in Nepal, modern medical institutional components are set up in such a way that modern health care is presently, and will continue to be, privileged "elite" medicine catering to a limited "elite" population and intensifying stratification within Nepali society along class lines.

DEVELOPMENT OF MODERN HEALTH CARE

Modern scientific medicine, or allopathic medicine as it is referred to throughout South Asia, was introduced in Nepal by missionaries who built the first hospitals and clinics, and also by Nepali medical practitioners trained abroad. Until 1951, Nepal remained closed to most outsiders. This was due to the fact that Nepal was never colonized and, secondly, under the Rana regime, the country and its people were strictly isolated from outside influences. Due to this isolation, all attempts at modernization, including the implementation of a modern health care system, are relatively new (Subedi 1989).

In Nepal, the modern health services were expanded primarily through the influence of international health assistance. The process was begun in the 1950s when a number of Christian missions, foundations, and trusts came to render services. Western drug companies also assisted. The primary contributors to public health and medical programs during the early years were the U.S., India, USSR, China, and the World Health Organization. During the past 25 years, the number of donors has multiplied many times (Justice 1981).

The growth and development of modern health care was carefully planned and initiated since His Majesty's Government's first Five Year Plan (1956–1961). Since then, the modern health care system has enjoyed access to valuable resources and aid from the government as well as from the agencies mentioned above. Hence, in spite of being a recent phenomenon in Nepal's pluralistic system of health care delivery, the modern health care system has clearly come to be identified as the dominant medical system. However, while modern medicine as a system of knowledge and procedures is undeniably valuable, the way it has been implemented and practiced in Nepal has led to access and improved health for only a limited urban population (see: Subedi 1992; Subedi and Subedi 1993).

THE DOMINANCE OF THE MODERN HEALTH CARE SYSTEM

According to Cockerham (1992), the professionalization of American medicine has led to, and assured, the dominance/power of the medical profession. The power, status, and prestige accorded to the physician in the United States by the general public is not the only criterion that explains their professional dominance. "A particular important factor is the organization of the medical profession itself" (Cockerham: 1992). With regard to this aspect, the author describes the role of hospitals, medical education, and interactions of physicians with clients, colleagues, and official agencies related to the medical profession to show how these help to consolidate and maintain the power structure of American medicine.

Similarly, in Nepal, four interrelated modern medical institutional components not only aid to consolidate the dominance of the modern health care system, but ensure that it remains a financially successful, capitalistic enterprise. Specifically, the role of physicians, hospitals, pharmaceutical companies, and medical education in Nepal are set up to maintain the power, prestige, autonomy, and monopoly of the modern health care system. In doing so, however, modern medicine has essentially become a marker dividing "elites" from the rest of society, not only in access to services but in providing opportunities to the non-elite population in becoming a part of the medical power structure.

Physicians

Until the twentieth century, in both Western and non-Western societies, physicians enjoyed limited social status. Starr (1982) described how medicine gained power and physicians became dominant professional authorities enjoying "elite" wealth, power, and social prestige since World War II. This positively affected the social status and prestige of modern practitioners throughout the world (Quah 1989).

Modern medical practitioners in Nepal are among the most wealthy, powerful, and socially desirable. For matrimonial negotiations (arranged), physicians are not only considered the most eligible bachelors in society, but also continue to fetch the largest dowries. This is because the legacy of Western imperialism has created a situation in which everything associated with "modern" (e.g., modern medicine) is considered superior, intellectual, sophisticated, and desired—in short, elite.

Until 1979–81 all modern physicians in Nepal (total 348) were trained abroad. Only a handful of them were employed in public institutions. Most preferred to live in the capital city of Kathmandu where basic amenities and comforts were available. Since 1982, Nepal has been producing some of its own modern physicians through the Tribhuvan University Institute of Medicine. To date, 250 students have graduated from this medical school.

Currently, Nepal has 1,212 physicians, 917 of whom work for the government, while 295 work exclusively as private practitioners, mostly in urban areas. Of the 917 physicians working for government hospitals and clinics, 334 are posted in urban areas and 583 are posted in rural areas. The disparity in the rural/urban spread of modern practitioners becomes evident because 91 percent of Nepal's population lives in rural areas. According to a bulletin published by the Ministry of Health (1991), there was one physician per 4,729 urban population versus one physician per 92,518 rural population. This problem is further exacerbated by the fact that, although modern physicians are posted in rural areas, many take leaves of absence, sick leave, and/or temporary administrative positions to avoid even minimal service in rural areas. For example, the district hospital of Rukum, which is situated in a hilly district in midwestern Nepal, has been devoid of physicians for the past six months. Although there is a vacancy/need for four physicians in this hospital, only one position is filled by a health assistant (a health paraprofessional) at present. As such, most rural hospitals, and virtually all health posts, are being run by health assistants, even though these assistants are not adequately trained or certified to prescribe medicines to patients. Currently, most of the trained health personnel are based in or around the capital Kathmandu. Yogi (1994) maintains that until the end of January 1994, more than 37 percent of the country's physicians were practicing in Kathmandu.

Modern physicians working for the government are not restricted from having private practice except those working at the Teaching Hospital, Institute of Medicine, Kathmandu. Hence, many physicians work at governmental hospitals/clinics during the day and practice at private clinics during evenings. All physicians working for the Teaching Hospital, however, continue to be involved in private practice even though they are paid much higher salaries than other physicians to keep them from being tempted to practice privately. In fact, private practice is the main source of income for most physicians. An average physician (working part-time) can expect to make an extra 30,000 rupees ($600 U.S.) or more per month from private practice alone.[1] The possibility of such heavy rewards creates a special interest and desire in physicians to spend as much time as possible in private practice. This, in turn, favors those in the population with the ability to pay for services (private), which generally includes better treatment/care, individualized attention, and facilities.

Unlike the situation in developed societies, in Nepal, there are very few external "checks and balances" to assure physician competence and prevent malpractice. There is no penalty for malpractice even for cases where it is clearly evident.[2] While the government and media choose to overlook and/or ignore the issue of malpractice, physicians also benefit, in part, from the cultural belief in fatalism. Hence, injuries, disabilities, and even death incurred during treatment are attributed to one's "karma" (fate).

The government does not mandate that physicians update their knowledge and undergo periodic recertification. For example, many physicians work as administrators or bureaucrats for several years, i.e., in nonclinical capacities. At the end of the term, most of these physicians resume general practice.

Overall, the authors argue that modern physicians in Nepal, reinforced through the Nepal Medical Association, are organized into a professional "caste" that allows them to act as a cartel to control the market for their services and reinforce their elite status. As there is no distinction between curative and preventive health care, physicians regulate the entire range of medical policy in their roles as ministers, secretaries, and planners. Hence, in Nepal, as in the U.S., the entire health care industry is subordinate to the modern physician's authority, regardless of whether the task is patient care, research, or administration (Cockerham 1992). No other group in society is in a position to challenge the power of this guild.

Hospitals

Historically, almost all hospitals were government sponsored. In 1951, Nepal had a few missionary (nonprofit) and government hospitals located mainly in the Kathmandu Valley. By 1956, Nepal had thirty-four hospitals with 625 beds. By mid-1977, there were forty-seven government operated and fifteen missionary and/or proprietary hospitals with 2,174 beds (USAID 1975; Nepal Janch Bujh Kendra 1976; UNICEF 1978). According to the latest available statistics, by 1991, Nepal had 111 hospitals (governmental, missionary, and proprietary) and nursing homes with a total of 4,768 beds (or 1 bed per 3,976 population). Of these, 20 hospitals and 1,980 (41.5 percent) hospital beds were located in Kathmandu Valley where 1.5 million of the country's 19 million population resided (Ministry of Health 1991). The majority of the hospitals outside Kathmandu Valley were located in cities or district headquarters/capitals. Other than a few hospitals in some major cities, most hospitals were small 15–25 bed units—relatively expensive to equip and staff, yet unable to provide comprehensive hospital services. Even where rural health centers and health posts (total 834) existed, they remained understaffed, undersupplied, and underutilized. According to Yogi (1994), there is a dire shortage/absence of trained physicians, personnel, medicines, and equipment in rural hospitals and health posts.

Basically, today there are two types of hospitals: governmental operated/affiliated public hospitals and proprietary (profit-making) hospitals/nursing homes. The former hospitals offer outpatient and inpatient (including emergency) services and are, technically speaking, equally accessible and nominally free for all citizens. The outpatient units are overcrowded and cater mostly to persons with limited resources. As such, individuals (other than those brought in due to an emergency) seeking public outpatient hospital services are often required to wait for several hours, or even days, to consult a physician. This time-consuming process creates a nightmare for most patients and their relatives (Yogi 1994). The inpatient units are divided into two types: general public wards and private wards. The latter are for those who can afford to pay for services. In contrast to the general wards, which are generally overcrowded, filthy, and lack adequate facilities (for example, rooms, toilets, or bathrooms), the private wards are cleaner, provide private rooms, bathrooms, and better attention/care. Thus, in government hospitals, not only is there differential treatment based upon an individual's ability to pay, but differential access as well. Entry to inpatient services is made easier by physician referrals from private practice and/or network connections. It is widely believed that bribery often figures in the access, speed, and quality of treatment for both outpatients and inpatients.

Needless to say, the private, profit-making hospitals/nursing homes cater to the rich. These hospitals are clean, well equipped, and offer quality services from well-known professionals in the field. Even then, it is common knowledge that the upper class and top level politicians/bureaucrats seldom seek modern health care services in Nepal. In general, this group utilizes private modern health care services for minor ailments from specialized Nepali practitioners. For more serious concerns, they seek services abroad, in such countries as India, Thailand, England, or the U.S. For example, in 1993, when the Minister of Health (who is himself a trained M.D. and who oversees the entire health care system/delivery of Nepal) was taken ill, he immediately left for England to seek treatment. Members of the upper-middle class resort almost exclusively to private care or seek modern health care services in India. Thus, it is mainly the lower-middle and poor classes that utilize government clinics and hospitals. In other words, where and what type of modern health care service is sought and what type of care is received is correlated with one's socioeconomic status.

Pharmaceuticals

According to Najman (1989), due to the shortage of qualified medical practitioners in most developing countries, pharmacies serve a central role in health care delivery. This is certainly the case in Nepal. The shortage of physicians, combined with limited access and expense involved in seeking modern professional health services, causes individuals to seek medical care from pharmacists, even though there is no effective licensing or training for pharmacists in Nepal. Pharmacists, in turn, are widely known to recommend and sell medicines, including prescription drugs, without prescriptions. Hence, most medicines can be readily obtained by anyone who can afford to buy them. Similarly, pharmacies are privately owned and operated, and virtually anyone with the resources can decide to open a pharmacy and claim himself or herself to be a pharmacist.

Nepal, like many other developing countries, does not sufficiently regulate the drug business. Many medicines enter the developing world through corrupt practices by multinational companies. According to Braithwaite (1984, 1986), multinational corporations pay substantial bribes to government officials, public servants, health inspectors, custom officials, and hospital staff. This is done in order to gain approval for unsafe products, set higher prices, and finally sell products. For example, sixteen of the top seventeen U.S. pharmaceutical companies (based on sales in 1977) admitted to bribery and corrupt practices in order to open foreign markets (Najman 1989).

Further, there is evidence that multinational pharmaceutical companies routinely "dump" in developing countries certain pharmaceutical products that have either expired or been banned in the United States. For example, Feagin and Feagin (1990) state that, until 1986, U.S. law prohibited drug companies from exporting drugs banned in the United States. Some drug companies ignored this law as there was little possibility of being caught, while others built production facilities overseas. Hence, Depo-Provera (a contraceptive injected into a woman's arm), which was known to produce serious adverse side effects, was produced in Belgium and made available without prescription in eighty countries. Feagin and Feagin (1990) allege that pressure from drug companies resulted in weaker U.S. laws in 1986, thereby allowing drugs not approved in the United States to be exported to twenty-one countries. Similarly, Greenhalgh (1986) reports that in recent years, chloramphenicol, an antibiotic with a high rate of serious and often fatal side effects, which had been banned by the U.S. Food and Drug Administration, accounted for 11 percent of all antibiotics sold in India. In fact, it was being sold as an over-the-counter drug. As most medicines sold in Nepal are obtained from India, some of the banned drug certainly must have reached the Nepali market. Rural areas in particular receive expired and/or banned drugs. Warnings on the negative effects of drugs are often removed because many countries, including Nepal, do not require them.

The authors argue that despite widespread knowledge and evidence of corrupt, unethical practices, the abuse of pharmaceutical products continues because: (a) pharmacies are part of the capitalistic, money-making modern medical enterprise; and (b) it is mainly the rural and/or lower socioeconomic population that is adversely affected.

The sale of drugs means big business to drug manufacturers and pharmacies. Physicians, drug manufacturers, and pharmacies often become linked together to generate positive outcomes (profit) for all. Physicians are known to recommend particular pharmacies and/or drugs to patients. Pharmacies, in turn, often refer persons to specific physicians and/or drugs. Both physicians and pharmacies are influenced, in turn, by sales/medical representatives of drug manufacturing companies. Employees of the drug companies may provide free samples, which are often sold to uninformed or unaware persons; entertain doctors at lavish parties; and, in some cases, share a percentage of their commission from sales in order to get physicians and pharmacists to recommend the company's products.

To further strengthen the profit potential of the modern health care industry, huge sums of money are being invested by drug manufacturing and pharmaceutical industries to advertise and popularize modern medicines through mass-media sources. Claims for the positive effect of drugs are often exaggerated (Feagin and Feagin 1990).

Medical Education

A major landmark in modern health care in Nepal was the establishment, in 1972, of the Institute of Medicine under Tribhuvan University. This medical school was primarily set up to meet the health care personnel needs of the country. Until 1978, the Institute trained only paraprofessional (technical and auxiliary) medical staff/workers. In 1978, the Institute began offering four-year M.D. (Medical Science Diploma for Doctor of General and Community Medicine) programs to train physicians. This program was basically initiated because: (a) until this time all physicians were trained abroad and most or all of them came from exclusive, well-to-do backgrounds. It was estimated that 50 percent of those trained abroad never came back to practice in Nepal. Among those who returned, almost all preferred to practice in Kathmandu; (b) the type of training received abroad was not appropriate for, or oriented to, Nepal's conditions; and (c) while the program would attract able students (traditional), the program would also encourage paraprofessional medical staff/workers (nontraditional) to continue their medical education by virtue of having already been involved in health care services. Finally, it was felt that the program, with its focus on "community medicine," would "remedy the bias" for "super-specialist hospitals and urban medical practice" and make it easier for its participants to work in rural settings (Shah 1980).

Although generous in its aim, the program has led to a status hierarchy (stratification) among medical students and physicians.

Despite the presence of a medical school in Nepal, many elites consider it more prestigious to obtain medical degrees abroad. These English-speaking, foreign-trained physicians return to Nepal with credentials to work at more lucrative and prestigious positions in urban areas. In general, medical education from the Institute of Medicine in Nepal is considered the last resort by many entering the profession, as its degrees carry much less prestige and promise of financial rewards than degrees earned abroad.

Further, there is significant disparity among medical students in Nepal. Most traditional students come from well-to-do backgrounds and English language schools. In contrast, most nontraditional students are from less affluent backgrounds, older in age, and not adequately trained in English. Hence, clear stratification seems to be emerging between traditional versus nontraditional students and the opportunities available to them.

Even though the school's original emphasis was towards "community medicine" and the recruitment and training of persons to work in rural areas, 145 traditional students and 125 nontraditional students have been enrolled in the M.D. programs since 1978. The traditional students tend to identify and interact with their own group and prefer to serve in urban hospitals and clinics. In contrast, nontraditional students are disadvantaged because: (a) they cannot identify or comfortably interact with their "traditional" peers, and (b) most instructors are trained abroad and come from the upper classes. Hence, although Nepal offers those from less elite backgrounds the chance for medical professional (M.D.) degrees, these same individuals are somehow considered "inferior" and tracked into the least prestigious or rewarding positions as physicians in small towns and rural areas.

Currently, in Nepal, there exists a three-tier status-hierarchy among physicians. These three levels are: the "elites," comprised of physicians with foreign degrees; the "middle class," consisting of traditional medical graduates of Nepal; and the "lower class," which is made up of nontraditional graduates of Nepal who are never able fully to escape their class status.

DISCUSSION

In 1990, an elected democratic government came into power in Nepal. Although the new government had generous plans for addressing some of the shortcomings in the modern health care system, not much has been achieved. According to a leading Nepali pediatrician, modern medicine in Nepal is not working well. While there is a tremendous urban/rural disparity, even urban areas such as Kathmandu lack basic supplies and cannot provide necessary health services (Sharma and Yogi 1994).

Instead of putting every effort and resource into improving modern health care implementation and outreach, the new democratic government seems to be actively pursuing a policy of privatization. It is noteworthy that Nepal does not have a School of Public Health. Clearly, then, public health is not a priority. Lately, the government has given permission to open three private medical schools in Nepal, even though the country does not have a national health education policy or any system for regulating medical education to assure quality control (Yogi 1994). Hence, these schools are not being established to fulfill gaps in Nepal's medical personnel resources, but purely as profit-making enterprises. Specifically, these schools are intended to attract students from neighboring countries, as well as other countries. These students generally do not have the credentials to enter medical schools in their own countries. Such students are being encouraged to enroll in medical schools in Nepal as long as they can afford to pay exorbitant admission and tuition fees. In other words, these new medical schools are being set up to cater exclusively to "elites" who have the ability to pay extravagant sums of money to obtain medical degrees.

Recently, while addressing a Parliamentary session, the Prime Minister of Nepal collapsed while standing at the podium. No physicians, provisions for first aid treatment, stretchers, or ambulances were available. Some Ministers and Members of Parliament carried the limp Prime Minister out of the building and to his car. He was taken to the Teaching Hospital, Tribhuvan University. A full nineteen minutes elapsed before he was admitted to the emergency unit at the Teaching Hospital (Yogi 1994). Here, a foreign-born and trained physician was rushed in to attend to him even though well-known, trained Nepali physicians were available. It is significant that this incident occurred in the capital city of Nepal and concerned the country's highest-ranking executive.

The opening of the above-mentioned medical schools has made modern medicine a hot topic of discussion in the mass media and among the urban public. Serious concerns regarding the current state and implementation of modern health care are being raised. These issues include: the disparity in modern health care availability and access; the differential treatment of patients; the various degrees of status accorded to physicians depending on who they are, where they are trained, and where they work; and the promotion of modern health care due to its profit potential while ignoring the needs of the general population. These concerns are being questioned and highlighted by the media.

The authors are convinced that, given the thrust of the present government, there will be no major changes in modern health care planning or policies. Effective health care would require the following: eliminating urban/rural disparity (not by increasing availability of modern health care facilities but making sure of their functional capabilities); applying checks and balances to physicians, hospitals, pharmacies, pharmaceutical products, and medical education; addressing the issue of differential treatment and status of patients/physicians; and paying greater attention to some of the options provided by the indigenous health care systems (which are easily available, less expensive, and meet the health care needs of large numbers of people [Subedi 1992]). Hence, the modern health care system in Nepal is and will remain the predominantly urban-based, profit-making medical enterprise that caters to and stratifies the elites from the rest of society.

NOTES

[1] This figure is based on research conducted by the authors in Kathmandu. The money earned from private practice is enormous. (The GNP per capita in Nepal was the equivalent of $160 in the U.S. This figure is based on the 1994 official exchange rate.)

[2] This information is derived from interviews the authors conducted in 1992 and 1993 with several patients and their families.

REFERENCES

BRAITHWAITE, JOHN. 1984. *Corporate Crime in the Pharmaceutical Industry*. London: Routledge and Kegan Paul.

―――. 1986. "The Corrupt Industry." *New Internationalist*, November (165): 19–20.

COCKERHAM, WILLIAM C. 1992. *Medical Sociology* (5th edition). Englewood Cliffs, NJ: Prentice-Hall.

FEAGIN, JOE R., and CLAIRECE BOOHER FEAGIN. 1990. *Social Problems: A Critical Power Conflict Perspective*. Englewood Cliffs, NJ: Prentice-Hall.

GREENHALGH, TRISHA. 1986. "Three Times Daily: Prescription Habits in India." *New Internationalist*, November (165): 10–11.

JUSTICE, JUDITH. 1981. *International Planning and Health: An Anthropological Case Study of Nepal*. Doctoral Dissertation. Berkeley: The University of California.

Ministry of Health. 1991. *Health Information Bulletin*, Vol. 7. Kathmandu, Nepal: Royal Palace, His Majesty's Government.

NAJMAN, JACOB M. 1989. "Health Care in Developing Countries," Pp. 332–46 in *Handbook of Medical Sociology* (4th edition). Howard E. Freeman and Sol Levine, editors. Englewood Cliffs, N.J: Prentice-Hall.

NEPAL JANCH BUJH KENDRA. 1976. Long-Term Health Plan. Kathmandu, Nepal: Royal Palace, His Majesty's Government.

QUAH, STELLA R. 1989. "The Social Position and Internal Organization of the Medical Profession in the Third World: The Case of Singapore." *Journal of Health and Social Behavior*, Vol. 30: 450-66.

SHAH, MOIN. 1980. "Tribhavan University Institute of Medicine, Nepal," Pp. 81-96 in *Personnel for Health Care: Case Studies of Educational Programs*. F. M. Katz and T. Fulop, editors. Geneva, Switzerland: World Health Organization.

SHARMA, SUSHIL, and BHAGIRATH YOGI. 1994. "Nepal's Health System Is Not Doing Well." *Spotlight Magazine*, (Kathmandu, Nepal), (March 11-17): 22-24.

STARR, PAUL E. 1982. *The Social Transformation of American Medicine*. New York: Basic Books.

SUBEDI, JANARDAN. 1992. "Primary Health Care and Medical Pluralism Exemplified in Nepal: A Proposal for Maximizing Health Care Benefit." *Sociological Focus*, Vol. 25 (4): 321-28.

SUBEDI, JANARDAN. 1989. *Factors Affecting the Use of Modern Medicine in a Pluralistic Health Care System: The Case of Nepal*. Doctoral Dissertation. Akron, OH: The University of Akron.

SUBEDI, JANARDAN, and SREE SUBEDI. 1993. "The Contribution of Modern Medicine in a Traditional System: The Case of Nepal," Pp. 110-21 in *Health and Health Care in Developing Countries: Sociological Perspectives*. Peter Conrad and Eugene B. Gallagher, editors. Philadelphia, PA: Temple University Press.

UNICEF. 1978. Annual Report on Nepal. Kathmandu, Nepal: UNICEF.

USAID. 1975. Reports on the Evaluation of Basic Health Services in Nepal. Kathmandu, Nepal: USAID.

YOGI, BHAGIRATH. 1994. "Dying, Dying, Dead?" *Spotlight Magazine* (Kathmandu, Nepal), (March 18-24): 16-20.

CHAPTER 5

Culture and Technology in Health Care, as Exemplified in Gulf Arab Medicine

Eugene B. Gallagher

INTRODUCTION

The contemporary social sciences have from their beginnings as a distinct mode and focus of inquiry been concerned with the implications of technology for social relationships. Sociologists in particular have defined the historical significance of macrosocial phenomena that are intimately intertwined with new technology. Mediated by urbanization and industrialization, technological change has exerted massive pressure upon social structure and the social identity of the individual (Gehlen 1980).

Sociological debate has crystallized around the question of whether the overall thrust of technology has been to enhance or to diminish human existence, and whether technology can be introduced in a controlled fashion that softens its jarring social impact and psychic dislocation (Fromm 1968). Key sociological concepts such as alienation, depersonalization, and anomie have been defined against a backdrop of relentless technological advance.

The empirical domain of health and medicine can be used to test and clarify concepts that have arisen in other parts of sociology. Medical sociology has taken up the foregoing society-and-technology discourse and imparted its own distinctive agenda and phrasings to it.

Consider for example alienation and depersonalization. These concepts acquire special meanings in medical care. If a factory or clerical worker is alienated from his or her job, there is at least the redemptive compensation of the paycheck. Often enough, the employer does not expect the worker to be psychically identified with his work; the familiar notion of "a fair day's work for a fair day's pay" implies a disconnection. Marxist and Christian humanists deplore and protest the widespread alienation of the worker from his or her work, but, in general, it has been accepted in industrial society. The usual view is that work is one thing, and the self or identity is something else—something more vital and central to the self—that finds expression in family, recreation, mass participation, or culture.

The view is different, however, in the world of health and medicine. Would we want care from a doctor or nurse who was "in it" sheerly for the paycheck? Probably not, because we expect medical workers to have a sense of concern, a motivation of caring in addition to their economic motivation. The image of the exploitable, vulnerable patient colors interpersonal and role relationships throughout health care. Even those patients whose lives and well-being are not at high risk—for example, most cosmetic surgery or arthritis patients—are, we feel, entitled to receive care from workers who care, who are at least somewhat committed beyond earning a living. Alienation and lack of identification with work are questionable stances in health care, however tolerated or expected they may be elsewhere.

Another window that medical sociology opens up for fresh perspectives into general sociology can be found in the concept of the patient as a **worker**. Does it make sociological sense to view the patient as working toward his own health improvement, assisted, or perhaps led, by the doctor and/or other health professionals? What then if the patient is alienated from, or dissatisfied with, the source of medical care? Do notions of exploitation and alienation apply only to the professional production of services, or can they be applied also to those on the receiving end of medical care? Whether or not we have personally experienced it, everyone is familiar with the common complaint of patients that they are being dealt with as a disease, a body part, an object of treatment, or an economic object. Does an alienated health worker alienate his or her clients?

The notion of the patient as an economic object is all too familiar to us in the era of health care reform and of concern with the commercialization of health care. Most medical sociologists, health policy analysts, and other sociomedical scientists share in the wider public sense of a crisis in health care. We experience moral apprehension, refined by our expert knowledge of the dynamics of health care, about the patient-as-a-commodity and about rampant profiteering by care providers. Beyond our indignation, however, we can raise sharp, critical, analytic questions about the economic stance of health care providers. For example, granted that the public justifiably expects health care providers to be attuned to the patient's welfare and not to be profit-driven like General Motors, what *is* the socially and morally viable economic stance of the health care provider?

If, as at one time, health care were provided on a purely free, voluntary, altruistic, and philanthropic basis, there would, of course, be no problem. But in the modern era, society expects that health care providers will find not only their vocation but also their livelihood or economic support from their work. They are expected to be clinically dedicated but not to be utterly altruistic. What level of remuneration is just and reasonable, and how is it to be determined? We have heard the formula "doing well while doing good" advanced in a delicate wrapping of irony. The implication: how wonderful it is that health profession-als can prosper while they are actually helping patients. When anyone else in the capitalistic economy does well their prosperity is thought to have a merce-nary taint to it.

The foregoing example shows that there is much work to be done, con-ceptually and empirically, in medical sociology, drawing upon general sociology for questions and answers—and reciprocally fashioning its own concepts to interpret health/medical phenomena that are not part of the received canon of sociology.

TECHNOLOGY IN MEDICAL CARE

The part that medical technology plays in creating distance between doctor and patient, the detachment of the physician, and the alienation of the patient, has been a major focus of concern in medical sociology (Reiser 1978). There is sub-stantial agreement that, though not alone in the forces that conspire to make modern medicine impersonal, technology is a leading factor. (Increasingly bureaucratic administration of services is another such force.)

Medical historian Stanley Reiser has studied the entry of medical devices and apparatus into routine medical practice over the past two hundred years (1978). He argues that practicing physicians nowadays do not like to use their subjective judgment and unassisted sense organs for diagnosing and treating patients. They distrust their own abilities. A few generations back, their prede-cessors embraced instruments such as the stethoscope and electrocardiograph for their objectivity. Currently, the newer, noninvasive imaging techniques such as NMR and PET are increasingly used despite their substantial cost and despite the often diagnostically inconclusive cognitive overload they sometimes generate.

These innovations are adopted for their presumptive benefit in medicine, but little attention is paid to the ways in which they shape the fabric of the doc-tor-patient relationship. The changes are subtle and cumulative. Communication between the two atrophies as the doctor becomes enamored of what meters and mechanical or electronic controls can deliver. Thus Reiser writes:

> The separation that has developed between the physician as a healer and the patient as human being continues to be viewed with concern in many quarters of medicine and society. . . . the healing of illness requires more than healing parts of the body; it also requires intensive efforts to communicate with patients. . . . Technologies that improve accuracy . . . are essential factors in mod-ern medicine. Yet accuracy, efficiency, and security are purchased at a high price when that price is impersonal medical care. . . ." (Reiser 1978, pp. 230–31)

I have briefly traced out the inroads that technology has made into the doctor-patient relationship. I have done this by design within a sociocultural vacuum. I have assumed what doctors, and society, usually assume about medical care: it is culture-proof. In this simplistic conception, patients have needs and illnesses, and doctors use their skills and techniques to cure or to help them. Beyond that, it makes no difference whether the patient is poor or rich; sophisticated about medicine or uninformed about it; rural or urban-dwelling; Chinese, American, German, or Malaysian.

The latter dimension—the cultural framework or background of the patient—is, however, critically important. Culture is a "fuzzy" yet insistent and powerful influence upon all manner of human behavior. Culture is conveyed and felt in the ways that personal needs are experienced: in food preferences, styles of habitation, apparel, personal appearance, and language.

Medical anthropologists have paid particular attention to the impact of culture on medical care—how cultural values shape the seeking and giving of medical care, especially among traditional peoples in developing areas of the world; and how culture affects the genesis and symptomatology of illness. However, neither anthropologists nor other social scientists have given much attention to the connections between technology and culture—for example, whether the alleged alienation of the patient that occurs with high-tech medicine is more severe in some cultures than others, and how culture shapes expectations regarding the role of technology in medical care.

In this chapter I focus on Arab culture. In the following section, I will set forth two features of Arab culture that are particularly salient for medical care. Following that, I will deal with medical trends in Gulf Arab society, where a rush to technology is currently in full swing.

ARAB SOCIETY AS PERSONALISTIC AND HELPING-ORIENTED

Sociologists and anthropologists who have studied developing societies often note that all social relationships in such societies are colored by the desire for interpersonal attachment and emotional warmth. Many sociological concepts that convey the difference between modern civilization and traditional society recognize this characteristic. In the terminology of Talcott Parsons' well-known pattern-variables, social relationships in traditional societies are particularistic, ascriptive, affective, and diffuse; they are suffused with the closeness of family and collectivity ties (Parsons 1951). It is for this reason that, in traditional societies, fictive kinship terminology is invoked in otherwise impersonal relationships such as buyer-seller. The fictive kinship ties enhance the aura of trust, reliability, and mutual concern. If I am a young person, my opposite in a commercial transaction becomes my "uncle" or my "grandfather." This fiction makes the relationship more satisfying and productive within the immediate social situation. It creates the illusion of a solidary, kin-bonded twosome—two people who are not strangers to each other, much less enemies.

Nowhere in the developing world is the striving for personal bonds, for affiliation, and for the glow of intimacy stronger than in Arab society. A well-known Arabic rhyming aphorism reads "Jarr qubla darr w rafeeq qubla tareeq." It translates literally into: [Choose] "the neighbor before the house, and [choose] the companion before the journey." Like all aphorisms and proverbs, it singles out and overemphasizes a single thread in the complex fabric of human rela-tionships. It distorts, but it clarifies. The idea of "the neighbor before the house" cannot be taken as a complete guide to the process of acquiring a residence— but neither can it be ignored. The aphorism gives direct insight into the per-sonalistic, personalizing nature of the culture that spawned it.

In *The Arab Mind* (1976), Patai argues that the personalism of Arab culture is rooted in, and expressed by, a Bedouin tribal psychology; by this means, even a person of low status living in a Baghdad or Damascus slum will feel pride in using the name of the tribe that his forebears came from, though he is many gen-erations removed from the nomadic desert life. Within the tribe or lineage, there are no real strangers. Though no member holds every other member in equal regard and affection, it is a united, solidary body vis-à-vis an indifferent or hostile world.

A second characteristic of Arab society with great relevance for medical care is the great extent to which it values helper roles and helping activities. This is certainly not a unique feature of Arab society. All human societies would cease to exist if parents did not nurture (nurture is a radical form of helping) their chil-dren into adulthood. Equally, all societies value the kind of help represented by timely aid in physical disasters; assistance in various forms to those who are poor, disabled, or otherwise disadvantaged; and heroic self-sacrifice and altruistic giving. Further, it must be acknowledged that helping as an altruistic, other-ori-ented disposition shades off imperceptibly into self-oriented attitudes, whereby the helper reaps gratitude from the helped. These cautionary notes notwith-standing, I would still argue that societies can be roughly graded in the extent to which they value helping activities—and that Arab society stands well beyond most societies on this axis of societal variation. More than most societies, it weaves helping activities into the social fabric, so that the giving of help becomes a constitutive social value, not merely an activity of benefit to the per-son who is helped.

The two features that I have set forth as pronounced characteristics of Arab culture coalesce into another strong cultural formation, namely, a high tolerance for dependency in the sick role. Medical sociologists will recall Parsons' formu-lation of the sick role, in which, according to prevailing social norms, the sick person is relieved of social responsibilities in proportion to the disabilities imposed by the illness or the demands of treatment (Parsons 1951).

The Parsonian formulation is sometimes thought by clinicians to imply that "anything goes"—that the patient is free to disregard norms and expectations just as he or she pleases. I have heard social workers use the phrase "sick-role behavior" in a tone of disapproval, meaning that patients are regressing, acting out, engaging in outrageous, dependent behavior. I do not doubt that patients sometimes do act this way but I dispute that this is in accord with Parsons' con-ception, which offers a theoretically informed description of the social reality of the sick role. In this conception, there are definite limits to socially permitted dependence on the part of the patient. As will be seen below, the Arab edition of the sick role affords an unusually strong cultural support for dependency.

Dealing with the position of the sick role in Arab society raises a related question: whether the sick role is to be understood as a cultural universal, or whether it is significantly nuanced or shaped by cultural values (Gallagher and Subedi 1992). Although the Parsonian model remains robust as an anchor point for understanding the sick role, there are important cultural variations in it. Compared with American society or most Western European societies, Arab society is indulgent regarding sick-role dependency. This cultural stance is congruent with the core values of Arab society as set forth above. It is virtually axiomatic that in a culture that values highly both interpersonal closeness and helping activities, dependent behavior will be comfortably tolerated. Dependent behavior promotes closer interpersonal ties than autonomous, independent self-sufficiency. Further, people who act in a dependent mode require the help of others to maintain them and to compensate for their own exemptions from social responsibilities.

I present here two case-examples which illustrate sick-role dependency in Arab society. To make the point that this is a basic cultural characteristic and not a function of other factors, such as regional and socioeconomic contingencies, I have drawn these cases from sharply contrasting social classes and nations—a poor Bedouin Arab in Israel, and a member of the royal family in Saudi Arabia.

The first case is that of a 56-year-old male chronic hemodialysis patient at Soroka Hospital in the Negev desert of southern Israel. He is married and, unlike many of the semi-nomadic bedu, lives in a stone house instead of a tent. Because of vascular complications from diabetes, which was also the cause of renal failure, his right leg was amputated. After that, he received a prosthesis, crutches, and a wheelchair. Members of the dialysis staff report, however, that he barely uses his prosthesis or crutches; instead, his sons and grandsons regularly carry him or push him in the wheelchair. The patient's dependence upon close relatives for mobility, and their readiness to meet his expectation, is consistent with a more general observation made by the staff (Lewando-Hunt 1980, p. 10):

> There is a specific cultural attitude amongst the Bedouin toward the chronically sick and the handicapped which both gives them support but also encourages them to be dependent on their family. One's family is expected to adjust to one's limited functioning. They have no expectations of rehabilitation. The blind are assumed to be unable to undertake any physical activity without guidance. The deaf are not expected to know how to lip-read. Their relatives and friends learn how to communicate with them by gesture. In the case of the dialysis patients, there is a readiness to care for them, even unnecessarily.

Soroka Hospital is an outpost of advanced biomedicine in a remote area. Whatever reservations the thoroughly Arab-Muslim bedu may have concerning the impersonality of such medicine, it does not deter them from seeking help— especially for such a symptomatically distressing, medically grave condition as chronic renal failure. From the nephrologists' accounts, it appears that the cultural/communications gap between patient and clinic was enormous. For example, Bedouin dietary practice did not accord with the restrictions that go with dialysis treatment. However, so far as patients' overdependency on relatives is concerned, this did not bother the staff in the least. These professionals confined themselves to the mechanics of effective dialysis and did not invest themselves in rehabilitation objectives.

The second example of culturally sanctioned dependency comes from the Saudi monarchy. The American physician Seymour Gray spent several years practicing medicine in Saudi Arabia. His observations are presented in the mode of participant ethnography in *Beyond the Veil* (Gray 1983). They include the following episode (p. 45):

> Since an ulcer diet was an important part of the treatment, the next step was to devise a diet that prince would be willing to follow. I consulted with the dietician and recommended rice, yogurt, and camel's or goat's milk to start with. These were among the prince's favorite foods. He seemed content, providing his servant prepared the food and fed him spoonful by spoonful. I watched this nursery scene for a few moments and then left.

The patient, cousin to the late King Khalid, was a 60-year-old man hospitalized for ulcer distress. He could easily have fed himself but his feeding dependency was well tolerated. It was based in part upon the tremendous wealth of the Saudi royal family, but to reduce it to that is too facile an explanation. Recall the dependency of the poor Bedouin father; it was supported by his sons. Lacking a servant, the prince could certainly have called in a family member to perform the same task. In other words, this is a parameter of Arab culture that cross cuts, but lies deeper than, socioeconomic status.

Modern biomedical care, drawing heavily upon technology, is relatively new—going back not more than three decades—in the Arab societies of the Middle East. However, the figure of the physician is a strong motif in the earlier history of that region (Khairallah 1946; Ahmad 1991). The historical literature on medicine in Arab societies, dating back to Islam's period of cultural flowering and scientific leadership (800–1300 A.D.), assigns great importance to the role of the physician.

Contemporary Islamic physicians take as role models famous physicians of that period and look to their teachings for guidance. The contemporary generation believes that, in the welter of new technology and multitiered medical bureaucracy that characterizes most health care systems in the Arab world, as elsewhere, patients have become confused and demoralized. Will the doctor—seen as a moral authority as well as a scientific expert—be able to rescue the patient? The following is a typical voicing of this sentiment:

> First and foremost the physician needs to gain back the respect of the patient he once enjoyed. Perhaps very humbly I should point out that the "Muslim physicians" that practiced one thousand years ago had achieved the respect of their patients. . . .
>
> If ever such a practice of Islamic Medicine is restored . . . I think that the physicians will regain the confidence of the patient and his respect will be restored. Unfortunately, until that happens we are going to face a decline in medicine for years to come (Nagamia 1985, p. 1).

Dr. Nagamia made this statement in *Journal of the Islamic Medical Association of North America*, a medical periodical that circulates among Muslim physicians who are currently practicing in the United States and Canada. This group of emigré physicians, drawn mainly from the Middle East, Pakistan, and India, make up a very substantial fraction of all the foreign-born physicians in North America. Although they are fully engaged, successful professionals, they cannot help but have, individually and collectively, the sense of dislocation and uprootedness that goes with migration. Dr. Nagamia's backward look to the days of patriarchal glory of Muslim-Arab physicians such as Al-Razi and Avicenna is a wistful, nostalgic projection into the past.

SOCIAL DYNAMICS AND THE RUSH TO MEDICAL TECHNOLOGY IN THE ARAB GULF

The oil-rich kingdoms of the Arabian Gulf have made a substantial commitment to medical education and health care resources for their people. The countries under consideration here are: Kuwait, Saudi Arabia, Bahrain, Qatar, the United Arab Emirates, and Oman. These countries share a conservative political outlook and a monarchical form of government. Their ruling families are well aware that the worldwide temper of the twentieth century is decidedly democratic and anti-monarchical; they try to keep such issues out of their domestic politics. It is characteristic of modern autocratic rule that health care, along with public education, becomes an important legitimating avenue; it can be seen as a modern-day expression of the same solicitude that the enlightened ruler of the past was expected to show for his people (Gallagher and Searle 1985).

The economic, political, and demographic situation in the Arabian Gulf is dauntingly complex, in ways that affect the organization and provision of health care. National affluence matters. Economically, it would be cheaper for these countries to continue, as they have in the past, to import foreign physicians (and other health professionals) than to train their own. However, their wealth permits them to assert their national pride and to pursue an expensive avenue of self-sufficiency. They desire to demonstrate that they can mount medical education of an international standard and train their own young nationals into doctorhood.

Medical nationalism, however, is tempered in a peculiar way by the demographic fact that Gulf Arab states all have many foreign workers in their midst—another consequence of their wealth. Thus, although the ambitious agendae for hospital construction and physician production are intended to benefit the national population, in fact they will also benefit the expatriate population. The powerful planners and administrators who stand immediately behind the royal families must constantly wrestle with delicate issues about how to promote national identity and how to introduce religious and political institutions that are culturally acceptable. Health care is, fortunately, a highly appealing, unchallengeable platform for modernization, less problematic even than mass education.

The Gulf Arab societies are ambivalent toward Western culture; it is not only democratic values that they view apprehensively but, like many other non-Western countries, they have their doubts about Western individualism, women's equality, unbridled free inquiry, cultural innovation, and all the other forces that threaten tradition and social cohesion. However, in a decisive, energetic compensation for the social values that they reject, they fervently embrace modern technology. This holds true in medicine as much as in communications, transport, and military technology.

European and American medical suppliers, equipment manufacturers, and pharmaceutical companies view the Gulf Arab portion of the Middle East as lucrative sales territory. Foreign construction firms negotiate and execute so-called "turnkey contracts," in which they build a hospital, then equip and furnish it down to the last and most modern detail, and finally turn the key over to the ministry of health officials whose bidding they have done. Vendors and advertisers engage heavily in health fairs and in promotional conferences for medical specialists.

Handsome, glossy catalogues are the order of the day. Additionally there are a number of medical journals that may have four parts advertising to one part medical content. *Middle East Health* (MEH) is a representative specimen of the latter. It is a monthly publication; Volume 19 is appearing in 1994. Among the many items advertised in the March 1994 issue were: a Japanese-manufactured small echo camera that can be inserted into the body through natural orifices as well as by surgical incision; a surgical laser device of British manufacture; blood glucose monitors for patient use, of American origin; Danish anesthesia machines, surgical prostheses, and "ostomy" devices; and Swiss-made dental products for patients with extremely tender gums.

The line between advertising and informing is blurred at many points in this journal. Many of its advertisements endorse brand-name products but also provide extensive information on how the products work and what their clinical uses are. There are also content articles, for example, current guidelines in the treatment of diabetes, that give no brand names but describe very specific kinds of monitoring and diagnostic equipment. From a marketing standpoint, these articles probably stimulate the desire of the physician, hospital administrator, or other professional with purchasing power to acquire the product.

In the rush for technology acquisition, doctors and hospitals sometimes acquire equipment that goes beyond the ability of staff to operate and maintain it. Through it all is a strong pro-technology bias that Fuchs (1974, 1986) has called "the technological imperative." This he describes as "the desire of the physician to do everything that he has been trained to do, regardless of the benefit-cost ratio" (Fuchs 1974, p. 60). This concept seems almost too mild to describe the rush to technology in the Arabian Gulf; there can be no doubt that physicians there and elsewhere wish to practice medicine as they have learned it in the course of medical education, which imprints into them a vigorous embrace of technological medicine. But technology acquisition in the Arabian Gulf seems more like an idolization of technology for its own sake, fueled strongly by financial imperatives—hospital and clinic capital equipment budgets that must be spent within the budget year, and the desire to buy now rather than later, when the price may be higher.

CONCLUSION

The Arabian Gulf societies present a natural experiment that permits us to see how medical care develops when there are few financial constraints. Rampant technology acquisition is one such development. A second development is the strong reliance upon medical and related health professional services provided by expatriates.

According my observation, there is in Gulf Arab medicine no detectable consumer lobby of the kind developed in the United States, which challenges doctors to spend more time with patients and to improve their communication skills. The intense personalism of Arab culture does not translate into an egalitarian mutuality between patient and physician, as for example represented in the early model developed by Szasz and Hollender (1956). Instead, Arab personalism seems to express itself in a doctor-patient relationship that leans heavily on medical patriarchalism: "doctor knows best." It also amounts to an asymmetrical form of helping.

Does medical technology interfere with, or detract from, the doctor-patient relationship? This is a difficult question to deal with even under ideal circumstances where a researcher might be able to hold doctor-patient encounters and relationships under an interactional microscope and search out the effects, in terms of patient compliance and satisfaction, of "medical machinery."

Doctors and patients in the Gulf Arab countries hold a high estimation of technology. A sweeping adulation of everything technologically modern is an important part of their contemporary culture. The patients are probably awed by the gadgetry and may even respect their technology-wielding doctors all the more for their use of it. However, it is probably not empirically accurate to suppose that medical technology always "interferes." To suppose that it does would be to take an over-sentimentalized, romanticized view of the matter.

The doctor-patient relationship is culturally more complex than allowed for above. Instead of having a culturally homogenous Arab doctor-patient dyad, to which technology may be added as an introduced element, the doctor and patient in the Arabian Gulf will not, as a rule, both be of Arab background.

Consider, for example, that some 55 percent of the Kuwait population in 1994 is non-Kuwaiti. (Before the Iraqi invasion in 1990, non-Kuwaitis comprised some 70 percent of the population.) Kuwait's demographic profile is approximated in most of the other Gulf Arab nations. Most of the expatriate laborers constructing the roads, family residences, and office buildings are from South Asia: India, Pakistan, Sri Lanka, Bangladesh, and Thailand. The same is true of the many domestic servants, predominantly female, who work for Gulf Arab families. Most nurses come from the Philippines and Thailand. Many clerical and service workers in the banks, insurance companies, restaurants, and shopping malls come from Egypt, Lebanon, Jordan, and Syria. These four countries also provide many of the higher-level professional workers: physicians, petroleum geologists and engineers, computer experts, and bank officers. A small minority of the top professionals are North American and European.

Focusing upon health service providers in the Gulf Arab states, the proportion of expatriates is undoubtedly higher among them than in the general work force. From this it may be deduced that the typical doctor-patient encounter is not between an Arab doctor and Arab patient. Instead, one or both parties will be non-Arab.

Rather than seeing these cultural disjunctions as an impediment to the delivery of medical care, it is possible to regard Gulf Arab medicine as a laboratory in cultural diversity. What happens to provider-patient relationships under the flux of extreme transiency, where local populations are in the minority and are served by a constant turnover of foreigners? This, of course, is not unique to Gulf Arab societies; many parts of the contemporary world are marked by rapid movements and shifts of population, which have tremendous implications for medical care as well as education, commerce, public services, and every other area of life.

Perhaps the most unique feature of the Gulf Arab situation is that the conservative, reticent culture of the region, with its deep Arab-Islamic religious roots and politically royalist ethos, is, among the world cultures, one that is ill-suited to absorb the clash and din of multiculturalism. In other words, Kuwait and Dubai are not Hong Kong or Los Angeles. Perhaps the rush into medical technology is, in addition to its intended instrumental value for medical care, an important defense against the stress of cultural diversity.

REFERENCES

AHMAD, M. BASHEER. 1991. "Contribution of Muslim Physicians and Scholars of Spain during the Period between the Ninth and Thirteenth Centuries." *Journal of the Islamic Medical Association of North America*. Vol. 23, 82–86.

FROMM, ERICH. 1968. *The Revolution of Hope—Toward a Humanized Technology*. New York: Harper and Row.

FUCHS, VICTOR R. 1974. *Who Shall Live? Health, Economics, and Social Choice*. New York: Basic Books.

———. 1986. *The Health Economy*. Cambridge, Mass.: Harvard University Press.

GALLAGHER, EUGENE B., and JANARDAN SUBEDI. 1992. "Studying Health in Developing Societies: A Conceptually-Informed Research Agenda." *Central Issues in Anthropology*. Vol. 10: 127–33.

GALLAGHER, EUGENE B., and C. MAUREEN SEARLE. 1985. "Health Services and the Political Culture of Saudi Arabia." *Social Science and Medicine*. Vol. 21, No. 3, 251–62.

GEHLEN, ARNOLD. 1980. *Man in the Age of Technology*. New York: Columbia University Press. [First published in German, 1949.]

GRAY, SEYMOUR. 1983. *Beyond the Veil*. New York: Harper and Row.

KHAIRALLAH, AMIN. 1946. *Outline of Arabic Contributions to Medicine*. Beirut, Lebanon: American Press.

LEWANDO-HUNT, GILLIAN, STANLEY RABINOWITZ, NAOMI SHOHAT, and GABRIEL M. DANOVITCH. 1980. "The Influence of Socio-Cultural Factors on Adaptation to Dialysis Treatment." Beersheba, Israel: Ben Gurion University of the Negev. Unpublished report.

NAGAMIA, HUSAIN F. 1985. *Journal of the Islamic Medical Association of North America*. Vol. 9 (April 1): 1–2.

PARSONS, TALCOTT. 1951. *The Social System*. New York: Free Press.

PATAI, RAPHAEL. 1976. *The Arab Mind*. New York: Scribner's.

REISER, STANLEY JOEL. 1978. *Medicine and the Reign of Technology*. New York: Cambridge University Press.

SZASZ, THOMAS, and MARC H. HOLLENDER. 1956. "The Basic Models of the Doctor-Patient Relationship." *Archives of Internal Medicine*. 97: 585–92.

PART II

ETHNOMEDICINE

CHAPTER 6

The Case of Hannah Azulai, Illustrating the Confluence of Western and Folk Medicine in an Israeli Immigrant Community

Ofra Greenberg

INTRODUCTION

This paper focuses on two aspects of folk medicine in Western society today.[1,2] First, it examines the factors that affect the individual's choice of treatment when faced with several alternatives (mainly between modern and folk medicine). More specifically, it seeks to clarify under what circumstances folk medicine is utilized alongside, or even in preference to, conventional Western medicine. Secondly, the paper presents a discussion of the main features of folk medicine versus Western medicine, with special emphasis placed on the role of the family and the use of kin networks in the treatment process.

These issues were studied in an Israeli immigrant town, most of the population of which stems from predominantly Islamic countries. The information used was collected according to anthropological research methods, particularly the participant-observer technique and a number of unstructured interviews. The research was carried out over a period of two years (1981–1982), during which the researcher resided in the town under study. Over this period, the researcher and research assistant met with some fifty patients who had simultaneously sought medical assistance from physicians and folk healers.

In order to demonstrate this argument I describe extensively a case in which a woman patient seeks help alternately from a Western physician and a folk healer. The sociocultural context in which she acts, and the set of considerations and constraints that direct her behavioral strategy and the reactions of her family are presented in some detail.

Western medicine is endowed with virtually exclusive legitimacy by the Israeli health authorities. For the most part, it is provided under government auspices, while alternative medicine is administered in private practice. Western medicine as practiced in Israel is considered to be of a high international standard.

The Israeli health establishment has generally viewed folk medicine as a remnant of traditional cultures imported from abroad, mainly from Islamic countries. Our research, on the other hand, has found this type of medicine to be an integral part of current Israeli social and cultural reality in general, and that of the immigrant town in particular.

The literature dealing with the forms of alternative medicine practiced in Western society rarely touches on the use of folk medicine. On the other hand, much has been written about various aspects of the simultaneous use of folk and Western medicine in developing countries (Gonzalez 1966; Press 1969; MacLean 1971; Frankenberg and Leeson 1976; Lieban 1976; Alland 1977; Fabrega and Manning 1979; Finkler 1981), and about difficulties encountered in the adoption of modern medicine by the population of such countries (Lewis 1965; Colson 1971; Woods 1977; Camazine 1980; Kunitz et al. 1981). The assumption made both by public administrators and by many researchers is that a traditional population transplanted to a modern milieu would undergo rapid assimilation and accept the behavior patterns prevalent in its new surroundings. We are, however, able to deduce from research studies dealing with various aspects of immigrant communities that, as in other areas, the process of adopting new patterns of health-related behavior is not at all rapid and is often fraught with many hardships. Our research confirms the findings of others (Garrison 1977; New 1977), that even in countries regarded as modern and that operate sophisticated Western medical services, part of the population encounters difficulties in utilizing modern medical methods and chooses to use traditional treatment and its agents.[3] This finding is particularly valid for countries that have recently absorbed heterogeneous immigrations, such as the United States and Israel. A few studies carried out in Israel have investigated the use of folk medicine. The treatment of male barrenness was studied by Shokeid (1974). Bilu (1978) and Palgi (1981) investigated the characteristic of folk treatment of mental illness among Moroccan and Yemenite immigrants.

Once the decision to try folk medicine has been made, the patient has to choose a particular healer to see or a type of healing he or she wishes to undergo. Fabrega (1973) enumerates several alternative treatment methods that may be chosen by the individual seeking relief for a particular condition. These possibilities range from self-treatment, through acceptance of advice from a layperson, to consultation with one of a number of "professional" healers. Chrisman (1977) views choice of treatment as one of several elements in the health-seeking process, which includes symptom definition, illness-related shifts in role behavior, and lay consultation.

The present study seeks to clarify the health-seeking process, and particularly the choice of healer, in an immigrant community. Conventional health services are available to this population, but the system of beliefs about illness, social networks, and family support encourage the use of traditional healers (some of whom live in the community, and others elsewhere throughout the country).

GENERAL BACKGROUND

Social Characteristics of the Population of Karnit[4]

The town of Karnit numbers some fifteen thousand inhabitants, 90 percent of whom are immigrants from Morocco and Iraq, and their Israeli-born children. The average level of education is low (relative to the rest of the Israeli population); roughly half the adult population have no more than elementary education. Most of the work force lacks professional skills and this is reflected in their mode of employment, which is typically unskilled and low-paying.

Government-Provided Services

Housing.   Eighty-five percent of the apartments and houses in Karnit are owned and administered by Amidar, the government-run housing corporation. The rental fees charged are minimal, in most cases less than thirty dollars a month. Payment is waived completely for needy tenants. Those suffering from illness are given preference in terms of location and quality of the apartment.

Welfare.   The number of families receiving support from the welfare department is 50 percent above the national average (2–3 percent as against 1.6 percent). Such support takes the form of allocation for specific needs such as clothing, travel, and religious articles. The welfare services participate in the fees for 70 percent of the children enrolled in daycare centers catering to the six-month to three-year age group (the national average is 12 percent). Assistance is also provided to cover unusual expenses in the field of health care, such as transport by ambulance, orthopedic aids, and home help for the incapacitated. A doctor's certificate is required for all such cases.

National Insurance.   The National Insurance Institute provides financial assistance to various categories of people in need. In addition, it allocates several types of allowances, such as those for children, the elderly, the handicapped, and others.

Official Medical Services.   All officially recognized services are provided by one of two organizations: Kupat Holim, the sick fund run by the Federation of Labor, and the Ministry of Health. The Ministry of Health runs five mother-and-child clinics staffed by primary-care nurses who also work as school and kindergarten nurses. Some medical services are supplied by the government hospital in a nearby town, which sends doctors to Karnit. Kupat Holim runs three neighborhood clinics, which are staffed by five general practitioners and two child specialists. Other specialists are brought from the central region of the country.

The doctors are predominantly young, of Ashkenazic (North American and

European) origin, and do not live in the town, preferring the surrounding kib-butz settlements. They are highly mobile, and most leave the town after a short period of time. Development of stable doctor-patient relationships is further hindered by the frequent transfer of practitioners from one of the town's clinics to another. Most of the population has no access to private medical care, which is virtually nonexistent, perhaps because of the inability of a low-income community to support such practice.

All these factors tend to have an adverse effect on the doctor-patient relationship, and contact between the two is often far from pleasant. In many cases, the doctor does not know the patient. The different socioeconomic backgrounds and the language barrier tend to limit the new immigrant doctor from Russia or Argentina, for instance, who attends to a patient who speaks Arabic better than Hebrew. The doctor's inability to understand the patient may lead to resentment. Patients tend to feel estranged and anxious. Medical attention is available only at fixed hours at the clinics. Appointments may be made, with some difficulty, only on the day on which treatment is required. Clinics are generally congested and waiting rooms filled with patients.

The Role of the Family in the Western Healing Process (As Observed in Clinics Run by Public Authorities)

In most cases, the doctor meets his patient alone and unaccompanied. The doctor generally does not know members of the patients' immediate family, unless they have also been patients in the past. Even when the need arises for the doctor to meet other members of a patient's family, they sometimes lack sufficient interest to make the contact.

The family often remains indifferent to the healing process even when its cooperation is required. For example, a man approached the nurse at the "after-care unit" to inform her of his elderly father's imminent discharge from the hospital. He was bedridden and in need of special arrangements at home, as well as constant care. The patient's son was direct in his approach: "So, now that you know he's coming home, take care of all that's necessary." According to the nurse, such behavior is fairly common among needy families; from the outset they expect things to be done for them, such as engaging a housecleaner or home-help aide, or purchasing special equipment, all expenses being borne, as a matter of course, by the authorities.

A second example is that of an elderly, bedridden woman who wished to return to the home of one of her several sons after a cancer operation. The sons insisted that she be cared for in a special institution for terminal patients. The welfare authorities finally acceded to these demands, and the woman died shortly afterwards.

The relationship with the folk healer, in contrast, generally involves the entire family, who play an active part in the treatment, and accompany the patient at every step. The following case demonstrates this aspect of folk medicine, as well as illustrates the simultaneous utilization of both types of health care available. The choice made at each stage and the reasoning behind it are examined.

HANNAH AZULAI: A CASE IN POINT

Hannah Azulai, aged 37, was born in Iraq. She immigrated to Israel with her family in 1950. Married at the age of 17, she has six children. Her parents and brothers moved to a distant agricultural settlement some time ago. Her husband, of Moroccan origin, grew up in Karnit, where part of his family still resides. He has a secure job as a senior worker with a large public company.

The history of her illness was related to me by Hannah, while developments over the past two years were directly observed. The first signs of a disorder appeared some five years ago, in the form of swelling and pain in one leg. Hannah approached a general practitioner, who diagnosed rheumatism after administering a blood test, and prescribed a pain-killing drug. Not satisfied with this, Hannah consulted a surgeon, whose diagnosis was the same.

Faced with increasing pain, and a long waiting list for an orthopedic examination, Hannah privately consulted a well-known doctor in a nearby town who, after having her legs X-rayed, diagnosed a growth on her right leg. He recommended that she undergo an operation and referred her to the regional hospital, sending the X-rays with her. Hannah spent fifteen days in the orthopedic ward, undergoing examinations by the head of the department, a psychologist, and a psychiatrist. She was discharged with no pathological finding having been discovered.

The pain continued, but Hannah received no treatment. Some three years ago her condition worsened. She underwent an orthopedic examination and was referred to a large hospital in the center of the country, where she was given an appointment for surgery several months later.

At the same time, Hannah's brothers, despairing of conventional treatment, decided to take her to a rabbi of Yemenite origin, who lived in the central region of the country. (He had, of late, figured prominently in the media, following his curing of some blind girls.) The brothers were prepared to bear the expenses incurred by the visit. On arrival, it transpired that a prior appointment was necessary. Men standing guard outside the rabbi's house set a consultation date three months hence, for which service payment was requested.

By coincidence, the date set for Hannah's hospitalization coincided with her appointment with the rabbi. One of the brothers suggested a solution to the dilemma, according to which they would visit the rabbi early in the morning and then decide whether to go ahead with hospitalization. This plan was indeed put into effect. After asking several questions about Hannah's parents, the rabbi diagnosed her illness as "evil eye," which, he said, had begun in her legs and subsequently spread throughout her body. He gave her a black charm (inscribed with religious verses), instructing her to wear it around her neck and to remove it only during menstruation. She was also instructed to apply a mixture of pure olive oil and baby oil to all parts of her body over a period of ninety days. Finally, once a fortnight she was to mix henna (a medicinal herb, used for hair coloring and in rituals), salt, oil, and vinegar and rub this on her feet at night.

A religious woman herself, Hannah had no doubt that this treatment, prescribed by a rabbi, would effect a cure. She followed all the instructions to the letter, assisted by her husband, but her condition worsened. She decided to resume treatment at the hospital, and underwent an operation for a growth on her leg. She returned home after six weeks of hospitalization, suffering from side effects from the operation. Shocked at her condition, a local specialist demanded that she be rehospitalized. She was referred to the same hospital for further examinations and remained there for another month. She was eventually told that she was suffering from an inflammation of the pelvis, an incurable illness. Physiotherapy would be effective only in easing the pain.

By this stage, Hannah's pain prevented her from sitting and she was mostly bedridden. She was referred to another prestigious hospital, where she received treatment by injections in the Department of Rheumatic Diseases. The head of the department recommended radiation therapy, but warned Hannah of the possible side effects, suggesting that she discuss the matter with her family.

Hannah was afraid of radiation therapy. Her family found it difficult to advise her, as they feared that they would be blamed should the treatment prove to have a damaging effect. The neighborhood primary-care nurse suggested that she see the local medical specialist again. He was against radiation therapy on the grounds that it was an outdated method of treatment. Hannah described her reaction: "I thought to myself, at the hospital they told me that (radiation therapy) was the last possible treatment. So I'll try the Eastern remedies." Thus began a series of consultations with various folk healers.

Her brother took Hannah in his car to a healer of Iraqi origin in the center of the country. She visited him twice and meticulously carried out his instructions (excluding certain foods from her diet and drinking various beverages that he gave her), but to no avail. Hannah did not bother to inform the healer that the treatment had failed.

Approximately six months after consulting this healer, on a visit to her sister in another town, Hannah heard about an Arab "sheik's wife" from Nablus who had helped many people. Hannah's brother volunteered to take her and they were accompanied on their journey by the sister and Hannah's husband. The sheik's wife requested substantial payment before beginning her treatment. Since Hannah could not afford the sum, her brother and sister bore the expense jointly. The healer asked a number of questions and cast lots in order to determine whether she would be able to treat Hannah. Her explanation of the illness was "evil eye." She promised to prepare a medicine that would be ready two days hence. Hannah remained at her sister's house for two days, returning together with her brother, sister, brother-in-law, and her sister's neighbor. The healer instructed the brother-in-law to gather wild plants, which Hannah was ordered to grind and boil in two liters of olive oil. After straining, this liquid was to be applied to the body for fifty days. During this period, Hannah was forbidden by the healer to leave her home, so as not to expose herself to the wind. She was also given several charms. When the fifty days passed without improvement in her condition, Hannah lost her hope and belief.

Hannah also consulted two local healers. She had known one since childhood, when their families had been neighbors. She went to see him after a friend of hers had been successfully treated by him for infertility. Twice, he prescribed a beverage, to no avail. The rabbi performed a ritual in which he used eggs, and gave her a charm, again without success.

At one stage of the illness, Hannah wrote to a rabbi in the United States for help. She had heard of this rabbi from a friend of her brother's, whose son's life had allegedly been saved by the rabbi. The letter was sent by a nephew who was studying at a religious college in Israel with which the rabbi was connected. No reply was received.

In the summer of 1981, Hannah found new hope. A neighbor told her daughter of a local woman who had been cured of cancer by a Muslim sheik in Haifa. The neighbor recounted further stories of the sheik's unusual success, which awakened in Hannah the desire to see him. Hannah was driven to the sheik by two friends, accompanied by the neighbor. The sheik's diagnosis (delivered after receiving information about Hannah's age, illness, and mother's name, and after some time spent in seclusion) was that Hannah had been punished by a spirit that she had angered by throwing some object to the floor. He assured her that she would recover within a year, provided that she follow all his instructions: daily bodily application of liquids that he would provide and bathing with an herbal essence. The sheik's fee was high, to be paid in installments. He promised to return it if Hannah failed to get well. She would have to arrange collection of fresh medicine once a fortnight. It was agreed that this task would be shared by her neighbor, husband, and daughter.

The fee was beyond Hannah's means. Part was paid by her brother, as a gift, while the remainder was obtained by her husband, who received a loan from his employer, ostensibly for renovating their apartment. Hannah persisted with the treatment, apart from a few short intervals. In the beginning she took to sitting in the sun outside her apartment building so as to facilitate absorption of the liquid. All the passersby, and in particular neighbors on their way to the grocery, stopped to inquire about the treatment, expressing strong confidence and hope in its efficacy.

A year-and-a-half has now passed since she began this treatment, with no marked change in her condition, but Hannah still has not lost hope. She conjectures that she may have been worse off without the sheik's treatment.

FOLK MEDICINE

Characteristics and Practitioners

Folk medicine is practiced at two distinct levels in Israel, that of popularly used home remedies on the one hand, and of specialist healing on the other. Home remedies are employed by women to treat members of their families suffering from minor ailments such as coughs, colds, stomach ache, and fever. Specialist healing is the province of a small number of practitioners who treat anyone, including strangers, and who deal also with serious illnesses.

We may distinguish further between local and external folk medicine; while local residents may travel considerable distances to visit a healer, a regular stream of outside visitors seeks help from Karnit's specialists. Occasionally an outside healer is brought in to treat a local patient. (The discussion here has been limited to specialist folk medicine practiced in Karnit.)

Five specialist healers practice in Karnit. They have no other occupation, and two of them devote a considerable amount of time to their work. All are long-time residents in the community, having arrived with the early waves of immigration some twenty to thirty years ago. They came together with their extended families and in most cases with part of their original community from abroad. Those who were active healers in their original communities have maintained a network of potential clients; their patients from preimmigration days continued to seek their assistance. This is true mainly of local residents, although the frequency of their visits has naturally declined and the range of treatment has become more circumscribed.

Many inhabitants reported that in their country of origin they often approached a rabbi or an Arab sheik, since very few Western doctors were available. Furthermore, the homogeneous traditional belief systems prevalent among some of the immigrant communities in their countries of origin (particularly in the Atlas mountains and the mountains of Kurdistan) obviously facilitated approaches to a rabbi or other healer. Two of Karnit's healers are recognized community rabbis, whose activities thus have religious legitimacy. One of the two female healers claims to be the daughter of a rabbi.

The healers' skills were handed down to them by their fathers and were developed during childhood under supervision by the father or mother. The general public attaches importance to this heritage, with the healer's stature considered to be a function of his forefathers' stature. Patients are thus predisposed to believe in the power of a particular healer on the strength of his family's tradition of healing.

It is interesting to note that no young healers have appeared on the scene. The majority of healers are elderly, and began practicing prior to immigration. The mode of treatment is fairly uniform, taking the form of either writing charms or of applying medication externally. Various types of illness are thus treated in a fairly undifferentiated manner. The only exception to this general pattern is one innovative healer, who employs a variety of healing techniques, some of which, such as naturopathy, are accepted by modern Western society. He has succeeded in building up a heterogeneous clientele.[5]

Treatment is administered in the healer's house, generally in a guest room. All the healers receive patients on any weekday and at any time. There is no need to make a prior announcement of a visit. The wives of male healers serve as assistants; they are generally present during the consultation, and at times administer treatment to women patients.

There is no uniformity in the matter of payment. Some healers charge a definite (and substantial) sum, others leave the decision about rate of payment to the patient, while the most active healer in Karnit makes no charge for treatment, accepting payment only for medicinal herbs which he himself buys.[6]

The Clients

This section deals with a number of issues related to the healer's clients. Among these are: the common cultural background shared by healers and clients; attitudes of the second generation towards folk medicine; the types of complaints commonly brought for treatment; simultaneous approaches to doctor and healer; and the role of the family in the healing process.

A healer's first clients are fellow members of his community who already knew him abroad or whose parents and neighbors knew him in preimmigration days. Information about a healer is initially passed among relatives and neighbors who are generally of similar ethnic origin. The healer's acquaintance with his patient thus goes beyond the purely medical context and covers many areas of life, such as kinship, neighborhood, membership in the same synagogue, relatives' place of employment, and the like. According to Chrisman (1977), traditional belief systems in the field of health tend to be conserved for relatively long periods of time in compact networks characterized by "multivalued" relationships, by which is meant strong social control, common sources of information (from within the network), and exclusion of outside sources of information. Such are the social features of the local community.

The folk healers share a common social background with the majority of their public, which is made up of people of non-Western origin with little secular education. Healers and clients also share a belief in the same value system and the same explanatory framework through which to interpret the surrounding world in general and medical phenomena in particular. For example, a belief in the existence of spirits invested with power to influence a person's state of health or illness is held by most of the healer's clients. Thus, a patient will accept without question the healer's diagnosis that an illness is caused by such a spirit.

This common belief system forms the basis for recognition of the healer's powers, acceptance of his diagnosis of the source of the illness, and willingness to employ the healing techniques recommended by him. For example, when a resident of Karnit, a married man who had become impotent, approached the Moroccan healer, it was determined that this disability had been incurred after a night-time shower. The evil spirits, who thrive in water and in dark, had injured the man when he showered at night. His wife subsequently recalled that she had warned her husband against showering at night, for fear of such evil spirits.

The public differentiates between proficient and ineffective healers. The greater his knowledge of religious matters, the more successful a healer is considered to be. (Such is the case regarding the rabbi healers, for instance.) Muslim sheiks are also highly ranked in terms of power. Some of Karnit's residents hold little respect for the local healers, believing more in the power of certain distant healers, considering it worth the effort to travel to see them.[7]

A somewhat surprising phenomenon is that young people, particularly women, visit the healers. Apparently, there is social permission for women to be less rational or modern in their search for medical treatment. (It is also possible that young women approach *conventional* doctors more often then do young men. This subject warrants further examination.) At any rate, this seems to indicate that the belief in the powers of such healers is handed down to a younger generation that has grown up in Israel in a heterogeneous culture, exposed to different thought systems. Some of these young people are brought to the healer by their mothers or aunts. In other cases, a mother, sister, or son will approach the healer alone, without bringing the member of the family for whom treatment is sought. The reason for this may be that the patient is bedridden, or that he refuses to visit the healer, either because he is ashamed to do so or because he lacks belief in him. The "go-between" provides the healer with the required information regarding the patient and may then administer the prescribed treatment, sometimes without the patient's knowledge. This procedure was carried out by a young woman who wished to put an end to her brother's liaison with a married woman. She was given a charm to put in his bed and instructed to perform an additional ritual, all of which was done without the young man's knowledge.

The types of complaints for which the healer's help is sought are extremely varied, ranging from transitory physical ailments such as stomach or backache, chronic and even incurable illnesses such as diabetes, asthma, or cancer, to psychological problems such as depression and anxiety. The healer's intervention is also sought for marital problems (finding a husband, unfaithfulness) and for ensuring success in some venture (an examination or new employment). Some healers deal with all complaints brought to them, others treat only certain ailments, such as infertility and depression.

While a doctor is preferred for treatment of physical illnesses, a direct approach to a healer is made for treatment of two categories of problem. The first includes psychological complaints, referred to by patients as "nerves," "fear," or "evil eye," with the latter also perceived as a cause of illness. Secondly, marital problems and everything concerned with relationships between the sexes are treated exclusively by healers.

As a result of various public figures' scornful and dismissive attitude toward folk medicine, the healer's clients often feel ashamed of having approached him. This feeling is expressed in attempts to conceal their use of folk medicine, and particularly their recourse to a healer, from "nonbelievers." Only in the company of relatives and like-minded people are such topics as the attributes of various healers and details of treatment freely discussed.

The Role of the Family in the Folk Healing Process

We have already touched upon the important role played by members of the family in the decision-making process leading to a choice between one type of medical treatment or another. Their experience, sources of information, and degree of commitment constitute weighty factors in this context. The family also extends much practical assistance during the course of folk treatment. Those and other aspects are demonstrated by the case study of Hannah, presented above.

The analysis of Hannah's case reveals two major aspects of health-seeking in this community: (1) The process of alternating or simultaneous choices between Western and folk medicine and (2) the exploitation of family ties in the context of folk medicine, as compared to the absence of this factor with regard to conventional doctors.

The phenomenon of folk medicine is best understood in the light of social processes that determine the choice of a certain type of medical treatment. Among the components of such processes we find relationships and commitments among family members, the individual's position in his social network, his financial position, and channels of information.

Faced with the necessity to choose a certain type of treatment, the individual does not generally make a clearcut decision. In the community studied here, a variety of factors interplay to favor folk medicine. Among these factors are: the failures of conventional medicine (for instance, medical doctors could not cure Hannah); the need for treatment of complaints that exceed the scope of conventional treatment; the stigma associated with psychological treatment; the relaxed atmosphere in which contact with the healers takes place (and their consideration towards the patient); traditional patterns of medical treatment that had been accepted by the entire community until recent times; the conception of illness (for example, belief in spirits); sources of information; and experiences of close relatives and friends (such as those of Hannah's neighbors).

The system of folk medicine is, to a large extent, built upon kinship ties, which are utilized for obtaining information, for assistance in reaching the healer (particularly when long-range transportation is supplied by relatives, who tend to accompany the patient even when their services are not essential), and for providing financial support needed to cover healers' fees, which are often substantial.

It is surprising to note that patients considered to be poor, who receive extensive support from the National Insurance and welfare services in many areas, manage to find the means to pay for treatment by a healer. Such financial self-sufficiency stands in sharp contrast to their various insistent demands of the welfare service system.

The explanation of this apparent paradox lies in the nature and functioning of Israel's welfare service system, and the place of health care within that system. Health services constitute an integral part of the system of welfare services provided by the authorities, all of which are interdependent. Thus, a patient's recourse to the agent of Western medicine (be it a doctor, nurse, physical therapist, or other professional), and manner of approach toward that agent depend, among other factors, on the extent of his requirements from other services, such as the National Insurance or housing corporation, and on the pattern of his contacts with them. An individual's interaction with representatives of the establishment affects his ties in other spheres, the most important of which are the relationships with his family.

On approaching the folk healer, the same patient is well aware that the authorities will not support him financially or in any other manner. Furthermore, he knows that the establishment does not believe in this type of medicine, and thus attempts to conceal his contact with the healer. Finding himself in need of assistance with regard to the practicalities of folk treatment, including finances, the patient makes use of a traditional means of support, whose help is now only selectively needed, but which once provided all necessary support—his close family.

The widespread utilization of kinship ties in the sphere of folk medicine is particularly significant in the light of the family's lack of involvement in conventional health care. The full utilization of the kinship network during the entire course of traditional treatment, and its absence during conventional medical treatment, and during interaction with the welfare services in general, reflects the function of the welfare services. These are designed to meet all the individual's needs, without depending on his family or neighbors; people lacking a source of income are supported by the National Insurance, while bedridden patients unable to pay for assistance are provided with home-help by the welfare bureau.

The same pattern is evident in the sphere of health: people who fall ill are treated virtually free of charge. Maintenance expenses charged by various types of specialized institutions are covered by the welfare bureau if the individual is incapable of paying them. Chronically ill patients in need of regular treatment and who are unable to reach their Kupat Holim clinic are transported at the health authorities' expense. With all his needs met by the public service, the client learns not to approach his family for help. Furthermore, he often demands public aid when quite capable of paying on his own. Families tend to renounce their commitment toward the patient, secure in the knowledge that the public service will bear responsibility and take care of him.[8]

Kinship ties are doubtless utilized in other areas of life that remain beyond the sphere of influence of the authorities and various welfare agencies. Such areas may be located and studied only by means of regular contact with people in informal frameworks. However, the access to Western medicine is controlled by bureaucracies where kin ties are often less relevant and useful, while folk medicine needs these ties for information, practical aid, and financial aid.

SUMMARY

Folk medicine was found to exist and thrive in spite of the dismissive attitude toward it exhibited by the medical establishment (with a few exceptions). This finding is somewhat surprising, considering the extensive dependence of the immigrant population on a wide range of welfare services, and in view of the exclusive legitimacy enjoyed by Western medicine and the subsidized nature of medical services.

Patients tend to try one healer after another, sometimes seeking help simultaneously from two healers. If the complaint is a physical one, the patient will generally approach a Western doctor first, turning to a healer only after the conventional treatment has failed to effect a cure. Many patients suffering from chronic illnesses continue receiving treatment simultaneously from both a doctor and a healer, without the former knowing about the latter.

Some first visit a doctor in order to receive a diagnosis, on the strength of which they decide to whom to turn for treatment. Such behavior points to the doctor's preferential status. Further evidence of this pattern is provided by a duality of treatment: while a certain ailment, such as high blood pressure, once diagnosed, is treated by the doctor, the same patient's depression may be simultaneously treated by the healer.

The new postimmigration social context produced changes in the patterns of consumption and functioning of traditional medicine. Not all sectors of the population utilize folk healers to the same extent. Different attitudes toward folk medicine, and particularly toward certain practices employed by folk healers, are expressed by members of various social categories. The potential clientele (mainly people of non-Western origin with little secular education) has developed new habits and adopted different criteria regarding use of the healers' services. This population has merged the healer and his services into a wider system of welfare services that include the agents of medicine recognized by the establishment, and has learned to utilize the healer alongside these services as an alternative, according to patterns of thought formed partly by the new social reality.

NOTES

[1] I gratefully acknowledge the assistance of the Sapir Center, Tel-Aviv University, which financed my initial research. I also wish to thank Dr. Edgar E. Siskin, Head of the Jerusalem Center for Anthropological Studies, whose grant enabled me to extend and broaden the research.

[2] The term "folk medicine" denotes a type of medicine that is part of the cultural heritage of various communities and that is not founded on Western biomedicine. Among other terms used are "traditional medicine" and "granny's remedies." My use of the term "alternative treatment" is a generalization for any kind of medical therapy which is not a Western one.

[3] Garrison (1977) describes the healers operating in a Puerto Rican immigrant community in New York and the characteristics of their clients. She does not regard spiritualism as folk medicine, since it was introduced to Puerto Rico simultaneously with Western medicine in the middle of the last century. Spiritualism and Western medicine are thus viewed by her as parallel systems that do not constitute a dichotomy between the traditional and the modern. New (1977) raises various possible questions which may be addressed by research in this field, in particular the process of approaching the folk healer. Although he makes no territorial distinction between developing and modern countries, the literature on which his discussion is based stems from the less developed countries.

[4] The name of the town discussed here has been changed.

[5] Landy (1977, p. 479) discusses various ways in which a folk healer confronted with Western medicine may react. According to his classification, most of Karnit's healers are conservative, while the above-mentioned innovator belongs to the category of healers who adopt modern ingredients in their work, thus undergoing a process of acculturation.

[6] Bilu (1978, pp. 421-29) analyzes in detail the structure and significance of the healer's payment.

[7] A parallel conception is evident among believers in Western medicine. They tend to explain failure of particular medical treatment in terms of the shortcomings of the doctor, without questioning the efficacy of the general medical system. This would indicate a propensity towards a cognitive system encompassed within a framework of beliefs, such as that described by Evans-Pritchard (1937, pp. 336-39) in his discussion of witchcraft among the Azande.

[8] This pattern of shedding family responsibility was observed by Marx (1973, pp. 36-37) in another immigrant town in Israel.

REFERENCES

ALLAND, ALEXANDER, JR. 1977. "Medical Anthropology and the Study of Biographical and Cultural Adaptation." Pp. 41-47 in *Culture, Disease, and Healing*, edited by David Landy. New York: Macmillan.

BILU, YORAM. 1978. *Traditional Psychiatry in Israel*. (Unpublished Ph.D. Thesis), Hebrew University, Jerusalem (in Hebrew).

CAMAZINE, SCOTT M. 1980. "Traditional and Western Health Care Among the Zuni Indians Of New Mexico." *Social Science and Medicine* 14B (1):73-80.

CHRISMAN, NOEL J. 1977. "The Health Seeking Process: An Approach to the Natural History of Illness." *Culture, Medicine, and Psychiatry* 1:351-77.

COLSON, ANTHONY C. 1971. "The Differential Use of Medical Resources in Developing Countries." *Journal of Health and Social Behavior* (September), 12:226-37.

EVANS-PRITCHARD, EDWARD EVAN. 1968 (1937). *Witchcraft, Oracles, and Magic among the Azande*. Oxford: Clarendon.

FABREGA, HORACIO, JR. 1973. "Toward a Model of Illness Behavior." *Medical Care* 11 (6):470-84.

FABREGA, HORACIO, JR., and PETER K. MANNING. 1979. "Illness Episodes, Illness Severity and Treatment Options in a Pluralistic Setting." *Social Science and Medicine* 13B (1):41-52.

FINKLER, KAJA. 1981. "A Comparative Study of Health Seekers or Why Some People Go to Doctors Rather than to Spiritualistic Healers." *Medical Anthropology* 5 (3):383-424.

FRANKENBERG, RONALD, and JOYCE LEESON. 1976. "Disease, Illness and Sickness: Social Aspects of the Choice of Healer in a Lusaka Suburb." Pp. 223-58 in *Social Anthropology and Medicine*, edited by Joseph B. Loudon. London: Academic Press.

GARRISON, V. 1977. "Doctor, Espiritista or Psychiatrist? Health Seeking Behavior in a Puerto Rican Neighborhood in New York City." *Medical Anthropology* 1:65-180.

GONZALEZ, NANCIE SOLIEN. 1966. "Health Behavior in Cross-Cultural Perspective." *Human Organization* 25 (2):122-25.

KUNITZ, STEPHEN J., HELENA TEMKIN-GREENER, DAVID BROUDY, and MARLENE HAFFNER. 1981. "Determinants of Hospital Utilization and Surgery on the Navajo Indian Reservation." *Social Science and Medicine* 15B (1):71-79.

LANDY, DAVID. 1977. "Role Adaptation: Traditional Cures Under the Impact of Western Medicine." Pp. 468-81 in *Culture, Disease, and Healing*, edited by David Landy. New York: Macmillan.

LEWIS, OSCAR. 1965. "Medicine and Politics in a Mexican Village." Pp. 403-34 in *Health, Culture, and Community*, edited by Benjamin Paul. New York: Russell Sage.

LIEBAN, RICHARD W. 1976. "Traditional Medical Beliefs and the Choice of Practitioners in a Philippine City." *Social Science and Medicine* 10 (6):289-96.

MacLEAN, UNA. 1971. *Magical Medicine: A Nigerian Case Study.* London: Penguin.

MARX, EMANUEL. 1973. "Coercive Violence in Official-Client Relationships." *Israel Studies in Criminology* 2:33-38.

NEW, PETER KONG-MING. 1977. "Traditional and Modern Health Care: An Appraisal of Complementarity." *International Social Science Journal* 29 (3):483-95.

PALGI, PHYLLIS. 1981. "Traditional Method of Dealing with Mental Health Problems among Yemenite Immigrants in Israel." Pp. 43-67 in *Community Mental Health in Israel*, edited by U. Aviram and I. Levav. Tel-Aviv: Tcherikover (in Hebrew).

PRESS, IRWIN. 1969. "Urban Illness, Physicians, Curers and Dual Use in Bogota." *Health and Social Behavior* 10 (3):209-18.

SHOKEID, MOSHE. 1974. "The Emergence of Supernatural Explanation for Male Barrenness among Moroccan Immigrants." Pp. 122-50 in *The Predicament of Homecoming*, edited by Shlomo Deshen and Moshe Shokeid. New York: Cornell.

WOODS, CLYDE. 1977. "Alternative Curing Strategies in a Changing Medical Situation." *Medical Anthropology* 1 (3):25-54.

CHAPTER 7

Ethnomedicine in the Context of Health Care Delivery in Ghana

Kodjo A. Senah

INTRODUCTION

Indigenous African beliefs and practices concerning health and therapy management have always been topical, especially for persons outside the continent. Early European explorers, traders, colonial administrators, and missionaries have recorded and extensively published their personal observations and impressions of ethnomedical systems often to show the "primitive" nature of the societies they had encountered and thereby justifying their missionizing efforts. For earlier students of ethnography or natural history, the study of African medical systems—indeed of African cultural configurations—was heavily influenced by the Comtian "law of three stages," which stressed the unilinear progression of human society beginning with the theological stage and culminating in the stage of positivism or scientificity.[1]

However, the early twentieth century saw the birth of a new breed of anthropologists and ethnographers whose scholarly works, based on extensive fieldwork in so-called primitive cultures, often showed the logic underlying the "irrational" and "primitive" practices found by earlier anthropologists. In this regard, the scholarly works of Evans-Pritchard (1937), Field (1937), Harley (1941), and Gelfand (1956; 1964) are pertinent. These works notwithstanding, in some quarters today interest in African medical systems is centered on such issues as religion and magic, spirit worlds, witchcraft and sorcery, and the shaman or med-icine man. As Maclean has rightly pointed out, "For many people, the mention of African Medicine is still apt to conjure up the fearsome image of the 'witch doc-tor' . . . clad in fur and feathers, (who) prances around a fire, to the inexorable rhythms of the tom-tom" (1971, p. 13). In spite of the increased interest in Africa and the spread of knowledge concerning the wealth and variety of African cul-tures, the character of ethnomedicine and the medico-religious functions of eth-nomedical practitioners (EPs) remain subjects of widespread ignorance and mis-apprehension. Even though it is fashionable in some intellectual circles to give them "credit," elsewhere ethnomedicine and its practitioners are cast in a nega-tive light. They are still viewed by most Westerners and the local elite, at least publicly, as the incarnation of a shameful legacy of paganism, barbarism, and black magic. EPs in particular project an image of the backward, the primitive, and the heathen, whom local elites regard as a thing of the past rather than a contemporary force to be reckoned with.

Local and international awareness of the role and contributions of eth-nomedical systems in African countries is essentially a postcolonial development. This emerging consciousness is a product of intertwining variables—the sociode-mographic and cultural characteristics of the African people, the poverty of African nations, and the political ideology of "Africanness" or "African Personali-ty."[2] However, the elixir to this emerging consciousness is the sudden realization by most African states that the kind of biomedical delivery system, which Good (1987) describes as the "aspirin and bandages" variety of Western health service, which was introduced by colonial administrations and subsequently inherited and nurtured by independent African governments, does not and cannot meet many of their societies' most pressing health needs. As Dorozynski (1975) has argued, this health service is of limited relevance to the conditions of life of people in developing countries because it renders insufficient care even in cen-tral urban areas, and practically no care in the rural areas where the majority of the population resides. Further, even where biomedical health services are phys-ically present, a number of studies have shown that prevailing social and cultur-al values render biomedicine an inappropriate option for many illnesses (Jahoda 1970; Twumasi 1975; Janzen 1978; Fosu 1981; Wondergem, Senah, and Glover 1989). The need to encourage medical pluralism is therefore clear.

In this chapter, attention is focused on the relationship between eth-nomedicine and biomedicine in Ghana by examining the social and historical factors which have influenced the ambivalent love-hate relationship between the two medical systems. This is a necessary backdrop to the understanding of the current status and modus operandi of ethnomedicine in Ghana.

GHANA: A DESCRIPTIVE PROFILE

In order to appreciate the present status and potential role of ethnomedicine, it is necessary to take a broad look at the national context within which this med-ical system operates. As Janzen (1978) has argued, a sufficient analysis of a local pluralistic medical system must begin with the "macro" level of colonial history and national policy. In support of this, Kleinman (1980) has advised on the need to see local health care systems in an ecological perspective that recognizes "external" influences such as political, economic, social structural, and historic factors. It is against this background that we offer a brief description of Ghana.

In 1957, Ghana, formerly the British colony of the Gold Coast, became the first black African country to gain political independence from colonial rule. It is situated on the Gulf of Guinea in West Africa and is bounded on the north by Burkina Faso; on the west by the Ivory Coast, and on the east by Togo. The capital city of Ghana is Accra.

Currently Ghana has a population of about 14.6 million and an annual population growth rate estimated to be between 2.6 and 3 percent. About 68 percent of the population are rural dwellers with subsistence agriculture as the mainstay of the rural economy. The per capita income is about 400 U.S. dollars per annum; life expectancy at birth is 54 years while the adult literacy rate is 47 percent (World Bank 1990).

In terms of health care delivery there are wide regional variations in the ratios of population per qualified health personnel. The population per doctor ratio ranges from 4,281 to 1 in the Greater Accra Region, to 67,818 to 1 in the Northern Region. The leading individual causes of deaths in hospitals have been pneumonia (12.1 percent), malaria (9.2 percent), and perinatal disorders (8.8 percent), while the leading causes of outpatient morbidity are malaria, diarrhea, respiratory infections, skin diseases, accidents, pregnancy-related disorders, and intestinal worms (Ministry of Health 1991).

Since 1979, the government has committed itself to the Primary Health Care Program in an attempt to reach the rural areas with affordable health care. This commitment has led to the institutionalization of such programs as Expanded Program on Immunization, Control of Diarrheal Diseases, Maternal and Child Health and Family Planning Clinics, Guinea Worm Eradication Program, and AIDS Control Program. Traditional birth attendants and some healers are among a number of health personnel trained for these programs.

DEFINITION

As a point of departure, the author prefers the concept "ethnomedicine" to "traditional medicine." The latter connotes a static state, a still-picture imagery although evidence abounds to show that "traditional medicine" is undergoing structural changes in harmony with the demands of the time (Last and Chavunduka 1986; Bonsi 1977; Wondergem et al. 1989). Throughout this chapter, therefore, the term "ethnomedicine" will be used in place of "traditional medicine."

Ethnomedicine generally refers to "the total body of knowledge, techniques for the preparation and use of substances, measures and practices, whether explicable or not, that are based on . . . personal experience and observations handed down from generation to generation, either verbally or in writing, and are used for the diagnosis, prevention, or elimination of imbalances in physical, mental or social well-being" (Bannerman 1983, p. 25). In a similar vein, WHO (1978) defines ethnomedicine as a corpus of knowledge which applies "vegetable, animal and mineral substances and other methods based on the social, cultural and religious backgrounds as well as on the knowledge, attitudes and beliefs that are prevalent in the community regarding physical, mental and social well-being and the causation of disease and disability." These definitions have a wide latitude: stretched to their logical limits, they may include popular folk medicine and "indigenized" use of pharmaceuticals. For our purposes, however, the concept includes all practices devoid of Western pharmaceuticals. Further, we are interested here in the public and not the private face of ethnomedicine.

As a consequence of the above definitions, in Ghana, Twumasi (1988) identifies four main types of ethnomedical practitioners: (a) traditional birth attendants; (b) faith healers; (c) herbalists; and (d) spiritualists. Traditional birth attendants focus on pregnancy-related problems. Traditionally they play crucial roles in child delivery, puberty rites, child care, and sex education. In the rural areas of Ghana, they do most deliveries.

Faith healers are leaders of religious movements. Such movements are often syncretic and thaumaturgical in orientation: they rely on spiritual wonder-working and employ holy water, incense, and perfume, among others, in their mode of worship. In Ghana today, some of these cults have hospitals that admit patients.

Herbalists are healers whose healing practices involve mainly the use of herbs, mineral substances, and/or the anatomical parts of animals. There are also a number of specialists in this group: bonesetters, herbalist-diviners, circumcisionists, and tribal- or body-markers.

Finally, the spiritualists include diviners, fetish priests or priestesses, and ritual leaders. A common feature of their therapeutic art is possession when a spiritualist is said to be in communion with the transcendental forces concerning the fate of the sick person. Spiritualists are often attached to shrines or temples of minor deities and act only according to the direction of the particular deity.

In Ghana today, there are also a few "fringe practitioners" who lie between allopathy and ethnomedicine: homeopaths and acupuncturists. Given their mode of operation and places of origin, they are most conveniently treated as the "third force." For this reason, they are not included in our discussion on ethnomedicine.

ETHNOMEDICINE IN THE COLONIAL SETTING

As mentioned earlier, an understanding of the role and status of ethnomedicine in contemporary Ghana requires attention to the historical circumstances that have created this situation. As Berger (1976) has rightly pointed out, this appreciation is necessary because there is nothing happening today that is free of ties with the past. The entire medical enterprise of Ghana is one institution whose form and operation can best be understood against the background of colonial history.

In 1844, the British formally gained control of the Gold Coast (now Ghana) when an alliance was formed by some chiefs along the coast. This event led to relative peace and stability in the southern half of the country and therefore to an increase in trade and missionary activities. A new medical dispensation was therefore instituted to curb the high morbidity and mortality rates, resulting from malaria and other infectious diseases, but it was limited to Europeans only. However, as colonial rule and European activities extended inland, it dawned on the colonial administration that the health of Europeans could not be protected unless efforts were made to protect the local population also. The attempt to do this led to a direct conflict with the indigenous medical system which was better known and more attractive to the local people. The colonial administration thus devised ways of neutralizing the influence of healers in order to promote the acceptance of the new colonial medical regimen. In 1868, under the Native Customs Regulations Ordinance, legislation was passed to liquidate indigenous medical practitioners. Official documents described them as "insincere jujumen living on the neurosis of their illiterate folk." This was followed by a campaign of "enlightenment" to persuade urban dwellers, educated persons, and opinion leaders to shun indigenous healers. African colonial civil and public servants were compelled to seek medical care from the new health service; only colonial medical officers could issue a certificate of disability. These campaigns were complemented by Christian missionaries through intensive proselytizing, Western education, and threats of excommunication. As a result, indigenous medical practitioners fled into the remote areas to practice their art.

In spite of official efforts to provide modern health care services for the people, a large segment of the population had no access to them. Even in areas where allopathic medical facilities were fairly accessible, indigenous response to them was cautious and pragmatic. Invariably, people tended to "shop" around or to design a "hierarchy of resort" according to their own nosological notions. Table 1 below shows the number of patients treated in government hospitals at the height of colonial medical care, when the colony had a population ranging between two and three million people. As the table shows, less than 9 percent of the population had access to colonial health care facilities in any of the given years.

Colonial rule began to face stiff local opposition in the early twentieth century. Opposition came mainly from local intelligensia with some degree of Western education. In defiance of colonial legislation, therefore, in the 1930s and 1950s two herbal practitioners' associations were founded to agitate for recognition of indigenous healers. These were: the Society of African Herbalists based in Sekondi in the Western Region and the Ga Medical Association based in Accra, respectively. According to Kwesi Aaba, his Society of African Herbalists intended "to raise the local practice of medical herbalism up to a high and refined standard and to seek for free or unhindered practice for its members." Although the

TABLE 1. PATIENTS TREATED IN GOVERNMENT HEALTH CENTERS (1992–1930)

Year	Total Treated	Percentage of Total Population
1922–23	70,821	2.7
1923–24	77,224	2.9
1924–25	81,957	3.0
1925–26	97,443	3.5
1926–27	104,811	3.7
1927–28	132,446	4.5
1928–29	214,605	7.5
1929–30	248,325	8.2

Source: Patterson, D. K. *Health in Colonial Ghana: Diseases, Medicine and Socio-Economic Change. (1900–1955)* Waltham, Mass: Crossroads Press 1981. Page 113.

colonial administration withheld both *de facto* and *de jure* recognition from these associations, they nonetheless had established an important precedent in the development of herbalism in the country.

HERBALISM IN POST-COLONIAL GHANA

At independence in 1957, while parasitic and infectious diseases still loomed large, Ghana inherited a health care system that was urban-biased and capital-intensive. Such was the enormity of the health problems of the young nation that Kwame Nkrumah, the first Prime Minister, declared: "We shall measure our progress by the improvement in the health of our people. . . . The welfare of our people is our chief pride and it is by this that my Government will ask to be judged." In support of this declaration, Nkrumah's government invested heavily in social welfare services. The health sector especially saw massive expansion in facilities and personnel.

However, as the leader of the first black independent African state, Nkrumah also took on the mantle of championing the African cause. Under the ideology of "African Personality"—the quest for an authentic African way of life—in 1963, he initiated steps "to study and organize traditional healers to form an association for the advancement of their art and techniques in the delivery of health care." This led to the formation of the Ghana Psychic and Traditional Healing Association in the same year. As envisaged, the aims and objectives of the Association were:

1. to uphold, protect, and promote the best in psychic and traditional healing
2. to encourage the establishment of advanced training programs in traditional healing
3. to introduce and train medical students to appreciate the work of traditional healing
4. to encourage research work into traditional medicine; and
5. to establish clinics in remote places and to educate traditional healers in the districts in order to improve upon their practices (Brew-Graves 1977, p. 7).

Given the personal interest Nkrumah had in this Association, it is not clear why he withheld *de jure* recognition from it. However, the Association operated in very high political circles and it was no surprise that it was marginalized following the overthrow of the Nkrumah government in 1966. The subsequent internal squabbles that ensued between psychic healers and herbal practitioners and between the educated and the illiterate members of the Association brought its activities to a stand-still for about ten years. Today, the original Association has to contend with a number of splinter groups: Ghana National Traditional Healers' Association; Ghana Psychic and Traditional Healers' Association; Ghana Psychic and Herbal Practitioners Association; Association of African Psychic and Herbal Practitioners; Ghana Traditional Medical Association; and Scientific Herbal Practitioners Association. In 1982, a committee appointed by the Ministry of Health to unite all these factions failed in the attempt.

The 1970s were very critical for Ghana and for most developing economies. Described as the "lost decade," it was a period characterized by a fall in the price of their exports on the world market, crippling debt-servicing burdens, balance-of-payment difficulties, and shortages of basic goods. The World Bank captured the essence of this crisis thus:

> . . . for most African countries, and for a majority of the African population, the record is grim, and it is no exaggeration to talk of crisis. Slow overall economic growth, sluggish agricultural performance coupled with rapid rates of population increase, and balance-of-payments and fiscal crises—these are dramatic indicators of economic trouble (World Bank 1981).

In the health sector, these problems manifested themselves in the exodus of health professionals, shortage of drugs and other equipment, and lack of professional commitment. For health policy makers, this period called for a rethinking of the existing health delivery strategy. Some form of primary health care with heavy infusion of local resources was proposed. From the 1970s, therefore, various experimental programs were initiated by both the government and other nongovernmental organizations to forge a link between orthodox Western medicine and ethnomedicine.

In 1970, the first of these, the Danfa Comprehensive Rural Health and Family Planning Project, was initiated. It had important components focusing on the training of traditional healers and traditional birth attendants and on their linkage with biomedicine. The Danfa Project worked with traditional birth attendants, a significant number of whom were also herbalists. Today, the program is suffering from lack of sustainability, and the traditional birth attendants trained are experiencing a number of operational difficulties (Twumasi 1987).

The next important project is the Centre for Scientific Research into Plant Medicine commissioned in 1974 at Mampong-Akwapim. Among its important functions, the Centre was to conduct and promote scientific research into plant medicines and to cooperate with the Ghana Psychic and Traditional Healing Association, research institutions, and commercial organizations on matters of plant medicine. The Centre formerly employed two herbalists on a permanent basis. They were a good source of information on medicinal plants. In addition, the Centre's silviculturist travelled around the country interviewing healers in the different regions from whom he obtained information. Healers and "quacks" also come to the Centre from time to time to volunteer information on various remedies. Many of these so-called remedies are said not to be genuine, the motives of the informants being to get some money for the false information they give—or to pick up some knowledge themselves. Today, although the Centre has lost the services of its herbalists, important work is being done in the improvement in methods of preparation and presentation of certain drugs that are already being used by herbalists: powders, ointments, tinctures, lotions, etc. Ten areas chosen for clinical studies are: (1) asthma; (2) diabetes; (3) hypertension; (4) peptic ulcer; (5) skin diseases; (6) sickle cell disease; (7) arthritic conditions; (8) malaria; (9) guinea worm infestation; and (10) hemorrhoids (piles).

According to Evans-Anfom (1986) considerable progress has been made in the evaluation of an antidiabetic plant *indigoferra*, and *canthium* has been found effective in mild hypertension. Recently also *cryptolepine*, an alkaloid extract from *cryptolepis angimoleta*, has been found to be effective in the treatment of fever and headaches. In spite of these achievements, the Centre experiences one serious drawback. As the Director of the Centre observed recently, "We are fighting a two-frontal battle: a battle against orthodox medical practitioners who do not want us to promote herbal medicine and against traditional healers who are suspicious of our activities."[3]

The third important project is the Brong Ahafo Rural Integrated Development Project established in 1975 at Kintampo. Like the others, this project was meant for the training of indigenous healers and other health functionaries for Ghana's primary health care program. Today this project is used mainly for the training of low- and middle-level personnel of the Ministry of Health only.

In 1978 the Alma-Ata Declaration gave international blessing to Ghana's effort to integrate its medical systems as an essential strategy for the promotion of primary health care and also for attaining the goal of "Health for All by the Year 2000." Soon after this, the first real effort for collaboration between indigenous healers and biomedical functionaries started in Techiman in 1979. The Primary Health Training for Indigenous Healers Programme (PRHETIH), a brainchild of Dennis M. Warren, an anthropologist at Iowa State University, was designed to provide better health care for the population of Techiman District by augmenting the knowledge and skills of local healers in biomedicine and fostering closer cooperation between the healers and biomedical practitioners. This project built heavily upon the rich experience of the Catholic Holy Family Hospital in training traditional birth attendants and using them within the hospital itself. By mid-1983 over eighty healers had been trained and there were plans to extend the program into surrounding rural communities. Various studies described this project as one of the most interesting and possibly the most successful collaborative experiments in Sub-Saharan Africa (Good 1987; Bannerman 1983; Fyfe 1987; Slikkerveer 1990). Some recommended that the positive results evident from the initial pilot program should be of great interest to health authorities in other areas of tropical Africa who are searching for ways to make appropriate health care more accessible to their populations. Commenting on the cost-effectiveness of the program, Warren observed:

> Indigenous healers have found oral rehydration techniques far superior to some of the local methods for dealing with diarrhea problems. It has now become a standard procedure not only among the healers who have taken part in the training sessions but the techniques have been taught by these healers to numerous other local practitioners. The multiplier effect has been extensive. It is very apparent that the primary health care skills of the healers have improved greatly (Warren 1988, p. 176).

In spite of these optimistic views, the PRHETIH program has collapsed. The main reasons for this will be investigated.[4]

Other integrative efforts worth mentioning are the Nazareth Healing Complex in Vane in the Volta Region, the Dormaa Healers' Project in the Brong-Ahafo Region, and the Nandom Healers Project in the Upper West Region of Ghana.

Significantly, these initiatives are all mission-based. However, like the others, they are all suffering from low sustainability.

At the national level, one significant boost to indigenous medicine is the creation of a directorate in 1990 to handle all issues relating to ethnomedicine. This directorate is located within the Ministry of Health. Currently, it is actively trying to forge a united front among the various herbal/healing associations. There is every indication, however, that, given its orientation and novelty, this directorate is a pariah among the other directorates.

THE GREAT DEBATE

The coexistence of various ethnomedical systems, such as: Yoruba, Unani-Tibbi, Ayurvedic, or classical Chinese, with each other and with biomedicine is a well-documented phenomenon. What is less certain, however, are the actual success rates of such coexistence, especially of the collaborative projects in Africa. Barbara Pillsbury, after surveying national health systems throughout Africa, Asia, and Latin America in 1982, noted:

> ". . . little progress has been made in actually utilizing indigenous practitioners, especially healers, in these national systems. It appears in fact that in the entire developing world there are only one or two countries in which traditional healers have actually been incorporated, as traditional healers, in the national health care system" (Pillsbury 1982).

In Ghana, as in other parts of Africa, the difficulties that have attended many collaborative efforts have often brought into question the desirability of collaborative effort. While health policy makers, at least publicly, proclaim the need for collaborative work, privately they are not sure whether such effort is desirable: ethnomedical practitioners remain, to them, a serious anachronism, a throwback to heathenism and primitivism. And even if it is agreed that such collaborative effort is necessary, the question still remains: with which group of healers? Ghana's collaborative efforts have so far shown that traditional birth attendants are the most preferred category: cooperating with other categories of healers is more difficult because as found in the PRHETIH experiment, "their underlying principles, concepts, techniques, and assumptions were found to be entirely different from biomedical theories. It was therefore not readily possible to seek their cooperation" (Twumasi 1982, p. 210). The recent controversy between the Ministry of Health and the late Nana Drobo over the latter's claim to have found a cure for AIDS brings the debate into sharp focus. Whether the impediment for cooperation was from the Ministry of Health or from Nana Drobo will be a topic for discussion for a long time to come. The incident nonetheless shows the extent of animosity and suspicion that clouds any relationship between ethnomedical and biomedical practitioners in Ghana.

The question may be asked: how have healers responded to all these overtures? This is a difficult question to answer because healers do not constitute a homogeneous entity. Studies have shown, however, that very often healers have cooperated in these programs essentially as a way of acquiring the needed recognition from the government (Ventevogel 1992). It may be said, however, that the failure of almost all the integrative efforts discussed is indicative of structural difficulties that surround such collaborations. The fact that such training programs are organized *for* and not *with* healers ipso facto shows the arrogance of biomedical practitioners. As Fink (1990) has observed, the PRHETIH project did not regard the healers to be genuine colleagues of biomedical practitioners. She writes: "It is a fact that healers who took part in the PRHETIH project complained that doctors and the hospital personnel continued to show a lack of respect to them and did not accept them as colleagues" (Fink 1990, p. 42).

In Ghana indigenous healers have responded to the challenges of the time by establishing professional associations and organizing occasional seminars. Some have established herbal clinics with all the paraphernalia of Western medical bureaucracy and equipment. Their moves have coincided with a crisis in the medical profession, a crisis among whose symptoms are doctors' strikes; shortages of equipment; a sharp rise in the cost of Western pharmaceuticals and in the unofficial costs to the public of obtaining treatment; and a realization on the public's part that hospital medicine might not cure everything. Today there are herbal drugs for all manner of ailments. These drugs are prepacked and labelled and leaflets are often distributed to advertise new herbal clinics and medicines. The health authorities look on these developments with ambivalence. As one government-owned daily recently lamented:

> It is about 15 years now since the UN recommended the integration of traditional medicine into the orthodox system to back the primary health care programme. It is at least a century now since scientific knowledge of traditional medicine was attained, and it is many, many years now that the successful practice of its integration into the orthodox (medical system) has been going on. And yet our own orthodox medical authorities talk and behave as if the integration is novel and far-fetched (*Ghanaian Times*, May 28th 1993, p. 2).

Such prejudice has prevented a formal and straight acceptance of herbal medicine in the national health care program because the prejudice happens to be strongest among the very official and professional quarters responsible for recommending its acceptance.

This situation, however, does not prevent people from utilizing the services of ethnomedical practitioners when the need arises. The future of ethnomedicine is enhanced by the fact that some Ghanaians will always suffer from health conditions perceived to be "unordinary," to have been caused by malevolence. Others will see their diseases as capable of being cured by herbal medicine only; yet others will prefer to enjoy the "best" of both worlds available in pluralistic medical systems. For public safety, however, it is necessary to control the proliferation of ethnomedical practitioners and for the practitioners themselves to control their members. A strong national association of healers is thus long overdue.

NOTES

[1] Auguste Comte, the putative father of empiricist sociology, influenced a number of earlier sociologists with his evolutionary view of society. He saw human societies developing through three invariable stages: the theological, the metaphysical, and, finally, the positive or scientific stage. Earlier

anthropologists such as Levy-Bruhl, influenced by this postulation, attempted a classification of the various cultural configurations they had studied.

[2] In the struggle for political independence, certain writers and nationalists emerged to champion the distinctive identity of the African and peoples of African descent. Among such personages were Kwame Nkrumah of Ghana, Leopold Senghor of Senegal, Leon Damas of Guyana, and Aime Cesaire and Frantz Fanon from Martinique. To them, "African personality" or "Negritude" was the cultural heritage, the values, and particularly the spirit of Negro-African civilization borne out of a time of search and conflict. These ideological orientations lived on after political independence and helped significantly to reorient the social structures of some African states.

[3] In 1990, at a meeting organized by the Royal Tropical Institute in Amsterdam to discuss research findings on herbal drugs in Ghana and Thailand, the Director of the Centre for Scientific Research into Plant Medicine made this statement in response to some of the problems of his organization.

[4] Currently, social scientists from the Universities of Leiden, Amsterdam, and Ghana have drawn up a proposal for a postmortem study of the PRHETIH project. This will start as soon as funds are available.

REFERENCES

BANNERMAN, RICHARD H. 1983. "The Role of Traditional Medicine in Primary Health Care." In: R. H. Bannerman, J. Burton and C. Wen-Chieh (eds.) *Traditional Medicine and Health Care Coverage: A Reader for Health Administrators and Practitioners.* Geneva: WHO. Pp. 318–27.

BERGER, PETER L. 1976. *Invitation To Sociology: A Humanistic Perspective.* Harmondsworth, England: Penguin Books.

BONSI, STEPHEN K. 1977. "Persistence and Change in Traditional Medical Practice in Ghana." *International Journal of Contemporary Sociology.* 14:27–38.

BREW-GRAVES, HARRY S. 1977. "The Evolution of Traditional Healing in Ghana." *Report of the First National Workshop on Traditional Medicine in Zambia.* Mulungushi Hall.

DOROZYNSKI, ANTHONIO. 1975. *Doctors and Healers.* IDRC-043e. Ottawa: International Development Research Centre.

EVANS-ANFOM, EMMANUEL. 1986. *Traditional Medicine in Ghana: Practice, Problems, and Prospects.* Accra: Ghana Publishing Corporation.

EVANS-PRITCHARD, EDWARD E. 1937. *Witchcraft, Oracles and Magic Among the Azande.* London: Oxford University Press.

FIELD, MARGARET J. 1937. *Religion and Medicine of the Ga People.* London: Oxford University Press.

FINK, HELGA. 1990. *Religion, Disease and Healing in Ghana: A Case Study of Dormaa Medicine.* Muenchen: Tricker Wissenschaft.

FOSU, GABRIEL B. 1981. "Disease Classification in Rural Ghana: Framework and Implications for Health Behaviour." *Social Science and Medicine.* 15B:471–82.

FYFE, CHRISTOPHER. 1987. Introduction. In: *African Medicine in the Modern World*, edited by U. Maclean and C. Fyfe. Centre of African Studies, University of Edinburg. Pp. 1–4.

GELFAND, MICHAEL. 1956. *Medicine and Magic of the Mashona.* Cape Town: Juta.

———. 1964: *Witchdoctor: Traditional Medicine Man of Rhodesia.* London: Harvill Press. *Ghanaian Times*, 1993 (May 28).

GOOD, CHARLES M. 1987. *Ethnomedical Systems in Africa.* London: Guilford Press.

HARLEY, GEORGE W. 1941. *Native African Medicine.* Cambridge, MA: Harvard University Press.

JAHODA, GUSTAV. 1970. "Supernatural Beliefs and Changing Cognitive Structures Among Ghanaian University Students." *Journal of Cross-Cultural Psychology.* 2:115–30.

JANZEN, JOHN. 1978. *The Quest for Therapy in Lower Zaire.* Berkeley, CA: University of California Press.

KLEINMAN, ARTHUR. 1980. *Patients and Healers in the Context of Culture.* Berkeley, CA: University of California Press.

LAST, MURRAY, and CHAVUNDUKA, GODFREY L. (Eds). 1986. *The Professionalization of African Medicine.* Manchester, Eng.: Manchester University Press.

MACLEAN, UNA. 1971. *Magical Medicine. A Nigerian Case-study.* Baltimore: Penguin Books.

Ministry of Health. 1991. *Ghana: Health in Brief.* Accra, Ghana.

PATTERSON, DAVID K. 1981. *Health in Colonial Ghana: Diseases, Medicine and Socio-Economic Change* (1900–1955). Waltham, MA: Crossroads Press.

PILLSBURY, BARBARA L. K. 1982. "Policy and Evaluation Perspectives on Traditional Health Care Practitioners in National Health Care Systems." *Social Science and Medicine.* 16:1825–34.

SLIKKERVEER, ISAIAH J. 1982. "Rural Health Development in Ethiopia: Problems of Utilization of Traditional Healers." *Social Science and Medicine.* 16:1859–72.

———. 1990. *Plural Medical Systems in the Horn of Africa: The Legacy of "Sheikh" Hippocrates.* London: Kegan Paul International.

TWUMASI, PATRICK A. 1975. *Medical Systems in Ghana.* Accra/Tema: Ghana Publishing Corporation.

———. 1982. "Improvement of Health Care in Ghana. Present Perspective." In: *African Health and Healing Systems*, edited by P. Stanley Yoder. Los Angeles: Crossroads Press. Pp. 199–215.

———. 1987. "Traditional Birth Attendant Review Programme in Ghana." Unpublished study commissioned by MOH, Accra.

———. 1988. *Social Foundations of the Interplay between Traditional and Modern Systems.* Accra: Ghana Universities Press.

VENTEVOGEL, PETER. 1992. "The Effects of a Training Programme for Indigenous Healers in the Techiman District, Ghana." Unpublished M. A. thesis. University of Amsterdam.

WARREN, DENNIS M. 1989. "Utilizing Indigenous Healers in National Health Delivery Systems: The Ghanaian Experiment." In: John van Willigen, Barbara Rylko-Bauer, and Ann McElroy (eds). *Making Our Research Useful. Case Studies in the Utilization of Anthropological Knowledge.* Boulder, CO: Westview Press.

WONDERGEM, PETER, KODJO A. SENAH, and EVAM GLOVER. 1989. *Herbal Drugs in Primary Health Care: An Assessment of the Relevance of Herbal Drugs in Ghana's PHC.* Amsterdam: Royal Tropical Institute.

World Bank. 1989. *Accelerated Development in Sub-Saharan Africa: An Agenda for Action.* (Berg Report), Washington, D.C.

———. 1990. *World Development Report.* Oxford: Oxford University Press.

World Health Organization. 1978. *The Promotion and Development of Traditional Medicine.* WHO Technical Report Series, 622. Geneva, Switzerland.

PART III

SOCIOPOLITICAL AND REGIONAL DIMENSIONS

CHAPTER 8

Development of Health Policy and Services for Rural Mexico

Margaret Sherrard Sherraden

At noon on the first day of July 1979, village authorities convened community assemblies in 890 remote villages in Mexico. On hand were government representatives from the coordinating office of the Plan for Depressed Zones and Marginal Groups (COPLAMAR) and the Mexican Social Security Institute (IMSS). Two months later, 873 clinics opened their doors. By 1985, IMSS-COPLAMAR officially provided services to more than 13 million of the rural poor through a network of over 3000 clinics and 65 rural hospitals. By 1991, the program, renamed IMSS-Solidaridad by Mexico's President Salinas de Gortari, expanded to cover an additional 3.4 million people (Solidarity 1993). It is now estimated that 71 percent of small communities (under 2,500 population) have access to basic health services (Rojas Gutiérrez 1991).

Far more than a "paper creation," IMSS-Solidaridad has contributed to a shift in Mexico's health policy from a primarily urban, hospital-based system to a system providing substantial rural primary health care (Table 1). To a more limited extent, the program addresses community health concerns in rural villages and has promoted community participation in the health program (Sherraden 1991b).

In this chapter we examine the development of IMSS-Solidaridad. Mexico ranks among only a handful of nations in Latin America that have seriously

TABLE 1.   SOCIAL SOLIDARITY, IMSS-COPLAMAR AND IMSS-SOLIDARITY, RURAL HEALTH SERVICES, 1975–1992

| | POPULATION (MILLIONS) | | RURAL CLINICS | RURAL HOSPITALS | COVERAGE[1] (MILLIONS) | PERCENT OF RURAL POP. |
	TOTAL (1)	RURAL (2)	(3)	(4)	(5)	(5÷2)
Social Solidarity (1973-78)						
1975	60.2	—	310	28	.7	—
1978	65.7	—	310	28	2.8	—
IMSS-COPLAMAR and Social Solidarity						
1979	67.5	23.6	2104	30	3.7	15.7
1985	77.9	23.9	3246	65	13.7	57.3
(Decentralization decision)						
1986[a]	79.6	23.9	2191	50	9.8	41.0
1988	82.8	23.7	2323	51	9.9	42.0
IMSS-Solidarity (1989-	)[b]					
1992[c]	83.3	22.5	3448	53[d]	14.3	—

Sources: World Bank 1993, IMSS-COPLAMAR 1980-87, Solidarity in National Development, 1993.

[1]Coverage refers to numbers of people registered (*adscrito*) in the program.

[a]Coverage decreases due to decentralization of 20 states to the public health system. These decentralized states are not included for the years after 1986.

[b]These figures are for IMSS-Solidarity; they do not include decentralized programs.

[c]Figures are for 1992 except (1) and (2), which are for 1991.

[d]In addition, 7 regional hospitals were constructed.

attempted to provide basic primary and secondary care to rural populations (Sherraden and Wallace 1992; Mesa-Lago 1992). Mexico's program is unlike other well-known examples in the region, such as the universal care models in socialist Cuba and democratic Costa Rica, and the free market model in Chile (Borzutsky 1991; Morgan 1993; Feinsilver 1993). Mexico's policy, which has followed a more incremental path, illustrates an alternative for providing health care to poor and ethnically diverse rural populations (Sherraden 1991a).

Why did Mexico shift its policy to provide substantially more rural health care? It is not entirely a coincidence that this major initiative occurred soon after the World Health Organization called for "health for all in the year 2000" (WHO 1978). But the political commitment to IMSS-Solidaridad has its roots in compromises following the Mexican Revolution, and the shape of current health policies bears the mark of policies forged in the last 60 years.

This chapter addresses the origins and historical development of rural health policy in Mexico. It examines the institutions that have been responsible for rural health care and suggests why, despite important antecedents in the public health sector, the social security sector has spearheaded the most successful rural health care initiatives. This contrasts with the experiences of most other Latin American nations, which historically have given ministries of health, not social security, responsibility for services to the rural poor.

THE STRUCTURE OF HEALTH SERVICES IN MEXICO

Like most other Latin American nations, the majority of people in Mexico receive medical care from government or government-affiliated institutions, primarily social security and public health. A relatively small private sector also provides health care. Each of these sectors tends to direct services to distinct social groups, resulting in a three-tiered system:[1]

Social Security

Social security institutions primarily serve the urban working classes, civil servants, and professionals. These institutions offer medical care and economic benefits to specific occupational groups. Each operates independently and is financed by some combination of employer, employee, and government contributions. They are parastate organizations, affiliated with the federal government, but administered by semi-independent councils.[2] In 1990, social security institutions officially provided coverage to 48.1 million Mexicans or 59.3 percent of the population (Valdés Olmedo 1991; Mesa-Lago 1992). The largest social security institution is IMSS, which provides benefits to blue-collar and white-collar workers and their families. Other social security institutions offer benefits to groups such as civil servants, petroleum workers, electrical workers, railroad workers, the armed forces, and the police. Historically, social security programs have been relatively well funded compared to public health programs.

Public Health

Public health institutions serve the so-called "open population," i.e., those not covered by social security institutions and who do not receive private care. This population includes the urban poor, most of the rural population, and workers in the informal sector (Mesa-Lago 1990). In 1990, the open population was estimated officially at 29 million (Valdés Olmedo 1991). The largest institution that serves the open population is the Ministry of Health. Several other institutions also provide services in the public health sector, including several specialized hospitals in Mexico City, the city's health department, and the National System for Integrated Development of the Family (DIF) and the National Indigenous Institute (INI). Estimates of how many of the open population lack access to health services tends to vary by source, from 6 percent (Salinas de Gortari 1990) to 17 percent (Consejo Consultivo 1990). Administration of public health programs is under direct government control and financing comes, almost entirely, from government funds and patient fees with some special projects financed by international development agencies.

In contrast to social security, public health historically has devoted a larger portion of its budget than social security to prevention and public health. It also receives the fewest resources and serves more people. Average annual per capita expenditures for those covered in the social security sector were more than two-and-a-half times those for the open population during the 1980s (Valdés Olmedo 1991). While the Ministry of Health was officially responsible for providing services to half the population, it received only 23 percent of the health budget in 1980, and received 24 percent in 1990 (Valdés Olmedo 1991).

Private Health Services

The private health services sector is relatively small and is utilized by two social groups. One is the wealthy, who pay for care directly or through private health insurance plans. This group is estimated at approximately 3.6 million (Valdés Olmedo 1991). Many families that are covered by social security plans often also use private care, depending on their financial ability. Twenty percent of medical facilities are private (Soberón and Ruíz 1984).

The second group is the population in poverty with little real access to public health and social assistance services who rely on traditional healing, domestic medicine, and over-the-counter pharmaceuticals.[3] Especially in the more isolated rural and underserved areas, such informal care predominates, including traditional health care, midwifery, and domestic medicine (Aguirre Beltrán 1986).

Among physicians, private practice is usually part time (López Acuña 1984a). State institutions train and absorb most medical professionals; physicians tend to affiliate early in their careers with one of the major government-affiliated health agencies and remain for their working careers. In rural areas there are even fewer formally trained private health providers.

Neither the public health nor the social security sector devoted much effort to rural areas until the creation of IMSS-Solidaridad. In 1970, when the Mexican population was more than 40 percent rural, the Ministry of Health devoted only 4 percent of its budget to rural health and IMSS devoted only 3 percent (Hewitt 1977). A scarcity of rural doctors resulted from these pro-urban policies. For example, in 1970, 80 percent of doctors were located in urban areas, there were 474 inhabitants per physician in the Federal District, and in the poorest states there were more than 4000 people per doctor (López-Acuña 1984a, p. 115).

The creation of IMSS-Solidaridad within social security profoundly altered the structure of health services and significantly increased the services and resources destined for the rural poor. It is critical to understand the historical context of reform, to which we now turn.

RURAL HEALTH SERVICES

Revolution to 1940

In an effort to maintain the support of peasants, who had been mobilized during the Mexican Revolution, framers of Mexico's 1917 Constitution included far-reaching social justice provisions to protect peasant land ownership and social welfare. In the words of historian Adolfo Gilly, "[Peasants] left their mark on the emergent bourgeois republic, so that [they] could never be disregarded in the political and social life of the republic" (1983). Nonetheless, in the fifty years following the Revolution, government policies tended to promote industrial and commercial agricultural growth at the expense of meeting peasant needs and demands. But there were periods when government policies aimed at improving economic development *and* peasant welfare. Overall, this has resulted in an ebb and flow of resources and attention to the rural sector (Fox 1992). The development of rural health policy paralleled these intermittent gains.

After the Revolution, health services were nationalized but little was done to build a health services infrastructure until the 1930s when the Depression and working class and peasant violence led to increasing support in government circles for social policies to relieve poverty and suffering (Alvarez Amezquita 1960; Frenk 1980). Under President Cárdenas (1934–40) the federal government turned its attention and resources to health and welfare policy for the poor.

Cárdenas proposed far-reaching social reforms that aimed at economic, political, and social integration of the rural sector into national society. This resulted in creation of many new state institutions, including the Rural Cooperative Medical Services in 1934 to provide health services in *ejidos*, communally held agricultural lands. (*Ejidos* were among Cárdenas' earliest rural reform efforts aimed at transforming agricultural production by helping formerly impoverished and landless peasants become prosperous rural producers [Sanderson 1981]). The Rural Cooperative Medical Services concentrated its efforts on the densely populated and commercial agricultural areas in northern Mexico, but provided some free preventive services to more remote and impoverished rural areas (Whetten 1984). Rural organizers taught groups of mothers, children, and youth about rural sanitation. By 1936, the program had constructed 11 hospitals, 56 clinics, 36 health centers, and 225 auxiliary centers (Moreno Cueto et al. 1982). This program was an important antecedent for IMSS-Solidaridad.

Another part of Cárdenas' rural development strategy involved sending medical doctors into underserved rural areas, a policy that continues today. Through *Servicio Social*, a program of mandatory social service by doctors in rural areas, the federal government hoped "to bring scientific medicine to backward rural areas" (Almada Bay 1985, p. 16), to encourage doctors to stay in rural areas, and give them firsthand experience (Hewitt 1977; Whetten 1984; Sherraden and Sherraden 1991). Officials hoped that not only would *Servicio Social* improve living standards in rural areas, but also would help integrate isolated indigenous ethnic communities into national life.

Following this, the Secretariat of Public Assistance was created in 1937, the first social assistance agency at the federal level with the mission "to realize the work of social solidarity [assist the poor]" (Moreno Salazar and Redorta Zúñiga 1984). At the same time, the Public Health Department moved beyond combating epidemics to: address infectious diseases, such as tuberculosis and leprosy; improve worker hygiene; provide potable water; pasteurize milk; and provide breakfasts for children (Almada Bay 1985). The Department of Social Assistance to Children, also created in 1937, provided social welfare services to indigent mothers and children in urban areas. This program evolved into the principal federal child welfare agency, the National Institute for the Protection of Children (INPI), and eventually became the national family assistance agency, Integrated Family Development (DIF).

The Post-Cárdenas Era

Despite growth of the health budget and important rural health reforms during the Cárdenas years, most rural areas still lacked health services. By 1940, only 8.7 percent of the doctors lived in rural areas that contained 67 percent of the population (Whetten, cited in Almada Bay 1985).

Cárdenas' broad agenda, which had achieved solid popular support during the first half of his term, was increasingly viewed as too radical. By 1940, a conservative alliance dominated state policymaking. Peasants increasingly were marginalized as government policy promoted large commercial agricultural enterprises at the expense of *ejidos* and small properties. Rural development was scaled back, even as the national economy expanded rapidly in the postwar period.

As the 1970s approached, however, strains began to appear. Resources flowing into the agricultural sector had not kept pace with the outflows, resulting in huge net losses of capital from the countryside (Sanderson 1981). The result was a decline in the average annual growth rate within the agriculture sector from 8.2 percent in the 1940s to 2 percent in the 1970s. Increasingly, the government relied on foreign borrowing to finance social capital investment and public enterprises (Sanderson 1981).

By the 1970s, reformers argued that the poor had been denied the benefits from the postwar "Mexican economic miracle" they helped to produce. Birth rates increased and poverty grew worse. Hewitt de Alcántara points out that the numbers of working people depending on each landholding increased markedly by 1954, resulting in 54 percent of landholdings (1.3 million) providing less than minimum subsistence requirements for bare survival (1977). Finding small farming untenable, more and more peasants migrated in search of work. The number of day agricultural laborers increased from 1.9 to 3.3 million (from 50 percent to 54 percent of the agricultural labor force) between 1940 and 1960, according to Hewitt de Alcántara (1977). After decades of exporting basic food items such as corn, Mexico began importing food in 1965.

In the meantime, urban health services captured ever larger portions of the federal budget. Between 1940 and 1970, rural health services, and health services for the poor in general, stagnated in favor of extending services to commercial and industrial workers in urban areas (López Acuña 1984a, pp. 101–105).

Some rural Ministry of Health programs survived, but their share of the budget declined steadily. The Rural Cooperative Medical Services claim on the Ministry of Health's budget declined from a high of 8.2 percent in 1937 to a low of 2 percent in 1944 (Hernández Llamas 1984).

Despite limited resources and little political commitment for services to the rural poor, reformers at the Ministry of Health continued to try to develop a rural health policy. In 1953, the Rural Social Welfare Program was created to provide medical services as well as programs in nutrition, sanitation, health education, community participation, and cottage industries and cooperatives. In 1963, international agencies lent support to rural development in conjunction with the Rural Cooperative Works Program and Mexico's food distribution program, CONASUPO, in distributing half a million food rations as incentives for the unemployed and underemployed to work on thousands of community development projects (Fujigaki Lechuga 1984). Other programs supplemented the diets of pregnant and lactating women and preschool children. But by the early 1970s, these programs suffered the fate of other rural programs and virtually disappeared (Alarcón Navarro et al. 1986). Rural health centers were absorbed into state public health services.

Broad-based rural health policies within the Ministry of Health took a back seat to programs that targeted specific illnesses such as antimalarial and antirabies campaigns. These "vertical" programs were not only less expensive, but with the creation of new vaccinations, they became increasingly effective.[4] The government only sporadically supported more expensive "horizontal" medical services and environmental health programs. For example, López Acuña reports that out of 97,653 localities in the 1970 census, only 2600 had professional medical services (1980), and 80 percent of doctors were concentrated in cities of more than 50,000, while more than 50 percent of municipalities in Chiapas, Oaxaca, Puebla, Yucatán, and Aguascalientes had no doctor at all in 1977 (1984a).

Throughout the 1980s, the Ministry of Health extended rural health services through the perennially underfunded state-based Coordinated Public Health Services.[5] This program provides volunteer services in remote areas, *casas de salud* operated by village health workers in small communities, clinics in communities of less than 5000, and secondary care in small city hospitals (Pineda 1984). The Ministry of Health's rural coverage in 1986 was estimated at 4.8 million, but it continues to suffer from lack of resources, especially since the economic crisis of the 1980s (Alarcón Navarro et al. 1986).

Even though public health institutions have been poorly funded and have concentrated their resources in urban medical services, such efforts as the Cultural Missions project (1920s); Cooperative Rural Medical Services (1930s–1950s); and the Rural Social Welfare Program (1950s) were important models for IMSS-Solidaridad. Furthermore, some of the reformers involved in the development of the Ministry of Health rural programs became influential later in federal rural health policymaking in the social security sector. In the words of one health official, IMSS-Solidaridad is really the "product of six decades of experience" in rural health planning.

RURAL HEALTH SERVICES UNDER SOCIAL SECURITY

Although both the Constitution of 1917 and the social security legislation of 1943 include provisions for protections for agricultural workers and *ejidatarios*, IMSS postponed extending social security to rural areas. Planners hoped to establish a solid organizational and financial footing before extending services to the impoverished rural sector, viewing redistribution to the poor as an impossible luxury before first making sure that IMSS was institutionally and financially stable.

Like other Latin American nations, financing of social security in Mexico poses an obvious obstacle to incorporating the poor (Mesa-Lago 1991). Mexico adopted the principle of tripartite financing based on employer, employee, and government contributions from Western Europe and North America. While the working and middle classes and their employers can afford to make contributions, workers and employers in the informal sector, peasants, and the poor frequently cannot (Mesa-Lago 1992). Generally, employment is too erratic and income is too low to support individual contributions. Likewise, employers frequently are unknown and difficult to locate, making institutional arrangements difficult. As a result, IMSS opted to include the rural sector at a later date. The 1943 legislation that founded IMSS left "open the possibility . . . that in an opportune moment new programs of incorporation could be brought about" (IMSS 1976a, p. 10).

Not until 1954 did IMSS make a tentative step to extend services to peasant areas. IMSS chose seven relatively densely populated, prosperous, and highly productive agricultural areas in northern Mexico to initiate rural social security. By 1958, nearly 98,000 rural beneficiaries and their families received services (Wilson 1981).[6] A series of small incorporations of agricultural groups followed, but according to one observer, the program soon developed into a "bureaucratic and administrative quagmire" (Spalding 1978, p. 228). The use of credit societies as brokers for financing was not working, employers were not registering most of their workers, seasonal workers were difficult to incorporate, and IMSS could not control the provision of services.

However, under the leadership of President López Mateos (1958–1964), who was committed to expanding social security, rural extensions received new impetus. New legislation attempted to deal with some of the administrative and financial problems in IMSS' initial efforts at rural coverage. Social security benefits and contribution structures were altered to allow coverage of agricultural workers, especially seasonal and self-employed farmers (Spalding 1978, Wilson 1981). Most notably, employee contributions in the case of seasonal workers were dropped, although the plan included fewer benefits. Despite these important initiatives, social security coverage of the total rural workforce in 1963 was only 1 percent (García Cruz 1972–1973).

New extensions to the rural sector were slowed and administration and finances were consolidated and managed more conservatively at IMSS in the late 1960s (Spalding 1978). Episodic violent confrontations between government, employers, and labor brought rural coverage to a standstill until the election of President Echeverría in 1970. At the beginning of the 1970s, IMSS covered only 1.4 percent of rural inhabitants and 8 percent of the economically active in rural areas (López Acuña 1984b).

During the Echeverría administration, reformers once again argued that the peasant sector was the "Achilles heel" of economic growth (Moreno Cueto et al. 1982, p. 75). Echeverría proposed rural reforms intended to redress inequalities through rural development. Echeverría called on the nation to make "ever greater efforts towards national solidarity [redistribution of the wealth] aimed at extending benefits to the weakest sectors" (Echeverría Alvarez 1973, p. 14). The reforms, funded largely through foreign borrowing, included extension of health care and other social welfare services. Rural expenditures increased from 4.1 percent of federal spending during the previous presidential administration to an average of 12.8 percent during the first five years of Echeverría's term (Spalding 1978).[7]

For the first time, in 1973, health programs were created that seriously addressed the unique structural qualities of the rural sector and agricultural work, including the presence of multiple employers, short-term employment, migration, combined subsistence and wage work, and high rates of poverty (Moreno Islas 1958). The initiatives took three forms: voluntary incorporation, modified schemes, and IMSS-Solidaridad's forerunner, Social Solidarity.

Voluntary Incorporation

This concept permitted domestic servants, workers in small family businesses, the self employed, professionals, small farmers, *ejidatarios*, and the temporarily unemployed to join IMSS provided that they made the entire financial contribution (Spalding 1978).

Modified Schemes

These programs allowed peasants with fewer resources to participate in a modified version of social security. Hemp workers, tobacco workers, cotton workers, palm workers, wax workers, and lumber workers in various states were covered under the new schemes between 1972 and 1974 (Cárdenas de la Peña et al. 1975; Spalding 1978). Under modified schemes, rural workers paid a smaller contribution to IMSS based on land size and crop value in return for modified social security coverage. Very often rural credit associations, *ejidos*, and cooperatives made contributions or guaranteed payments to IMSS. The modified schemes excluded most economic benefits, concentrating efforts on "urgent necessities" such as medical services.[8] Workers covered under these programs were regular beneficiaries of IMSS and specialized services of IMSS, such as urban specialty hospitals, were available, at least theoretically.

Social Solidarity

This program, which ran from 1973 to 1979, was particularly important to the emergence of IMSS-Solidaridad because it brought together elements of prior rural health programs into the social security structure and provided a model for the present day program. The name, "solidarity," which has historical and symbolic meaning in Mexico, recalls the social justice goals of the Mexican Revolution and the nation's responsibility to redistribute resources to the poor.

The goal of Social Solidarity was to create an infrastructure of health services for the rural poor, the single largest social group without access to institutional health services. Although it began as a rural hospital program, it soon evolved into a network of clinics. By 1976, IMSS had built 30 rural hospitals and 310 clinics in 27 states (Table 1). Beneficiaries received free medical assistance, medications, and hospitalization. Maternal and infant care, preventive dentistry, and rural sanitation were emphasized (IMSS 1976b). Community participation was seen as a way for families to "pay" with in-kind contributions for medical care and to promote family and community health (IMSS 1976b; Sherraden 1991b).[9]

IMSS extended Social Solidarity by region, beginning in the north in 1973 (Cárdenas de la Peña et al. 1975). By 1978, nearly three million "profoundly marginal" people were officially covered (Table 1). The population served included agricultural workers, but, by and large, it did not include the indigenous ethnic communities which later became the focus of IMSS-Solidaridad.

Despite the fanfare surrounding these new programs, officials were careful not to threaten existing social security programs. IMSS emphasized that they would not interfere with the "effective delivery of benefits to the workers and beneficiaries of the [regular] social security regimen" (IMSS 1982, p. 40). In other words, solidarity with the poor would not be pursued at the risk of losing support of unionized workers or employers affiliated with IMSS. These assurances, along with support by IMSS bureaucrats and the president, permitted Social Solidarity to get underway with little opposition (Spalding 1978). Planners minimized Social Solidarity program costs by emphasizing low-cost preventive and primary health services instead of more expensive hospital-based services. Beneficiaries had access only to Social Solidarity facilities; they were not permitted to use IMSS hospitals.

But Social Solidarity enjoyed the support of the president and reformers in IMSS, some of whom were veterans of previous rural health initiatives. Social Solidarity was favored by the president in order to increase rural food productivity and political legitimacy in rural areas (Spalding 1981) and reformers in IMSS were pushing hard for expansion of social security among uncovered population groups.[10] By 1976, the program used 14.8 percent of IMSS budget surplus, resulting in a small net transfer to the poverty program from IMSS' regular program (Spalding 1981).

Nonetheless, the rural population continued largely uncovered. Out of an estimated 24 million rural people without institutional health services, only 5.4 million rural inhabitants had been incorporated into some rural social security program by 1976 (Zamarripa Torres 1984). IMSS only increased its coverage from 8 to almost 10 percent of the rural work force between 1970 and 1978 (Wilson 1981; López Acuña 1984b). Coverage remained concentrated in the North and Gulf states except Chihuahua and Tabasco, leaving the poorer Central, South, and West largely uncovered. Furthermore, redistribution effects were small; costs per beneficiary in the Social Solidarity program were less than one quarter of costs in the regular social security program. Annual per capita expenditure for urban beneficiaries was approximately U.S. $158 in 1986 dollars, while per capita expenditure for modified scheme beneficiaries was approximately U.S. $79, and for Social Solidarity beneficiaries was only approximately U.S. $39 (Cárdenas de la Peña et al. 1975). Thus, in spite of efforts to move towards universal social security coverage, services were designed to provide only minimum protection.

HEALTH CARE AND RURAL DEVELOPMENT: COPLAMAR, 1977–1983

Expansion of rural social security slowed by the end of President Echeverría's term in office as concerns about the financial stability of IMSS and economic, political, and social problems in Mexico intensified. Rural health reforms were placed on the back burner for the first three years of President López Portillo's term in office (1976–1982). By the end of the decade, Social Solidarity's budget had fallen from 1.3 percent of IMSS's budget in 1976 to only 0.4 percent in 1979 (Cárdenas de la Peña et al. 1975, Spalding 1981). The number of Social Solidarity clinics and hospitals stagnated as well (Table 1).

But the president did not entirely turn his back on the poor. González Navarro recounts that even in his inaugural speech, López Portillo "asked [on behalf of the nation] for forgiveness from the dispossessed and marginals for not having considered removing them from prostration . . . the country is conscious and ashamed of this and therefore he had decided to 'conquer the rights of justice' " (1985, p. 18).

In 1977 the president created COPLAMAR to promote and coordinate rural development activities in impoverished rural areas.[11] At the time, the "marginal population" was estimated at 20 million, with only one in ten people receiving services in health, education, employment, housing, roads, water, and other support services (COPLAMAR 1982). Although given very few funds at first, COPLAMAR officials formulated policies intended to deal with the causes and consequences of marginality. The guiding concept of "marginality" employed by COPLAMAR planners referred to the condition of groups involved in the production of the nation's wealth, but who are not benefitting from it (COPLAMAR 1982). This definition marked a major conceptual shift towards viewing rural poverty from a structural perspective rather than as the result of cultural "backwardness" (Hewitt de Alcántara 1984, p. 174).[12]

A major function of COPLAMAR's small but dedicated research staff was to document the level of "marginality" and needs of the impoverished rural sector. They produced an impressive series of volumes documenting existing and projected basic needs in health, nutrition, education, and housing, by geographical area of the country, thereby providing an empirical foundation for future rural development (COPLAMAR 1983).

At the same time, in the late 1970s, international pressures to increase social security and health coverage for the rural poor were also intensifying. International endorsement of primary health strategies peaked in 1977 when the World Health Organization (WHO) and UNICEF, in a historic meeting at Alma Ata, called on nations to provide "health care for all by the year 2000" (WHO 1978). Although Mexico's efforts to provide primary health services to rural communities often preceded or occurred simultaneously with these international developments, reformers could utilize international pressures to press their case for reform (Spalding 1978). The Alma Ata declaration, for example, provided an opportune moment for Mexico to announce health policy reforms of its own and, as a result, has been viewed as a vanguard in development of rural primary health care (ILO 1986).

The IMSS-COPLAMAR Decision

Pressure to do something for the rural poor intensified. A former COPLAMAR official reported that President López Portillo was "vexed" by the unwillingness of federal entities and agencies to cooperate with COPLAMAR, which could theoretically earmark portions of agency budgets for the rural poor, but had little say over the final allocation of funds.

In 1979 the president gave COPLAMAR, which operated out of the Office of the Presidency, direct control of funds destined for impoverished rural areas. This was made possible by additional public revenues, and swelled as a result of massive foreign loans, which were backed by the promise of huge profits from Mexico's newly discovered oil reserves. The president seized the moment to announce a major rural development initiative, with health care at its very center. The objectives of COPLAMAR's rural development program were to increase employment and the productive capacities of communities, to distribute resources to underserved communities, to improve the planning capacity of the poor, and to strengthen the negotiating capacities of poor communities (COPLA-MAR 1982). COPLAMAR continued its research and coordination functions, while specific agencies contracted to provide services.

There is ample evidence that COPLAMAR was successful in channeling additional resources to rural areas. Through the various programs, COPLAMAR officially invested approximately $5 billion in 1986 dollars, over 87 times the original amount of resources originally destined to these agencies for impoverished rural areas between 1979 and 1982 (COPLAMAR 1982).[13] IMSS-COPLA-MAR, the health program, swiftly built over 3000 village clinics and 61 hospitals. The national food agency built 276 warehouses and 14,000 small village stores to provide subsidized food (Fox 1992). Other agencies built bilingual boarding schools and community centers, created jobs, built and rehabilitated water systems, reconstructed roads, made home improvements, and provided agricultural support services (COPLAMAR 1982).

COPLAMAR planners aimed at involving the rural poor in planning and implementing their own development rather than incorporating them into the system that had marginalized them in the first place (COPLAMAR 1982). In order to receive benefits of the health program, COPLAMAR, like Social Solidarity, required families to contribute ten days a year to development projects, as long as it did not conflict with "normal productive activities." Yearly reports on compliance with community participation goals authorized continuation of services for the following year. (Former officials report, however, that communities were rarely "deauthorized.") During the first two-and-a-half years, 108 million *jornadas* (day's work) were performed, resulting in an estimated savings to the government of over $747 million in 1986 dollars (COPLAMAR 1982).

Although substantial community contributions were realized, participation designed to "break patterns of paternalism" was less successful, according to a former COPLAMAR researcher. According to research in other Latin American countries, this is not unusual. Ugalde (1985) and Morgan (1993) have pointed out the challenges and contradictions of government-initiated community participation. In the case of COPLAMAR, a lack of beneficiary participation in decision making and evaluation reduced local control. However, former COPLAMAR officials agree that, among COPLAMAR programs, IMSS-Solidaridad and CONA-SUPO-COPLAMAR were most successful. Analyses show that community participation successes appear to depend on the ability of bureaucrats and reformers within federal agencies to ensure that participation objectives are addressed (Sherraden 1991b; Fox 1992).

Continuing the cycle of support and withdrawal of support for rural development programs, COPLAMAR disappeared by presidential decree in April 1983. Reformers were unable to save COPLAMAR because of Mexico's economic problems and political problems with the incoming president, de la Madrid, and his allies (Cornelius and Craig 1984).

But despite COPLAMAR's demise, IMSS-COPLAMAR survived the presidential transition. Observers attributed IMSS-COPLAMAR's survival to the popularity of the program both among reformers and rural beneficiaries, administrative support within IMSS, relatively low operating costs, and international recognition. In particular, IMSS-COPLAMAR provided an opportunity for IMSS to increase substantially its coverage and move significantly towards its historical mandate of universal coverage (ILO 1986).

ECONOMIC CRISIS AND DECENTRALIZATION OF THE HEALTH SECTOR

Mexico experienced severe economic difficulties in the 1980s as massive external debt combined with a stagnating economy. Between 1977 and 1987, total health sector expenditures fell as a percent of GDP from 2.4 percent to 1.8 percent, but began to recuperate by 1988 at 2 percent of the GDP (Valdés Olmedo 1991).

Coinciding with economic crisis, President Miguel de la Madrid announced several new health policies which had profound impact on rural health care. In 1983, he decreed the social guarantee to health services for all Mexicans and, in 1984, a national health system was created. Decentralization of health services was announced as part of a national policy to "decentralize national life," an important political platform of the president (de la Madrid 1986, pp. 31–32).

In what since has become a standard challenge to member nations by international agencies, decentralization was proposed as a way to make health policies more responsive to local needs, less bureaucratic, more representative, more productive, and more efficient. One of the first tasks of the newly created national health system was to decentralize health services to the open population. A presidential decree ordering the decentralization called for state-by-state transfer of IMSS-COPLAMAR and Ministry of Health programs to individual State Departments of Health under authority of the Ministry (de la Madrid et al. 1986). Between 1985 and 1986, twelve states were transferred to state control, with states assuming some responsibility for funding (Soberón et al. 1988).[14]

Decentralization halted in 1986 because the transfer process ran into problems. These included a lack of public health infrastructure and resources to contribute to the program's operations, central government reluctance to grant autonomy to some states, and institutional footdragging.[15] According to IMSS-COPLAMAR personnel and other observers, there were also implementation problems: local inhabitants also objected to having to pay fees for service (under state public health rules), staff abandoned their posts, and supplies and medication were not delivered and, in fact, were being diverted elsewhere. A year later, in 1987, two more states were transferred, but decentralization of IMSS-COPLAMAR did not resume after that. Currently, responsibility for serving the rural poor in Mexico continues to be shared, making coordination of health services to the open population difficult (Soberón and Ruíz 1984).

IMSS-SOLIDARIDAD AND THE NATIONAL SOLIDARITY PROGRAM, 1988–PRESENT

The most recent developments in the health program occurred with the election of President Salinas de Gortari in 1988. Having won by a slim (and questionable) margin, the president has made a concerted effort to regain the support and votes of the urban and rural poor, who comprise somewhere between

20 and 50 percent of the population. The president's inaugural speech once again invoked the goals of redistribution, although perhaps somewhat less forcefully than earlier presidents: "The welfare of each family must be the measure of the nation's prosperity. The great proposition of equality is that the standard of living improves for everyone, but that those who have less benefit more and those who have more benefit less."

President Salinas traveled the country initiating rural and urban development programs aimed at the provision of basic services. After a decade of slow growth and belt tightening, the president began to release large sums for social welfare under the National Solidarity Program (Moffett 1991). Charged with documenting need, and coordinating and designing strategies "to combat low standards of living," Solidarity recalls the objectives of COPLAMAR: to provide health, education, food, housing, and urban services to the needy, and to promote agricultural and regional development (Consejo Consultivo 1990; Salinas de Gortari 1991; Solidarity 1993).

Expansion of health services for the poor is one of several explicitly stated strategies. IMSS-COPLAMAR became IMSS-Solidaridad, harkening back to its days as Social Solidarity. After undergoing a period of slow growth during the mid- to late 1980s, the program grew more rapidly again. Between 1989 and 1992, over 1000 rural primary care clinics and seven regional hospitals were added and others were rehabilitated to serve an additional 3.4 million people (Solidarity 1993). The Ministry of Health also expanded its coverage of urban populations under the direction of Solidarity.

The model of community participation that had evolved in health policy since 1973, one that emphasized community and family contributions, has become a pillar of the new Solidarity program. President Salinas promotes a mode of participation that not only capitalizes on historical participation patterns in Mexico, but also captures current trends in poverty discussions in the United States (one editorial refers to the program as a "workfare poverty program") and international aid agencies (Asman 1991). In Salinas' words:

> Solidarity is breaking down the populist links between the government and the poor and erecting popular links instead. By popular, I mean not paternalistic, not for free, and respect for people's mobilization and their own initiative. In a word, co-responsibility (Asman 1992).

CONCLUSION

What explains Mexico's bold efforts to extend rural health services in the last fifteen years? Why did a languishing rural health policy suddenly flourish in the late 1970s? After all, the need for rural health care had been recognized long before, but relatively little had been done.

Several theoretical perspectives have been proposed by analysts to help explain the development of health policies in Mexico and other Latin American nations. Some researchers have proposed that social policies are expressions of the interests of the dominant capitalist classes in a "pact of domination" over subordinate classes (Cardoso 1979, p. 38). This perspective has emerged as a prominent explanation for social policy development in Latin America (Eckstein 1982).

As we have seen, an analysis of the overall context of health services in Mexico lends support for this view. Services had indeed developed along a two-tiered system in which extensive health services for industrial and large, commercial workers were covered by the resource-rich social security sector, while others—the majority of whom were poor—received care from the resource-poor public health sector. Thus, the class perspective contributes to understanding the overall conditions and context of policy making and quite clearly points out the inadequacies of simplistic appeals for redistribution to the poor. However, it tells us little about the timing and nature of reforms that have led to dramatic policy reforms in this case and have led to sustained and serious efforts to provide health services to the rural poor.

Policy developments are often assumed to be the result of socioeconomic growth (Cutright 1965). In the case of rural health policy in Mexico, however, we see little expansion in rural health care during periods of strong and sustained economic growth, such as the decades following World War II. On the other hand, we see expansion during hard economic times, such as the economic recovery period of the 1990s. Thus, although economic development and availability of financial resources undoubtedly have provided opportunities for health services expansion, it would appear that other factors explain policy advances in this case.

From a bureaucratic politics perspective, institutional factors help explain policy developments (Heclo 1974; Wilensky 1975). In fact, in the case of Mexico, it is clear that policymakers at IMSS were interested in fulfilling the constitutional mandate for universal coverage by expanding coverage to the rural poor. Another example of the power of bureaucratic politics was the decentralization attempt that was sidelined, in large part, by resistant institutions (Sherraden and Wallace 1992).

The corporatist-authoritarian perspective suggests that political elites, especially the president, utilize corporate state structures to control the policy agenda, to build political legitimacy, and to bring sectors of the population under the ruling party's control (O'Donnell 1977; Stepan 1978; Malloy 1979; Cardoso and Faletto 1979). In fact, the history of rural development efforts, health services included, reflects central government concerns about the perils of uneven development and loss of political legitimacy and support for the regime. The latest example is the National Solidarity Program, which has been utilized by the president to increase support for the party after a decade of worsening living standards and electoral threats to one-party rule (Brachet-Márquez and Sherraden, forthcoming).

Fox (1992) has proposed that different "policy currents" within the state forge alliances with other groups and are able to steer policymaking at different times. In the case of rural health policy, where we observe historical periods when reformers have been able to press their agenda, this observation makes a good deal of sense. Some of the reformers involved in the creation of IMSS-Solidaridad had been active in planning and implementation of early rural health programs. Repeatedly, we see that reformers have been most successful when presidential receptivity to rural reforms was high; such as when the president was attempting to consolidate central government control, to promote balanced urban-rural development, to gain international recognition, or to augment rural political support for the regime.

Historical patterns also demonstrate that rural health care had often been integrated into a broader rural development agenda. With political attention focused on the rural poor, reformers in health institutions were able to boost rural health services. During these periods, they could capture some of the resources that were usually won by urban industrial and large-scale agricultural concerns. This happened during the Cárdenas, Echeverría, and López Portillo presidencies and has also occurred, most recently, under Salinas. The National Solidarity Program once again has presented an opportunity for reformers to channel health resources to the rural sector.

NOTES

[1] Although theoretically separate, the boundaries between service sectors are blurred in reality. For example, many employees in the public sector "moonlight" in the private sector; many social security beneficiaries utilize private health services including the services of homeopathic doctors; many people self-medicate in addition to seeking the advice of a physician; and many rural inhabitants utilize both institutional health services (such as IMSS-Solidarity) and some form of informal care.

[2] See Mesa-Lago (1978), Moreno Cueto et al. (1982), Spalding (1978), and Wilson (1981) for detailed discussions of the development of social security in Mexico.

[3] It should be noted that 65 percent of medications are sold privately. Prescriptions are not required for most pharmaceuticals.

[4] "Vertical" health programs refer to "categorically specific, hierarchically organized, discrete disease control programs," as opposed to "horizontal" health systems based on "a mixed group of disease control/health promoting activities" (Gish 1982, p. 1049).

[5] However, numerous smaller regional programs were created in the 1970s. These are reviewed in Pineda (1984).

[6] Spalding discusses two principal financing mechanisms: "For agricultural wage earners, the financial mechanism was the same as that used in the urban program. The tripartite financial structure was utilized in which employers paid 50 percent of the contribution while workers and the State each paid an additional 25 percent. The amount of this contribution was to be determined based on employer reports of the land cultivated and the type of crop produced, IMSS estimations of the hours required for that production, and the wage structure of the area. Agricultural workers affiliated through their credit societies which administered member contributions equal to half of the total contribution while the State paid the other half. Again, this contribution was based on data presented by the societies estimating the annual income of their membership" (1978, p. 253fn).

[7] It should be noted that social spending as a proportion of total government spending did not increase much over the period. Social spending during Diaz Ordaz averaged 21 percent and during Echeverría's term averaged 23 percent. However, economic expenditures increased from an average of 45 percent during 1964–1970 to 56 percent during the following sexennium (Newell and Rubio 1984).

[8] Funeral costs, disability pensions, old-age pensions, and survivor benefits were included in the modified scheme (Cárdenas de la Peña et al. 1975).

[9] Even during periods when government attention has been turned to providing health services to the rural population, the poor are required to pay. Rural health programs, in contrast to urban programs, typically incorporate payments "in kind" instead of—or in addition to—monetary payments. Collective work, which traditionally served mutual aid functions, have "been relegated to tasks such as building the school house, houses, roads, etc., almost always under State control, thus effecting considerable savings in labour costs" (Bartra 1978, p. 435). For example, Rural Cooperative Medical Services expected beneficiaries to contribute labor and materials for community projects in exchange for food and medical services. Between 1959 and 1964, communities made contributions worth more than U.S. $1.9 million in 1964 dollars to the program (Vargas Lozano 1984, p. 125). Likewise, programs such as Social Solidarity and IMSS-Solidaridad in the social security sector require that beneficiaries contribute land, labor, money, and materials.

[10] The World Bank has recently emphasized the importance of health improvements for the poor in increasing agricultural productivity (World Bank 1993).

[11] The other major initiative was the Mexican Food System (1980–1982) which was aimed at generating food self-sufficiency and food distribution (Redclift 1981; Spalding 1984; Fox 1992).

[12] Planners and policymakers observed that the nation had drained capital and labor from the rural sector for too long and ignored the welfare of peasants. They proposed reversing the flow of wealth

back to rural areas. In addition to sending resources to villages, villagers would be encouraged to organize and become involved in guiding their villages' development.

[13] Estimates by Schumacher (1982) are much smaller. He calculates that $62.5 billion pesos (U.S. $2.7 billion) were spent on basic social infrastructure between 1980-1982.

[14] The states' share of costs increased from 3 percent in 1985-1986 to between 6 and 12 percent in 1986-1987 (González Block 1988, p. 31; Soberón et al. 1988, p. 121).

[15] With only one exception, the poorest and most rural states with the most clinics and hospitals were not transferred. Even with fourteen states transferred—almost half the states in the nation—the program lost only approximately 23 percent of its clinics and 25 percent of its hospitals. (The exception was Guerrero.) There is some indication that officials from the poorest states were reluctant to take over the health program because they lacked resources and administrative infrastructure to support it (Mares 1986; González Block 1988, p. 320). Likewise, the federal government may have been reluctant to relinquish central control (González Block 1988). In fact, the states *not* decentralized, such as Oaxaca, Chiapas, Hidalgo, and Puebla are among the states where local and regional elites continue to compete with the federal government for control over land, labor, and resources. By 1987, the states that were easiest to transfer had already been decentralized, leaving the poorest and most problematic states in the hands of IMSS-COPLAMAR. Finally, although publicly supportive of decentralization, many in IMSS and IMSS-COPLAMAR opposed the new policy. Although they were unable to challenge the policy early in de la Madrid's term, they may have been able to lobby effectively to halt decentralization during the presidential transition of 1987-1988.

REFERENCES

AGUIRRE BELTRÁN, GONZALO. 1986. *Antropología Médica*. Mexico, D.F.: Centro de Investigaciones y Estudios Superiores en Antropología Social, Ediciones de la Casa Chata.

ALARCÓN NAVARRO, FRANCISCO, HIRAM BRAVO BARRIENTOS, and ALBERTO PURIEL MARTÍNEZ. 1986. "El Medio Rural Mexicano y los Servicios de Salud." Pp. 13–50 in *Planificación familiar, población y salud en el México rural*, edited by J. Martínez Manatou. Mexico: IMSS.

ALMADA BAY, IGNACIO. 1985. "Las Políticas de Salud de la Administración Cárdenas: Una Primera Aproximación." Mexico: El Colegio de Mexico. Photocopy.

ALVAREZ AMEZQUITA, JOSÉ. 1960. *Historia de la Salubridad y de la Asistencia en México*. Mexico: Secretaría de Salubridad y Asistencia.

ASMAN, DAVID. 1991. "The Salinas Reforms Take Root." *Wall Street Journal*, December 2:12A.

———. 1992. "Attention U.S. Politicians: Take Note of Mexico's War on Poverty." *Wall Street Journal*, May 29:12A.

BARTRA, ROGER. 1978. *Estructura Agraria y Clases Sociales en México*. Mexico: ERA.

BORZUTSKY, SILVIA. 1991. "The Chicago Boys, Social Security, and Welfare in Chile." Pp. 79–99 in *The Radical Right and the Welfare State*, edited by H. Glennerster and J. Midgely. Hertfordshire: Harvester Wheatsheaf.

BRACHET MÁRQUEZ, VIVIANE, and MARGARET S. SHERRADEN. Forthcoming. Fiscal Austerity, The Welfare State and Political Change: The Case of Health and Food Policies in Mexico (1970-1990). *World Development*.

CÁRDENAS DE LA PEÑA, ENRIQUE, et al. 1975. *Nuevos Rumbos: Seguridad Social en México*. Mexico: IMSS.

CARDOSO, FERNANDO HENRIQUE. 1979. "On the Characterization of Authoritarian Regimes in Latin America." Pp. 33–57 in *The New Authoritarianism in Latin America*, edited by D. Collier. Princeton, NJ: Princeton University Press.

CARDOSO, FERNANDO HENRIQUE, and ENZO FALETTO. 1979. *Dependency and Development in Latin America*. Berkeley: University of California Press.

Consejo Consultivo del Programa Nacional de Solidaridad. 1990. *El Combate a la Pobreza*. Mexico, D.F.: El Nacional.

COPLAMAR. 1982. *Memoria de Actividades 1976-1982*. Mexico: Presidencia de la República.

———. 1983. *Necesidades Esenciales en México: Situación Actual y Perspectivas al Año 2000*. Five volumes: Nutrition, Education, Housing, Health and Geography of Margination. México: Siglo Veintiuno Editores.

CORNELIUS, WAYNE A., and ANN L. CRAIG. 1984. *Politics in Mexico: An Introduction and Overview*. La Jolla: Center for U.S.-Mexican Studies, University of California, San Diego.

CUTRIGHT, PHILLIPS. 1965. "Political Structure, Economic Development, and National Social Security Programs." *American Journal of Sociology*, 70:537-50.

DE LA MADRID, MIGUEL, et al. 1986. *La Decentralización de los Servicios de Salud: El Caso de México*. Mexico: Miguel Angel Porrúa.

ECHEVERRÍA ALVAREZ, LUÍS. 1973. "Editorial Comments." *Revista Mexicana de Seguro Social*, No. 5-6: 14.

ECKSTEIN, SUSAN. 1982. "Impact of Revolution on Social Welfare in Latin America." *Theory and Society*, 11(1):43-94.

FEINSILVER, JULIE M. 1993. *Healing the Masses: Cuban Health Politics at Home and Abroad*. Berkeley, CA: University of California Press.

FOX, JONATHAN A. 1992. *The Politics of Food in Mexico: State Power and Social Mobilization*. Ithaca, NY: Cornell University Press.

FRENK, JULIO. 1980. "Medical Modernization in Mexico: Paradigms, Labor Markets, and the State." Paper presented at the Latin American Studies Association Meeting, New Orleans, March, 1988.

FUJIGAKI LECHUGA, AUGUSTO. 1984. "Los Programas de Bienestar Rural en Mexico." Pp. 253-67 in *La atención médica rural en México: 1930-1980*, edited by H. Hernández Llamas. Mexico: IMSS.

GARCÍA CRUZ, MIGUEL. 1972-1973. *La Seguridad Social en México, Volume I: 1906-1958, Volume II: 1958-1964*. Mexico: B. Costa-Amic.

GILLY, ADOLFO. 1983. *The Mexican Revolution*. Thetford, Great Britain: The Thetford Press. Translated by Patrick Camiller.

GISH, OSCAR. 1982. "Selective Primary Health Care: Old Wine in New Bottles." *Social Science and Medicine* 16:1049-63.

GONZÁLEZ BLOCK, MIGUEL. 1988. "Decentralization of the Health Sector in Mexico, 1930-1987." Paper presented at the Latin American Studies Association Meeting, New Orleans, March, 1988.

GONZÁLEZ NAVARRO, MOISÉS. 1985. *La Pobreza en México*. Mexico: El Colegio de México.

HECLO, HUGH. 1974. *Modern Social Politics in Britain and Sweden*. New Haven: Yale University Press.

HERNÁNDEZ LLAMAS, HÉCTOR. 1984. "La Atención Médica en el Medio Rural Mexicano." Pp. 21-32 in *La atención médica rural en México: 1930-1980*, edited by H. Hernández Llamas. Mexico: IMSS.

HEWITT DE ALCÁNTARA, CYNTHIA. 1977. "Mexico: A Commentary on the Satisfaction of Basic Needs." Pp. 153-63 in *Another Development: Approaches and Strategies*, edited by M. Nerfin. Uppsala, Sweden: Dag Hammarskjöld Foundation.

———. 1984. *Anthropological Perspectives on Rural Mexico*. London: Routledge and Kegan Paul.

IMSS. 1976a. *Extensión de la Seguridad Social en el Medio Rural*. Mexico: IMSS.

———. 1976b. *Servicios Médicos de Campo y Solidaridad Social*. Mexico: IMSS.

———. 1982. *Memoria Institucional*. Mexico: IMSS.

IMSS-COPLAMAR. 1980-87. Sistema Unico de Información. Mexico, D.F.: IMSS.

International Labour Organisation (ILO). 1986. *Primary Health Care and Health Strategies in Latin American Social Security 1986*. Geneva, Switzerland: ILO.

LÓPEZ-ACUÑA, DANIEL. 1980. "Health Services in Mexico." *Journal of Health Policy* 1:83-95.

———. 1984a, 5th ed. *La Salud Desigual en México*. Mexico: Siglo Veintiuno Editores.

———. 1984b. 8th ed. "Salud, Seguridad Social y Nutrición." Pp. 177-219 in *Mexico Hoy*, edited by P. González Casanova and E. Florescano. Mexico: Siglo Veintiuno Editores.

MALLOY, JAMES. 1979. *Politics of Social Security in Brazil*. Pittsburgh: University of Pittsburgh Press.

MARES, MARCO A. 1986. "El Programa IMSS-COPLAMAR, casi paralizado por la descentralización del sector salud." *UnoMás Uno*, Mexico. July 7, page 3.

MESA-LAGO, CARMELO. 1978. *Social Security in Latin America: Pressure Groups, Stratification and Inequality*. Pittsburgh: University of Pittsburgh Press.

———. 1990. *La seguridad y el Sector Informal*. Santiago de Chile: ILO.

———. 1991. *Social Security and Prospects for Equity in Latin America*. Washington, D.C.: The World Bank Discussion Paper #140.

———. 1992. *Health Care for the Poor in Latin America and the Caribbean*. Washington, D.C. and Arlington, VA: Pan American Health Organization and the Inter-American Foundation.

MOFFETT, MATT. 1991. "'Los Yuppies': A 1980s-Style Boom is Just Now Reaching an Awakening Mexico." *Wall Street Journal* December 18:1A.

MORENO CUETO, ENRIQUE, and JULIO MOGUEL VIVEROS, MIGUEL A. DÍAZ DE SANDI, MARTHA E. GARCÍA UGARTE, and EDUARDO CÉSARMAN VITIS. 1982. *Sociología Histórica de las Instituciones de Salud en México*. Mexico: IMSS.

MORENO ISLAS, MANUEL. 1958. *La Extensión del Seguro Social al Campo de México*. Mexico: Editorial Carnaval.

MORENO SALAZAR, PEDRO H., and G. ESTHELA REDORTA ZÚÑIGA. 1984. "Notas para el análisis de la política del sector salud: el caso del IMSS-COPLAMAR." Mexico: CIDE, Departamento de Administración Pública. Photocopy.

MORGAN, LYNN M. 1993. *Community Participation in Health: The Politics of Primary Care in Costa Rica*. Cambridge: Cambridge University Press.

NEWELL, ROBERTO, and LUIS RUBIO. 1984. *Mexico's Dilemma: The Political Origins of Economic Crisis*. Boulder: Westview Press.

O'DONNELL, GUILLERMO A. 1977. "Corporatism and the Question of the State." Pp. 285-318 in *Authoritarianism and Corporatism in Latin America*, edited by J. M. Malloy. Pittsburgh: University of Pittsburgh Press.

PINEDA, CUAUHTÉMOC. 1984. "Los programas de salud rural en Mexico." Pp. 275-96 in *La Atención Médica Rural en México: 1930-1980*, edited by H. Hernández Llamas. Mexico: IMSS.

REDCLIFT, MICHAEL R. 1981. *Development Policymaking in Mexico: The Sistema Alimentaria Mexicana (SAM)*. La Jolla: Center for U.S.-Mexican Studies, University of California, San Diego, Research Report No. 24.

ROJAS GUTIÉRREZ, CARLOS. 1991. "Avances del Programa Nacional de Solidaridad." *Comercio Exterior* 41 (5):443-46.

SALINAS DE GORTARI, CARLOS. 1990. *Segundo Informe de Gobierno*. Mexico, D.F.: Poder Ejecutivo Federal.

———. 1991. "Tercer Informe de Gobierno." *Comercio Exterior* 41(11):1069-84.

SANDERSON, STEVEN E. 1981. *Agrarian Populism and the Mexican State: The Struggle for Land in Sonora*. Berkeley: University of California Press.

SCHUMACHER, AUGUST. 1982. "Agricultural Development and Rural Employment: A Mexican Dilemma," in *The Border That Joins*, edited by P. J. Brown and H. Shue. Totowa, NJ: Rowman and Littlefield.

SHERRADEN, MARGARET S. 1991a. "Community Influences on Implementation of Health Policy in Rural Mexico." *Social Development Issues* 13(3):44-63.

———. 1991b. Policy Impacts of Community Participation: Health Services in Rural Mexico. *Human Organization* 50(3):256-64.

SHERRADEN, MARGARET S., and MICHAEL W. SHERRADEN. 1991. "Social Service by University Students in Mexico: Thoughts for the United States." *Children and Youth Services Review* 13(3):145-70.

SHERRADEN, MARGARET S., and STEVEN A. WALLACE. 1992. "Innovation in Primary Care: Community Health Services in Mexico and the United States." *Social Science and Medicine* 35(12):1433-43.

SOBERÓN, GUILLERMO, JESUS KUMATE, and JOSÉ LAGUNA, eds. 1988. *La Salud en México: Testimonios 1988, Tomo I, Fundamentos del cambio estructural*. Mexico: Fondo de Cultura Económica.

SOBERÓN, GUILLERMO, and LEOBARDO C. RUÍZ. 1984. *Hacia un Sistema de Salud 1933-1983*. Mexico: Comisión de Salud y Seguridad Social, Coordinación de los Servicios de Salud, Universidad Nacional Autonoma de México.

Solidarity in National Development. 1993. Mexico, D.F.: Secretaria de Desarrollo Social and Programa Nacional de Solidaridad.

SPALDING, ROSE J. 1978. *Social Security Policy Making: The Formation and Evolution of Mexican Social Security*. Unpublished doctoral dissertation, University of North Carolina.

———. 1981. "State Power and Its Limits: Corporatism in Mexico." *Comparative Political Studies* 14:139-61.

———. 1984. *The Mexican Food Crisis: An Analysis of the SAM*. La Jolla: Center for U.S.-Mexican Studies, University of California, San Diego, Research Report No. 33.

STEPAN, ALFRED. 1978. *The State and Society*. Princeton, NJ: Princeton University Press.

UGALDE, ANTONIO. 1985. "Ideological Dimensions of Community Participation in Latin American Health Programs." *Social Science and Medicine* 21(1):41-53.

VALDÉS OLMEDO, CUAUHTÉMOC. 1991. *Bonanza, Crisis, Recuperción? Financiamiento de la Salud: 1970-1990, Una Prospectiva Hacia el Año 2000*. Mexico, D.F.: Fundacion Mexicana Para la Salud. Photocopy.

VARGAS LOZANO, RENÉ. 1984. "Dirección de Servicios Médicos Rurales Cooperativos." Pp. 109-25 in *La Atención Médica Rural en México: 1930-1980*, edited by H. Hernández Llamas. Mexico: IMSS.

WHETTEN, NATHAN L. 1984. "Salud y mortalidad en el México rural." Pp. 147-79 in *La Atención Médica Rural en México: 1930-1980*, edited by H. Hernández Llamas. Mexico: IMSS.

WILENSKY, HAROLD L. 1975. *The Welfare State and Equality: Structural and Ideological Roots of Public Expenditures*. Berkeley, California: University of California Press.

WILSON, RICHARD R. 1981. *The Corporatist Welfare State: Social Security and Development in Mexico*. Unpublished Ph.D. dissertation, Yale University.

World Bank. 1993. *World Development Report: Investing in Health/World Development Indicators*. Oxford: Oxford University Press.

World Health Organization (WHO). 1978. *Declaration of Alma Ata, Report on the International Conference on Primary Health Care*. Alma Ata, U.S.S.R.: ICPHC/ALA/78.10, September.

ZAMARRIPA TORRES, CARLOS. 1984. "Servicios médicos del Seguro Social en el medio rural." Pp. 321-38 in *La Atención Médica Rural en México: 1930-1980*, edited by H. Hernández Llamas. Mexico: IMSS.

CHAPTER 9

Health and Development in the Third World: The Political Economy of Infant Mortality in Brazil

Ande Kidanemariam

It is widely recognized that infant mortality remains a major health problem in Third-World countries despite its general decline over the past three decades. Less widely recognized, however, are *the considerable variations in infant mortality decline that are to be found in Third-World countries that stand at an equivalent level in economic development*. The expectation that a rapid decline in infant mortality in the Third World would follow the trends that occurred in the industrialized countries in the wake of economic development and/or modernization appears not to have been borne out in general.

By the standards of Third-World countries, Brazil is a highly economically advanced country, comparable to South Korea and the others in the so-called "gang of four" in South Asia. Brazil's economy grew at an impressive 11.5 percent annually during the economic "miracle" period that began in the mid-1960s. Brazil's health resources (health manpower as well as health services) were also quite impressive by Third-World standards. Yet, Brazil's spectacular development both in the economic and health arena was plagued by a dismal record in its social welfare, exemplified especially in its pervasive inequality and its high infant mortality. The infant mortality rates for 1975 and 1980 were 89 and 77 per 1000 live births, respectively. The comparable infant mortality rates for South Korea for the same years were, respectively, 40 and 34 per 1000 live births

(World Bank 1987), less than half of Brazil's rates. What explains such high infant mortality in the midst of spectacular economic development and enormous health resources?

The purpose of this study is to address the socioeconomic and political causes of inequality and high infant mortality in Brazil from the mid-1960s to the mid-1980s. In explaining the high infant mortality rates in Brazil during this period, infant mortality (and health in general) is conceptualized as the outcome of an interconnected web of social, economic, political, and medical conditions. The persistently high rates of infant mortality during the mid-1960s to the mid-1980s in Brazil will be analyzed within the context of the sociohistorical and political structure of the country. More specifically, we will examine Brazil's external links (world economic system) and its internal social forces (state-society relations) to gain some insight into how the interplay of these forces shaped development and the particular health/welfare outcomes in the country over the course of twenty years (1964–1984).

THEORETICAL BACKGROUND

Proponents of modernization theory emphasize that development—and hence the improvement in the health and well-being of Third-World societies—is likely to occur only as the values of hard work, punctuality, achievement, and other "industrial" values are inculcated through deliberate efforts. In other words, development occurs when a broad set of modern values and institutions, including modern education and health care services, are present (Seligson 1984). The modernization focus is on the absorption of modern values and services with little or no consideration for their distribution in a society. The underlying assumptions are that modernization is a total process that encompasses transformations in social, economic, and political organizations at the macro level and the transformation of human personality at the micro level, and that this process constitutes a universal pattern.

Since the early 1960s, during which time modernization/development theories have been at their peak, the dependency/world system perspective challenged these theories as the dominant paradigm in the study of socioeconomic development in the Third World. In sharp disagreement with modernization theory, proponents of dependency/world system perspective argued that development in the Third World is not simply a matter of removing internal obstacles to development by infusions from the developed countries of a "modernization repertoire" consisting of values, institutions, capital, and technology. Rather, they contend, the real obstacles to development in the countries of the Third World lie in the external relations between these countries and the developed capitalist countries of the First World. Consequently, dependency/world system analysts gradually came to dismiss the usefulness of the modernization theory as an explanation of the lagging development of the Third-World countries (Frank 1972; Portes 1973; Wallerstein 1976).

Dependency/world systems theory maintains, in contrast, that a country's structural position in the world capitalist system is a main determinant of development and underdevelopment.

Development in the core and underdevelopment in the periphery are deemed to be interdependent processes of a single global system, i.e., the capitalist world economy. According to the proponents of dependency/world perspective, underdevelopment of Third-World countries results from their incorporation into the world economy, which is characterized by asymmetric economic relations in the processes of exchange and commerce. Specifically, empirical studies have shown that the investment dependency of Third-World countries leads inevitably to severe domestic income inequality within these countries (Wallerstein 1976; Seligson 1984).

How, one may ask, does the incorporation of Third-World countries into the world capitalist economy affect infant mortality in these countries? The causal chain has several links, which will now be set forth.

First, the dependency/world systems perspective maintains that relationships between core countries and the peripheral nations promote inequality through exploitative economic linkages such as investment dependence (Wimberly 1990). Second, they slow down economic growth, mainly through factors such as decapitalization and displacement of domestic firms by multinational corporations (MNCs). Third, they promote income inequality, partly because the success of the politically and economically powerful foreign investors depends on wage exploitation of the local populace. Fourth, they obstruct progressive domestic political processes that oppose the core economic interests. Fifth, they divert land from food production for domestic use to export commodities, and displace poor farmers who have little alternative for livelihood. Sixth, and last, they corrupt local consumer tastes (Wimberly 1990).

One limitation in many dependency/world system studies is that they remain focused at the world level. Studies that locate the causes of underdevelopment in the exploitative relationships imposed from the outside do not, by themselves, tell us much about internal political economic processes and their impact on social welfare outcomes such as infant mortality. The equally important effects of internal structures—the state apparatus and class structure—are also largely ignored.

In order to comprehend fully the larger context that influences infant mortality, a political economy approach—that is, a framework that integrates both the external and internal factors, namely, the world economic system and the internal state-society relationships—is used here (for more on this, see Koo 1984). Economic development and its effects on infant mortality in Brazil over a span of twenty years will be examined in terms of the interplay among the world economic system, the state apparatus, and the class relations. Admittedly, there is a wide explanatory gap to bridge, moving between the macrostructural influences and the immediate causes of infant mortality, such as infections and malnutrition at the microlevel. Disease and death are undeniably biological phenomena at a basic individual level. Death is the end product of disease, which itself can be the consequence of biosocial interaction (Mosley 1984). Biomedical experts are usually concerned with immediate, clinical causes of infant mortality. However, causes such as malnutrition and diseases/infections are influenced by social and economic factors in the form of standard of living—amount and quality of food/nutrition, sanitation, housing, water supply, and access to medical care. The standard of living of a society, in turn, is influenced by the pattern of distribution of development/modernization benefits (e.g., income, education, health services, etc.) and productive resources (e.g., land).

In most Third-World countries, where land is a vital source of subsistence for millions of peasant households, the ownership or lack of ownership of this productive resource makes a critical difference in the survival chances of infants among such households. Differential access to land (hence to income) dramatically affects life chances. The same is true with education and health care services.

The pattern of distribution of development benefits and productive resources in a given country is determined by development policies and strategies that are the direct consequences of the interplay of the three political-economic structures described above (the world economic system, the state, and the society within it), with the specific and concrete socio-historical circumstances unique to a given country. I have dealt with this on a theoretical level more thoroughly elsewhere (Kidanemariam 1994).

Here, by means of historical method, it is helpful to analyze the nature of the state and society relationships in Brazil (i.e., state and class relations) and the way the world system impinges on the state in order to explain the pattern of distribution of land, income, education, and health as it directly and indirectly affects infant mortality. This is followed by an analysis of the development policies and strategies pursued in Brazil from the mid-1960s to the mid-1980s. Finally, a detailed account of the pattern of the distribution of development benefits (income, education, and health services) and productive resources (land) is presented, with the aim of shedding light on how such patterns have affected the level of infant mortality in Brazil.

Two statistical measures of distribution are used. The first one is the Gini coefficient of inequality. The Gini coefficient is especially useful for the kind of analysis that enables us to find out what is happening to the poorest segment of a population, the middle, or the richest segment (Mason et al. 1980). The Gini coefficient theoretically varies between 0 (maximum equality) and 1 (maximum inequality). As a convention, Gini coefficients of 0.3 or below reflect low levels of inequality, and those above 0.5 reflect high inequality (Haggard 1990). Where the Gini coefficient on income distribution is not available, the percentage of income obtained by various population percentiles (e.g., top 10 percent, bottom 40 percent, etc.) will be used instead. It must be pointed out that, given the nature of the history and politics of Brazil, the analysis given here is, while accurate, a preliminary venture into a complex phenomenon.

The thrust of our analysis is on the period of time spanning 1964–1984. The mid-1960s provided a turning point in the history of Brazil for several reasons, among which the economic and the political forces figure most prominently. In 1964 the military took the reins of power in the country, which completely changed the political scene for the next twenty years. At the same time, with rapid economic growth in the late 1960s and early 1970s, economic inequality increased sharply. Since this period has marked a watershed in the history of Brazil, I address this particular historical experience because of its direct relevance to the understanding of the problem being analyzed.

Data on social, economic, and health indicators as well as measures of income inequality as represented in the form of income share of the top 10 percent come from various secondary sources.[1]

THE POLITICAL ECONOMY OF INFANT MORTALITY IN BRAZIL

State and Society in Brazil

Formerly a Portuguese colony, Brazil became independent in 1822. It is the largest country in South America, occupying more than half of the South American continent. Brazil is characterized by diverse climatic zones, heterogeneous topography, and varied population densities (Horn 1985). Although one of the most rapidly industrializing countries in the world, Brazil still has a high proportion of rural population.

If there is any one thing that most observers of Brazil agree on concerning the political system of the country, it is the fact that from the mid-1960s to the mid-1980s, an authoritarian state represented the interest of the dominant classes. The government under the First Republic (1894–1930) earlier adhered to economic policies that benefited the landed elite (Nyrop 1982). The transformation over ensuing decades from an agricultural country dominated by a landed oligarchy to an economically diversified nation with broader-based popular participation was formidable. By 1930, democratic forces began to appear on the political scene. Urban industrial, commercial, and financial elements had wrested political control from the conservative land owners. A rapidly growing urban middle class was gaining political strength; urban labor, although susceptible to political manipulation, became an important element of the political scene. Yet the power of conservative forces did not entirely diminish. They continued to wield considerable political power (Schneider 1971).

With the inauguration of a constitutional regime in 1945 came the addition of political parties. These political parties had uniquely Brazilian characteristics, eschewing ideology and radical mass mobilization in favor of regional electorate organizations dedicated primarily to capturing the presidency and seats in the legislature. Essential to the governance of Brazil between 1945 and 1964 was the maintenance of a balance among its dominant players—rural elites, business elites, the military and others—through the state's promotion of a growing industrial economy (Wynia 1984).

The year 1964 marked a watershed in Brazilian politics. The military seized power and turned the country into a repressive authoritarian state that prevailed for two decades. By early 1964 it appeared that Brazil was headed for a confrontation between leftist revolutionaries and the anti-communist military junta. The military had the upper hand, for the leftists were not only poorly armed but also relatively disorganized and not up to the task. This confrontation drove the propertied classes to align themselves with the military to prevent a socialist coup that would transform the socioeconomic structure of the country. Thus the authoritarian regime was installed in an atmosphere of growing class conflict in which the bourgeoisie provided the social base for the new regime, whose first course of action was to dismantle and disarticulate the political organization of the working class, using its coercive powers (Stepan 1985). All opposition to the military state was muted either by cooptation or outright suppression. Political parties of the popular sector were in fact incorporated into the system of legitimation of the state; they did not attempt to present anti-authoritarian and anti-capitalist political alternatives (Cotler 1979).

The Brazilian state of that period fits the model of a bureaucratic-authoritarian state as described by O'Donnell (1979). A bureaucratic-authoritarian state is characterized by political and economic exclusions. The political exclusion involves the suppression of citizenship. In particular, this suppression includes the liquidation of the institution of political democracy. Economic exclusion involves the alienation of the popular sector; it promotes a pattern of capital accumulation that is highly skewed toward benefiting the large oligopolistic units of private capital and some state institutions. The preexisting inequities in the distribution of societal resources were thus sharply increased.

The military regime embraced a concept of development inimical to basic human needs: an economic model favoring growth over equity, development over social welfare, and budget priorities favoring the vocal urban middle sectors at the expense of marginal populations (Horn 1985).

Development Policies/Strategies

Spectacular economic growth in the 1964–1984 period did not benefit all segments of Brazilian society. The development strategies that were pursued led to gross inequalities along regional, sectoral, geographic, and class lines. Brazil was the most pronounced advocate of the theory that growth-oriented strategy will, in the long run, also benefit the poor and that "the cake has to grow before it can be eaten" (Brundenius 1981).

Clear priority was given to *economic growth*, with the objective of building an economy modelled on those developed Western industrial nations. This strategy was concerned with more aggregate output: the assumption was that, as aggregate production increases, the equity question will take care of itself. That is, growth would be accompanied by improved social and economic conditions. This assumption did not come to fruition. On the contrary, the economic expansion led to the concentration of the economic benefits and a legacy of unmet social needs. Grindle (1986:37) notes that "in 1980 rural Brazil was marked by a notable difference among regions, by highly visible maldistribution of resources and wealth in the sectors . . . , by policies that discriminated among crops, producers, and regions. Brazilian development was pursued with little regard to issues of equity, poverty, distribution, or employment. Policies in agriculture, for example, were frequently decisive in encouraging the concentration of resources in the hands of large land owners and in creating extensive regional disparities."

Brazil's dependent development and its attendant problems took shape under a powerful repressive state that closely allied itself with local dominant and entrenched industrial/commercial and land-owning classes as well as multinational corporations. This collusion of powerful forces, which Evans (1979) described as the "triple alliance," (the state, the bourgeoisie, and multinational corporations) had far-reaching impact in terms of shaping development policies that resulted, as noted above, in the alienation and polarization of Brazilian society. While it could be argued that the penetration of international capital had strengthened the hand of the state in suppressing domestic opposition groups, the same process also imposes structural constraints the state cannot escape. For, as Evans (1979:290) writes "the entire success of the dependent development is predicated on multinationals willing to invest, international bankers willing to extend credit, and other countries willing to consume an ever increasing volume of Brazilian exports." The world capitalist economy does indeed exert tremendous influence in shaping development policies. But this is, for the most part, mediated through the state apparatus and in alliance with the dominant domestic classes, all of which stand to benefit from such alliance.

Distributional Patterns of Development Benefits

During the economic "miracle" period (1967–1974), Brazil's GNP doubled, reflecting an average growth rate of 10 percent per year (Fields 1980). Brazil produced most of its own capital goods and it was a major exporter of manufactured goods to markets in the developed countries. The nation's industrial plant had made it the leading "NIC" (Newly Industrialized Country) (Evans et al. 1984). However, the gap between the rich and the poor widened considerably, thereby making Brazil the object of great and curious fascination, at least partly because "it epitomized both the hopes and disillusionments of Third-World development" (Evans 1984:1).

Land Distribution.   During the period of time under consideration, land ownership in Brazil remained highly concentrated, and subsistence agriculture was widespread. Minifundia (small landholdings) and latifundia (large landholdings) existed side by side, with the former often serving as a labor reserve for the latter during planting and harvesting seasons.

The distribution of land is an important factor in determining the distribution of income, as land is the principal source of income generation. The inequality in land distribution increased from .838 in 1970 to .853 in 1980 (Table 1).

Income Distribution.   As in the case of patterns of landholding, income concentration and inequality became pervasive in Brazil following the "economic miracle." Such a tendency was reinforced by government policies and development strategies, especially, from 1964 to the mid-1980s (Andrade 1982). While the income share of the bottom 50 percent of the economically active strata continued to decline from 1970 to 1976, those of the middle to top 15 percent and top 5 percent grew for the same period of time (Table 2). The income share of the top 5 percent of the economically active population was a large 39 percent

TABLE 1.   LAND DISTRIBUTION INEQUALITY IN BRAZIL, 1970–1980

	1970	1975	1980
Gini coefficient	.838	.850	.853

Source: Thiesenhusen and Melmed-Sanjak, 1990.

TABLE 2.   INCOME DISTRIBUTION IN BRAZIL, 1970–1976

STRATA OF ECONOMICALLY ACTIVE POPULATION	SHARE OF TOTAL INCOME PERCENT	
	1970	1976
Bottom 50 percent	14.90	11.80
Top percent	34.90	39.00
Gini coefficient	0.56	0.60

Source: Adapted from Andrade, 1982.

in 1976, those of the bottom 50 percent was a mere 12 percent. The income distribution deteriorated so much that income inequality—(as measured by the Gini coefficient) rose from 0.56 in 1970 to 0.60 in 1976.

The rich benefited enormously from Brazil's remarkable economic growth. The gains of the rich were enormously larger than those of the poor in absolute terms. Brazil's income distribution remained extremely uneven throughout the 1960s, 1970s, and the early 1980s (Pfefermann and Webb 1979).

The inequality was especially marked in the rural areas. Brazil has the largest concentration of rural population in South America, and the rural poor represent 67 percent of the rural population (International Labor Office 1979).

While the richest 10 percent received over 50 percent of the national income in 1975, the poorest 40 percent of the population received less than 10 percent (Table 3).

The shares of the poor in total income are extremely low. Further, Brazil's economic growth and industrial expansion did not eliminate the sharp regional inequalities that have characterized Brazil's development. The Northeast region of Brazil was the hardest hit. Over one-third of the poor were in rural areas in the Northeast, which seemed to be the geographic center of Brazil's poverty. The Northeast region, which includes nine of the country's twenty-three states, has about 29 percent of Brazil's population (Thomas 1987).

Education.   There were at least three kinds of inequality that one could identify in Brazilian education during the period under study. First, regional disparities in literacy were wide. The Northeast was one of the most deprived regions of the country.

Adult literacy rates for the Northeast in 1978 were far lower (56 percent) than the national average (76 percent). Second, there were inequalities in rates of enrollment: the top socioeconomic strata had greater participation in higher educational levels. Enrollment rates in the primary level (grades 1–8) in rural areas in 1974 were about half the level of those in urban areas (Knight 1979). Third, inequalities in the allocation of resources for education across educational levels were significant; the system clearly benefited the more affluent strata of Brazilian society (Pfefermann and Webb 1979). In short, the distribution of education showed extreme disparities between different regions, urban/rural sectors, and socioeconomic groups.

TABLE 3. ESTIMATES OF INCOME SHARE, BRAZIL, 1970–1980

YEAR	BOTTOM 40%	TOP 10%
1970	8.4	51.5
1975	8.5	51.9
1980	9.0	48.0

Source: Pfefermann and Webb, 1970; World Bank, 1987.

Health. The pattern of health care service distribution in Brazil also showed a characteristic concentration. During the nineteenth century, the little health care available was confined largely to the big cities, with virtually none for the majority of Brazilians outside these cities (Horn 1985). The emergence of a strong, curative-oriented medical care in the 1960s was further consolidated following the 1964 military-authoritarian takeover in Brazil. There were two principal components of Brazilian health care: the collective-preventive and the individual-curative. The two subsystems grew at widely divergent rates. The collective-preventive subsystem, which was composed of the Ministry of Health and the State Secretaries of Health, began to fall behind the individual-curative subsystem in terms of its share of total public expenditure for health following the Second World War (Knight 1979). The share of the collective-preventive subsystem fell from 87 percent of total health outlays in 1949 to about 30 percent in 1975. On the other hand, the share of the individual-curative subsystem increased from 13 percent in 1949 to 70 percent in 1975 (Knight 1979).

The individual-curative health care system, which was urban-biased, was consolidated under a social security system. The health care coverage of the urban population rose from 43 percent in 1960 to about 80 percent in 1980/1981, with little or no coverage extended to rural areas (Pfefermann and Webb 1979).

The extreme concentration of the health manpower and facilities in the industrialized Southeast as compared with the Northeast and Frontier is testimony to the urban-biased nature of the Brazilian health care system. Based on 1970 data, 80 percent of the physicians, 73 percent of the nursing persons, and 79 percent of the hospital beds were concentrated in the most urbanized region of the country—the Southeast. Clearly, the two regions, the Northeast and the Frontier (largely rural) were at a disadvantage in terms of the share of national health resources, as with many of the other benefits of development.

There was a great rural/urban imbalance in health personnel. As Knight (1979:15) noted, "the ratios of population per physician and dentist were four times higher in smaller towns and rural areas than in the cities. For other health personnel, such as nutritionists, nurses, and nursing auxiliaries the differential was on the order of 10 to 1."

The infant mortality rates in the Northeast were as high as 122 per 1000 live births in 1978, a figure that was the average infant mortality for the whole of Brazil in 1960. The profound effect of extreme forms of inequality on infant mortality in Brazil was poignantly described by women in a small town in the

Northeast, where infant mortality rates were very high. When the women were asked why so many babies between birth and six months were dying, their replies were a reflection of the overall macro-socioeconomic inequality described above: "They die because we are hungry; they die because the water we drink is filthy with germs; they die because we can't keep them in shoes or away from this human garbage dump we live in; they die because we get worthless medical care; street medicine; . . . they die because we have no safe place to leave them when we go off to work" (Scheper-Hughes 1984:539).

One notable failure of the health care system in Brazil during the mid-1960s to the mid-1980s in reducing infant mortality was the direct outcome of a government's deliberate development policy failure to make health services available and accessible to as many people as possible, especially the rural poor. The unavailability and inaccessibility of the health services situation was further exacerbated by extreme concentrations of development benefits.

CONCLUSION

Inequality in the distribution of land, income, education, and health services in Brazil worsened when the country came under repressive military rule from 1964 to 1984. Indeed, under the *bureaucratic-authoritarian state*, Brazil saw rapid economic growth, which came to be labled as an economic miracle. However, as I have indicated in detail, the benefits of growth were accompanied by extreme maldistribution of wealth.

The authoritarian state was both politically and economically exclusive. Development policies clearly benefited the elites. The state allied itself with the domestic bourgeois classes and multinational corporations, which played an important political as well as economic role in sustaining inequality and structural distortions in the country. The alliance of these forces engendered a bulwark that operated against any social reform or egalitarian development strategies.

The net effect of all this was the exclusion of major sectors of Brazilian society from the political and development process and the benefits of development, which, in turn, is reflected in glaring and gross social inequality. The paradoxical nature of Brazilian development was that the rapid advance of a few into the world of postindustrial society came at a heavy social cost—the marginalization of the vast majority of the population.

Indeed, the Brazilian economic "miracle" in a sense presented a sort of a Faustian bargain for which the vast majority of Brazilians paid dearly in the form of high infant mortality, among other things. What I have tried to show in this study is that the rate of decline in infant mortality was determined primarily by the way the benefits of development (income, education, health services, etc.) and productive resources (such as land), which have both direct and indirect bearing on health and welfare, were distributed in Brazil. Not only were health resources highly concentrated, but also health (medical) interventions could not attain the desired goal—the reduction of infant mortality—because they were not carried out in synergism with other social and economic interventions as part of an integrated state development policy.

The social, economic, and political conditions that prevailed during the mid-1960s through the mid-1980s were detrimental for infant survival. Whether health care services will have positive impact on infant mortality works in one way or a combination of two different methods. One way in which health care services can enhance the social welfare of a society in general and reduce infant mortality in particular is through extensive medical coverage of the population. This is often the outcome of a direct government policy designed to make health services available and accessible to as many people as possible, especially the rural poor. The emphasis here is on primary health care based on preventive approach. The second way to achieve good health is through an indirect route: egalitarian distribution of income, education, and other income-generating resources, such as land and employment opportunities. Equitable distribution of such benefits of development improves the health of the population by enhancing a better standard of living, as well as by increasing families' purchasing power for goods and services including medical care services. Clearly, as I have tried to show in this study, neither of these approaches were given any priority in Brazil.

NOTE

[1] From *World Development Report* by the World Bank and other related sources. (See References.)

REFERENCES

ANDRADE, REGIS DE CASTRO. 1982. "Brazil: The Economics of Savage Capitalism." Pp. 165–88 in *The Struggle for Development: National Strategies in an International Context*, edited by Manfred Bienefeld and Martin Godfrey. New York: John Wiley and Sons.

BRUNDENIUS, CLAES. 1981. "Growth with Equity: The Cuban Experience." *World Development* 9:1083–96.

COTLER, JULIO. 1979. "State and Regime: Comparative Notes on the Southern Cone and the 'Enclave' Societies." Pp. 255–82 in *The New Authoritarianism in Latin America*, edited by David Collier. Princeton, NJ: Princeton University Press.

EVANS, PETER. 1979. *Dependent Development: The Alliance of Multinational, State, and Local Capital in Brazil*. Princeton, NJ: Princeton University Press.

EVANS, PETER, ELIDA RUBINI LIEDKE, and ENNO D. LIEDKE FILHO. 1984. *The Political Economy of Contemporary Brazil: A Study Guide*. Albuquerque, NM: University of New Mexico.

FIELDS, GARY. 1980. *Poverty, Inequality, and Development*. Cambridge: Cambridge University Press.

FRANK, ANDRE. 1972. "Sociology of Development and Underdevelopment of Sociology." Pp. 341–97 in *Dependency and Underdevelopment: Latin America's Political Economy*, edited by James D. Cockcroft, Andre G. Frank, and Dale C. Johnson. Garden City, NY: Doubleday.

GRINDLE, MERILEE S. 1986. *State and Countryside*. Baltimore: The Johns Hopkins University Press.

HAGGARD, STEPHAN. 1990. *Pathways from the Periphery*. Ithaca, NY: Cornell University Press.

HORN, JAMES. 1985. "Brazil: The Health Care Model of the Military Modernizers and Technocrats." *International Journal of Health Services* 15:47–67.

INTERNATIONAL LABOR OFFICE, 1979. *Profiles of Rural Poverty*. Geneva International Labor Office.

KIDANEMARIAM, ANDE. 1994. "Development and Health in Third World Countries: A Theoretical Analysis." Unpublished manuscript, Lexington, KY: University of Kentucky.

KNIGHT, PETER. 1979. *Brazil*. Washington, D.C.: World Bank.

KOO, HAGEN. 1984. "World System, Class, and State in Third World Development." *Sociological Perspectives* 27:33–52.

MASON, EDWARDS, MAHN JE KIM, DWIGHT H. PERKINS, KWANG SUK KIM, and DAVID C. COLE with LEROY JONES, IL SAKONG, DONALD R. SNODGRASS, and NOEL F. MCGINN. 1980. *The Economic and Social Modernization of the Republic of Korea*. Cambridge, MA: Harvard University Press.

MOSLEY, HENRY. 1984. "Child Survival: Research and Policy." Pp. 3–23 in *Child Survival: Strategies for Research*, edited by W. Henry Mosley and C. Lincoln Chen. Cambridge: Cambridge University Press.

NYROP, RICHARD F. (ed.). 1982. *Brazil: A Country Study* (Foreign Area Studies). Washington, D.C.: The American University.

O'DONNELL, GUILLERMO. 1979. "Tensions in the Bureaucratic-Authoritarian State and the Question of Democracy." Pp. 285-318 in *The New Authoritarianism in Latin America*, edited by David Collier. Princeton, NJ: Princeton University Press.

PFEFERMANN, G., and RICHARD WEBB. 1979. *The Distribution of Income in Brazil*. World Bank Working Paper # 356. Washington, D.C.: World Bank.

PORTES, ALEJANDRO. 1973. "Modernity and Development: A Critique." *Studies in Comparative International Development* 8:247-79.

SCHEPER-HUGHES, NANCY. 1984. "Infant Mortality and Infant Care: Cultural and Economic Constraints on Nurturing in Northeast Brazil." *Social Science and Medicine* 19:535-46.

SCHNEIDER, RONALD M. 1971. *The Political System of Brazil*. New York and London: Columbia University Press.

SELIGSON, M. A. 1984. *The Gap between Rich and Poor*. Boulder, CO, and London: Westview Press.

STEPAN, ALFRED. 1985. "State Power and the Strength of Civil Society in the Southern Cone of Latin America." Pp. 317-43 in *Bringing the State Back In*, edited by Peter B. Evans, Dietrich Rueschemeyer, and Theda Skocpol. Cambridge: Cambridge University Press.

THIESENHUSEN, WILLIAM C., and JOLYNE MELMED-SANJAK. 1990. "Brazil's Agrarian Structure: Changes from 1970 through 1980." *World Development* 18:393-415.

THOMAS, VINOD. 1987. "Differences in Income and Poverty within Brazil." *World Development* 15: 263-73.

WALLERSTEIN, IMMANUEL. 1976. "Modernization: Requiescat in Pace." Pp. 131-35 in *The Uses of Controversy in Sociology*, edited by Lewis A. Coser and Otto N. Larson. New York: Free Press.

WIMBERLY, DALE W. 1990. "Investment Dependence and Alternative Explanations of Third World Mortality: A Cross-National Study." *American Sociological Review* 55:75-91.

World Bank. 1987. *World Development Report*. Oxford: Oxford University Press.

WYNIA, GARY W. 1984. *The Politics of Latin American Development*. London and New York: Cambridge University Press.

CHAPTER 10

Demographic and Spatial Aspects of the Health Care Delivery System in Malawi

Ezekiel Kalipeni

INTRODUCTION

As Meade, Florin, and Gesler (1988) note, a health care delivery system consists of more than ill people and the practitioners who diagnose and treat illnesses. The system, if it is to be successful in its objectives, should also try to enhance health. Prevention, a healthy care environment, and good relationships between patients and medical personnel are also essential components of a health care system (Schaefer 1974; Gesler 1984; Meade et al. 1988). While realizing that a health care delivery system is a complex entity, which consists of disease complexes as well as a number of factors, such as the governmental system, economic system, cultural system, resources, environment, etc., plus the interplay among all these, the main focus of this paper is to assess briefly the demographic and spatial aspects of the health care delivery system in Malawi.

Specifically, the paper examines the current structure of the health care delivery system in Malawi within the Central Place Theory framework or spatial/functional organization of facilities. The basic question under examination in this paper is the extent to which regional inequalities in the distribution of health care resources exist in the country. The role and responsibility of the Ministry of Health, its spatial philosophy, and overall objectives are especially emphasized. The policy implications of a rapidly expanding population for the provision of adequate health care facilities are also highlighted. Using the most recent available data from the Ministry of Health (MOH) of the Government of Malawi and other governmental agencies, the paper discusses the provision of health care facilities in relation to population distribution and the relative accessibility of the services, taking into consideration the "distance factor." In light of the spatial structure of the health care delivery system, the general state of health in the country as revealed by recent data on mortality and fertility rates, and main causes of morbidity and mortality are given as a background to the rest of the discussion.

Located in southeastern Africa astride the Great Rift Valley of Eastern Africa, Malawi is one of the poorest countries in the world. In terms of the World Bank's basic economic indicators, Malawi is ranked sixth from the bottom of the list of Fourth-World African states (World Bank 1990a). The per capita GNP in 1989 was estimated at U.S. \$240 (UNICEF 1990). Based on the 1977 mortality conditions, the life expectancy at birth is estimated at 45 years (UNICEF 1990). Although mortality rates have been declining, albeit slowly, fertility rates have remained stubbornly high. The total fertility rate, which is the average number of children that a Malawian woman would expect to give birth to if she experiences the 1977 fertility pattern throughout her reproductive years, is estimated to be 7.6 (Malawi National Statistical Office 1984). The population growth rate, estimated at 3.6 percent, is among the highest in the world (Malawi National Statistical Office 1991). This growth rate translates into a population-doubling time of less than 19 years. Considering the country's relatively poor resource endowment, it is unlikely that the living and health standards of the majority of the people in the country will improve unless the rate of population growth is curbed.

DEMOGRAPHIC TRENDS
AND THE ECOLOGICAL CONTEXT

Since independence in 1964, Malawi has more than doubled its population—from 4 million in 1966 to an estimated 8.75 million in 1992 (Malawi National Statistical Office 1984 and 1987a; World Bank 1992a). The final results of the 1987 Population and Housing Census give a total of about 7.98 million persons as compared to 5.55 million in the 1977 census. This implies that the total population had increased by 44 percent during the 1977–1987 intercensal period with an implied intercensal annual population growth rate of 3.6 percent, considerably higher than the previous 1966–1977 intercensal growth rate of 2.9 percent. The large influx of Mozambican refugees into Malawi during the past decade is partly responsible for the high population growth rate (Morna 1988; House and Zimalirana 1992b; Kalipeni 1992b). But even if the refugees, numbering about 1 million, were excluded from the computations of the growth rate, it would still stand at 3.3 percent, high by both African and world standards. Africa's population is estimated to be growing at a rate of 2.9 percent.

As far as the spatial distribution of population is concerned, Malawi is one of the most densely populated countries in Africa, at 85 persons per square kilometer in 1987. This is the fourth highest population density figure in Africa.

Administratively, the country is divided into three regions (Northern, Central, and Southern) and twenty-four districts (counties) as shown in Figure 1. There are marked regional and district variations in population density in the country. For example, in 1987, the densities varied from 34 in the Northern Region to 88 in the Central Region to 125 in the Southern Region (Malawi National Statistical Office, 1991). At district level the range in densities is even greater, from 16 persons per square kilometer in Rumphi district in the Northern Region to 300 persons per square kilometer in Blantyre and Chiradzulu districts in the Southern Region (Kalipeni 1992a and 1992b; House and Zimalirana 1992b). When arable density is used, population pressure is even heavier. Arable land in the country amounts to only 48 percent of total land area (Malawi Department of Town and Country Planning 1987). The national population density per square kilometer of arable land is now estimated at 171, and densities in the range of 230 to 460 are common in districts of the Southern Region and parts of the Central Region (World Bank 1990b and 1992b).

The age composition of the population is heavily skewed towards the younger age groups. In 1987, 48 percent of the total population was under the age of 15, as compared to 45 percent in 1977 and 44 percent in 1966 (Kalipeni 1992b). A very young population such as this one results in a high dependency ratio. In 1966 the dependency ratio was 92 dependents per 100 persons in the economically productive age group of 15–65. In 1987, the ratio had risen to 103 dependents for every 100 persons. The significance of this large contingent of young people can best be appreciated in terms of pressures it imposes upon the social and demographic system. As will be discussed below, Malawi has failed to achieve its economic and health provision goals. What is gained by technological development is absorbed by the high consumption rate of an expanding population (Kalipeni 1992b). With so many dependent young people who are vulnerable to the vagaries of an unforgiving environment, the country's health and educational facilities have become overburdened. The failure to provide adequate educational and health facilities is reflected in the low rate of literacy, estimated at 25 percent, and a high infant mortality rate, estimated at 151 infant deaths per 1,000 births (Kalipeni 1993).

The physical and ecological structure of the country is as varied as the population densities and demographic characteristics. The altitude ranges from less than 200 feet above sea level in Nsanje district in the Southern Region to over 7,000 feet on the plateaus of the Central and Northern Regions with annual rainfall of 28 inches in some parts of the Southern Region to over 100 inches in some parts of the Northern Region (Msukwa 1981; Pike and Rimmington 1965). Within a small country like Malawi, with a land area of 119,000 square kilometers (46,000 square miles) of which 26,000 square kilometers (10,000 square miles or 21 percent of the total area) is occupied by Lake Malawi, one finds remarkable ecological differences from region to region and district to district. There are extremely hot and relatively dry areas, especially in the Rift Valley Zone, and relatively cool and wet areas on the plateaus. Different microclimates imply a diversified agricultural base, with various areas specializing in the production of certain cash and food crops.

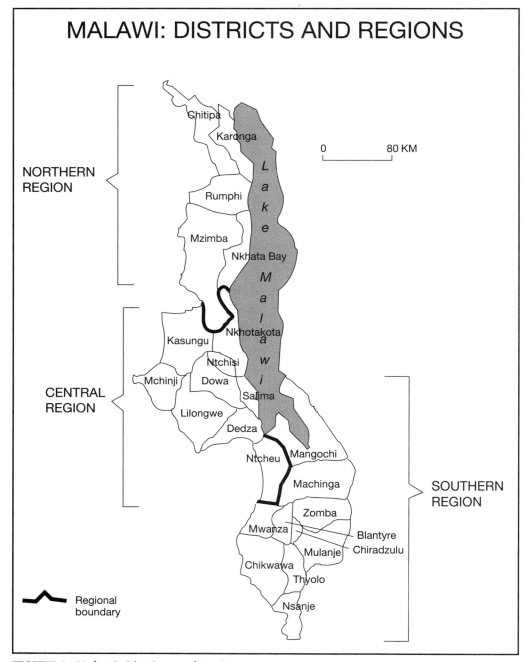

MALAWI: DISTRICTS AND REGIONS

FIGURE 1. Malawi: Districts and Regions

As Msukwa (1981) notes, the ecological variations within the country are crucial to health planning since temperatures are closely connected to specific diseases and, together with rainfall, can determine what particular crops can be grown in each area suitable for improving the nutritional standards of the resident population. For example, the hot climate of the Shire Valley and the Lakeshore area make them ideal places for mosquito breeding and, therefore, lead to a higher prevalence of malaria (Msukwa 1981). Due to the absence of iodine in mountain soils the incidence of goiter is higher than expected in such areas as the Misuku Hills of the Northern Region. In contrast, bilharzia is likely to be rare in mountainous regions because of the unfavorable habitats for bilharzia snails, which require stagnant water (Kalipeni 1985; Msukwa 1981). In short, as Msukwa (1981) states, if any health policy is to succeed in Malawi, the physical and demographic aspects of the population will have to be taken into account, especially in regard to the health education of the population.

In short, Malawi's living environment is a significant part of the determinants of the disease patterns in the country. Without sanitation, almost any level of curative clinical interventions by the medical profession would still leave their environmental causes more or less intact (USAID 1977 and 1979). In addition, broad-scale public health measures and "environmental sanitation" efforts produce limited benefits when they are not accompanied by significant public health education. As USAID (1979) notes, to be truly effective, public health programs must be integrated into a variety of social services and development programs that address the ecological variations found within the country.

HEALTH STATUS OF THE POPULATION

Many of the environmental and cultural factors associated with ill health elsewhere in Africa are also present in Malawi. As noted in the preceding section, the mildly warm tropical environment of Malawi encourages a host of microorganisms, disease agents, and insect carriers, which are responsible for killing or debilitating thousands of Malawians, especially children. The varied microclimates in the country favor the presence of important vectors such as mosquitoes, which make malaria difficult to control; the water snails that transmit bilharzia; and the flies that transmit onchocerciasis, to mention a few (USAID 1979; Teesdale, Chitsulo, and Werler 1983; Choudhry and Teesdale 1984; Kalipeni 1985). The high population densities that have resulted in degraded environments, massive soil erosion, and acute shortages of arable land mean that agricultural output in many areas is inadequate to meet basic subsistence needs. The end result has been widespread malnutrition in the country (Msukwa 1984; Nankumba 1989).

The Government of Malawi recognizes that, with an infant mortality rate of 151 per thousand, a crude death rate of 21.8 per thousand, and an estimated life expectancy of 45 years, the current health status of the population is unsatisfactory (Malawi Government 1986, p. 112). Females in Malawi report a large proportion of children who die by the time they reach various ages of childhood (Malawi National Statistical Office 1987b, 1987c; Srivastava and M'manga 1991; M'manga and Srivastava 1991). For example, three-tenths of children die before they reach the age of 5 years; one-third die before they reach the age of 10 years (Malawi National Statistical Office 1984, p. 54). Table 1 gives an indication of the common causes of death in hospitals in the 0–4 age group in 1989. Malawi does not have comprehensive data on causes of morbidity or mortality. The only data available is that collected from government and nongovernment health facilities on causes of death among inpatients; morbidity statistics are drawn from outpatient facility reports (Msukwa 1987). These statistics are inherently limited in that most deaths occur in the communities and not all illnesses are brought to health facilities. In the absence of more reliable data, the facility statistics can be used with caution to show general trends in the causes of death among infants and can be assumed to reflect valid orders of magnitude (Kalipeni 1993). The figures in Table 1 illustrate that relatively few diseases are responsible for most deaths of infants and young children. In terms of Omran's (1971, 1974, and 1977) epidemiologic transition, the major causes of death among infants and children are still largely infectious and nutritional diseases. With the exception of diseases of the nervous system and, to some degree, accidents and injuries, all the important causes of illness and death in Malawi are preventable, or at least treatable, by means of the primary health care approach, particularly immunization or early

TABLE 1.   TEN LEADING CAUSES OF MORTALITY AMONG ADMISSIONS TO HOSPITALS

DISEASE/CONDITION	NO. OF DEATHS	AS PERCENT OF ALL DEATHS	CUMULATIVE PERCENTAGE
a) Ten leading causes of mortality among under age 5 in-patient admissions[a]			
1. Avitaminosis, nutritional deficiencies	1470	17	17
2. Pneumonia	1139	14	31
3. Anemia	1097	13	44
4. Malaria other than cerebral	839	10	54
5. Causes of perinatal morbidity	723	9	63
6. Measles	672	8	71
7. Cerebral malaria	639	8	79
8. Enteritis, other diarrheal	549	7	86
9. Diseases of the nervous system	269	3	89
10. All other infective diseases	123	1	90
b) Ten leading causes of mortality among all admissions[b]			
1. Avitaminosis, nutritional deficiencies	1780	12	12
2. Pneumonia	1662	11	23
3. Anemia	1514	10	33
4. Malaria other than cerebral	1319	9	42
5. Cerebral malaria	922	6	48
6. Enteritis and other diarrheal	905	6	54
7. Measles	775	5	59
8. Causes of perinatal morbidity	723	5	64
9. Diseases of the nervous system	607	4	68
10. TB of respiratory system	572	4	72

Notes: [a]Total number of under age 5 deaths: 2,409.

[b]Total number of all deaths: 14,837.

Source: Malawi Ministry of Health. 1989. *Health Information System Reference Tables*. Lilongwe: Ministry of Health, Tables 4.7 and 4.8.

case detection and treatment (Kalipeni and Kamlongera 1987). Implementation of primary care will, however, require a higher level of female education than prevails at present.

In a recent study of the determinants of infant mortality in the country, Kalipeni (1993) has identified significant regional differentials in infant mortality rates. There is a clear cluster of spectacularly high infant and childhood mortality in the districts of the Central Region, particularly the districts of Mchinji, Dowa, Salima, Dedza, Kasungu, and Lilongwe, with infant mortality rates ranging from 185 to 228 infant deaths per 1,000 births. From these districts, infant mortality levels fall progressively in the Northern and Southern Regions. Districts in the Northern Region have some of the lowest infant mortality rates in the country, with Chitipa district's rate of 106 as the lowest in the country. The results in Kalipeni's (1993) study also indicate that, at the regional and district levels, the variation of infant mortality is strongly associated with a number of demographic and socioeconomic variables such as female education, age at first marriage of females, and availability of hospital facilities. Indeed, female literacy rates and age at first marriage of females are generally higher in the Northern and Southern regions than in the Central Region. A number of other spatial variables were also identified in this study.

Adult mortality is also quite high by African and world standards. Results of the 1977 census gave a crude death rate of about 25 per 1,000 population per year. Recent estimates indicate that the crude death rate has declined to 21 deaths per 1,000 people (Malawi National Statistical Office 1984, 1991). As noted above, the expectation of life at birth gives a summary measure of the level of mortality in any population. It is estimated that, on the basis of derived age-sex patterns of mortality prevailing in Malawi during the 1977 census, males and females are expected to live approximately 38 and 41 years, respectively. Recent data shows that life expectancy has increased to 43 and 46 for males and females, respectively. At the regional level, the three regions of the country present a markedly different picture of the level of mortality in the general population. As measured by crude death rates, the probability of dying and life expectancy in 1977, the Northern Region had the lowest level of mortality among the three regions with crude death rates of 22 and 18 for males and females, respectively. The Central Region had the highest crude death rates—31 and 27 for males and females, respectively. The Southern Region, with crude death rates of 25 and 21 for males and females respectively, occupied a place in between, but closer to the Northern Region than to the Central Region. Recent data from the 1987 census confirms the persistence of these regional differences in the status of health as measured by infant and adult mortality. One other interesting aspect to note is that in all three regions, males consistently show a higher crude death rate compared to females, with a difference of about 4 per 1,000 persons. However, female death rates are generally higher than male death rates during the active reproductive years of ages 15–35 (UNFPA 1983).

Fertility is exceedingly high throughout Malawi by any standards, at a national total fertility rate (TFR) of 7.6 births per woman (Malawi National Statistical Office 1987b). There are moderate variations by region and district. Urban fertility is slightly lower than rural fertility although the difference is not statistically significant. Overall the Central Region exhibits higher fertility rates in comparison to the Northern and Southern Regions. In the matrilineal and patrilineal societies of Malawi, a woman is expected to bear as many children as possible for her maternal lineage or that of her husband (Chilivumbo 1975; Demographic Unit 1987; Kalipeni and Zulu 1993). Malawian women marry at early ages. It is estimated that by the age of 17 half of all women in Malawi are married, and almost all eventually marry. Remarriage is common and immediately after widowhood or divorce a woman is expected to find another partner. Since marriage is universal at early ages, the process of childbearing also starts early, resulting in extremely high fertility rates across the regions. As noted above, frequent childbearing takes its toll in the form of high maternal death rates due to complications of pregnancy. Although official statistics indicate that maternal mortality is estimated at 2 deaths per 1,000 or less (UNFPA 1983, Malawi Ministry of Health 1989), this is a gross underestimation since the data on which the rate is calculated is collected from government and nongovernment health facilities. These statistics are inherently limited in that most women (about 70 percent in rural areas) deliver at home outside the health institutions (Malawi National Statistical Office 1973, 1987b). One study gives an estimate of 16 maternal deaths per 1,000 births (Malawi Government 1986).

The most recent scourge to hit the people of Malawi is the AIDS epidemic. The speed and intensity of its spread have reached alarming levels. Within 5 years of its start in 1985, over 7,000 AIDS cases had been reported, of which most had already ended in death (World Bank 1992; House and Zimalirana 1992a). Although cases have been reported from every district, the population groups most gravely affected so far have been urban dwellers and those living or working along major transportation routes. This is in keeping with the usual dissemination pattern of African AIDS epidemics where rural areas are spared in the initial stages of diffusion. It is the young, highly educated by Malawian standards, the future leaders of the country, that have been heavily hit by this scourge. Women in the childbearing age range in urban areas have also been affected. Thus unlike the Western pattern, the AIDS epidemic in Malawi has affected both sexes equally, since it is transmitted through heterosexual contacts rather than through homosexuality and the sharing of needles.

Nationwide data on seroprevalence are not yet available although efforts are underway to measure the scale and characteristics of the epidemic. Prevalence estimates for around 1990 range from 2 to 10 percent for the adult population, compared to 7 percent for Uganda (from a national seroprevalence survey in 1988), which is one of the worst-affected countries (World Bank 1992b). If the higher estimates were to prove correct, Malawi would rank among the world's most heavily affected countries. The AIDS epidemic is likely to have a major impact on population dynamics in the country. Life expectancy, which is already low by African standards, could begin to decline. Although its demographic impact is yet to be seen, it is estimated that the population growth rate could be reduced from its current 3.3 percent to 2.3 percent within a short period of twenty years. There is ample evidence of widespread deaths of young people between the ages 20–40 with AIDS as the major culprit. AIDS-related opportunistic diseases, such as tuberculosis and pneumonia, are also taking their toll. The AIDS pandemic in Malawi has grave implications for the socioeconomic development of the country.

In short, the health status of the population of Malawi is dreary. Preventable communicable diseases and poverty-linked disorders related to poor environmental sanitation are the main causes of ill health and the high mortality rates. The major causes of death among infants and children under five years are measles, upper respiratory infections, diarrhea and gastroenteritis, malaria, and malnutrition. For the general population, the leading causes of morbidity and mortality are respiratory infections, measles, diarrheal diseases, malaria, anemia, tuberculosis, nutritional deficiencies, and complications of pregnancy. The rising incidence of promiscuity, particularly in urban areas, has cultivated a fertile ground for the uncontrollable spread of AIDS. As noted above, infant mortality, crude death rates, and life expectancy exhibit marked regional variations. It is important that the underlying factors behind these regional variations should be clearly researched and understood in order to combat effectively ignorance, poverty, and disease in the country. Such an undertaking is, however, beyond the scope of this paper.

In the following sections, I concentrate on the policies and strategies of the health care delivery system in Malawi.

SPATIAL ORGANIZATION OF THE HEALTH CARE SYSTEM

This section is concerned with the spatial aspects of the health care delivery system in Malawi. On paper, the Malawi health care delivery system closely resembles Central Place Theory—a complex geographic concept applied to the delivery of goods and services in general. Shannon and Dever (1974) showed how health care delivery systems can be modeled and then compared to actual systems using the tenets of Central Place Theory. The basic ideas are familiar to geographers: threshold and range, spatial/functional organization, and hierarchies of central places. As Gesler (1984) notes, the model is generally applied to facilities that deliver Western care. Services range from lowest-order aid posts up through highest-order teaching hospitals. Each service requires a certain threshold population to be viable and provides health care over a corresponding range or territory. In theory, each level of services is provided by facilities spread evenly throughout an area. Of course there are many distortions to this model caused by such factors as uneven population distribution and geographic barriers (for more on Central Place Theory see Christaller 1966).

In Malawi the health services are centrally directed by the Ministry of Health. The Principal Secretary under the Minister of Health is responsible for all technical and administrative branches. The administrative branch is headed by the Under-Secretary, and the technical branch is headed by the Chief Medical Officer, who has responsibility for the professional divisions. The Chief Medical Officer is assisted by two assistant Chief Medical Officers and a number of senior professional officers based in the various districts of the country (USAID 1979; UNFPA 1983; Malawi Government 1986). Thus the administrative structure of the Ministry of Health is of a hierarchical nature.

Although the Ministry of Health is the largest health service provider in the country, the 13 church denominations in Malawi provide more than 40 percent of the health services. Especially active in the rural and remote areas, the church organizations operate 20 district hospitals, 19 rural hospitals, and 97 primary health centers with a total bed capacity of 5,000 compared to the Ministry of Health's 6,800 beds. The health activities of the church groups are coordinated through the interdenominational Private Hospital Association of Malawi (PHAM). PHAM collaborates closely with the Ministry of Health in the planning and implementation of health services (Zulu 1989, UNFPA 1983 and 1984).

Besides these two major agencies, there are other small modern health care providers in Malawi, including private practitioners not affiliated with any church, private company, or estate-financed health facilities for employees, and other government agencies such as the army and police. Altogether these account for another 200 health facilities and more than 600 beds. Beyond the modern health care sector, there also flourishes in Malawi a very large, traditional health care sector including about 18,000 traditional healers and 1,000 traditional birth attendants. So far, this group of health care providers has been entirely ignored by the modern health care system and governmental officials. However, as has been noted by a number of scholars, coopting this sector into the modern health care delivery system would yield great benefits towards provision of primary care to the rural communities (Good 1977 and 1979; Kalipeni 1979; Rapparport 1980). The training of traditional healers in the basics of modern medicine and of traditional birth attendants in maternal and child care would certainly go a long way to complement the overworked personnel in the Western-style health care delivery system.

The Ministry of Health (MOH) is responsible for the development of working objectives, plans, and strategies within the government's overall health goals. The working objectives of the MOH are derived from the government's national health goal, which is "to raise the level of health of all the people of Malawi by providing a network of sound health facilities capable of reducing disease, protecting life, promoting better health, increasing productivity, and ultimately, promoting well being" (Malawi Government 1986). However, the rigid hierarchical administrative structure has its own inherent problems in the effective provision of health care. Apart from the perennial severe understaffing at all levels, the remoteness of some health facilities makes it difficult to provide adequate logistical support. In a number of cases, poor transportation and communications facilities present serious problems in communicating policy goals from top to bottom. The Ministry could benefit organizationally from the decentralization of certain functions and decision-making processes.

At the geographic or spatial level, the country is divided into three regions and twenty-four districts for the purposes of providing health services (Figure 1). The existing health services are delivered at six levels of hierarchy, namely, (1) health posts, (2) health subcenters, (3) primary health centers/rural hospitals, (4) district hospitals, (5) central hospitals, and (6) special hospitals (UNFPA 1983 and Kandawire 1989). Each district has a district hospital. Two of these, in the cities of Blantyre and Lilongwe, have been designated central hospitals, and one, in Zomba, is a general hospital. These three hospitals provide specialist services in medicine, surgery, pediatrics, obstetrics and gynecology, ophthalmology, and so forth. The other twenty-one district hospitals are staffed by physicians, senior clinical officers, or, in some cases, medical assistants. There are three special hospitals in selected localities that provide specialized services relating to mental illness (one hospital) and leprosy (two hospitals).

One level below the district hospitals is a network of forty-one primary health centers, each of which is supposed to serve a population of 50,000 people and to provide support and supervision to four adjacent health subcenters. The services provided at primary health centers vary. The established standard services include basic curative treatments; taking care of referrals from outreach posts; prenatal, natal, and postnatal care; well-baby care; nutrition clinics; and all outreach services. On the other hand, the subcenter, serving a population of 10,000, is the basic health facility and the base for the provision of primary health care and health education. Health posts, the most peripheral units, are sometimes located in public buildings, such as schools. In certain agricultural development areas, a few units, staffed by maternal and child health (MCH) assistants, have been built. The health posts are generally served by the staff of the nearest health subcenter. In remote rural areas the post's activities are supplemented by mobile clinics operating from subcenters or primary health centers. The distribution of these facilities at the regional level is given in Table 2. The hierarchical arrangement of these subcenters is given in Figure 2.

As indicated in Table 2, there are only 48 district-level hospitals and 41 primary health centers that are supposed to serve the 8.7 million people in the country. Under the principles of Central Place Theory, in order to provide adequate health services at a population threshold of 50,000 per primary health center, there would be need for an additional 85 primary health centers. Similarly, the number of subcenters and health posts would have to be increased from current levels to meet the basic needs of the rapidly expanding population. The idea of a well-structured, national hierarchy of health facilities is logically appealing, but the issue at stake is whether these facilities are adequate in meeting the basic needs of the population. In the following sections we analyze avail-

TABLE 2.   DISTRIBUTION OF HEALTH INSTITUTIONS BY TYPE AND REGION, 1989

DISTRICT	DISTRICT HOSPITALS	PRIMARY HEALTH CENTERS	HEALTH SUBCENTERS			HEALTH POST	LEPROSARIA AND MENTAL HOSPITALS
			Full	*Disp.*	*Mat.*		
Northern Region	9	11	45	54	20	4	0
Central Region	15	16	80	77	30	7	1
Southern Region	24	14	94	178	41	20	2
Total	48	41	219	309	91	31	3

Notes: Disp. = dispensary; Mat. = maternity; Full = both maternity and dispensary in the same unit.

Source: Malawi Ministry of Health. 1989. *Health Information System Reference Tables*. Lilongwe: Ministry of Health.

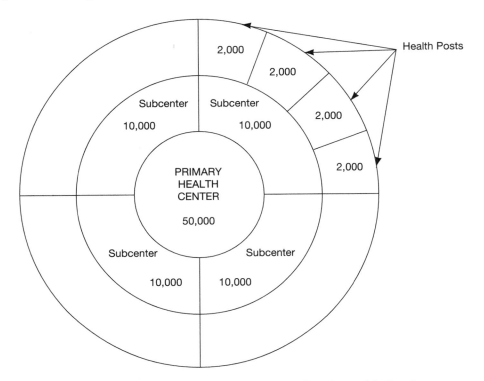

FIGURE 2. The Hierarchical/Spatial Organization of Basic Health Services Facilities in Malawi.

Notes: One primary health center covers 50,000 people, and also functions as a subcenter for its immediate catchment area. Each subcenter covers 10,000 people and also functions as a health post for its immediate catchment area.

Source: World Health Organization. 1973. *National Health Plan for Malawi*. Lilongwe: WHO.

able data to determine whether there exists spatial inequality in the distribution of these services in relation to population distribution as well as accessibility in terms of actual and social distance.

SPATIAL INEQUALITIES AND ACCESSIBILITY ISSUES

When looking at the spatial organization and distribution of facilities, a basic question one needs to ask is whether there is equality or inequality. One also needs some standards of equality to compare with actual distributions. To this end, a number of measures have been developed in the subdiscipline of medical geography. A simple type of standard—the Hill-Burton idea from American legislative history—requires that doctor/population ratios or hospital bed/population ratios be approximately equal across certain spatial units (Gesler 1984; Pyle 1979). One-way analysis of variance can also be used to measure the extent of equality in the indicators across regions or districts. These are some of the techniques employed in this section to measure the extent of regional inequality in the provision of health services in Malawi. It must also be realized that there are inherent flaws in most of these techniques since the geographic unit of analysis, in this case, the district, is itself arbitrary. There is a need for a comprehensive study of the location of health facilities in Malawi in relation to the population served in order to demarcate areas of service and identify those areas that are underserved by the current distributional pattern of health services.

The distribution of health facilities at regional levels in 1989 is given in Table 2. Altogether there were 48 district hospitals, 41 primary health centers, 219 full health subcenters, 309 dispensaries, 91 maternity centers, and 31 health posts. The district hospitals appear to be evenly distributed across districts with at least 1 in each district (not shown in Table 2), but there are marked district and regional inequalities in the distribution of the other facilities. Table 3 gives the distribution of the facilities in relation to population. In this table, the spatial distribution of the facilities has been assessed in terms of the number of people served by each facility and the population per hospital bed. Clearly, results in Table 3 indicate that the standards set in the 1973 "National Health Plan for Malawi" are far from being attained 20 years later (see World Health Organization 1973 for the plan; see also Figure 2). As noted above, one of the priorities emphasized in the Plan was the establishment of a network and hierarchy of health infrastructure, particularly in rural areas (Malawi Department of Town and Country Planning 1987). In the hierarchical system of health service, the higher-level units were to supervise the lower-level units; and the lower-level units were to refer patients to the higher-level units when required.

In 1989, only one district, Rumphi in the Northern Region, met the 1973 planned standard of one primary health center per 50,000 persons (Table 3). The rest of the districts in the country were far from achieving this. However, 1983 data showed that 7 districts, most of them concentrated in the Northern Region, had populations of less than 50,000 persons per primary health center (Malawi

TABLE 3.   DISTRIBUTION OF FACILITIES AND BEDS IN RELATION TO POPULATION, 1989

	MALAWI	**NORTHERN REGION**	**CENTRAL REGION**	**SOUTHERN REGION**
Facility/Population Ratio				
Total Population (1989)	8,496,215	950,269	3,325,795	4,220,251
Pop. per bed	644	413	740	660
Pop. per hospital	177,004	105,585	221,720	175,844
Pop. per primary health center	202,291	86,388	195,635	301,447
Pop. per health subcenter	38,796	21,117	41,572	44,896
Ranking				
Pop. per bed rank	—*	1	3	2
Pop. per hospital rank	—*	1	3	2
Pop. per primary health center rank	—*	1	2	3
Pop. per health subcenter rank	—*	1	2	3

*The national average is not ranked.

Source: Data obtained from Malawi Ministry of Health. 1989. *Health Information System Reference Tables*. Lilongwe: Ministry of Health.

Department of Town and Country Planning 1987, p. 231). The goals set forth by the government of Malawi twenty years ago are still far from being achieved. In general terms, as depicted by the rankings in Table 3, districts in the Northern Region have better population/facility ratios than districts in the Central and Southern Regions.

A simple one-way analysis of variance confirms the existence of regional imbalances in the distribution of population/facility ratios (Table 4). For example, the *F* ratio(s) in Table 4 indicate that population per hospital bed is significantly smaller in the Northern Region than the Central and Southern Regions. This is also true of population per district hospital and population per primary health center. The regional differentials of population per health subcenter were not statistically significant, although the Northern Region was still in a favorable position compared to the other two regions. In most instances, the Central Region appears to have the worst ratios. Thus, apart from the government's failure to meet its own standards in the provision of health facilities using Central Place Theory's guiding principles, the available facilities are inequitably distributed across region and district.

Maldistribution of health facilities is not the only problem. There is also the problem of access to many of the facilities. One of the important objectives of the Ministry of Health's plan is to improve access to modern health services. In the plan, accessibility is seen mainly in terms of walking distance, as walking is the most common means of transport for at least 90 percent of the total population. Indeed, in developing countries, many people, perhaps the majority, walk to obtain health care (Jackman 1972) although many other forms of transportation are also used (e.g., buses, bicycles, boats, motorcycles, etc.). Apart from one comprehensive survey conducted by the Malawi Department of Town and Country Planning in the early 1980s in preparation for the national physical

TABLE 4.   ONE-WAY ANALYSIS OF VARIANCE OF HEALTH FACILITIES IN RELATION TO POPULATION BY DISTRICT WITH REGION AS CLASS VARIABLE

VARIABLE	REGION	MEAN	*F* RATIO[a]
Population per hospital bed	Northern	433	5.18*
	Central	780	0.01
	Southern	698	
Population per district hospital	Northern	112,519	4.06*
	Central	230,013	0.03
	Southern	178,677	
Population per primary health center	Northern	86,855	5.89*
	Central	182,249	0.01
	Southern	311,158	
Population per health subcenter	Northern	20,896	0.84
	Central	43,827	0.45
	Southern	104,167	

Notes: [a]First value in each cell of this column is the *F* ratio and the second value is the probability value at which the *F* ratio would be statistically significant.

*Implies *F* ratio is significant at the 5 percent level of significance.

development plan, data on accessibility to the health facilities is virtually nonexistent.

Based on the sample survey carried out in various parts of the country by the Malawi Department of Town and Country Planning, 89 percent of people who reported visiting an under five (for children under five years of age) clinic travelled by foot; in the case of visits to dispensaries and hospitals, 82 percent and 36 percent, respectively, went by foot (Malawi Department of Town and Country Planning 1987). For those visiting hospitals, the most common mode of transport was travel by bus, which accounted for 39 percent. Those walking to health facilities tended to travel long distances—often beyond five kilometers although generally not beyond fifty kilometers. Of the respondents travelling by foot to under-five clinics, 34 percent walked beyond five kilometers to reach the clinics. The corresponding figures for dispensaries and hospitals were 44 percent and 67 percent, respectively. These figures clearly indicate that the majority of the people do not live close to health facilities.

The new national health plan provides locational planning standards for health centers, as well as district and central hospitals, based on the sole criterion of accessibility in terms of distance or travel time. In the new plan, the locational and accessibility standards are eight kilometers (or five miles) radius for a primary health center, with at least one district hospital in each district and one central hospital in each region. District hospitals are already in place. However, the question of accessibility does not involve distance or travel time alone. It is clear from the new national health plan that health planning has tended to adopt the rather narrow view of accessibility, relating it to the maximum distance people are willing to travel to obtain a particular health service. Consequently, much emphasis is being placed on building new facilities at great capital and recurrent cost to the state without necessarily improving absolute access to rural or even urban inhabitants.

In a study by Kalipeni and Kamlongera (1987) it was found that people within walking distance to health facilities did not take advantage of their proximity. They were impeded from using the facilities, not only by distance, but also by social and psychological barriers. They found the modern buildings too imposing and the conduct of the young nurses to be unacceptable to their traditions. Older women and men avoided visiting nearby facilities in times of need for fear of being ordered to undress in front of a nurse or doctor of the same age as their daughter. What this suggests is that facilities can be made available on the basis of distance and/or Central Place Theory tenets, but this does not necessarily mean that they will be utilized by the people most in need of them, even if they are provided free of charge. Cultural barriers should also be taken into consideration when planning the provision of health care facilities. The barriers can be reduced or broken through intensive health educational campaigns.

IMPLICATIONS OF RAPID POPULATION GROWTH

As noted earlier, any efforts at trying to meet the basic health needs of the people of Malawi are likely to be frustrated by a rapidly growing population. Social services such as health and educational facilities not only directly improve welfare and living standards, but also make an essential contribution to the development of human capital, itself a major factor in the speed and effectiveness with which a country can develop (World Bank 1992b). At current population growth rates, maternal and child health clients will treble over the next 30 years if fertility does not fall in the near future (World Bank 1992b; Srivastava 1989). With no change in fertility, the annual budget allocations to health services would have to grow at between 3.5 and 4 percent per year simply in order to maintain existing services. A moderate or rapid decline in fertility would mean huge savings of health expenditures allocated to merely keep up with population growth and such savings could be meaningfully used to expand service coverage and improve quality.

From a spatial and social equity perspective, the impact of rapid population growth on social services would adversely affect the poorest families in Malawi. Since such families tend to live furthest away from schools and health facilities, they are the last to be reached if service expansion is constrained by lack of funding, and the first to suffer from any enforced cuts in coverage or service quality (World Bank 1992b). Similarly, since their incomes are lowest, they also tend to suffer most if attempts are made to introduce fees for the health facilities (World Bank 1990b).

Srivastava (1989) has estimated that by the year 2002 the health facilities will have to be expanded to the order of 70 percent just to meet the population increase at the same level of service as in 1987. Growth of the population in the various age categories during the new health plan period of 1986–1996 is expected to be between 32 and 35 percent. The reported number of general (nonmaternity) beds in various health units of Malawi in 1986 was 7,699. This implied the availability of just over one bed per 1,000 estimated population in 1986, or about 8 beds for every 100 square kilometers of land area. Srivastava (1989) calculates that to maintain the service level of 1986, by the years 1995 and 2000, the need for nonmaternity beds in Malawi as a whole, as a result of population growth alone, will go up to 10,049 and 11,940 respectively (i.e., increases of 30.5 and 55.1 percent respectively). These calculations are also true for maternity beds.

In terms of budgetary provision, the estimated expenditure on the provision of health services by the Ministry of Health was 45 million Kwacha (=K) in 1986. This expenditure in per capita terms was K6.18 or U.S. $1.50. Using the same per capita expenditure and taking the size of population into account, the estimated annual budget for 1996 is K123 million, allowing for an inflation rate of 7 percent per annum (Srivastava 1989; Kalanje 1989). Thus, the Ministry of Health would have to come up with an additional K71 million in 1996 in order to provide the 1986 level of health to the population of Malawi. It is clear that population growth will continue to play a major role in the decline of the quality of health services in Malawi. With a poor resource base, it is doubtful that the government will be able to provide the same level of service in the future as today. Indeed, evidence indicates that the health care infrastructure is on the decline largely due to lack of funding and rapid population growth.

CONCLUDING REMARKS

The discussion in this paper clearly paints a bleak picture for the health care delivery system in Malawi in the years to come. According to epidemiologic transition theory, Malawi, like many other countries in the developing world, finds itself trapped on the borderline between the first stage of the transition, the age of pestilence and famine, and the second stage, the age of receding pandemics. While mortality rates have experienced a considerable decline during the past 30 years, there is no guarantee that they will continue to decline. The brief analysis in this discussion indicates that modern health care facilities in the country are inadequate on two fronts.

First, basic indicators of health care provision have not been able to achieve the standards set forth in the health plan of the Government of Malawi that was launched twenty years ago. For example, population/facility ratios are higher today than they were ten years ago. Generally, there are over 100,000 people per primary health center, twice the 50,000 people per primary health center set in 1973. Although the budget allocation for health activities has increased from a low of 3.3 percent to well over 7 percent of the total budget allocation, the government has failed to provide adequate health facilities largely due to a rapidly expanding population that is doubling its size every twenty years or less. The failure to provide adequate health facilities over time is reflected in the prevailing high rates of national infant mortality (151/1,000), 0–4 age group cumulative mortality (330/1,000), and maternal mortality (16/1,000). Second, there are conspicuous regional imbalances in the provision of health care facilities. The districts in the Northern Region have more facilities per capita compared to districts in the Central and Southern Regions. The Central Region has some of the highest population/facility ratios in the country. It is no wonder that basic indicators of health, such as infant and adult mortality rates, are highest in the Central Region in comparison to the other two regions. Life expectancies for districts in the Central Region are far below the national average.

It was also pointed out in the above discussion that the chief causes of both infant and adult mortality are preventable. Although the causes of Malawi's anomalously high levels of childhood mortality are still not entirely clear, evidence from agricultural surveys of the 1980s and examination of the available health statistics point to extremely severe prevalences of malnutrition and malaria as the major determinants (World Bank 1992b). Adult mortality is also on the increase due to the AIDS epidemic and the proliferation of communicable diseases such as tuberculosis. Given the current resource constraints, the Government of Malawi cannot continue to rely on building more and more hospitals to keep up with population growth. It is the strong conviction of this author that the way out of the current health crisis lies in the extension of peripheral services, particularly community and primary health care-based facilities. This can be easily achieved by the incorporation of the traditional healers into the system. The traditional healers can then be charged with the task of motivating the various communities in which they live. The various Christian denominations in the country have largely remained silent on issues of primary health care. They could also play a direct and prominent role of disseminating information on basic health care issues. Active community participation and involvement is vital in the success of any health care program, especially where communicable diseases are concerned. It is time the government seriously considered implementing the primary health care recommendations put forth by notable scholars such as Bennet and Cole-King (1982), Kalipeni and Kamlongera (1987), and Msukwa (1987).

However, one of the critical factors in the deterioration of health care facilities is rapid population growth. Unless serious steps are taken to reduce the high fertility rates, the population will continue to explode, thereby frustrating any development efforts or investments in the health and education services sector. The government has taken the first step in addressing population matters by launching the child-spacing program (Malawi Ministry of Health 1992). But as its name suggests, the program simply emphasizes the proper spacing between two successive births rather than direct birth prevention. While this program might, if successful, have the desirable effect of reducing fertility, it needs to be complemented by other measures, including incentives and disincentives to discourage large families.

REFERENCES

BENNET, F. J., and S. M. COLE-KING. 1982. *Guidelines for the Development of Primary Health Care.* Lilongwe: Ministry of Health, PHC Working Committee, Government of Malawi in Collaboration with WHO/UNICEF.

CHILIVUMBO, ALIFEYO. 1975. "Malawi: Cultural Consequences of Population Growth." In *The Consequences of Population Change.* A report on a seminar held in Bucharest, Romania, 14–17 August, 1974. Washington, D.C.: The Center for the Study of Man, Smithsonian Institution.

CHOUDHRY, A. W., and C. H. TEESDALE. ed. 1984. *Bilharzia: A Manual for Health Workers in Malawi.* Nairobi, Kenya: Geigy Trading and Marketing Services Ltd.

CHRISTALLER, WALTER. 1966. *The Central Places of Southern Germany.* Englewood Cliffs, NJ: Prentice-Hall.

GESLER, WILBERT M. 1984. *Health Care in Developing Countries.* Washington, D.C.: Association of American Geographers.

GOOD, CHARLES M. 1977. "Traditional Medicine: An Agenda for Medical Geography." *Social Science and Medicine* 11:705-13.

——— . 1979. "The Interface of Dual Systems of Health Care in the Developing World: Toward Health Policy Initiatives in Africa." *Social Science and Medicine* 13D:141-54.

HOUSE, WILLIAM J., and GEORGE ZIMALIRANA. 1992a. *Malawi's Population Dynamics: Future Prospects.* Lilongwe: UNFPA/ILO.

——— . 1992b. "Rapid Population Growth and Poverty Generation in Malawi." *Journal of Modern African Studies* 30:141-63, 1992.

JACKMAN, M. E. 1972. "Flying Doctor Services in Zambia." Pp. 97-103 in Neil D. McGlashan, ed. *Medical Geography: Techniques and Field Studies.* London: Methuen and Co.

KALANJE, N. N. 1989. "The Role of Population and the Impact of Population Growth on the Planning and Delivery of Health Services in Malawi." Paper presented at the national seminar on *Population and Development in Malawi* held at the Demographic Unit, Chancellor College, University of Malawi, Zomba, Malawi, June, 5-9.

KALIPENI, EZEKIEL. 1979. "African Traditional Healing of Mental Illness as Compared with Western Psychiatry." *Dansk Psykolog Nyt (Danish Journal of Psychology)* 14 and 15:377-81 and 402-9.

——— . 1985. "The Natural Nidus of Schistosomiasis with Reference to Malawi." *The Malawian Geographer* 24:28-47.

———. 1992a. "Population Redistribution in Malawi Since Independence in 1964." *Geographical Review* 82(1), January 1992, pp. 13–28.

———. 1992b. "Population Growth and Environmental Degradation in Malawi." *Africa Insight* 22 (4):273–82.

———. 1993. "Determinants of Infant Mortality in Malawi: A Spatial Perspective." *Social Science and Medicine* 37 (2):183–98.

KALIPENI, EZEKIEL, and CHRISTOPHER KAMLONGERA. 1987. *Popular Theatre and Primary Health Care in Malawi.* Zomba, Malawi: University of Malawi, Demographic Unit.

KALIPENI, EZEKIEL, and ELIYA ZULU. 1993. "Gender Differences in Knowledge and Attitudes Toward Modern and Traditional Methods of Child Spacing in Malawi." *Population Research and Policy Review* 12(2), 1993.

KANDAWIRE, KAMCHITETE. 1989. "Health and Development in Malawi." Paper presented at the national seminar on *Population and Development in Malawi* held at the Demographic Unit, Chancellor College, University of Malawi, Zomba, 5–9 June.

Malawi Department of Town and Country Planning. 1987. *National Physical Development Plan.* Lilongwe: Office of the President and Cabinet.

Malawi Government. 1986. *Statement of Development Policies: 1987–1996.* Lilongwe: Office of the President and Cabinet, Department of Economic Planning and Development.

Malawi Ministry of Health. 1989. *Health Information System Reference Tables.* Lilongwe: Ministry of Health.

———. 1992. *Child Spacing Policy and Contraceptive Guidelines for the Republic of Malawi.* Lilongwe, Malawi: Ministry of Health.

Malawi National Statistical Office. 1973. *Malawi Population Change Survey, February 1970–January 1972.* Zomba, Malawi: Government Printer.

———. 1984. *Malawi Population Census 1977: Analytical Report, Vol. II.* Zomba, Malawi: Government Printer.

———. 1987a. *Malawi Population and Housing Census 1987: Preliminary Report.* Zomba, Malawi: Government Printer.

———. 1987b. *Malawi Family Formation Survey 1984.* Zomba, Malawi: Government Printer.

———. 1987c. *Malawi Demographic Survey.* Zomba, Malawi: Government Printer.

———. 1991. *Malawi Population and Housing Census 1987: Summary of Results.* Zomba, Malawi: Government Printer.

MEADE, MELINDA, JOHN FLORIN, and WILBERT M. GESLER. 1988. *Medical Geography.* New York: Guilford Press.

M'MANGA, W. R., and M. L. SRIVASTAVA. 1991. *Socio-Economic and Demographic Determinants of Family Size in Malawi: A Multivariate Analysis.* Zomba: Demographic Unit, University of Malawi.

MORNA, C. L. 1988. "Shouldering the Refugee Burden," *Africa Report* July–August 1988, pp. 51–54.

MSUKWA, LOUIS. A. H. 1981. *Meeting the Basic Health Needs of Rural Malawi: An Alternative Strategy.* Monograph XII. Swansea: Centre for Development Studies, University College of Swansea, University of Wales.

———. 1984. "Agriculture and Nutrition in Malawi." Paper presented at the conference on *Malawi: An Alternative Pattern of Development* held at Edinburgh University, Scotland, 24–25 May.

———. 1987. "Primary Health Care in Malawi: A Search for Relevance." Zomba, Malawi: Center for Social Research, University of Malawi. Unpublished Report.

NANKUMBA, SINOYA J. 1989. "Food Requirement and Agricultural Production, Cropping Patterns and Land Ownership in Malawi." Paper presented at the national seminar on *Population and Development in Malawi* held at the Demographic Unit, Chancellor College, University of Malawi, Zomba, Malawi, 5–9 June.

OMRAN, ABDEL R. 1971. "The Epidemiologic Transition: A Theory of the Epidemiology of Population Change." *Milbank Memorial Fund Quarterly* 49:509–38.

———. 1974. "Changing Patterns of Health and Disease during the Process of National Development." Pp. 259–74 in *Community Medicine in Developing Countries,* edited by Abdel R. Omran. New York: Springer Publishing Co.

———. 1977. "Epidemiologic Transition in the U.S.: The Health Factor in Population Change." *Population Bulletin* 32(2).

PIKE, JOHN G., and GERALD T. RIMMINGTON. 1965. *Malawi: A Geographical Study.* Oxford: Oxford University Press.

PYLE, GERALD F. 1979. *Applied Medical Geography.* Washington, D.C.: V. H. Winston and Sons.

RAPPARPORT, H. 1980. "The Integration of Scientific and Traditional Healing." Pp. 81–98 in *Traditional Health Care Delivery in Contemporary Africa,* edited by P. Ulin and M. Segall. Syracuse: Syracuse University Press.

SCHAEFER, MORRIS. 1974. "Planning and Organization of Community Health Systems." Pp. 383–402 in *Community Medicine in Developing Countries*, edited by Abdel R. Omran. New York: Springer Publishing Co.

SHANNON, GARY W., and G. E. A. DEVER. 1974. *Health Care Delivery: Spatial Perspectives*. New York: McGraw-Hill.

SRIVASTAVA, M. L. 1989. "Implication of Population Growth in Planning for Health Services in Malawi." Paper presented at the national seminar on *Population and Development in Malawi* held at the Demographic Unit, Chancellor College, University of Malawi, Zomba, Malawi, 5–9 June.

SRIVASTAVA, M.L., and W. R. M'MANGA. 1991. *Traditional and Modern Methods of Child Spacing in Malawi: Knowledge, Attitude and Practice; A Survey Report*. Zomba, Malawi: Demographic Unit, University of Malawi.

TEESDALE, C. H., L. CHITSULO, and C. WERLER. 1983. "The Bilharzia Control Program in Malawi." *Malawi Epidemiological Quarterly* 4:10–37.

UNICEF. 1990. *The State of the World's Children, 1990*. Oxford: Oxford University Press.

UNFPA. 1983. *Malawi: Report of Mission on Needs Assessment for Population Assistance*. Report Number 64. New York: UNFPA.

———. 1984. *Report on the Evaluation on UNFPA Assistance to the Maternal and Child Health Programme of Malawi: Project MLW/78/P03*. New York: UNFPA.

USAID. 1977. Southern Africa Task Force, *A Framework for U.S. Assistance in Southern Africa: Country Resource Paper—Malawi*. Washington, D.C.: Office of Southern and East African Affairs, Africa Bureau, USAID.

———. 1979. *Malawi: A Report to Congress on Development Needs and Opportunities for Cooperation in Southern Africa*. Washington, D.C.: USAID.

World Bank 1990a. *World Development Report 1990: Poverty*. Oxford: Oxford University Press, published for the World Bank.

———. 1990b. *Malawi: Growth Through Poverty Reduction*. Washington, D.C.: World Bank.

———. 1992a. *World Development Report 1992: Development and Environment*. Oxford: Oxford University Press, published for the World Bank.

———. 1992b. *Malawi Population Sector Study, Vol. 1*. Washington, D.C.: Population and Human Resources Division, Southern Africa Department, African Regional Office, World Bank.

World Health Organization. 1973. *National Health Plan for Malawi*. Lilongwe: WHO.

ZULU, M. C. J. 1989. "Community Based Health Programs in Malawi." Paper presented at the national seminar on *Population and Development in Malawi* held at the Demographic Unit, Chancellor College, University of Malawi, Zomba, Malawi, 5–9 June.

PART IV

SOCIETAL DISLOCATION

Planning of National Primary Health Care and Prevention Programs: The First Health Insurance Law of Russia, 1991–1993

Irina V. Mckeehan

INTRODUCTION

After the disintegration of the Soviet Union, which led to the August Coup of 1991 and the formation of the Commonwealth of Independent States (CIS), international aid became available to the novice sovereign nations. The Perestroika of the political and economic system in Russia also affected population health programs and policy. Proposed legislative reform was designed to establish privatized, for-profit market relations in the general economy, as well as in the health sector. An unintended consequence of the broad economic changes was an increase in the acute shortage of staples, such as food, drugs, and medical supplies, especially for the vulnerable segments of the population. After the Coup of 1991, humanitarian relief organizations, like CARE (Centers for Disease Control 1992a; 1992b) and the U.S. Food and Humanitarian Assistance Bureau, as well as the World Bank (1993) and IMF, undertook a series of assessments of the risk factors that were affecting the political stability in Russia and the communities targeted to receive foreign aid.

The International Monetary Fund (IMF) made aid to Russia contingent upon the enactment of legislation that encouraged market forces of supply and demand. In outlining the strategy of foreign assistance programs to Russia in

April 1992, IMF Director Camdessus (*New York Times* 1992) pointedly noted that the hallmark of a sound democracy was the functioning of a well-developed social welfare system. A nation's health, quality of life, and sense of well-being were contingent upon the integrity of its educational, public health, and social security programs. In changing from a centralized bureaucratic planned economy to market regulation of supply and demand, the IMF urged Russia to focus on providing effective government safety nets for the most vulnerable segments of the population, as well as establishing an adequate private sector in social services. The IMF emphasized the fact that the Russian Federation exhibited a low standard of living similar to other ethnic republics. All showed the signs of having borne similar cultural and economic costs of Communist party ideology. Foreign aid was necessary to curtail political upheaval and speed the transition to a democratically oriented market economy. Social reforms needed to be made in macroeconomic stabilization, including interest rates, exchange rates, and the formation of legal, public administration, and institutional mechanisms to execute policy. The International Monetary Fund, therefore, declared that Russia would receive about $25 billion in foreign aid, primarily in the form of loans over a period of five years, as would the smaller republics.

The Russian Parliament anticipated IMF policy requirements to encourage market relations, grappling with these fundamental issues in formulating the Health Insurance Act of 1991: free government health care vs. private, fee-for-service medicine; universal access vs. choice of providers within a range of cost and quality constraints; direct financing through taxation vs. mixed public and private insurance mechanisms of financing; central budgetary allocation of resources vs. competitive market distribution of medical goods and services; and bureaucratic accountability for quality vs. provider responsiveness to consumer choice. Russia's first health insurance legislation was signed into law by President Yeltsin in June 1991. It was scheduled to take effect October 1991, with full implementation by January 1993. The Insurance Act was tabled in 1992 pending reassessment of several provisions. These were presented in November 1992 by the Interministerial Working Group on Health Insurance to the Parliament of the Russian Federation and the President for approval. The modified legislation was signed into law in April 1993 by President Yeltsin while he was attending the Vancouver Summit with President Clinton (Potapchik 1993, p. 1).

Russia, as the most influential member of the Former Soviet Union, is central in defining the direction of social change in the CIS. Therefore, the public policy and health legislation debated and implemented in Russia may be a precedent-setting model for other newly independent states and member nations of the former Warsaw Pact.

HEALTH POLICY: WHAT ARE THE ISSUES?

Health is an international phenomenon, situated in the larger socio-ecological context of a global community. Not only does each individual's health status affect others, but the health of one group in a society can influence the welfare of other groups. The diffusion of medical technology and health systems research can affect positively a nation's health much like, in a negative direction, the spread of infectious diseases can affect communities. International diffusion of health systems reform was institutionalized by the philosophical investment in health care as a universal human right rather than a sellable commodity. The United Nations Charter of 1948 adopted Article 25, the Universal Declaration, which stipulated that all people had the right to a standard of living that guaranteed health. In 1960, the Universal Declaration of Human Rights further specified health positively as the highest attainable standard of physical and mental well-being, achieved through the promotion of maternal and child health, reduction of mortality and morbidity rates, environmental sanitation, and provision of adequate medical services. Susser (1993) has outlined how the United Nations reaffirmed health as an intrinsically valuable end after the Second World War by emphasizing that poor health is caused predominantly by poverty and environmental conditions. A 1978 World Health Organization Conference in Alma-Ata, the capital of Kazakhstan, a republic of the former Soviet Union, supported the global issue of equity through accessibility to "Health for All by the Year 2000," by recommending the implementation of primary health care and disease prevention in national policies.

The human rights movement in health raised the issue of equity in health status, which was tied to universal access and comprehensive medical and health services for different social groups. Universal access implies the availability of services to all individuals and groups. Comprehensive treatment of disease also requires preventive services that promote health through population-based programs of education, nutrition, sanitation, vaccinations, industrial safety, and so forth. Evaluating the distinctions between individual medical care and public health care became important as a means of monitoring health status as the outcome of equity and quality of care. Equity in access, measured as an input to the health system did not, however, categorically lead to equity in health status. Equity in the differential health status among social groups was constrained by the process of delivering health care, as well as by the sociocultural, economic, and political arrangements of the community in which the delivery system was functioning. The case of the Soviet Union with regard to equitable health care and public well-being is especially instructive because the disparity between ideology and implementation has been so great in socialized medicine.

Soviet health policies during the 1970s and 1980s proposed preventive and primary care programs but lacked effective strategies to promote them administratively within the existing medical delivery system. Before Perestroika, Soviet health policy promoted medical care, allocating resources that emphasized an increase in supply, the volume of hospital beds, and the number of physicians and curative resources as the primary factors for optimizing public health. Rigid central health planning and budgeting, pharmaceutical shortages, management problems, and patient dissatisfaction were not recognized by the USSR Ministry of Health as factors contributing to declining population health status.

The health reform proposals of post-coup Russia departed sharply from previous policy. Post-coup proposals argued that the determinants of health status, especially chronic diseases, were related less to medically controllable biological factors than to the quality of life and to social conditions, such as environmental pollution, nutrition, and lifestyle.

Although the initial version of the 1991 Health Insurance Act of Russia was primarily concerned with the financial mechanisms of medical care, several provisions did attempt to link quality of life to two basic issues that have relevance for American health care reform as well. The first issue asks whether health is valuable in itself, or only as a means for enhancing economic production; and the second assesses interrelations between various indicators of health care financing, management, quality, and general population well-being. In Russia, a private health system had to be built upon public hegemony, whereas in the United States, health reformers were grappling with the issue of how to make a private health system more responsive to public demands.

Comparative Research

Data from cross-cultural research in health services is often viewed with scientific disdain because it is fraught with more exceptions than generalizations. The very value of comparative research, however, lies in the testing of the historical, spatiotemporal limits of theoretical generalizations and in the specification of the extent to which there is a universal model of social behavior. One central problem in drawing cross-cultural comparisons is the linguistic and cultural nonequivalence of concepts. For example, does self-perceived poor health have the same meaning in Russia as in the United States?

The search for a common scientific terminology has led to a premature demand for the cross-cultural identity of meaning as the golden criterion for construct validity. Equivalent but nonidentical concepts have often been confused with being incongruous or invalid. Cross-cultural equivalence does not necessarily imply identity, even under conditions of *ceteris paribus* (all other things being equal). Sociocultural norms are tacitly imbedded in health assessments and sociomedical indicators. What is accepted as healthy in rural Siberian villages, for example, may not be tolerated as healthy to the same extent in Moscow or on an Arkansas farm. The universalism of scientific validity has often been assumed to be independent of culture, although researchers, such as Kohn (1987) and Elder (1976) have long argued that scientific activity is situated in a sociocultural community. Comparative research is thus not only confounded by the social context of research methods, but also by the social context of the research problem. The limitations of specific comparative research must be articulated and acknowledged, but they are not insurmountable.

A comparative analysis of Soviet health policy is useful in clarifying the extent to which variations in health status can be weighted by structural factors of a centralized, planned social system and economy, or by such factors of culture as social choice, individual preferences, and values. Factors such as cultural values influence individual choice in lifestyle and thereby individual quality of life, whereas social structural factors directly affect medical care organization and indirectly affect individual choice in navigating the delivery of health care. It is important to understand at the policy level which health issues are subject to individual control, and which require structural change.

Health promotion and disease prevention policies in the early twentieth century emerged in industrialized nations as a response to social pressure from workers. Health care services and costs have subsequently escalated without concomitant improvements in population health status. This has forced many countries, such as Israel, Canada, and Britain, to reorganize their health systems (Chernichovsky 1992a). Primary care and preventive health policy in the USSR made an ideological leap after the Communist Revolution of 1917, promulgating the intrinsic value of health, but they lacked implementation. Later, after the success of the 1960s in decreasing mortality and morbidity rates, the economic resources that fed the Cold War gradually crowded out health spending. This myopic approach to public health eventually led to the current decline in economic indicators and the present health crisis in the Russian Federation.

Social costs in lost years of productive life, medical expenditures, and increased debility from chronic diseases have become a major concern for both the public and private sectors in the new democracies of the Eastern bloc, as much as the West (World Bank 1993). The crises in national health policies have arisen in both market- and centrally planned economies. The fulcrum of policy goals rested on relating population health as a human right to promoting quality of life and to the means for furthering economic objectives, without relinquishing consumer choice.

In the United States, policy debates have centered on who was responsible for providing what type of health care, to whom, and at what cost, in the public and private sectors (Davis 1992). The Former Soviet Union (FSU), in contrast, seeks to improve workers' health as a way to increase economic productivity. The motivating thrust behind the former debate has been the lack of relation between increased health care costs and better health, while the latter debate was concerned with the interaction between a declining national domestic product and increasing morbidity and mortality rates. The more general question of viewing health, like education, to be guaranteed by government policy principally as a right, distinguishes the two issues at a more fundamental level. The American federal government has articulated a minimal philosophical commitment to individual health as an end in itself after the Medicare and Medicaid legislation (among the poor and elderly), while the FSU institutionalized a concern with health principally as a means (among industrial workers) for ensuring the goal of economic productivity.

Health Status

Medical research in industrialized countries, especially within the past two decades, shows an increase in the prevalence of chronic diseases. This is related to unhealthy social environments, ecology, and individual behaviors, as well as a lack of accessible medical services. Public health planning, in both the United States and the FSU, established programs that addressed the issues of individual lifestyle; environmental protection; and primary, secondary, and tertiary prevention. Primary prevention was understood by health care professionals as the care taken prior to the development of the disease process, measures such as health education, water fluoridation, and immunizations. Secondary prevention involved the diagnosis and detection of disease before symptoms appear, as by screening tests. Tertiary prevention concerned curative medicine that prevents the progression of disease by means such as surgery and medication. Poor individual health habits, such as alcohol consumption, smoking, overeating; environmental pollution; and sociopolitical aspects of the management of medical delivery systems, were related by Berkman and Breslow (1983) to poor health and by Thornberry, Wilson, and Golden (1985) to the development of specific preventive public health programs.

National health goals, such as increasing the effectiveness of the medical system in curtailing morbidity and mortality, were measured by macro population indicators of health. Changes in the health status of the Soviet population before Perestroika were shown by Schultz and Rafferty (1990) to undergo a marked deterioration: cardiovascular mortality rates increased by 50 percent since the 1960s, comprising half of all Soviet deaths in 1980. Life expectancy for men in 1980 declined to 62.2 years from 67 years in 1964 (Feshbach 1982b). Average number of annual deaths per 1000 males increased steadily from 8.9 in 1970–1971 to 9.7 in 1974–1975 to 11.1 in 1980–1981. The rate of increase was slightly less for women (Feshbach 1985b; Moscow Executive Committee 1991).

Soviet infant mortality increased to 27.3 in 1980 from 24.7 per 1000 live births in 1970. Infant deaths due to infectious diseases in the first year of life increased from 122 deaths per 100,000 births in 1970 to 360 per 100,000 births in 1980, and to 383 in 1986; or about 66 percent over 16 years (Moscow Executive Committee 1991, p. 33). The number of new cases of infectious diseases, such as acute poliomyelitis, pertussis, diphtheria, and measles, increased from a low in the mid-1960s to a new high in 1981–1982 (Feshbach 1985b, p. 83). Alcohol consumption accounted for 20 percent of all premature mortality in 1980 and for 30 percent of household budgetary expenditures in one-fourth of Russian, Ukrainian, and Byelorussian households (Schultz and Rafferty 1990).

The rate of chronic diseases in the FSU, including the number of cardiovascular deaths, suggested the pattern typical of industrialized societies (Ryan 1990; Feshbach 1982b). As in the U.S., the leading killer in Russia and the Baltic Republics was heart disease, highest among urban men and lowest among rural women. Mortality and morbidity rates for the FSU fell into two distinct patterns when divided by republic. A differential pattern of disease distribution was due to the disparate levels of socioeconomic development within and between the fifteen Republics.

The developing and industrializing Asian Republics had the greatest incidence of water- and air-borne infectious diseases. Susceptibility to disease was increased by lack of vaccinations, crowding, poor sanitation, inadequate nutrition, and exhausting working conditions. Acute infectious diseases, such as measles, diphtheria, scarlet fever, cholera, typhoid, tuberculosis, bronchitis, whooping cough, and smallpox were more prevalent than in the European republics (Ryan 1990; Goskomstat 1989). The Central Asian and Caucasian Republics exemplified the developing nation pattern of infectious diseases, while the Baltic Republics exhibited the pattern of urban, industrial society similar to the United States.

The longest life expectancy was found in Estonia, Latvia, Lithuania, Byelorussia, Ukraine, and Georgia, while the shortest was evident in Armenia, Turkestan, Kirgizia, Moldavia, Kazakhstan, and Russia (Goskomstat 1988). Russia also had the highest death rate from accidents, trauma, and violence between 1980–1987. In 1988, only Armenia reported a higher death rate from accidents and violence than Russia, probably due to the intensification of the armed conflict over Nagorno-Karabakh with Azerbaijan.

Developing areas, such as the Asian Republics, have higher birth rates and higher infant and maternal mortality rates (Ryan 1990; Moscow Executive Committee 1991). The converse is true in urbanized industrial centers, like the Slavic and Baltic Republics, where families are smaller and more isolated, but live longer and are exposed to a different set of health conditions, which cause cancer, cardiovascular disease, and atherosclerotic heart disease. The pattern of diseases shifts to chronic, noncommunicable disease, which are caused by social and psychological stressors such as crowding, poor housing, and environmental pollution, as well as lifestyle patterns of smoking, drinking, "fat-rich" diets, and lessened physical activity from the automation and mechanization of everyday life.

The international ranking of the Soviet Union on a number of health indicators, published by the USSR itself, slipped significantly after 1970 as compared to other nations, which were making steady improvements in infant, maternal, and disease-specific mortality rates (Vestnik Statistiki 1991). The health policy of the five-year plans from 1970 to 1985, before Perestroika, were formulated during the 24th, 25th, and 26th Communist Party Congresses, which addressed the changes in population health status not as consequences but as antecedents to a general economic slump.

Socialized Medicine

Recognizing that health policy was imbedded in the larger socioeconomic context, the debates around the Health Insurance Act, which began in the 1990s in the Russian Parliament, examined such factors as the centralization of sociopolitical institutions; the extensiveness of the decision-making role of government for individual lifestyles; the economic organization of competing insurance markets; and market distribution vs. government monopoly of medical goods and services. Several of the provisions of the Health Insurance Act of Russia attempted to revise the model of Soviet socialized medicine prevailing at the time of Perestroika.

This model of socialized medicine, established in the 1930s, was categorized by Davis (1988) for analytical simplicity into seven basic input components: (1) the central state health bureaucracy (overall control of the health production process through allocation of resources); (2) the medical care system (production of hospital and physician services); (3) the pharmacy system (distribution of medical goods); (4) the medical industry (production of medical goods); (5) biomedical research and development (production of medical knowledge and technology); (6) foreign trade organizations (distribution of foreign medical goods); (7) consumer behavior (production of household and individual health).

The centralized state bureaucracy acted as manager of medical care finances, employer and provider of hospital and physician services, producer and consumer of medical goods, and administrator of health planning and policy. The Soviet Ministry of Health made all health policy decisions for the individual consumer and the medical profession, as well as for the fifteen separate republics of the Soviet Union through republic ministries of health. Although Soviet socialized medicine has often been described as universally accessible, egalitarian, and monolithic, regional and local health policy was implemented by a myriad number of organizations. These were accountable to two sources: first, to the central administration and budget of the Ministry of Health, and second, to the local medical authorities, which functioned quasi-independently of the ministries of health.

Local health care organizations were responsible to the institution in which they were housed. Feshbach (1985a) and Davis (1987) described how medical care was delivered by facilities attached to specific institutions in the economic sector: industries; factories; government agencies such as the ministries of transportation, secondary education, defense, railroads, KGB (State Security); and department stores. Only employees of these institutions had access to the medical facilities, creating a multitier delivery system, with widely disparate levels of available medical services. Urban and rural teaching and nonteaching hospitals were open to the population residing within the geographic service area of the hospital. Quality of medical care and public access to medical goods and services varied greatly depending upon the location of the medical facility. Health care for the government and management elite resembled services routinely available in the West but was inaccessible, for example, to teachers, factory workers, or the general public.

Differential access and poor quality care resulted in an informal and illegal mechanism of private fee-for-service payments, given "under the table" as bribes, commonly known in Russia as "blat." Medical necessities, surgery, drugs, bandages, clean sheets, even food, often had to be bought by inpatients from hospital administrators, physicians, nurses, or orderlies. For those without the economic resources to purchase private medical care, the minimal prevailing level of government care had to suffice. This often meant being hospitalized for extensive observational periods without receiving any specific treatments because of an intermittent lack of equipment and adequately trained specialists. Shortages in intravenous fluids, sutures, antibiotics, vaccinations, and durable goods such as tape and bandages were endemic and even openly criticized in the press by the Communist Party Congresses (Brezhnev 1981; Feshbach 1982a, 1985a).

Although Soviet socialized medicine was based on systematic health planning, public administration, and financing, Robbins, Caper, and Rowland (1990) explain how the difficulties with providing universal coverage, comprehensive services, high-quality care, integrated treatment and prevention, and rational distribution of medical personnel remained as substantial problems for the Soviet state. Salaried government medical providers were accountable to professional bureaucrats, not patients. The Health Ministry had little control at the local level of monitoring such things as quality and physician-patient relationships. It also lacked the mechanisms or resources to impose sanctions. Many health providers were working under squalid conditions. Some were performing small daily miracles given available resources; others developed opportunistic practice patterns, shielded by equally culpable public administrators. Reassessments of the socialized model of medicine were undertaken by both the USSR and Russian Federation Ministries of Health only after Gorbachev's appointment as the first President of the USSR. Fiscal restructuring of the socialized health care system to promote a self-financing medical industry was the primary orientation of the new policy. Provider accountability, quality of care, and administrative efficiency were considered secondary issues at best.

PRE-PERESTROIKA HEALTH POLICY

Soviet health policy, prior to the advent of Perestroika in 1985, enumerated broad program goals based on economic exigencies. Lowering disease-specific mortality and morbidity rates were specified as goals in the Soviet five-year health plans of the 1970s and 1980s. Other principal goals included expansion of rural health services; expansion of preventive, genetic-counseling, and maternal-child services; improvement of sanitation, quality of medical care and education; increased availability, distribution, and production of pharmaceuticals and medicinal supplies; organization of specialty diagnostic centers accessible to the rural population at the republic and oblast levels. Soviet health policy research was dominated by an economic model that related health status primarily to the needs of a centralized economy (JPRS 1982).

Macro health measures such as mortality and morbidity rates were applied in the human capital model of health for assessing the social and economic costs of illness, disability, or death within Soviet society. This approach linked health and the production process, placing a monetary value on human life. The value of saving or increasing the quality of life was measured in direct and indirect costs to gross domestic income due to premature loss of human life and future earnings. The socialized state valued the individual based on the extent of individual contributions of labor to the state, which could be lost through illness or death. Cutting such losses and obtaining more accurate assessments of the need for, and provision of, curative and preventive health services were the fundamental goals of the five-year health plans. The model of human capital in health planning was not only widely used in the Soviet Union for prioritizing resource allocation in the health care system, but was also popular in the 1970s among health planners in the United States, Canada, and the United Kingdom (Black and Pole 1975; Mushkin and Dunlop 1979; Rice 1967).

Soviet health policy was limited in maximizing national economic output by demographic changes in the structure of the working population: there were twice as many pensioners in the Slavic and Baltic Republics of the 1980s as in the 1970s, but twice as many births in the Asian Republics of the 1980s as in the Slavic Republics of the 1970s (Feshbach 1982b). The health services required by the older Slavic population were determined by age-related disease patterns different from those prevalent among younger Asian populations: chronic disabling diseases such as heart disorders and cancer required primary preventive services and specialized tertiary preventive services, as well as custodial long-term care. The younger republics required maternal-child services and sanitation, vitamins and nutritional supplements, immunization and infectious-parasitic disease control, as well as adequate environmental protection from toxic pollutants and unpotable water.

The problem for Soviet decision-makers became even more apparent when almost two-thirds of all industrial output was centered in the Slavic Republics, where demographic projections indicated a population decrease of two million in 1981-1995 compared with 1971-1975. The rate of growth in the Slavic industrial labor force was reduced from an average of 0.9 percent per year during 1971-1985 to 0.5 percent per year in 1986-1990 (Feshbach 1978). The size of the available working-age population is projected to decline by one-fourth over the 1990s and into the next century. This labor shortage coincided with a decrease of 2.8 percent in productivity between 1971-1975 and 1976-1980 (Feshbach 1982b). There was a decline in Soviet fertility, which resulted in a national population growth of only 0.4 percent between 1980-1990, compared to the 1.8 percent growth in population during the 1960s. The skilled labor pool was further reduced by the general aging of the population and the rising mortality among males in the productive ages of 20-59 years. This pool, which increased by 30 million in the working-age population during the period 1970-1985, was projected to decrease by 6 million between 1985-2000 (Baldwin 1979).

The regional variation in fertility and mortality rates by republic also affected the skilled labor supply. Skilled workers were located primarily in the urbanized European republics, like the Russian Federation, which also had the lowest fertility rates (Brui 1991). Besides the size of available manpower, skilled labor depended on industry location, technical training, and education. Manpower, more abundant and youthful in the Asian Republics, was predominantly unskilled and part of the agricultural sector. The proportion of males in the population was less than the number of females, but more likely to comprise the skilled labor sector. Thus, an imbalance in the male:female ratio had important consequences for productivity. Male mortality rates were higher in the European Republics, as well as three-and-one-half times higher than female rates, compounding the projected scarcity of skilled labor. The growth rate of a workforce of 130 million was estimated to increase only 0.6 percent during 1990-2000, while a projected two million industrial jobs continued to remain unfilled (Feshbach 1982c; 1985b; Moscow Executive Committee 1991).

PERESTROIKA HEALTH POLICY

In 1985, more than one billion workdays were lost to illness, or about 3 percent of the daily workforce. The government expressed concern with the 0.7 percent increase, between 1986-1990, in workdays lost in the USSR as a whole, and 10-19 percent in Moldavia, Byelorussia, and Lithuania. The productively employed sector was further reduced by permanent disability, about 0.5 million in 1990, due to cardiovascular disease and cancer. The Baltics and Slavic Republics had the largest proportion of disabled workers in the Soviet Union, between 50-64 persons per 10,000 employed workers, compared to the national average of 47/10,000 employees. More than 60 percent of deaths were due to cardiovascular disease, accidents, homicides, and suicides; this percentage was three to six times greater among men than among women (*Vestnik Statistiki* 1991). Deaths due to chronic diseases, accidents, and violence increased between 1985-1990 in the Baltics and Slavic Republics, as did the number of deaths due to infectious and parasitic diseases in the Asian Republics.

Two other major health problems, which became more acute during Perestroika (and after the explosion of the nuclear plant at Chernobyl in 1986), were alcoholism and mental illness. It was acknowledged that one out of four cases of mental illness was due to mental retardation. Russia, the Ukraine, Lithuania, and Moldavia again reported the highest rates of mental illness (127–152/100,000 pop.) as compared to the union average (123/100,000). Moldavia reported 13 percent higher rates than the union average of 105 mentally ill/100,000 population; Lithuania—25 percent higher rates, and the Ukraine—31 percent (*Vestnik Statistiki* 1991). The rate of infectious diseases in the Soviet Union had increased dramatically, and the Asian Republics of Uzbekistan, Kyrgistan, and Turkmenistan were faced with the difficulty of controlling the spread of tuberculosis due to crowded housing, poor nutrition and sanitation, and lack of medications. Deaths from cancer between 1985–1990 increased significantly from 6–18 percent above the union average in the Ukraine, Kazakhstan, and Estonia, comprising between 22–33 percent of total morbidity.

Women's health issues received greater recognition during Perestroika, primarily because of declining fertility and population growth rates, projected to fall 75 percent below 1980 levels in 1995. The infant mortality rate had not significantly decreased during the 12th health plan, as compared to other industrial nations. New cases of congenital anomalies affected about 60,000 children every year and chronic diseases affected 20 percent of children younger than 15 years old. By the time children finished secondary education, the number with chronic diseases increased to 60 percent. Divorce and single-parent families affected about 20 percent of children, increasing their susceptibility to illness. Nosocomial infections (contracted as a result of being hospitalized) also increased during Perestroika. In 1990, more than 30,000 cases of septicemia were reported in hospitals among infants less than one month old, about 12,000 puerperal, and 27,000 postoperative infections. The greater flow of information during Perestroika permitted the official reporting of AIDS as a national concern. By July 1991, there were 1242 registered cases of HIV infections, half of which were children under 14 years of age (Vestnik Statistiki 1991).

For all the ideological bravado of Perestroika, health spending was not appreciably increased. In 1990, there were 28 percent fewer hospitals built and 15 percent fewer polyclinics than in 1989, even with an estimated shortage of 160,000 pediatric and 30,000 maternity beds. An evaluation of the progress made in 1991 of meeting the health goals of the 11th and 12th health plans indicated that 24 percent of polyclinics and hospitals did not have running water; 39 percent did not have toilets, and half lacked bathing facilities; 31 percent did not have central heating; 29 percent of polyclinics and 49 percent of hospitals lacked hot water. These conditions were exacerbated in small rural areas, affecting up to 80 percent of local facilities. In government polls, more than half the population expressed dissatisfaction with the inadequacies of the Soviet health care system, particularly with poorly trained medical staff, technological and pharmaceutical shortages, and the lack of basic sanitation and hygienic conditions (Brui, 1991).

The politically tumultuous period of Perestroika interfered with the implementation of several proposals: increasing GNP spending on health from 3.6 percent to 6 percent by the year 2000; increasing funding for medical equipment by 25 percent; construction of diagnostic clinics and over 1.4 million beds; and annual preventive health exams for children, veterans, pregnant women, and agricultural workers. The government encouraged fee-for-service polyclinics and physician-owned group practices by giving some tax breaks and permitting profits, to be retained as income, which were generated through private or group practice. In 1986, Moscow had 20 self-financing clinics which registered 2 percent of all outpatient visits out of an annual total of 126 million ambulatory visits. But, as Schultz and Rafferty (1990) point out, the enormous growth rate of cooperative clinics in 1988 was curtailed by state regulations concerning profits and types of services permitted. The government reasserted control, thus generating revenue for the state from the 74 percent of the population who paid for private medical services. As a result, an estimated 1350 clinics or 30 percent of cooperative clinics closed, pending the enactment of health reform legislation (Schultz and Rafferty 1990).

In regulating resource allocation and costs, policy during Perestroika followed previous health plans by altering input factors without adequately evaluating concomitant changes in health status as output. Optimization of health status was achieved by increasing the *volume* of services as the most important type of input to the delivery system. Improvements in medical services were specified as increases to the number of beds, number of visits per shift for outpatient polyclinics, number of rural outpatient clinics, number of physicians and midlevel personnel. The assumption that increases in the volume of medical services would improve general health status persisted during Perestroika.

Although the organizational impediments to preventive care were recognized as serious drawbacks to implementing health policy, no immediate recommendations were made until the provisions of the first Health Insurance Act in 1991. Health was viewed rhetorically as a social right at a basic if minimal level, but untested as the expected outcome of specific policies during Perestroika. The notion that the organization of medical care, financing mechanisms, and health policy had been threatening population health began to be generally accepted only after Perestroika, when the health reform debate finally culminated in the insurance legislation of the Russian Federation.

POST-PERESTROIKA HEALTH POLICY

The concern with establishing safety nets for resolving the social problems in Russia after the August Coup of 1991 speeded up the diffusion of Western social insurance mechanisms to Russia. Russia wanted to set up the administrative and legal structures to guarantee free market and democratic social relations. The Supreme Soviet adopted ideas for decentralized, self-financing medical care organization, but exercised caution regarding the importation of foreign health programs. The organizational form of provider-controlled, private insurance medicine has persisted over government-administered health programs in the United States, while Canada developed "single-payer" national health insurance and, in Great Britain, a national health service was maintained.

In their search for private medical care, Russian health reformers rejected the monolithic British health bureaucracy that gave government control over providers, financing, and public administrative decision-making. The Russian Federation combined the financing mechanisms of health alliances from the reform proposals of the Clinton Administration and the U.S. Congress with public administration techniques from the Canadian system. Russian legislative proposals addressed the necessity of separating the functions of providing, financing, and managing health care in the initial phase of privatizing the Soviet behemoth. Initial health reform sought to mix seedling private enterprise with state social insurance. The primary question for Russia centered on the extent to which public functions could be privatized.

Private insurance medicine was seen as a major cause of escalating costs. This form of medical financing also resulted in the growth of a huge industry in health technology, pharmaceuticals, surgical technology, and related ancillary services. Although often criticized for accumulating unprecedented profits, this business sector, according to Roemer and Roemer (1982), has contributed to a significantly higher quality of life for the general public over the past three-quarters of a century, and was almost completely lacking in the government medicine of the Former Soviet Union (Townsend, 1981). Stimulating a self-financing health care industry was a major factor in health sector privatization proposed by the first health insurance legislation of the Russian Federation.

A draft law was published in October, 1990, entitled "The Principles of Legislation of the USSR and Union Republics on the Financing of Health Care." The draft law permitted physicians and medical facilities to charge fees for services. The draft also established a minimum level of health services to be provided free by the government, with any additional services to be paid for by the patient. Financing was to be available from three sources: premiums paid by the government to a network of health care funds; tax-deductible premiums from employers; and voluntary purchase of insurance by individuals.

The deputies of the Supreme Soviet of the Russian Republic moved swiftly to propose their own version of insurance medicine. A planned transition to insurance medicine in Russia was based on the implementation of three basic principles: decentralization to the local level of all financing and administrative regulations; establishment of economically independent, self-financing medical facilities for preventive and curative care; and the formation of a more rational structure to the delivery of medical care. Ryan (1991) indicates that two regions in Russia, Kuibyshev and Kemerovo, began to apply these rudimentary principles in demonstration projects of insurance medicine in 1990.

A series of conferences with American and other international health care experts was organized in the Soviet Union. Medical technology and pharmaceutical trade exhibitions were sponsored in Russia by the U.S. Department of Commerce, and cross-cultural health systems analyses by GOSPLAN reformers were published in the American public health literature (Rowland and Telyukov 1991). Critiques from health economists (Chernichovsky 1992b) were actively sought from the World Bank. Russian deputies visited Japan and the United States to assess the experience of existing health care systems, and examined the health legislation of other developed nations in preparation for drafting a final bill. The political crisis in August 1991 established the national sovereignty of the Republics and accelerated the progress towards health reform.

The health care crisis facing Russia after the 1991 Coup was one of cost and access, as much as the sharp decline in population health status, quality of medical services, and availability of pharmaceuticals and health-related goods. Feshbach and Friendly (1992) state that the health plans and policy revisions enacted during Perestroika had little beneficial effect on the demographic and health trends from previous Soviet administrations. Russian physicians intensified a rolling strike in May 1992, protesting continued low wages, scarce supplies, and insufficient allocation of GNP resources to health care. In 1990 3.6 percent of the GNP in the FSU was allocated to health care, compared to 10.6 percent of the GNP in the U.S. in 1988, 12.4 percent in 1992, and an estimated 21 percent of the U.S. GNP by the end of the decade (Davis 1992). The life expectancy of Moscow residents in 1990 was ten years shorter than it had been in 1970. In 1989, the infant mortality rate was 22.3 infant deaths per thousand live births, compared with 10.1 for the U.S.; life expectancy for the Soviet Union was 69.8 years, compared with 75 years for the U.S. in 1987 (Rowland and Telyukov 1991; Mezentseva and Rimachevskaya 1990). The reformers of the Russian Federation set out to chart the direction of economic change by enacting health legislation.

1991 Health Insurance Act of Russia

The 1991 version of the Russian Health Insurance Act (HIA) initiated the transition from a universal, government-provided health service to private insurance. The Act was comprised of 28 articles specifying the legal, economic, and organizational basis of medical insurance for the Russian Federation (*Zakon* 1991). Article 1 defined the forms of medical insurance. Articles 2 to 5 defined the insured, the insurers, and the conditions of the agreement between them as the insurance policy. Articles 6 to 9 specified the rights and responsibilities of the insured and the insurers. Articles 10 to 13 concerned the sources of financing and structure of insurance funds. Articles 14 to 19 summarized the structure, rights, and responsibilities of insurance companies. Articles 20 and 21 outlined the rights, responsibilities, and licensing of medical care provider organizations. Finally, articles 22 to 28 defined the programs, contracts, tariffs, taxes, and regulations between the parties of the medical care system and government agencies.

As an initial step toward decentralization and privatization of government medicine, a network of health insurance agencies was authorized, similar to the Clinton Administration's proposal for market-based health alliances. A basic change in financing shifted direct tax revenues from centrally administered health care to individual- and employer-based insurance premiums for a private, profit-oriented delivery system. Such market incentives were provided to motivate the formation of competing insurance plans. Risks to the insurance plan were constrained by the type of benefits provided.

Insurance plans were divided into two categories: mandatory and voluntary. Mandatory insurance would be provided from two sources: through the workplace, such as the "play or pay" proposals or employer-based insurance as used in Hawaii; and directly through the government for those on pensions or unemployment. Voluntary insurance plans with supplemental benefits would be available to anyone at an additional out-of-pocket cost, similar to the indemnity and service-benefit plans of Blue Cross-Blue Shield. Indemnity plans, which also act as claims processors, reimburse directly to the consumer while service-benefit plans reimburse the provider. The burden of administrative control and the profitability of fiscal control was transferred from the Russian government to either the consumer of competing indemnity plans or the provider (hospital, third-party, physician) in service-benefit plans.

The HIA made health insurance compulsory for all employees. Mandatory insurance had to be provided by employers. Employees could not chose individual policies for themselves. Basic benefits included the right to choose medical facilities and physicians within health plan packages, and the right to seek redress for medical malpractice. This last provision was the primary mode of controlling the quality of medical care provided to consumers. Lack of professional accountability to the patient has been a major reason for patient dissatisfaction. Employers could choose among competing private health plans at different prices, much like the Health Insurance Purchasing Corporations considered by the Health Reform Task Force of the U.S. Senate Finance Committee. Although the choice of health plan was made by the employer, the Russian health care consumer was given greater access than going to the nearest polyclinic in their geographic medical district, where the medical staff was employed and accountable to the government.

Financing of the health care system with direct taxation to the central budget was replaced by local government budgets and premium payments to health care and insurance funds. Health care funds were to be publicly subsidized and administered by local government agencies and could receive credit from banks. The provision that permitted financing with bank credit, however, undermined the principle of developing a coherent, self-financing health market and a balanced health care budget, insofar as any budget deficit or deficit spending could be covered by government loans. The health care funds were responsible for financing professional medical education, biomedical research, catastrophic insurance, geographic redistribution of medical care for underserved populations, and public health programs in the case of epidemics or natural calamities. Insurance funds were financed exclusively through compulsory employer and voluntary individual insurance premiums for the payment of medical treatment. Health insurance premiums were tax deductible. Insurance funds had legal status as private corporations, differentiated from the government-financed health care funds. In the interests of decentralization, health care and insurance funds were restricted to an accounting role as claims processors that collected and disbursed funds, but could not give medical care directly.

Given the cumbersome bureaucratic heritage of socialized medicine that the insurance legislation was designed to replace, the drafters of the HIA acknowledged the difficulty and complexity of encouraging market forces, regionalization of services, decentralized decision-making, and individual choice and responsibility. A transitional redistribution of power between consumers, physicians, and insurance companies was therefore proposed. The HIA attempted to provide for a balance of power between vested interests by prohibiting insurance companies from functioning like HMOs or polyclinics, or from acting as health services providers. This ensured that the insurance companies acted as administrative intermediaries, and not as medical decision-makers, as is often the case in the United States.

Given the provisions of universal coverage in a basic benefits package of mandatory insurance, the medical professionals were empowered to run medical facilities and group practices based on consideration of health needs and quality rather than minimizing expenditures. The insurance companies could choose which medical providers and facilities would participate in their benefit plans, and shared responsibility for the legal accreditation of the facilities. The insurance companies could not refuse to provide the minimal levels of mandatory insurance, but were given the authority to offer many different benefit plans. The structure of insurance plans varied in the size of the insurance premiums and the domain, duration, and quality of medical services provided under specific benefits. Profits derived by insurance companies from the provision of mandatory insurance benefits were exempt from taxation. Medical facilities, physicians, and research centers had the right to own stock in health insurance ventures, thereby influencing company decisions through their private interests. Individual consumers, however, were at a disadvantage in developing a dominant interest in these ventures, which favored the control by health care providers.

The provisions of the HIA assumed that competition between financial packages offered by insurance plans and between different organizational forms of delivering medical care offered by private providers would contain the cost of premiums. Voluntary insurance rates were to be determined by costs and demand for medical programs in a fee-for-service insurance mechanism. The mandatory public rates were based on local health department budgets. Any regional deficits would be subsidized by the Council of Ministers of the Russian Federation. Competition between plans was assumed to provide the market incentives for the growth of a new health care industry. It was the hope of the Russian legislation that this revenue-generating industry would have an innovative impact upon the educational and scientific sectors in Russia, upon other depressed industries such as chemicals and plastics, as well as upon the overall quality of life and well-being of the work force.

The health care market is not one of self-regulated, unconstrained supply and demand between providers and consumers. There are costs to placing industry decision-making predominantly in the hands of the sellers or suppliers of goods and services. There are costs to constraining market relations by employers making health care decisions for consumers or the buyers. There are also unintended consequences of the HIA related to the development of uneconomical physician practice styles and increased expenditures for unnecessary services and defensive medicine, unrelated to health status outcomes.

Legislative mandates notwithstanding, progress in public health improves quality of life to a point partly dependent upon individual choice in taking health risks. The well-being and health of the public and private sectors converge in insurance rates that are based on risk assessment. Risks quantify the effects of various physical, social, occupational, and environmental hazards on mortality or life-expectancy. The costs of individual health habits (such as smoking) are distributed among the general public in the form of higher insurance premiums and more expensive medical care. Not only access to health care services, but the general quality of life, health habits, and lifestyle have been shown to affect the level of being at risk for a particular illness. Many diseases can be prevented by changing lifestyle patterns or health habits. The premium provisions of the 1991 Health Insurance Act of Russia attempted to grapple with these factors by linking health habits to premium costs, providing incentives for changing lifestyle patterns and preventive medical care.

Under the market incentives provided by the HIA, an insurance plan had the option of changing premiums based on the changing health needs of the patient after a three-year period. Although this prevented rejecting consumers based on preexisting conditions, it did permit dropping patients or increasing their premiums because they became high-risk clients. An inequitable scenario could arise, with government being forced to provide the premium subsidy for mandatory insurance if the employer chose not to bear the cost and dismissed the high-risk employee. The insured was obligated to eliminate voluntary risk factors that could adversely affect health status or, alternatively, pay higher premiums. The insurance company could reinvest its profits in commercial ventures that would enhance the public health sector, such as pharmaceutical companies. Although the issue of noncoverage of preexisting conditions was glossed over in the HIA, the emphasis on preventive health care and individual responsibility for health status had a financial justification. In the United States, for example, the Deputy Secretary of Health and Human Services Moley (1992) pointed out that, in 1991, one out of every six deaths and $65 billion in health care costs and lost productivity were related to cigarette smoking.

Despite the preventive health habits provisions, the HIA mechanisms did not encourage consumer well-being or market competition between providers as much as it fostered the expansion of the health care industry. The American experience of risk-based private insurance indicates that opportunistic behavior by Russian insurance plans to maintain high premiums would also be likely. This would constrain market competition by favoring an all too familiar private/government two-tier system that enrolled the economically and medically "healthy" in private plans and pushed the rest into less adequate public care.

1993 Health Insurance Act of Russia

Privatization of medical care was hindered in Russia by the lack of a legal framework to undergird the operation of market forces within the post-Coup Russian economy. Russia's struggle to join the international community of democratic nations has been a painfully slow process of transferring state-owned and operated industries, factories, and medical facilities over to private ownership. Before the HIA could be implemented, an insurance infrastructure had to be developed. The Insurance Law of the Russian Federation was published in late 1992, providing mechanisms for the general regulation of all insurance companies, including mandatory and voluntary health insurance. The World Bank provided assistance to the Russian Federation Interministerial Working Group on Health Insurance to reassess the appropriateness of the 1991 HIA, which was written and voted into law before the August Coup. Several revisions of the HIA dealing specifically with the functioning of the insurance funds were passed in quick succession by the Supreme Soviet of the Russian Federation (Potapchik 1993).

On December 25, 1992, a law was proclaimed "On Insurance Contributions to the Fund of Social Insurance of the Russian Federation, to the State Employment Fund, and to the Compulsory Health Insurance of Citizens for the First Quarter of 1993." The act provided for the concrete financing of health care funds by requiring employers to pay 3.6 percent of their payroll to a health insurance fund rather than the pension fund. The employers tax was similar to the 7.5 percent proposed by the Clinton Administration to be paid by American business towards purchasing employee health insurance (APHA 1993). On February 24, 1993, this legislation was followed by "The Law on the Amendments and Additions to the Health Insurance Legislation"; "The Enactment of the Supreme Soviet of the Russian Federation on the Procedure of Financing Compulsory Health Insurance of the Citizens in 1993"; and "The Enactment of the Supreme Soviet of the Russian Federation on the Procedure of Implementing 'The Law of the Russian Federation on the Amendments and Additions to the HIA'." These revisions were consolidated and signed into law by Yeltsin in April 1993, while he was attending the Vancouver Summit with President Clinton (Potapchik 1993).

The public health care funds of the 1991 HIA were redefined in 1993 as part of government social insurance, which provided compulsory health insurance, financed as a percentage of employee wages. The compulsory health insurance funds (CHI) were established as independent, nonprofit, noncommercial administrative agencies at the federal and local level. The CHI were subsidized by government funds to permit universal access and comprehensive coverage, and were the main mechanisms for implementing the Health Insurance Act. For those who were unemployed or who could not afford private insurance, the CHI would act as a direct insurer by paying the mandatory insurance premiums.

In removing mandatory insurance from the private market, the 1993 Health Insurance Act followed the Canadian model of guaranteeing universal access through public health insurance. In keeping an employer payroll tax as the primary financing mechanism rather than direct taxation, the 1993 HIA followed the American model. The benefits of economy of scale in group purchases of insurance rather than individual policies was built into the mandatory package. In creating CHI funds, the public administration of private employer premiums was to prevent escalation of claims processing and administrative overhead costs, curtailing but not eliminating the growth of private insurance companies. The breakup of the socialist health bureaucracy was accelerated with the separation of administrative and financing functions in the independent, nonprofit structure of CHI funds. The funds were also legislatively prevented from becoming giant providers of medical care, resembling Health Maintenance Organizations. The structure of the CHI funds removed the monitoring of accountability, quality, and cost from the self-regulating private sector, and defined it as function of public administration.

Seven interest groups were specified as part of the administrative boards of the CHI at the local level: consumers, trade unions, medical professionals, health insurance companies, the central bank, representatives from federal health funds, and legislators. The administrative boards had the responsibility for developing the regulatory norms for implementing the HIA; managing the claims processing data base on insurance premiums; providing payments to insurance companies; developing capitation rates for premiums; and providing incentives for medical facilities to operate more efficiently.

The 1993 revisions of the Health Insurance Act emphasized medical social security in guaranteeing universal access and a basic comprehensive benefits package in the compulsory insurance component, which was equally available to the employed, unemployed, and indigent through the CHI. The clause permitting a change in premiums if the health status of the insured changed within a three-year period was eliminated to protect against losing coverage from risk-based insurance. All risk-based insurance was removed from the mandatory package and relegated to the supplementary benefits available in voluntary insurance plans, thus establishing a private insurance sector.

The health funds were designed to function as fiscal intermediaries between consumers and providers, encouraging the growth of insurance companies and the gradual privatization of health care, thereby differentiating and restricting government activities. The health funds were designed to act as conduits for government subsidy of insurance premiums, purchased from insurance companies but insurance companies would be the direct fiscal agents to health care providers. Providers, rather than continue as salaried government workers, would be paid from premiums, which introduced performance incentives to medical practice. The exact mechanisms of the transition to private ownership of the health care delivery system were left ambiguous in the 1993 revision of the Health Insurance Act. The opportunity for providers and consumers to invest in medical group practices and insurance ventures, which could benefit from tax breaks and retain profits, however, opened the way for the growth of a profitable, commercial health industry.

SUMMARY

The 1993 Health Insurance Act constructs an array of incentives for the development of private ownership of a state-controlled health care system; it also assures that health care is a human right rather than a function of income and privilege. However, there are some persistent flaws in the health reform legislation. Consumer satisfaction, protection and elimination of the inequitable "parallel" health care system for elite bureaucrats have not been addressed by the HIA. Government health funds determine capitation levels for controlling the costs of mandatory insurance, while voluntary fee-for-service reimbursements, although costly, inequitable, and inefficient, encourage a competing plurality of providers, consumer choice, and satisfaction. Private suppliers of health care can still generate high incomes for themselves and escalate health care costs.

There is the danger that mandatory public insurance will lead to lesser care for the greater number, whereas voluntary private insurance will lead to luxury-level care for the smaller elite. The issue of consumer health education and unconstrained access to information on the operation of CHI funds needs to be specifically guaranteed by the legislation. However, the separation of government functions from being the sole agent to finance, administer, and provide health care will be an ongoing process, with Russia finding its own solution to the health care crisis.

Progress has been made by the Russian Federation in recognizing health as intrinsically valuable, not just a convenient ideological platform or instrumental component of government economic policy. It is easy to understand why Russia, in reacting to the Soviet legacy of socialized medicine, did not opt for either a national health service or national health insurance, administered by the state and financed wholly through income taxes. The health market is not a free market in any nation; everywhere it is a mix between the private and public sectors. Canada, Germany, Japan, France, and the United States have market-oriented health systems with varying degrees of government regulation and management. Great Britain has also considered introducing economic incentives into its limited profitable markets among the public hospitals and allowing private physicians to deliver medical care within the National Health Service. The enactment of the 1993 amendments to the Health Insurance Act of the Russian Federation thus introduces Russia to the health care debate, which is intensely preoccupying Western governments.

The mix between the public and private health sectors is converging among most industrialized democracies to include several common elements. Some form of public finance exists in all health systems to assure universal access to health care. Competition between groups purchasing health care, such as sickness funds or employers, rather than individuals, is intended to act as a cost-containment mechanism in health care. The differentiation of management and finance from the actual provision of health care exists to some degree in all efficient health systems. Keeping these functions separate prevents the concentration of financial and medical decision-making into supply-induced demand for health care, on the one hand, and profit-oriented rationing of medically necessary services on the other. A balance of power between management, finance, and providers also increases competition between sectors, assuring provider accountability, higher quality, and greater consumer access (choice), insofar as cost of basic services would not be directly regulated by the medical care provider.

The Russian Federation has incorporated several of these structural elements into the Health Insurance Act of 1993, trying to balance the issues of health care quality and equity for the public with the lack of private ownership of a self-financing medical industry. Several revisions of the Russian Health Insurance Act remain to be completed. Specific delineation of basic benefits, the services that are included in the mandatory package and those in the voluntary package, is still missing. It is also important to set out which prevention services, (immunizations, for example) will be available from the individual packages and which from the public health departments. The current provisions of the HIA do not address the issue of private ownership of hospitals, clinics, and other medical facilities. How exactly the changes in financing health care will accelerate the private ownership of health care facilities is left to subsequent amendments of the HIA. This issue, however, is of pivotal importance to dismantling the socialized system of medical care. The government centralization of management, finance, and provider functions not only did *not* guarantee universal access and comprehensive coverage, but it also created a corrupt fee-for-service delivery system for the privileged elite.

The health insurance crisis of the 1990s placed the problem of health reform legislation and preventive health policy on the agenda for nations everywhere. There has been a broad consensus concerning the health care crisis facing the United States, which, in turn, influenced the Russian Federation policymakers. Of particular concern are: large numbers of uninsured; unprecedented growth in profit margins for the insurance industry; decreased workplace mobility due to fear of changing jobs and losing medical benefits; and reduced government budgetary allocations for other important areas such as housing, transportation, and education. The United States spent, on a per capita basis, 43 percent more on health care than Canada and 131 percent more than Japan in 1992, but its population was no healthier. The lack of a direct relationship between health status and cost of medical services has remained a topic of sophisticated debate among American policymakers (Centers for Disease Control 1992c) and researchers (Vogt 1993; Young 1993).

The proposed Clinton Health Security Act argued for the right of each American to have access to health by eliminating risk-based insurance. The diffusion of health models from free market economies influenced Russian Federation reformers to modify the 1991 Health Insurance Act. They revised the mechanisms of financing health care, which included employer and risk-based insurance, to conform to a more balanced private-public mix of financing, which is universally accessible, publicly administered, and hopefully privately owned (in the future). The availability of health insurance was removed from being contingent upon employment. This provision thus allowed for more fluid occupational mobility and reduced the role of the employer in making medical decisions for employees.

There is, however, a noticeable lack of even a philosophical commitment in the legislation to emphasize primary care and preventive programs in either the public or private sector. Setting national priorities for health promotion and disease prevention requires attention to the following: reduction in smoking, drug, and alcohol abuse; improvements in nutrition and physical fitness; control of violence, stress, accidents, and traumatic injuries; water fluoridation and improvements in dental health; control of infectious diseases and increase in immunizations; preventive education about high blood pressure; increase in family planning and maternal and child health services; control of sexually transmitted diseases; monitoring occupational safety and health; and control of toxins and pollutants.

Health reform legislation needs to organize a uniform data collection system to track the progress towards the preventive goals outlined above. Balancing equity in health care as a human right with the efficient allocation of resources requires a monitoring system that focuses on evaluating health status as the most meaningful outcome of health programs (World Health Organization 1993). Planning, enacting, and implementing legislation are functionally as far apart as changing beliefs and changing behavior. The enactment of health reform legislation exemplifies which beliefs about the health care system need to be modified. The implementation of the legislation is the crucial link between changing such beliefs as the fundamental right to health into observable, measurable behavior, at both the individual and systemic levels (Vladeck 1993). The monitoring of health status indicators, as the gold standard for assessing the quality of health care outcomes, provides the rationale for legislative institutionalization of the set of beliefs underlying health reform. The HIA addressed beliefs concerning the need to: change the health output of Soviet socialized medicine; eliminate the inequities and corruption in an elitist practice of medicine; provide universal access to high-quality medical care with basic comprehensive health benefits; spur growth of medical research, technology, and pharmaceuticals; guarantee professional accountability to the individual patient; and increase the options available to consumers in making medical decisions or choices which affect their quality of life.

Russia needs to consider further avenues for implementing the goals of the 1993 amendments to the HIA, including provision for the private ownership of hospitals, clinics, and group practice. A commitment to the quality of health care requires modernizing the standards for health education and medical training. The specific provisions of the basic mandatory benefits package should be guaranteed and delineated by the legislation, as should the essential primary care and prevention programs. Administrative mechanisms need to be enumerated that prevent the centralization of decision-making at the level of federal and regional health funds. A quality assurance outcomes-based data system needs to be developed to monitor quality, patient satisfaction, provider practice patterns, and medical care effectiveness. The formula for determining capitation levels for local CHI funds from the federal budget, based on risk factors such as age, sex, health indicators, and other factors describing utilization and cost patterns, has been left to discretionary mechanisms. Further, it is unclear how primary care will be promoted in medically underserved populations.

The final issues that lawmakers ought to consider for evaluating the intended and unintended consequences of the amended HIA are: how much money for health will be allocated by the central budget to subsidize local CHI funds for administration and management instead of disease prevention and health promotion programs; what will be the health status impact, if any at all, of shifting payroll taxes from employee pensions to health insurance; and how can quality of care be assured along with equity in access. The factors that are likely to result in a higher quality of life being distributed more equitably in a community have traditionally been the responsibility of preventive public health programs rather than clinical medical intervention. Technologically sophisticated medical treatment, even if provided in a wealthy nation with a universally accessible comprehensive health plan, will be impotent to resolve the inequities of health status without promoting public education.

Russia's first step in privatizing the health care sector has necessitated a high-wire balancing act of encouraging private delivery with public financing in order to maintain health as a universal human right. The Soviet socialist model of medical care had extolled the virtues of free health services at the beginning of the twentieth century, only to converge with Western industrial democracies as the century draws to a close.

REFERENCES

American Journal of Public Health Editors. 1993. "APHA Rates Major Planks in White House Health Plan." *The Nation's Health.* 10:1-20.

BALDWIN, GODFREY. 1979. "Population Projections by Age and Sex for the Republics by Major Economic Regions of the USSR, 1970 to 2000." *International Population Reports.* Series P-91, No. 26. Washington, D.C.: Bureau of the Census.

BERKMAN, LISA, and LESTER BRESLOW. 1983. *Health and Ways of Living: The Alameda County Study.* New York: Oxford University Press.

BLACK, D. A. K., and J. D. POLE. 1975. "Priorities in Biomedical Research: Indices of Burden." *British Journal of Preventive Social Medicine* 29:222-27.

BREZHNEV, LEONID I. 1981. "Rech Tovarischa L. I. Brezhneva nam Plenume TsK KPSS 16 Noyabrya 1981 goda." *Partiinaya Zhizn* 23:6.

BRUI, E. MIKHAILOV. 1991. "Nekotoriye Osobennosti Demograficheskoi Obstannovki v RSFSR." *Vestnik Statistiki* 7:17-24.

Centers for Disease Control. 1992a. "Public Health Assessment—Russian Federation." *MMWR.* 41:89-91.

———. 1992b. "Nutritional Needs Surveys Among the Elderly—Russia and Armenia." *MMWR.* 41:809-11.

———. 1992c. *Health, United States, 1991 and The Prevention Profile.* #340867 P.O. 337 [MRDF] U.S. Department of Health and Human Services, Public Health Service, Washington, D.C. [distributor].

CHERNICHOVSKY, DOV. 1992a. "Health Systems Reforms in Industrialized Democracies: An Emerging Paradigm." Prepared for the World Bank Human Resources Unit, Country Dept. III. Washington, D.C. Unpublished manuscript.

———. 1992b. "A Right to Health Insurance Versus A Right to Health Care: A Critique and Amendment Proposals—The Health Insurance Law of the Russian Federation." Prepared for the World Bank Human Resources Unit, Country Dept. III. Washington, D.C. Unpublished manuscript.

DAVIS, CHRISTOPHER MARK. 1987. "Developments in the Health Sector of the Soviet Economy, 1970-1990." Pp. 312-35 in Joint Economic Committee of the Congress of the United States. *Gorbachev's Economic Plans, Volume 2.* Washington, D.C.: U.S. Government Printing Office.

———. 1988. "The Organization and Performance of the Contemporary Soviet Health Service." Pp. 95-142 in *State and Welfare USA/USSR: Contemporary Policy and Practice,* edited by Gail W. Lapidus and G. E. Swanson. Berkeley, CA: University of California, Institute of International Studies.

DAVIS, KAREN. 1992 May 6. "Comprehensive Health Care Reform." Testimony before the U.S. Senate Committee on Finance, Washington, D.C. Unpublished manuscript, p. 5.

ELDER, JOHN W. 1976. "Comparative Cross-National Methodology." *Annual Review of Sociology* 2:209-29.

FESHBACH, MURRAY. 1978. "Employment Trends and Policies in the USSR." *Il Politico* 43:650-81.

———. 1982a. "Issues in Soviet Health Problems." Pp. 203-27 in Joint Economic Committee of the Congress of the United States. *Soviet Economy in the 1980's: Problems and Prospects, Part 2.* Washington, D.C.: U.S. Government Printing Office.

———. 1982b. "The Soviet Union: Population Trends and Dilemmas," *Population Bulletin* 37:1-44.

———. 1982c. "Between the Lines of the 1979 Soviet Census." *Population and Development Report* 8:350-60.

———. 1985a. "Health in the USSR—Organization, Trends, and Ethics." Paper presented July 23-26 for the International Colloquium on Health Care Systems. Moral Issues and Public Policy. Bad Homburg, West Germany.

———. 1985b. "A Compendium of Soviet Health Statistics." CIR Staff Paper No. 5, p. 60. Center for International Research. Bureau of the Census. U.S. Department of Commerce. Washington, D.C.

FESHBACH, MURRAY, and ALFRED FRIENDLY, JR. 1992. *Ecocide in the USSR.* New York: Basic Books.

GOSKOMSTAT. 1988. *Zdravoohraneniye v SSSR.* Moskva: Ministerstvo Zdravookhraneniya SSSR.

GOSKOMSTAT RSFSR. 1991. *City of Moscow Statistical Bulletin.* Moskva: Mosgorstat.

GOSKOMSTAT SSSR. 1989. *Naseleniye SSSR 1988: Statisticheskii Ezhegodnik.* Moskva: Statistika.

Joint Publications Research Service (JPRS). 1982 August 26. "Resolution on Improving Health Care in the USSR." No. 82311 (November 24): 34-39.

KOHN, MELVIN L. 1987. "Cross-National Research as an Analytic Strategy." *American Sociological Review* 52:713-31.

MEZENTSEVA, ELENA, and NATALIA RIMACHEVSKAYA. 1990. "The Soviet Country Profile: Health of the USSR Population in the 70s and 80s—An Approach to a Comprehensive Analysis." *Social Science and Medicine* 31:869-73.

MOLEY, KEVIN. 1992 May 7. "Statement by the Deputy Secretary of Health and Human Services." Testimony before the U.S. Senate Committee on Finance. Washington, D.C. Unpublished manuscript.

Moscow Executive Committee. City Soviet of the Peoples Deputies. 1991 March 21. *Average Moscow Basic Indicators of the State of All Preventive and Curative Organizations of the Mai Medical Directorate of Mosgorispolkom.* Main Directorate of Public Health. Bureau of Medical Statistics. Moskva: Municipal Executive Committee. Pp. 31–38.

MUSHKIN, SELMA, and DAVID DUNLOP. 1979. *Health: What Is It Worth? Measures of Health Benefits.* New York: Pergamon Press.

New York Times. 1992 April 16. Sec. A1, A8:1, 8.

POTAPCHIK, ELENA. 1993 May 31. "Recent Legislation in the Russian Health Sector Finance and Its Correspondence to the Recommendation of the Working Group on Health Insurance." The World Bank Moscow Office: Washington, D.C. Unpublished manuscript.

RICE, DOROTHY. 1967. "Estimating the Cost of Illness." *American Journal of Public Health* 57:1954–56.

ROBBINS, ANTHONY, PHILIP CAPER, and DIANE ROWLAND. 1990. "Financing Medical Care in the New Soviet Economy." *Journal of the American Medical Association* 264:1097–98.

ROEMER, MILTON I., and JOHN E. ROEMER. 1982. "The Social Consequences of Free Trade in Health Care: A Public Health Response to Orthodox Economics." *International Journal of Health Services* 12:111–29.

ROWLAND, DIANE, and ALEXANDRE V. TELYUKOV. 1991. "Soviet Health Care from Two Perspectives." *Health Affairs* 3:71–86.

RYAN, MICHAEL. 1990. *Contemporary Soviet Society: A Statistical Handbook.* Hants, England: Edward Elgar Publ. Ltd.

———. 1991. "Health Care Insurance in the Soviet Union." *British Medical Journal* 302–303.

SCHULTZ, DANIEL S., and MICHAEL P. RAFFERTY. 1990. "Soviet Health Care and Perestroika." *American Journal of Public Health* 80:193–97.

SUSSER, MERVYN. 1993. "Health as a Human Right: An Epidemiologist's Perspective on the Public Health." *American Journal of Public Health* 83:418–26.

THORNBERRY, OTIS T., RONALD W. WILSON, and PAUL GOLDEN. 1985. "Health Promotion Data for the 1990 Objectives." *Advance Data From Vital and Health Statistics.* DHHS-PHS 86-1250(126). Washington, D.C.: U.S. Government Printing Office.

TOWNSEND, PETER. 1981. "Toward Equality in Health Through Social Policy." *International Journal of Health Services* 11:63–75.

Vestnik Statistiki Editors. 1991. "Meditsinskoye Obsluzhivaniye Naselenia." *Vestnik Statistiki* 11:57–61 (in Russian).

VLADECK, BRUCE. 1993. "Editorial: Beliefs vs. Behaviors in Healthcare Decision Making." *American Journal of Public Health* 83:13–14.

VOGT, THOMAS. 1993. "Paradigms and Prevention." *American Journal of Public Health* 83:795–96.

White House Domestic Policy Council. 1993. *Health Security: The President's Report to the American People.* New York: Times Books.

World Bank. 1993. *World Development Report 1993: Investing in Health.* New York: Oxford University Press.

World Health Organization Non-Communicable Disease Collaborating Centers and Key Officials. 1993. "Needed: Universal Monitoring of All Serious Diseases of Global Importance." *American Journal of Public Health* 83:941–43.

YOUNG, QUENTIN D. 1993. "Health Care Reform: A New Public Health Movement." *American Journal of Public Health* 83:945–46.

Zakon Rossiiskoi Sovetskoi Federativnoi Respubliki o Meditsinskom Strakhovania Grazhdan v RSFSR. 1991 June 28. Moscow: No. 1499-1 (in Russian).

CHAPTER 12

Migrants, Refugees, and Health: Some Policy Implications of Israel's Experience

Judith T. Shuval

Large-scale movement of populations, within and across political boundaries, is a prominent characteristic of societies in many parts of the contemporary world. It is expected that migratory pressures will increase in the coming decades as a result of economic imbalances, population pressures, political unrest, wars, ethnic conflict, and globalization of multinational enterprises. Together these will bring about a convergence of refugee- and economically motivated patterns of migration. An assessment by Appleyard (1991) of the dimensions of all categories of migration in the early 1990s indicates that: as many as 70 million persons, largely from developing countries, are working, legally or illegally, outside their nation of citizenship; over one million emigrate permanently each year to other countries; about a million seek asylum outside their country of birth; and over twelve million refugees live outside their homelands (Appleyard 1991; United Nations Development Programme 1991; Widgren 1990).

The traditional receiving countries—the United States, Canada, Australia, and Israel—continue to draw substantial numbers of permanent immigrants, which include unskilled as well as highly skilled and professional workers. Western Europe attracts increasing numbers of asylum seekers and displaced ethnic groups seeking to resettle in their original countries or elsewhere. In almost all cases these individuals tend to stay permanently in the country of asylum. In addition, illegal immigration is well established and increasing in all parts of the world: in Europe alone there will be an estimated three million illegals by the year 2000. The globalization of multinational enterprises has greatly increased the flow of contract-labor migration between countries at different stages of modernization. There are at least fifteen million refugees and twelve million displaced persons who live within the borders of their countries of origin (Appleyard 1991).

Over the past fifty years, Israel has faced many of the problems currently confronted by other immigrant-receiving countries. Immigration has been an ongoing process in Israel during its entire history, including the period predating independence in 1948. The centrality of immigration has affected not only the demographic structure but core elements of Israel's social, economic, and cultural life, many of which have important implications for health and health care on the individual and group level. The most recent groups of immigrants have come from the former Soviet Union (about 450,000 between 1989–1993) and Ethiopia (14,000 in 1991).

It is the purpose of this chapter to focus on Israel's experience with regard to health and health care of immigrants, noting both accomplishments and failures in an effort to formulate some generalizations on the policy level that may be relevant in other societies.

HISTORIC AND THEORETICAL PERSPECTIVES

A two-way process of mutual interaction and influence takes place between immigrants and hosts in all societies characterized by immigration. Immigrants bring with them resources, needs, and problems; the host society is characterized by its own array of resources, priorities, and problems. Processes of change and adaptation take place among the immigrants but no less among individuals and groups in the host society. When, as in the case of Israel, the proportional number of immigrants is particularly large, their impact on the host society is considerable.

On a theoretical level, a non-Marxist conflict perspective is useful in considering these processes. Thus society may be viewed as composed of unequal interest groups competing for scarce resources among which power is one of the most compelling rewards. From this perspective, the health care system may be viewed as a mechanism of social and political control on the macro as well as on the micro level (Collins 1975; Scambler 1987).

Historic and culturally determined circumstances help explain the location of various groups in relation to the centers of power and influence in a society. Inevitably, representatives of the host society occupy positions of greater influence and power relative to the immigrants at the time of the latter's arrival. Over time, this may change but much of the ongoing process focuses on efforts of entrenched groups to retain their positions by limiting or blocking the encroachment of immigrants and by presenting their own values and norms as "correct" and appropriate for newcomers. These efforts are legitimized by ideologies and mythologies that seek to provide authority and legitimacy.

One of the first legislative acts passed by the Knesset, Israel's parliament, after the declaration of independence in 1948 was the Law of Return, which stated that every Jew has the right to immigrate and settle in Israel. Pragmatic considerations of economic need, job availability, or health status have not served as criteria for admission as is the case in most other countries. The open-door policy continues to represent one of the cardinal values of Israeli society, which has always accorded it high priority and has allocated major resources to the absorption process. Table 1 shows the numbers of migrants that have entered the society since independence, as well as the continents of origin, each of which includes an extensive array of culturally diverse groups. The cultural heterogeneity of the countries of origin of immigrants to Israel has resulted in a special variety of ethnic pluralism that has repercussions in many areas, not least with regard to health and health care (Shuval 1989, 1992b).

Among the more tenacious cultural traditions that have persisted among immigrant groups from different countries of origin are many that are relevant to health. These include food preferences, patterns of nutrition, response to and expressiveness with regard to pain, traditions of infant and child care, personal health behavior, reliance on traditional and home remedies, patterns of solidarity, and social support among family members, levels of dependency, occupational and gender roles, and others. Differential use of contraceptives and family planning is associated with religious orthodoxy and level of education but also with ethnic origin. Health educators who have sought to change patterns that are viewed by them as unhealthful, have frequently met with resistance and mixed success—largely because some of the patterns are rooted in meaningful traditional cultural contexts that remain viable even in the host society.

TABLE 1.   IMMIGRANTS TO ISRAEL BY CONTINENT OF ORIGIN 1948*-1991 (THOUSANDS)

	TOTAL	ASIA	AFRICA	EUROPE	AMERICA	NOT KNOWN	PERCENT OF TOTAL FROM ASIA/ AFRICA
1948*-91	2,209	360	453	1,183	181	31	37.4
1948*-51	686	237	93	326	5	23	49.9
1952-54	54	13	27	9	2	—	76.4
1955-57	164	8	103	48	3	—	68.3
1958-60	75	13	13	44	3	—	36.0
1961-64	228	19	115	77	14	—	59.4
1965-68	81	15	25	31	9	—	49.7
1969-71	116	19	12	50	33	—	27.3
1972-74	142	6	6	102	26	—	9.2
1975-79	124	11	6	77	29	—	14.3
1980-84	83	6	15	35	25	—	27.1
1985-89	70	6	7	36	19	—	20.4
1990-91	375	1	24	341	7	—	7.0

*15 May, 1948

Source: *Statistical Abstract of Israel*, 1992, pp. 170-71.

Following Israel's independence, during the period of mass immigration, the official ideology of the society proposed a "melting pot" approach, by means of which it was believed that an integrated new society would be created. This policy was expressed by overt denigration of some modes of behavior imported by immigrants as well as efforts to change behavior and attitudes that were seen as inappropriate, or "primitive," in order to bring about conformity to what was defined by those in positions of power as appropriate. Among these behavior and attitude patterns were many relating directly and indirectly to health. The aftermath of resentment generated by this approach, especially among those of Asian-African origin, is still to be seen, after forty years, among the children and grandchildren of some of the early immigrants.

Over the years, this policy has been modified as those in decision-making roles became aware of the dysfunctional effects of the early approach. Nevertheless, residual strands of the earlier ideology and practices remain. They tend to reemerge when large groups of immigrants arrive from underdeveloped parts of the world: the Ethiopian Jews are the most recent example.

MIGRATION AND STRESS

Immigrants are faced with major changes in their lives brought about by leaving one society and entering another. The extent of such change depends on the social and cultural "distance" of immigrants' countries of origin from the host, and on the presence in the host society of earlier arrivals from the countries of origin. When there are enclaves providing a familiar setting and social support, the stress of change may be partly alleviated. But inevitably the changes induced by migration pose stressors requiring the utilization of effective coping resources. Individuals and groups differ in the resources at their disposal and in their coping skills. In some cases, coping resources and mechanisms that were effective in the countries of origin are also effective in the new society; in other cases, such resources are absent, reduced, or less effective in the new society. The transformation of prior coping mechanisms to meet new needs or the development of alternative ones geared to address unfamiliar situations takes time and skill. It may therefore be assumed that many immigrants are under stress for varying periods of time (Antonovsky 1979; Shuval 1992a).

Certain subgroups among immigrants are at relatively high risk. These include persons migrating as individuals (not part of a family or group), mentally handicapped, elderly, families in which there are intrafamilial problems, one-parent families, and large families.

In Israel, many first- and second-generation Holocaust survivors carry scars of trauma and persecution for indefinite periods of time. Immigrants from a large number of societies—most recently Ethiopia and the former Soviet Union—cannot quickly slough off the impact of their earlier experiences, the effects of which may only become evident at a much later date. Among such persons, earlier traumatic experiences have weakened their coping skills and the ensuing stress makes them more vulnerable than others to local diseases and new stressors. For example: there is some evidence that the traumatic impact of the Gulf War was greater on Holocaust survivors than on others, despite the fact that many years had passed since World War II (Hantman, Solomon, and Prager 1992; Shuval 1992b).

Israeli society is characterized by important stress-mitigating factors. The very fact that immigration is widely accepted as normative and immigrants comprise such a large proportion of the population, serves to normalize the phenomenon and reduce the feeling of newcomers that they are "outsiders" or "strangers." Informal social support is widespread, especially since many recent arrivals have family members who arrived earlier: these often serve as informants and personal facilitators who assist in dealing with the formidable bureaucracies that provide formal support facilities (Horowitz 1989). It is of interest that, among recent immigrants from the former Soviet Union, the immediate demoralizing effects of the Gulf War passed fairly quickly, apparently because of the sense of belonging and commonality shared with other Israelis and the widespread social support given to immigrants. Despite some indications of change in recent years, family solidarity remains relatively strong in Israeli society (Lerner 1992; Shuval 1992).

The effects of stress are not easily documented nor are they confined to the immigrant population. In Israel the high utilization rates of the primary care system, smoking, and the high motor accident rates have been viewed, at least partially, as behavioral expressions of stress. Recent growth in consumption of alcohol and drugs, violence, and deviant behavior among young people may be viewed as further evidence of long-term effects. While a variety of other factors—poverty, marginality, relative deprivation—play a role in determining these patterns, the need to cope with the many problems and pressures induced by migration provides an underlying background.

For some immigrants, Israel presents stressors in the form of changes in climate and food patterns. On the whole, adjustment to such change is relatively rapid, although the elderly often find the process difficult. Immigrants may be susceptible to endemic diseases and health problems to which long-term residents and native-born persons develop a natural immunity.

MIGRATION AND HEALTH STATUS

As physical fitness has not been a criterion for admission to Israel, the number of immigrants requiring health care has varied over the past fifty years, depending on the countries of origin and the age distribution of the immigrants at various periods. Incipient health problems often take years to show themselves.

A variety of diseases, both chronic and infectious, have been imported into Israel at various times. In some cases, these have required massive intervention by the health authorities. In the long run, as in other countries where migration has taken place, there tends to be a secular pattern of convergence over time toward morbidity patterns characterizing the indigenous population (Kliewer 1991).

The extent of importation of chronic diseases is determined in major part by the age of immigrants and by the quality of health care in the countries of origin. High proportions of older immigrants result in a high frequency of chronic diseases and an increased burden on the local health care system. When treatment facilities in the countries of origin were deficient, as in the case of the former Soviet Union, immigrants were found to bring with them a variety of health problems that were inadequately treated for prolonged periods before they left (Field 1990; Garbe and Garbe 1990; Rowland and Telyukov 1991).

Styles of life and environmental conditions in the countries of origin play a role in the health status of immigrants, thereby creating problems that may not be evident at the time immigrants arrive. For example: The former Soviet Union was characterized by a high frequency of smoking, alcoholism, drug abuse, poor dietary practices, inadequate attention to physical fitness, and poor living conditions. Some immigrants to Israel were exposed to the Chernobyl atomic disaster. Widespread use of abortion and ignorance of other means of birth control pose a health problem for immigrants from the Soviet Union until they become acquainted with alternative methods. The latter problem is especially serious among women from the Caucasus and other Asian parts of the former USSR (Ben-Barak 1988; Remennick 1991, 1993). Drug use among young immigrants to Israel from Western Europe and the United States has played a role in introducing these health problems to Israel.

Over the years a variety of infectious diseases have been brought into Israel by immigrants. During the early 1950s, living conditions in the transit camps were conducive to the spread of disease because of crowding and poor sanitary facilities. Holocaust survivors from Displaced Persons camps in Europe brought body lice, which transmit epidemic typhus fever. In the same period, immigrants from Yemen brought tuberculosis, trachoma, bilharzia, and malaria; those from Cochin in India imported filariasis; from Iraq, bilharzia and schistosomiasis. During this period, many immigrants suffered from undernourishment and brought health habits that tended to facilitate the spread of contagious diseases. Most of the contagious diseases were controlled through active intervention by the health authorities. On the whole, Israel has low rates of most infectious diseases (Grushka, 1968; Shuval 1992b).

The most recent importation of infectious diseases has been by immigrants from Ethiopia. The Ethiopian Jews are similar in many ways to other groups that have migrated from a Third-World setting to a Western country. Most originated in small rural villages where they worked as farmers or as artisans. Since life expectancy in Ethiopia is low, the arriving immigrants were young; many of the older, would-be immigrants did not survive the extreme hardships en route to Israel. Traditional healers and health practices were widespread in the Ethiopian villages from which the immigrants came, in both the Jewish and non-Jewish sectors (Berger, Schwartz, and Michaeli 1989; Hershko et al. 1986; *Israel Journal of Medical Sciences* 1991).

A number of contagious diseases are endemic in Ethiopia, where poor sanitary conditions as well as contaminated water and food are widespread. Upon arrival in Israel, immigrants were found to have relatively high rates of tuberculosis, syphilis, and viral hepatitis, type B. There has been a high prevalence—over 80 percent—of intestinal parasites. Twenty-five percent of the immigrants carried malaria parasites. Two percent of the Ethiopian immigrants who arrived in 1991 are HIV positive, about fifty times the overall rate in Israel. Central Africa has one of the highest rates of this disease in the world and there was little knowledge among the Ethiopian immigrants about the use of condoms.

Chronic disease is not common in Ethiopia because life expectancy is low. Among the immigrants, however, there is a relatively high prevalence of genetic diseases as a result of frequent intermarriage among kin. It has been found that immigrants are characterized by low blood sugar levels and genetically inadequate regulation of insulin level. This could cause heightening of blood sugar levels among them and eventual development of relatively high rates of diabetes.

Upon arrival in Israel, cholesterol levels are low among Ethiopian immigrants. Their diet before immigration consisted principally of beans, vegetables, corn bread, and little meat. In Israel, their diet tends to change and to include increased consumption of rich foods that are associated with higher blood pressure and increased heart disease. There is some evidence for an increase in dental caries as a result of consumption of sweets. More exposure to cigarettes, alcohol, drugs, and tranquilizers is likely to result in an increase in health problems that are endemic in Western societies.

Observers have noted that overly high expectations with regard to the effectiveness of modern Western medicine have resulted in some disillusionment in the face of actual experience. Local health care practitioners have in some cases been uninformed about the customs and practices of the Ethiopian immigrants and intolerant of their slow or incomplete acceptance of recommended health practices. Traditional healers have in some cases drawn patients from dissatisfied users of the official health care services.* Since immigrants and healers are aware that traditional health care does not conform to ongoing norms of the society, it is difficult to estimate the number of such practitioners or the extent to which they are utilized.

With regard to the mental health of immigrants, studies of psychological well-being among recently arrived immigrants from the former Soviet Union show them to be characterized by more symptoms of anxiety, depression, and somatization than a comparable sample of veteran Israelis. The immigrants to Israel showed more positive scores regarding somatization on the above symptoms than a comparable group of immigrants to the United States, even though the latter reported a greater improvement in their standard of living than the Israeli immigrants (Flaherty, Kohn, Levav, and Birth 1988; Lerner, Mirsky, and Barasch 1992). There is as yet no evidence with regard to long-term patterns.

There is no evidence that severe psychopathology such as schizophrenia is higher among immigrants than in the veteran population; however, the stress of migration apparently causes a higher rate of admissions to psychiatric hospitals. In 1990-91 the admission rate of immigrants was 35 percent higher than in the general population (3.5/1,000 and 2.5/1,000 respectively), and a prolonged inpatient stay of over one year was 50 percent more likely. Among the immigrants, 20.6 percent of those admitted were suffering from depression as compared to 13.4 percent of the veteran population (Popper and Horowitz 1992).

During immigrants' initial period in a new society, their help-seeking behav-

---

* Cf. Greenburg's chapter in this volume.

ior for health problems generally reflects patterns internalized before immigration. Thus it has been found that immigrants from the former Soviet Union tend to somaticize their complaints and prefer to turn to a primary care physician rather than to a mental health clinic, a pattern which can cause delay in appropriate mental health care (Kohn, Flaherty, and Levav 1989; Lerner, Mirsky, and Barasch 1992).

THE IMPACT OF MIGRATION ON THE QUANTITY AND QUALITY OF HEALTH CARE PERSONNEL

Over the years, immigrant physicians and other health care personnel have regularly augmented the population of Israeli-trained health care personnel. The open-door policy has meant that the number of immigrants in these occupations has been unplanned and has been a function of circumstances extraneous to needs of Israeli society. This has resulted in one of the highest ratios of physicians to population in the world: 292/100,000 (Anderson and Antebi 1991; Rosen 1987). Table 2 shows the ratios of several types of health personnel to population in Israel during the late 1980s, before the arrival of 400,000 immigrants from the former Soviet Union. With the exception of nurses, the ratios are high in comparison to the European average.

Beginning in 1989, a large wave of immigration from the former Soviet Union brought unprecedented numbers of health care personnel to Israel. By 1994, over 12,000 physicians had arrived from the former Soviet Union, thereby increasing the population of doctors by close to 100 percent and posing severe problems with regard to their professional employment. Dentists, nurses, and paraprofessionals also came in large numbers. (See Table 3.)

Dovetailing to the ideological commitment to an open-door policy for Jewish immigrants has been the commitment to provide them with employment. Indeed, until the late 1980s, general unemployment in Israel was kept relatively low. In 1992, however, it rose to 11.1 percent and was recognized to have assumed disturbing political and economic proportions.

Until the 1990s, 95 percent of all immigrant physicians were employed in

TABLE 2.   HEALTH PERSONNEL IN ISRAEL AND IN SELECTED EUROPEAN COUNTRIES* IN THE 1980S**

HEALTH PERSONNEL PER 100,000 POPULATION	ISRAEL	DENMARK*	IRELAND*	EUROPEAN AVERAGE
Physicians	292	237	148	278
Dentists	67	63	32	41
Pharmacists	61	29	57	43
Nurses (RN)	357	610	726	392

*Denmark and Ireland were chosen for comparison because they are comparable to Israel in size, while Denmark has a relatively high GNP and Ireland has a relatively low GNP. Data are not always from the identical time period but all are from the 1980s.

**Before the large immigration from the former Soviet Union.

Sources: Israel Ministry of Health, 1990; Rosen, 1987; World Health Organization, 1986.

TABLE 3.   IMMIGRATION OF HEALTH PERSONNEL FROM THE FORMER SOVIET UNION TO ISRAEL, 1989–1993*

YEAR	TOTAL IMMIGRANTS	PHYSICIANS AND DENTISTS	NURSES AND OTHER PARAPROFESSIONALS
1989	12,898	508	350
1990	184,429	5,820	4,013
1991	147,117	3,350	3,460
1992	64,648	1,430	1,580
1993	41,126	800	1,060
TOTAL	450,218	11,928	10,463

Source: Israel Ministry of Absorption, which does not publish separate information regarding physicians and dentists. The Israel Ministry of Health estimates that about 90 percent of the combined category are physicians.
*Data for the first eight months of 1993.

their profession in the health care system, although in most cases not in their area of medical specialization (Ofer, Flug, and Kasir 1991). This allocative process was functional in controlling potential conflict in the society by keeping unemployment among immigrant physicians to a minimum.

Maximum employment of physicians was facilitated by the structure of the licensure process. Until 1987, that procedure was flexible with regard to licensure for general practice but considerably more stringent with regard to recognition of specialty status. This made it possible to employ 95 percent of the immigrant physicians in the health care system. Most worked as general practitioners in the primary care clinics rather than in the more prestigious hospital system, which has been the preferred practice setting of graduates of Israeli medical schools (Shuval 1983, 1985).

In 1987 a more rigorous licensure procedure brought Israel closer to the standards of other Western countries. It required physicians trained outside Israel to pass formal qualifying examinations administered by the Israel Medical Association before they can be licensed for general practice. As of 1992, immigrant dentists and pharmacists are also required to pass a licensing examination. As a gesture to the open-door policy and those who felt that immigration of physicians might be curtailed if they were obligated to pass licensure examinations, exemptions were given to physicians with over twenty years of experience. In 1992, this requirement was reduced to fourteen years.

In 1990, with the large influx of immigrant physicians from the former Soviet Union, major changes in their patterns of employment became inevitable. There is a widespread feeling among Israeli professionals and health care administrators that the standard of medical practice in the Soviet Union was, with some exceptions, lower than that viewed as acceptable in Israel and a negative image of the professional standard of Russian physicians became widespread. Although this image has an objective base, it also serves the needs of the Israel medical profession to reassert its elitism in the face of a real threat to its status. In a society that has managed in the past to employ large numbers of immigrant physicians and more or less control the dysfunctional effects of ongoing oversupply, the excessive surplus now poses a growing threat of competition for resources and patients to Israeli doctors, and a potential for the erosion of their professional status. To the consumer population, there is a growing danger of "over-doctoring" (Frenk 1990, 1991; Ha Doan 1990; Rosenthal, Butter, and Field 1990).

The uneasy coexistence of conflicting sets of values—control of the quality of health care vs. the open door and provision of employment—was evident in 1990–92 in the paradox of publicly sponsored efforts to assist immigrant physicians to prepare for the licensing examination despite a saturated market. The licensure examinations impose a quality barrier. At the same time, immigrants have been provided with major public support to overcome this barrier in the form of a publicly subsidized six-month course focused on updating of medical vocabulary and practice procedures in the Israeli health care system. Participants receive financial subsidies during the course and pay no tuition. In 1991, 60 percent of those who took the licensing examination after taking the course passed. For comparison, it is of interest to note that during the period 1987–89, of seventy-three Soviet immigrant physicians who resettled in Chicago, only four had passed the examinations for licensure. In Australia the comparative figure is 15 percent (Vile 1990).

The present period is the first time in Israel's history that the job market for physicians is fully saturated. Experts estimate that positions in the medical profession will be available, at most, to 10–15 percent of all new arrivals who practiced medicine in the former Soviet Union. Indeed the 2,800 who received medical licenses by mid-1992 are not assured employment in their profession. On the psychological level, one cannot ignore the widespread view among immigrant doctors that the license provides at least a minimum of self-respect by reassertion of their professional identity and hope for future employment. Said one immigrant physician: "I'd rather be unemployed or make a living in some other field *with* a medical license than *without* one. . . ."

The immigrants themselves generate some jobs by their own needs for health care and until recently there were still some shortages in a few specialities, for example: anesthesiology, pathology, nuclear medicine, internal medicine, and geriatrics. However, by 1993 most of these had been filled. Some jobs can be generated in Magen David Adom (emergency casualty services) and in the army. Some doctors can be retrained as nurses, physiotherapists, occupational therapists, or as specialists in alcohol and drug abuse. But all of these options taken together will yield too few jobs, given the number of immigrant physicians. It is therefore inevitable that many will change their occupation or, if they have the option, emigrate.

DISCUSSION: SOME POLICY IMPLICATIONS

While Israel has a formal open-door policy for Jewish migrants, other nations are also experiencing large streams of population movement of migrants, asylum seekers, and refugees. Many of the reasons motivating such migrants to leave their homes and seek to settle elsewhere are similar to those that motivated migration to Israel; some are different. However, the net effects of large-scale movement of populations into a new political, social, and cultural context are in many respects similar to those seen in Israel. Rather than focusing on the unique issues of specific countries, we will attempt to spell out some general implications for health policy of the Israeli experience.

The Health Care System

Israel has provided health care for migrants through its existing health care system but has activated ad hoc outreach programs at certain times to meet the health needs of specific groups of migrants. Upon arrival, immigrants are automatically insured for six months by one of the sick funds that provide comprehensive health care. In principle, the health care system provides universal service for all segments of the population, veterans as well as immigrants, generally in the same clinic setting. Indeed, a universal health care system can be viewed as one of the most important integrating mechanisms in an ethnically differentiated society. The formal, visible entitlement to, and delivery of, health care on a universal basis provides a symbolic integrating effect that can be compared to the effects of a universalistic school system (Shuval, Antonovsky, and Davies 1970).

A full assessment of the health problems imported by the newcomers is essential if the health care system is to be geared to meet needs and identify at-risk groups. In addition to basic demographic data, this requires background information with regard to health practices and health care in the countries of origin. Immigrants are vulnerable to endemic diseases to which the host population has developed immunity. They also include high-risk groups—for example, the elderly, persons with a background of psychiatric problems, and individuals previously exposed to environmental hazards such as Chernobyl.

High-level policy decisions are required so that the host society can realign its resources to deal with these problems in order to minimize real or perceived deprivation in the veteran population. In societies where there is ambivalence with regard to the desirability of immigration, a sense of deprivation is likely to be felt in the veteran population because of competition for scarce resources, for example, housing, jobs, and health care. A strong pro-migration ideology has controlled this feeling in Israel but such an ideology is less likely to exist in most other countries. Zenophobia accompanied by overt violence have been seen recently in Germany and in other European countries against such a background and can only be controlled by stringent, unambiguous law enforcement.

Transit centers or camps in which immigrants and refugees are often accommodated, while planned as temporary facilities, often turn into long-term or even permanent centers of residence, which develop social pathologies and major health hazards. In Israel they have tended to turn into slums. Poor environmental conditions and inadequate preventive and curative services are conducive to the spread of infectious diseases and the exacerbation of chronic health and social problems of long duration. Policy makers need to be aware of the long-range importance of the conditions in these ostensibly temporary facilities.

Migration and Stress

It may be assumed that migration leads to stress. Coping mechanisms that were effective in the past are in many cases diminished by the act of migration or are ineffective in the host society. Changes in climate and food patterns are stressors that are especially salient for vulnerable groups such as the very young and the elderly. Traumas of earlier experiences among refugees and asylum seekers may have immediate effects but also long-term results that are seen many years after migration.

Jobs, housing, schools, and health services are structural conditions that provide a setting in which people can themselves deal with the stress of migration. Informal social and psychological support are critical means of mitigating the impact of stress. It is important to prevent long-term dependence on service-providers. Immigrants are best served by specialists who know their language and culture and can minimize barriers of communication. It is also important to note the long-term effects of stress, which may not become evident until years after the basic practical needs of immigrants are met.

Cultural Heterogeneity and Health

What are the optimal means of bridging the cultural distances between migrants and hosts so as to minimize the dysfunctional effects of migration on newcomers and hosts?

As already noted, knowledge of languages and sensitivity to the cultural contexts of immigrant groups are a *sine qua non* for interaction with them. Health care, both preventive and curative, inevitably involves ongoing interaction between providers and receivers; in most cases, the former are representatives of the host society while the latter are immigrants. One way of reducing communication blocks is to utilize appropriately trained immigrants as providers (Lerner, Mirsky, and Barasch 1992).

However, knowledge of languages is more than a mere technical requirement. Experience indicates that the provider-recipient relationship in health care is a sensitive one that requires in-depth understanding of the nuances and meaning of cultural symbols, traditions, and body language (Pliskin 1987). There is a real danger of elitist assumptions regarding the "appropriateness" of health behavior of groups stemming from different cultural origins and a tendency on the part of health practitioners to denigrate what may appear to them to be "primitive" behavior. Effective health promotion requires tolerance and openness to alternative practices that may be functional in the immigrants' cultural context even though they are different from the ones defined as acceptable in the host society. Health practices and behavior show remarkable tenacity over time.

Migration of Health-care Practitioners

In the most general sense, host societies benefit from an influx of trained personnel who, after appropriate adjustment to local needs, can supply underserviced areas with expertise. But this benefit depends on the level of saturation of the market. Few countries have as saturated a market with regard to health care personnel as Israel. Most societies, even developed ones, can utilize immigrant health care personnel in underserviced areas, for example, inner cities and rural areas. Location of immigrant professionals in less-sought-after loci of practice is likely in the early stages but options for mobility need to be assured and barriers that might be imposed by vested interest groups must be minimized.

When health care practitioners are abundant among the migrants, it is necessary to consider ways of integrating them into the host occupational system. Clearly, employment is one of the basic requirements for all immigrants. The high level of commitment of physicians to their profession, and the centrality of their work to their self-image, makes this issue a particularly salient one for them. Depending upon the size of the immigrant groups, they, themselves, will generate a need for some jobs in health care. The downward mobility that characterizes most occupational groups among immigrants is highly problematic for immigrant physicians and is likely to take its toll in their feelings of well-being and mental health.

Host societies need to balance two sets of needs: (a) those of immigrant professionals to gain acceptable employment, and (b) the need to maintain or improve the health standards of the host society. Decisions regarding formal licensure procedures for immigrant health practitioners reflect this balance. Policymakers need to be aware that the licensure process is a mechanism that is manifestly geared to quality maintenance but in fact fulfills several additional functions. It has been used selectively and manipulatively by those controlling entry to the professions in order to regulate the number and qualifications of entrants. Thus, the standards of skills or knowledge required of immigrant practitioners have been widely varied to meet functions that are, in many cases, not related to health (Butter and Sweet 1977; Kunz 1975; Mick 1975; Stevens, Goodman, and Mick 1978).

It is reasonable to expect that local professional pressure groups will be concerned about maintaining their own status and position and will utilize a variety of mechanisms to prevent competition or diminution of their status. Such measures are likely to be political, ideological, and value-laden; for example, tightening the licensure requirements for immigrant practitioners, denigration of the level of practice of immigrant professionals, and reiteration of the superior quality of locally trained practitioners. In some cases overt conflict can be expected and needs to be controlled.

SUMMARY

The health implications of large-scale movement of populations within and across political boundaries are considered against the background of Israel's extensive experience in dealing with health and health care of immigrants from a wide array of ethnic and cultural traditions. Some policy implications that are relevant to other societies experiencing large-scale migration are drawn from this experience.

Four principal issues have been discussed: (a) the implications for health care providers and recipients of cultural dominance as contrasted to tolerant pluralism with regard to varieties of cultural patterns in health behavior; (b) the relation of migration, stress, and well-being in terms of the effectiveness of previous and newly structured coping mechanisms; (c) health outcomes resulting from migration in terms of infectious and chronic diseases imported by migrants; and (d) the migration of health care personnel, especially physicians, with regard to their licensure and employment in the host society.

REFERENCES

ANDERSON, GERARD F., and SHLOMI ANTEBI. 1991. "A Surplus of Physicians in Israel: Any Lesson for the United States and Other Industrialized Countries?" *Health Policy* 17:77–86.
ANTONOVSKY, AARON. 1979. *Health, Stress and Coping.* San Francisco: Jossey Bass Publishers.
APPLEYARD, REGINALD T. 1991. *International Migration: Challenge for the Nineties.* Geneva: International Organization for Migration.

BEN-BARAK, SHALVIA. 1988. "Abortion in the Soviet Union: Why Is It So Widely Practiced?" Pp. 201–17 in *The Soviet Union: Party and Society*, edited by P. J. Potichnyj. Cambridge: Cambridge University Press.

BERGER, STEPHEN A., TIBERIO SCHWARTZ, and DAN MICHAELI. 1989. "Infectious Disease among Ethiopian Immigrants in Israel." *Archives of Internal Medicine* 149:117–19.

BUTTER, IRENE, and REBECCA R. SWEET. 1977. "Licensure of Foreign Medical Graduates: An Historical Perspective." *Milbank Memorial Fund Quarterly, Health and Society* Spring: 315–40.

COLLINS, RANDALL. 1975. *Conflict Sociology: Toward an Explanatory Science*. New York: Academic Press.

FIELD, MARK G. 1990. "Noble Purpose, Grand Design, Failing Execution, Mixed Results—Soviet Socialized Medicine after Seventy Years." *American Journal of Public Health* 80:144–45.

FLAHERTY, JOSEPH A., ROBERT KOHN, ITZHAK LEVAV, and SUSAN BIRTH. 1988. "Demoralization in Soviet-Jewish Immigrants to the United States and Israel." *Comprehensive Psychiatry* 29:588–97.

FRENK, JULIO. 1990. "The Political Economy of Medical Underemployment in Mexico: Corporatism, Economic Crisis and Reform." *Health Policy* 15:143–62.

FRENK, JULIO. 1991. "Patterns of Medical Employment: A Survey of Imbalances in Urban Mexico." *American Journal of Public Health* 81:23–29.

GARBE, SYLVIE, and EDOUARD GARBE. 1990. "La Sante en URSS a l'heure de la Peristroika." *Cahiers de Sociologie et de la Demographie Medicales* 30:6–45.

GRUSHKA, THEODORE. 1968. Editor, *Health Services in Israel*. Jerusalem: Ministry of Health.

HA DOAN, BUI DANG. 1990. "The Debates on the Numbers of Physicians." *Health Policy* 15:81–89.

HANTMAN, SHIRA, ZEHAVA SOLOMON, and EDUARD PRAGER. 1992. "The Effect of Previous Exposure to Traumatic Stress on the Reactions of the Elderly During the Gulf War." Paper presented at the 10th Congress of the Israeli Association of Gerontology, Tel Aviv, December, 1992.

HERSHKO, CHAIM, GIDEON NESHER, AMOS M. YINNON, GISELLA ZANDMAN-GODDARD, MARK KLUTSTEIN, AYALA ABRAHAMOV, ITZHAK ALON, BERNARD RUDENSKY, and MEIR ISACSOHN. 1986. "Medical Problems in Ethiopian Refugees Airlifted to Israel: Experience in 131 Patients Admitted to a General Hospital." *Journal of Tropical Medicine and Hygiene* 89:107–12.

HOROWITZ, TAMAR. 1989. *The Soviet Man in an Open Society*. Lanham: University Press of America.

Israel Journal of Medical Sciences. 1991. 27, 5 (The whole of issue #5 devoted to papers on the health of Ethiopian immigrants to Israel.)

Israel Ministry of Health. 1990. *Health and Health Services in Israel*. Jerusalem.

Jerusalem Report, August 12, 1993, p. 6.

KLIEWER, EUGENE. 1991. "Immigrant Suicide in Australia, Canada, England and Wales, and the United States." *Journal of the Australian Population Association* 8:111–28.

KOHN, ROBERT, JOSEPH A. FLAHERTY, and ITZHAK LEVAV. 1989. "Somatic Symptoms among Older Soviet Immigrants: An Exploratory Study." *International Journal of Social Psychiatry* 35:350–60.

KUNZ, EGON F. 1975. *The Intruders: Refugee Doctors in Australia*. Canberra: Australian National University Press.

LERNER, YAACOV, JULIA MIRSKY, and MIRIAM BARASCH. 1992. *New Beginnings in an Old Land: The Mental Health Challenge in Israel*. Jerusalem: JDC-Falk Institute for Mental Health and Behavioral Studies.

MICK, STEPHEN S. 1975. "The Foreign Medical Graduates." *Scientific American* 232:14–21.

OFER, GUR, KARNIT FLUG, and NITSA KASIR. 1991. "The Absorption in Employment of Immigrants from the Soviet Union: 1990 and Beyond." *Economic Quarterly* 148:135–71. Hebrew.

PLISKIN, KAREN L. 1987. *Silent Boundaries: Cultural Constraints on Sickness and Diagnosis in Israel*. New Haven: Yale University Press.

POPPER, MIRIAM, and RUTH HOROWITZ. 1992. *Psychiatric Hospitalization of Immigrants: 1990–91*. Statistical Report No. 7, Jerusalem: Mental Health Services, Israel Ministry of Health. Hebrew.

REMENNICK, LARISSA I. 1991. "Epidemiology and Determinants of Induced Abortion in the USSR." *Social Science and Medicine* 33:841–48.

———. 1993. "Reproductive Health: Selected Risk Factors." Institute of Epidemiology, Sheba Medical Center, Tel Hashomer. Unpublished paper.

ROGERS, ROSEMAY. 1992. "The Politics of Migration in the Contemporary World." Paper presented at the Conference on Migration and Health, Brussels, 29 June–1 July, 1992. Geneva: International Organization for Migration.

ROSEN, BRUCE. 1987. *The Health of the Israeli People: An International Comparison Based on the World Health Organization's "Quantitative Indicators for the European Region."* Jerusalem: Brookdale Institute of Gerontology and Adult Human Development.

ROSENTHAL, MARILYNN, IRENE BUTTER, and MARK G. FIELD. 1990. "Setting the Context." *Health Policy* 15:75–79.

ROWLAND, DIANA, and ALEXANDRE V. TELYUKOV. 1991. "Soviet Health Care from Two Perspectives." *Health Affairs* 10:71–86.

SCAMBLER, GRAHAM (editor). 1987. *Sociological Theory and Medical Sociology*. London and New York: Tavistock Publications.

SHUVAL, JUDITH T., AARON ANTONOVSKY, and A. MICHAEL DAVIES. 1970. *Social Functions of Medical Practice*. San Francisco: Jossey-Bass Publishers.

SHUVAL, JUDITH T. 1983. *Newcomers and Colleagues: Soviet Immigrant Physicians in Israel*. Houston: Cap and Gown Press.

_____. 1985. "Social Functions of Medical Licensing: A Case Study of Soviet Immigrant Physicians in Israel." *Social Science and Medicine* 20:901–09.

_____. 1989. "The Structure and Dilemmas of Israeli Pluralism," in *The Israeli State and Society*, edited by Baruch Kimmerling. Albany: State University of New York Press. Pp. 216–36.

_____. 1990. "Medical Manpower in Israel: Political Processes and Constraints." *Health Policy* 15:189–214.

_____. 1992a. "Migration and Stress," in *Handbook of Stress*. Edited by Leo Goldberger and Shlomo Breznitz. Second edition. New York: Academic Press.

_____. 1992b. *Social Dimensions of Health: The Israeli Experience*. Westport, Connecticut: Praeger-Greenwood.

Statistical Abstract of Israel, 1992. 43. Jerusalem: Central Bureau of Statistics.

STEVENS, ROSEMARY, LOUIS W. GOODMAN, and STEPHEN S. MICK. 1978. *The Alien Doctors: Foreign Medical Graduates in American Hospitals*. New York: John Wiley and Sons.

United Nations Development Programme (UNDP). 1991. *Human Development Report 1991*. New York: Oxford University Press.

VILE, PATRICIA. 1990. "Study of Soviet Physicians Resettling in Chicago, 1987-89." *Journal of Jewish Communal Services* 67:137-45.

WIDGREN, JONAS. 1990. "International Migration and Regional Stability." *International Affairs* 66:753.

World Health Organization. 1986. *Indicators for Monitoring Progress Toward Health for All: Quantitative Indicators for the European Region*. Copenhagen: Regional Office for Europe.

World Refugee Statistics. 1991. *World Refugee Survey—1991*. U.S. Committee for Refugees. Washington, D.C.: American Council for Nationalities Service.

CHAPTER 13

Postwar Health Care in Rural El Salvador: Healing the Wounds of War

James V. Spickard[1]

Melissa Penn Jameson

Most industrialized countries see health care as a right: something everyone deserves. Other countries treat it as a privilege: reserved for those with wealth or social status. In a few times and in a few countries, it has become a weapon: a way to control the population, especially rebellious groups within it. El Salvador has been one of these countries. During the 1980s, the government and the military manipulated the civilian health care system as part of its effort to isolate and destroy its guerrilla opponents—the Faribundo Martí National Liberation Front (FMLN). With the signing of Peace Accords in 1992, both sides began a long and painful transition from civil war to peace. The country's health care system also began to change. Today, the future of that system is in dispute. It is no longer a weapon of war; but will health care become a right, or merely a privilege?

This chapter explores the changing status of health care in rural El Salvador as of early 1994. It focuses on the health problems associated with the war's aftermath and on the struggles of various grassroots groups to improve the lives of the rural poor. Because official statistics are scarce and likely inaccurate, the authors spent several weeks in-country, interviewing participants in the struggle to rebuild a decimated medical system. We focused particularly on the area around Suchitoto, near the Guazapa volcano—the site of some of the war's heaviest fighting. We wanted to uncover the structural realities of providing health care to this rural area. We wanted to find out what health problems predominate. We were particularly concerned with the role international health workers could play in helping Salvadorans develop a better health care system for the rural population.

A few of the structures, problems, and potential international contributions that we found are peculiar to El Salvador. Most, however, are relevant to any country in which access to health care has become a weapon of war. The situation in El Salvador is, unfortunately, typical of much modern social conflict. A close look at rural health care in postwar El Salvador will thus highlight the kinds of problems aid workers will encounter in any similar situation (see Muller 1991).

BACKGROUND

From 1980 to 1992, El Salvador was engulfed in a brutal civil war. Springing from the country's deep social divisions and from years of repressive military rule, that war left more than 70,000 dead, two-thirds of them civilians. At least three-quarters of a million people fled the country; twice that many became internal refugees (Barry 1990, pp. 1, 6). These figures are shocking in a total population of 5.5 million. An equivalent war in the United States would have killed 3 million and displaced 100 million. The scope of the trauma would be unprecedented were it not for similar proportions in countries like the Sudan, Bosnia, and Somalia.

Throughout this century, El Salvador has been a poor country, hamstrung by social inequality. In the 1930s, an American military observer saw "nothing between the high-priced cars and the ox-cart with its barefoot attendant" (quoted in Grieg 1971, p. 152). The rich grew and exported coffee; the poor worked as sharecroppers or owned farms barely large enough to feed their families. Attempts at reform were cruelly suppressed: in 1932, as many as 30,000 peasants were murdered in the space of a few weeks, in an event Salvadorans still call *la matanza*—the massacre.

As the economy began to diversify in the 1950s, a small middle class developed. The agroexport sector expanded beyond coffee to include cattle, cotton, and sugar. Sharecroppers were pushed off their land as more modern agricultural methods reduced the demand for labor. Many migrated to the cities, seeking low-wage industrial jobs. Through it all, economic and political power remained in very few hands. By the 1980s, less than 1 percent of the population controlled most of the country's wealth; another 24 percent were middle-class professionals, bureaucrats, and small-business owners; the remaining 74 percent were workers, peasants, and the unemployed. Almost all of that 74 percent lived in extreme poverty: the poorest 20 percent of the population earned only 2 percent of the national income (Montes 1988). The country had the second lowest amount of medical resources in the region, as measured by the number of hospital beds and trained doctors and nurses relative to the population, and even at that, its resources were declining (PAHO 1988). Most of these resources were concentrated in the capital, and so were not available to the majority of the people, who lived in rural areas (Muñoz 1985).

The civil war arose because of these social divisions, and because the landed oligarchy would not relinquish its control of politics. Beginning in the late 1960s, various urban "popular movements" lobbied for change. They sought land reform, labor law reform, democratic elections, new tariff and trade laws that would benefit light industry and its workers, and greater public spending on health and housing.

Though able to put pressure on the government, the popular movements were unable to change many policies. The military and the established powers altered the vote count in the presidential elections of 1972 and 1977, and "won" the legislative election of 1974 only by fraud and intimidation. Seeing no democratic recourse, some activists joined the Popular Liberation Forces (FPL) and the People's Revolutionary Army (ERP), the first of the guerrilla groups to form. Many others fell victim to death squads, which were intent on terrorizing the opposition.

Anyone working against the regime was suspect, no matter how peaceful their approach. The Jesuit Father Rutilio Grande was murdered in 1977 at the behest of the military; seven other priests and hundreds of civilians died in the next two years. In return, the guerrillas assassinated several major Government figures. Over six-hundred people were killed in 1979, mostly at the hands of the military and right-wing death squads. In October of that year, a group of junior officers overthrew President General Carlos Humberto Romero, but the new junta was quickly taken over by the right-wing. Its more liberal members resigned and went into exile.

With the assassination of Archbishop Oscar Romero in March 1980—ordered by Robert D'Aubuisson, the founder of the currently ruling ARENA party (*Los Angeles Times* 3/15/1993)—much of the opposition decided that peaceful protest was no longer possible. The political opposition formed the Democratic Revolutionary Front (FDR) in May of that year; the five major guerrilla groups simultaneously formed the Faribundo Martí National Liberation Front (FMLN). A full-scale civil war began.

THE EFFECTS OF THE WAR

In the ensuing years of war, the plight of the poor worsened. As military spending grew, money for social services plummeted. Agriculture, education, and especially public health have taken the most serious cuts. Between 1980 and 1988, for example, the Ministry of Health budget fell by 40 percent (SMRF n.d.). In the same period, per capita national income dropped by 25 percent while inflation pushed up prices by 360 percent. By 1988, urban unemployment stood at 50 percent, while 71 percent of the rural population was jobless or underemployed (Barry 1990). Even among the employed, real wages in 1989 were less than 40 percent of their level ten years earlier (Instituto de Investigaciones Económicas n.d.). In 1993, the minimum wage was about forty cents an hour in the city and twenty cents in the countryside. The average monthly earnings of a two-income family can provide only half the minimum cost of a basic nutritious diet (National Labor Committee 1989). Forty-five percent of Salvadorans cannot afford food—let alone other necessities like health care and housing (Montes, Meléndez, and Palacios 1988).

Even in the farming areas, where people can grow some food, 70 percent of the population is unable to meet minimum nutritional needs. Despite a proforma land reform, 1 percent of the landowners still have 71 percent of the farmland—typically, the most productive plots (Barry 1987). Nevertheless, much of that land lies idle. Cotton exports, for example, all but disappeared during the 1980s, in part because of guerrilla sabotage but also, in part, because landowners failed to convert from DDT to new systems of pest control and so found their cotton barred from U.S. markets (Economist Intelligence Unit 1993).

Most of the rural poor have no land at all, or are crowded onto heavily eroded land in the north, the least productive part of the country. As a result, rural life expectancy has fallen to 46 years; perhaps as many as 25 percent of children die before age five (SMRF n.d.). UNICEF estimates that several hundred children die each week from malnutrition, preventable diseases, and lack of medical care. In 1980, three of every ten Salvadorans had easy access to safe drinking water; by 1988, that number had fallen to one in ten (*New York Times* 10/16/1988).

Furthermore, the war destroyed much of the country's infrastructure. Roads and bridges were bombed by both sides and stand unrepaired. The country's railroad was bombed into nonexistence; the resulting growth in truck traffic ruined the remaining road surfaces. Money was diverted from public works to pay for the war; what remained was often spent on useless projects like the "golden kilometer"—a road east of the capital that goes nowhere. Guerrilla sabotage to the power grid cost over $2 billion—about the same amount that the U.S. Agency for International Development (AID) has pumped into the country for economic stabilization. The guerrilla offensive of late 1989 alone (and the military's response) caused at least $30 million damage to the infrastructure. In addition, it cut economic production by nearly $90 million (*Processo* 12/6/1989).

The 1986 earthquake exacerbated the many preexisting problems. Over ten thousand families in the capital lost their homes; several rural areas were completely destroyed. Eight years later, many public buildings and nearly all private ones damaged by the quake are still unrepaired. The Catholic Church and popular organizations like the Union of Disaster Victims were able to get some private international funds for rebuilding. The government spent almost nothing, instead channeling to the military the international relief funds it received.

As hard as the civil war was on urban residents, the rural situation was even worse. For example, the area around the Guazapa volcano, north of the capital, was almost totally depopulated. The air force dropped bombs and napalm on peasant villages to drive out their inhabitants. The military and its American advisors saw this policy as "draining the sea to get the fish": if, as Mao Tse-tung taught, guerrillas live like fish in the sea of the people, one must remove the people to isolate the guerrillas. But in the words of one military commander, "For us, there is no sea, only fish" (Lundgren and Lang 1989). The enemy was no longer the guerrillas, but whole populations; anyone living in certain areas was labeled "subversive" and subject to death or deportation. The results of this policy were striking: for example, health workers in one Chalatenango village reported that half the children who died between 1980 and 1988 were killed by the army (Myers and Epstein 1988–1989).

As the military expanded its campaign against the rural population, the cutting off of health care became a weapon of war. As the army cordoned off rural areas, it prevented health workers from entering. Sick peasants had to go to towns or to the capital for treatment. If they tried to return, their medicines were often confiscated. Carrying a bottle of aspirin could bring summary execution for "aiding the guerrillas"; what peasant, after all, would need fifty aspirin? Medical personnel, including village health promoters, were routinely targeted for torture and execution. Merely owning a copy of "Donde No Hay Doctor" ("Where There Is No Doctor"), a medical self-help manual, could bring death in an army sweep (Clements 1984; see also Lundgren and Lang 1989). By denying access to medical care, the military hoped to make peasants leave.

This repression, plus the disease and lack of food that resulted from it, were particularly harmful to the health of rural women. Because Salvadoran culture makes a strong role division between the sexes, and assigns household and child-rearing tasks to women, women's burdens grow in times of emergency and privation. Men were conscripted to fight (many fled to avoid conscription), or they migrated to find work; they traded one kind of hardship for another. Women were left in the villages without resources and with young mouths to feed—increasing their hardship without granting them the resources with which to meet it. Military strikes against "the sea" of guerilla resistance increasingly destroyed women and children. Interestingly, this struggle led some rural women to take a more active role in village life—as community leaders and organizers and as rural health workers.

At first, people escaped from their farm homes to the rural towns; as the civil war intensified, the towns in turn became too dangerous. The town of Suchitoto, for example, saw all but 500 of its 30,000 citizens flee due to heavy fighting. Its hospital was occupied by the military and subsequently destroyed, as were many houses. Though many people moved back after the truce was signed, little has been rebuilt. Bullet holes still cover many walls. The water system works most of the time, as does electricity. But sewage is not treated, and more than half the population suffers from water-borne parasites. A woefully underequipped Ministry of Health clinic tries to serve as many people as it can. Yet refugees who have tried to repopulate the surrounding countryside have few or no resources—not even clear title to their lands.

THE CURRENT POLITICAL SITUATION

As of early 1994, the Salvadoran political situation is still in flux. The signing of the Peace Accords in late 1992 led to the demobilization of the rebel FMLN as well as of several elite Army battalions—including those guilty of the most egregious human rights abuses. The various semimilitary police forces are being disbanded, to be replaced by a new, civilian "National Police," made up of former government and FMLN partisans. A "Truth Commission" has identified the perpetrators of the major human rights crimes; as a result, most of the senior military officers have been retired, including the Minister and Vice-Minister of Defense. The military retains its influence over the ruling right-wing ARENA party, however. Though right-wing death squads are still active—a few political abductions and killings are reported in the papers each week—no one expects outright war to return.

The FMLN is now a legal political party and the largest part of the political opposition. There are five primary "tendencies" under the FMLN umbrella, however, each with its own political platform and bureaucracy. Significant differences have arisen between these "tendencies," and they have not been able to unite behind a common platform. Some of its more prominent leaders have been publicly censured for their wartime murders of rural ARENA mayors and for the recent discovery of hidden arms caches.

The fast pace of events would quickly outdate any detailed account of Salvadoran politics. At the time of writing, the outcome of the forthcoming elections scheduled for March and April 1994 will change the picture drastically, particularly if the FMLN and its allies win. Certain structural aspects of the political situation are apt to remain for some time, however, and will influence the provision of health care, especially in rural areas. These structural aspects are as follows:

First, the 1992 Peace Accords did not solve the major socioeconomic causes of the civil war. In essence, they were an agreement by the two sides to continue the conflict by political means. While the Accords did contain provisions for limited land reforms, these cover only the areas formerly under FMLN control. Even here, disputes over land title are being resolved very slowly. As a result, many rural communities lack legal title to the their land, even if they have farmed it for years. It is against the interests of the landowners to allow any short-run health improvements in these "squatter" villages, much less to allow government-sponsored development for the long run. Without a change of regime, villagers cannot expect the Ministry of Health to do much to address their needs.

Second, though the armed forces have supposedly been "purified" through forced retirements, current and former military personnel are still active and powerful. Parts of the old military police have been transferred to the new national police force, in violation of the Peace Accords. Some decommissioned soldiers have found jobs in the private militias of the large landowners. Others have joined the criminal classes. But most importantly, retired senior officers retain much wealth, which came both from wartime corruption and from their retirement fund. This fund is a major player in the Salvadoran financial scene. Significantly, this wealth is not all invested in land, making the military's financial interests different from those of the old landed elite. Instead, it has built tourist hotels, donut shops, malls, electronics plants, and other manifestations of a growing light-industrial and service economy. Salvadoran politics will certainly be influenced by these new economic interests; the new elite will likely use political means to protect itself, as did the old.

On the side of the civilian and guerrilla opposition, legalization has brought problems as well as opportunities. For the FMLN, the transition from revolutionary army to political party has been neither easy nor instant. Besides a major organizational restructuring, the process has involved a radical redefinition of tasks. The change from *comandante* to press secretary, for example, obviously requires some new job training. On an ideological level, both party activists and rank-and-file members have had to change their thinking about FMLN identity and goals. The fact that the five FMLN "tendencies" do not agree on these matters has made cooperation difficult. Many no longer share resources with each other; all are competing to keep themselves going until the upcoming elections.

This factionalization has had a direct impact on rural health care. As we shall see below, both the government and the FMLN see village health promoters as the front line of the battle for better rural health. But in many areas, including the Suchitoto area we visited most extensively, it is the FMLN and not the government that has funded these workers. During the war, the FMLN guerrillas saw rural health care, carried out by health promoters, as a way to get their soldiers treated while simultaneously winning the loyalty of the civilian population (Metzi 1988; Clements 1984). The Salvadoran Army responded to this by targeting the health promoters for assassination. Because current FMLN funding is low, however, its health workers must compete with other priorities to obtain resources. And because each of the five FMLN strands sponsors its own health organization, those groups must compete with each other for outside aid. Too often, the political effort of maintaining separate organizations has taken precedence over channeling funds to the villages.

These problems are exacerbated by the recent drying up of international health funding. Charitable contributions to North American and European organizations working in El Salvador have declined as the civil war ended and other world crises took center stage. Both civilian and guerrilla organizations now get less international aid, forcing them to cut back their programs. One very worthy mental health program was recently closed because it lost a grant from a North American charity. The support of two other international, nongovernmental organizations (NGOs) was not enough to keep it going. Given the tendency of First World donations to focus on the latest world disaster, continued "peace" seems unlikely to generate large outside resources.

THE CURRENT HEALTH CARE SYSTEM

Our interviews with Salvadoran medical workers reveal that, like most of the country's human services, the health care system is fractured and grossly inadequate. Indeed, to speak of a "health care system" implies more of a cohesive structure than is, in fact, present. There are currently several health care systems, which are only tangentially integrated with each other.

Theoretically, the Instituto Salvadoreño de Seguro Social—ISSS, the Salvadoran Social Security Institute—provides health care to part of the population. Under this scheme, employees of industry, the state, and other "urban" professional sectors pay into a fund. So do their employers and the government. This fund then runs four ISSS hospitals and about 30 clinics to which the employees have access—a kind of health insurance. The Ministry of Health, in theory, provides a "safety-net" to those not covered through the ISSS: 15 major hospitals, 15 "centros de salud" (health centers), and a network of health promoters in more remote areas (Ministerio de Salud 1991). Nearly 50 percent of the Ministry's beds are in the capital; most of the rest are cots in rural clinics, not designed for long-term care (PAHO 1986). Beyond this, private doctors, clinics, and hospitals exist only for those who can afford them.

The ISSS covers only 7–10 percent of the population; the vast majority must depend on the Ministry of Health (Morán Quijada 1988). Though its program was once an international model (see Dajer 1989), today the Ministry is completely incapable of meeting the demands that are placed upon it. It has much less funding than it did before the war (*Links* 1989). Furthermore, Ministry services have been, and continue to be, manipulated for political and military gain rather than directed at public health needs.

This manipulation manifests itself in many ways. The Ministry clinic in Suchitoto, for example—in an area of FMLN strength—serves almost the same number of patients as do clinics in other areas, but with one-fifth of staff and one-third of the facilities of the other centers. The surgical room listed for it in Ministry of Health official statistics does not exist. Similarly, while civilian hospitals are overcrowded and undersupplied, military hospitals are fully equipped. There is only one public maternity hospital in the country to serve a population of over 5 million. "Patients entering public hospitals are told to bring their own sheets, food, soap, toilet paper, surgical supplies and sutures" (Barry 1990, p. 109). Private health care is available and is the only source of many medical services, but only a small proportion of the population can afford it. Like other forms of health care—and like all public resources—it is concentrated in the nation's capital, an urban bias common in Third World societies (Donahue 1989). Private health care is practically nonexistent in the rural areas where most Salvadorans have traditionally lived (see Muñoz 1985).

VILLAGE HEALTH PROMOTERS

Thus most health needs are not met by the usual public and private institutions. Besides the FMLN, various nongovernmental organizations (NGOs) try to fill this gap: churches, Salvadoran "popular organizations," folk practitioners, and international "solidarity" groups, as well as worldwide agencies such as the Red Cross and UNICEF. Often these categories overlap; a Salvadoran church may support folk practitioners with international funds, for example. Clearly, such NGOs do not have the capital to fund the modern hospitals and medical clinics that Salvadorans need, though the rural health situation would be much worse were they not present (see Arias n.d.). Much of the work of these NGOs, especially on the village level, involves building a network of local health promoters and trainers. As the first line of support for poor people, these health promoters are supposed to treat the cases that they can manage while directing other cases elsewhere in the health system. (This model of health care has a long history in El Salvador; see Dajer 1989).

Local health promoters are needed because El Salvador lacks the physical and cultural resources to sustain a health care system based on trained physicians (see Aizenberg 1968). Our interviews with dozens of health promoters made it clear, however, that they are not simply a substitute for physicians. Their goals in working with patients are more subtle and far-reaching than that. *De facto* objectives may include (from the most idealistic to the most cynical): empowering people to have control over their own bodies and thus their lives; attempting to stem the spread of infection and disease among major populations;

making health care accessible to those in remote areas; easing the demand on overtaxed central clinics; and/or placating the underclasses.

As in so many other parts of Salvadoran life, political outlooks shape programs. While many NGO workers claim to be trying to "empower the poor," the current funding crisis makes this "empowerment" less effective than it might otherwise be. During the war, for example, many village health promoters were funded by international groups involved in solidarity work. As solidarity funds have dried up, less money gets to the villages. Several village-level health workers complained to us that they are not getting the international money they expected because their urban coworkers need it to keep their organizations alive.

Another widespread problem in rural health care is a lack of communication and a struggle for authority between the community health promoter(s) and the villagers they serve. Class, gender, age, and political dynamics, as well as personality problems, influence health care delivery at the village level. A health worker's effectiveness depends on social status as much as on expertise.

In one of the "repopulated communities" (villages of returned refugees) near Suchitoto, for example, the two village health promoters are women in their late twenties or thirties, who have many years of experience. They are well-connected politically (to one of the FMLN factions), and have thus been able to bring very concrete resources to their communities. These include a water system (from the Red Cross), a village clinic (built by a church group), and a visiting university medical team. As a result, the general level of health in this village is relatively high. People pay more attention to these health promoters than they would to others with less expertise or fewer connections.

In a neighboring repopulated village, on the other hand, the health promoters are three teenagers with very little training. The village is poorer and less healthy. The Red Cross has piped in water, and the village has built latrines, which are used by some. But the medicine stocks are low, and the health promoters do not seem to know how to use them. Many children have running skin sores; several people have come down with typhoid, which the health workers lack the knowledge to diagnose or treat. The villagers see no progress, and thus pay little attention to the health promoters' efforts to improve public sanitation, which would in fact improve their health greatly.

But these villagers are lucky compared to some. A third village in the same area lacks water, latrines, and health workers. Mixed packs of dogs and pigs run between the houses; villagers drink from, bathe in, and eat fish from the same lake into which their refuse is dumped. Their health is understandably poor, and the villagers seem to see no way of bettering their situation. They cooperate with none of the political organizations, and so lack even the rudimentary benefits those organizations can bring.

In most communities, at least in the Suchitoto area, there is a clear connection between a village's health and its degree of internal political organization. But organization alone is not sufficient. The health workers in the first two villages have not been paid for months because the organizations that sponsor them have run out of funds. As of early 1994, they were still working, but doubted that they could do so for long. Like others, they have children to feed and families to support. Good pay for health workers would attract more effective workers, but villages cannot support health workers on their own. The Ministry of Health recognizes the need, but is also facing a severe budget shortage.

Even if there were enough money to fund health promoters in each village, there would still be a disagreement about what qualifications they should hold. The government currently will certify (and pay) health promoters who have a 9th grade education and have taken a 14-month training course (free but unpaid) in the capital. Many of the promoters who served various factions of the FMLN during the war have little or no formal education. But they have years of experience doing field surgery, delivering babies on kitchen tables, and other basics of medical care. These workers cannot afford the several years of schooling required for them to meet government requirements, and so cannot be employed. Government policy would discard their experience and skills, certifying instead educated urban young people, who typically know little about rural conditions and have much less commitment to the rural population.

This conflict over certification is about politics as much as about health care. Government agencies are reluctant to recognize or pay FMLN health workers, because to do so would acknowledge the programs and training sponsored by their adversaries. Similarly, the former guerillas are none too ready to embrace government standards, especially when they hurt FMLN supporters in the villages. This political deadlock is undoubtedly heightened by the fact that many FMLN health workers are women, who are unwilling to return to their culturally submissive roles. Some of these women find themselves fighting the male hierarchies of their own organizations, whom they see as too wedded to centralized control. The battle over health promoter certification is thus not only about politics but about gender dominance, as well.

No matter what kind of certification is eventually established, there must be some kind of national health system into which village-level health workers are integrated. This, too, is a source of political conflict. People working in the popular organizations often express distrust of any government-run plan; on the other hand, any attempt to establish a nationwide health care system without significant involvement by the government would be unworkable. On both sides there seems to be a desire for greater communication and coordination between health professionals, educators, practitioners, and facilities. Yet there is no clear consensus about what type of structure a national health network would have, and who would hold positions of power in it. Such issues will undoubtedly continue to be the object of intense debate as decisions are made about the future of health care in El Salvador.

In short, funds for both the government and the FMLN are shrinking and are being directed away from health care and toward other areas. Everyone agrees that there is a need for some form of nationally coordinated network of health trainers and workers. And everyone agrees on the need for a national plan that includes government-paid health workers at the village level. But each political tendency has its own perspective about what should be done and how it should be implemented. Of course, those in the government have disproportionate power to make decisions about what steps are ultimately taken.

CURRENT HEALTH PROBLEMS

The health problems facing rural Salvadorans are somewhat different from those that North American medical personnel deal with. Besides malnutrition, which at times has affected as much as 70 percent of the refugee population (US-AID 1985), there are various water- and pest-borne diseases: typhoid, dengue, malaria, and amoebic dysentery. Exact diagnosis of these diseases is often prohibitively expensive and available only in the capital. Though endemic, they are best combatted by increased food supplies, improved latrine- and water-systems, and other infrastructure advances carried out as part of a comprehensive development program.

To its credit, the Ministry of Health provides some full-time senior staff members for work on such public health measures in rural branches like Suchitoto. Good latrine- and water-systems are, however, costly. The Ministry staff hopes to get donations from the European Economic Community to build water systems in three villages—out of the several dozen that need help. Yet even the village systems that exist are minimal, consisting of a few concrete block pit toilets, plastic pipe, and some spigots. The only other sources of funding are NGOs like the International Red Cross, the Salvadoran Medical Relief Fund (a North American group) and CONCERN (an Irish volunteer organization)—all of which are active in the area. But they can typically fund only small projects. Despite its commitments in the Peace Accords, the Salvadoran government seems unwilling to spend its money on rural public health projects. The fact that title to village lands is still in dispute does not help matters; government spending on infrastructure would amount to taking the side of "squatters" against absentee "landowners," even though the land in question was long ago occupied by the former and abandoned by the latter. Yet the terms "landowner" and "squatter" imply more stability to the formal land tenure system than is in fact the case. Williams (1991) describes a centuries-long dynamic throughout Central America in which land is alternately occupied by "squatters" and "landowners," depending on the salability of cash crops on the export market. "Title" to land is a sometime thing for each; there is no reason to presume that the rights of the "landowners" are superior to those of the "squatters." No Salvadoran government, however, has been willing to side with the latter.

In the Suchitoto area, at least one public health program has been successful. Most area residents have been vaccinated against the major inoculable diseases. Though Ministry and FMLN health personnel both claim credit for this, in fact, the work was carried out by the committed representative of an international NGO.

There is no general survey of health problems in the Suchitoto area, nor does the Ministry clinic maintain complete records of the cases that its staff sees. Such records would not give an accurate picture in any event, because richer patients go to private doctors and the poorest ones only come to the clinic *in extremis*. We can get some sense of the general health picture from the report of a team of doctors from the Salvadoran Medical Relief Fund that visited several of the villages in the area in April 1993. Of the 43 potential surgery patients they examined, they found 16 whom, they felt, were treatable locally. Among the needs of those patients were: 6 hernia treatments, 5 growth removals, 1 stump modification, and 2–3 removals of shrapnel. Several other patients had problems severe enough to require specialized work in the capital. Still others showed the aftereffects of war wounds without needing more surgery. This team did not attempt to survey the many cases of parasites, skin sores, influenza, and so on. The widespread presence of untreated minor surgical problems, however, shows a low level of health care in most of the villages, a fact that our visits confirmed impressionistically.

All of the health workers with whom we spoke mentioned a further problem, which has as yet received little medical attention: mental health. Rural Salvadorans have been through tremendous trials; the signs of posttraumatic stress are apparent among them. In the Suchitoto area, for example, every village family has some tale of horror to tell. Nearly all have lost close relatives to the fighting. Many children were orphaned; many parents had to watch their children die. Some were tortured by government troops. As the "sea" was "drained," they were driven from their lands at gunpoint. All this pain remains untreated, salved only by whatever inner strength or religious belief surviving villagers possess.

Soldiers, too, have suffered. While the FMLN fighters were volunteers, and thus committed to their cause, government troops were often conscripts, brutalized by their commanders. Just as U.S. draftees returned from Vietnam unprepared for civilian life, Salvadoran soldiers have suffered the flashbacks, depression, and mental deterioration typical of posttraumatic stress syndrome. Unfortunately, there are few or no mental health resources available to them.

VIOLENCE AS A HEALTH ISSUE

These mental problems, together with the incidence of shrapnel injuries, old gunshot wounds, landmine damage, and so on, underscore another continuing Salvadoran health problem: violence. The country is no longer at war, but to speak of "peace" in El Salvador is far too simplistic. Violence in many forms still prevails. An understanding of how the violence has changed is essential to a picture of the current health situation.

Salvadorans are experiencing the violence common to postwar periods in many countries. Street crime is skyrocketing, undoubtedly because of the collapsing economy, whose major industry—war—has been shut down. Thousands of former fighters from both sides join the soaring numbers of the unemployed; too often, their weapons come with them. Besides "standard" street violence, such as robbery, rape, and other forms of assault, carjackings are becoming increasingly common. These trends result in a general state of insecurity that plays into the hands of those who would strengthen the military and the police. That the owners of the major media that publicize the increased street violence would benefit from police militarization does not mean, however, that the increase is just a matter of publicity. As was the case in the 1970s, the line between the private armies and the criminal classes is now extremely thin.

Besides crime, random bombing and political violence still continue, though at a lower rate than during the war. Late 1993 saw a wave of political killings, however: three high-ranking FMLN leaders were gunned down near the capital, and two FMLN ex-combatants were murdered in the Guazapa region. Such events may well escalate as the 1994 elections approach.

Domestic abuse is a second growing form of violence in El Salvador. Many popular organizations report that wife-beating is on the increase. Sexual assaults are more common now, and are usually carried out by relatives or acquaintances. One urban women's organization claimed that as many as 80 percent of homes have experienced domestic violence. True, more women report abuse now than in the past; yet this alone does not account for the change. Women's wartime need to care for their families on their own may have altered gender-based power relations; currently high unemployment levels also may have given more economic power to those women who found jobs during the conflict. Domestic violence may, in part, be an attempt by men to reestablish their traditional dominance. Legal attitudes toward domestic abuse reinforce this tactic. Such violence has not traditionally been considered a crime; the police and the state typically aim only "to unite couples." A similar attitude is reflected in the legal treatment of rape cases: two witnesses to the crime are necessary to prosecute. Many of those to whom we spoke believe that domestic abuse will continue to climb as soldiers return home—especially if they cannot be adequately integrated into civilian society. This interpersonal violence is a direct threat to Salvadoran women's health and well-being.

Furthermore, the political violence has not ended. While almost everyone acknowledges with relief the end of all-out war, political killings and threats continue throughout the country. The political situation remains highly charged, and involvement in political issues is still dangerous, though less so than before. The results of this violence shows up in the health clinics, doctors' offices, and emergency rooms—and is a key element in the health situation facing the country.

WHAT CAN INTERNATIONAL HEALTH WORKERS DO?

Most of the foregoing is typical of Third World rural health care in the aftermath of civil war. Details differ, but the general problems facing Salvadorans as they rebuild their rural health system are much like those health workers find in Uganda, Nicaragua, Mozambique, Somalia, Sudan, and other recent zones of conflict, including perhaps even the former Yugoslavia. The problems are daunting, but there is a definite role for international health workers in rural El Salvador, as there is in these other countries. To be helpful, however, they must recognize the political and social realities of the region. Naive aid may provide a few bandages and improve a few lives; but only intelligently targeted aid can help Salvadorans develop a sustainable health care system for their rural population. In closing, we shall note some of the political obstacles such aid must currently overcome. Then we shall suggest a few areas toward which aid could well be directed.

The first obstacle is the fact that there are many on the political Right, including significant parts of the government and military, who do not want good health care in rural areas. A centralized health care system is easier for them to control, and good health care in the villages might encourage people to stay there, making it more difficult for landowners to clear the land for cattle, cotton, and other export crops. Starving health care in the countryside is thus a "peacetime" continuation of the government's wartime policy. So is the common harassment of incoming health care personnel and the impounding of medical equipment. Despite the dedicated work of many in the Ministry of Health, international health care personnel have to expect government noncooperation. Those currently active in the country have learned various ways to get around such roadblocks, but these take considerable time and energy.

Second, there is the current factionalism on the political Left. The various FMLN health organizations are trying to survive, and so are likely to spend some of the aid they receive on organizational overhead. They also gain political support for every bit of health care they seem to deliver. They will thus attempt to get international workers to help "their" villages rather than those of their rivals. Foreigners must be aware of the appearance of favoritism; sometimes even visiting the projects of one faction will alienate another. This factional competition is discouraging to international aid workers, and makes their job more difficult. Each international agency must decide whether to work exclusively with a single faction, or balance ties among several groups.

Several of the FMLN factions have recognized the need to cooperate, especially given the limited resources available to them. They have formed a committee of "concertación" (cooperation) in Suchitoto, which has met sporadically since late 1992 to iron out differences. In the absence of significant outside resources to share, it still meets but has not made much practical progress.

A third significant obstacle is the atmosphere of mistrust that lingers as a result of the war. Simply doing rural health work then was dangerous, whether or not it was politically motivated. As a result, people still are not open about their identities, work, or goals, especially over the phone or to strangers. Most nongovernmental organizations do not have a sign in front of their offices announcing their presence. Smaller organizations do not make their factional ties explicit. Few names or phone numbers of community organizations appear in any commonly available publications. Beyond these specific practices, the survival mentality necessarily adopted by so many leads to a pace of work that is far different and at times frustratingly slow by First World standards. International health workers must learn to adjust to this and often to copy it; death squads still sometimes target those seeking to help the rural poor.

If international health workers are willing to take these political circumstances into account, then there are several aid projects that can make a very real impact on Salvadoran rural health. International aid can strengthen existing programs and services, and can introduce resources or programs not yet available in El Salvador—at the village, the regional, or the national level.

Chief among the programs needing international support is the network of village-level health promoters described above. More such workers are needed, and those currently serving need better training and pay. International groups can provide both, and also can help establish neutral standards for health promoter certification, avoiding the political strife over these matters described above. Financial support for field-trained health workers while they attain government certification is crucial if the villages they currently serve are to retain the little health care they now enjoy.

There is a great need for popular educational materials, both for the general population and for the specific training of health promoters. Such items would include posters illustrating symptoms, causes, and treatments of common diseases, including sexual functioning, knowledge of which is shockingly low. Similar attention could be paid to literature, charts, or posters showing the uses and effects of common drugs, preventive measures, treatment procedures, or diagnostic decision-making. The latter, particularly, would help village health promoters decide which cases to treat on their own, which to send to the clinics in the smaller cities, and which to send to the larger hospitals. These materials need to be designed for the semiliterate villagers who will be their primary audience. And aid workers should remember that, until recently, mere possession of such materials made one a target for repression.

Mental health care is another fruitful area for international attention. Not that North American or European psychiatry should be transplanted unchallenged to El Salvador; Salvadoran culture calls for much different techniques. But U.S. mental health workers have experience dealing with posttraumatic stress—particularly the aftereffects of the Vietnam War. This experience could prove useful to Salvadorans who work with the victims of violence.

Besides these projects, international NGOs can support more capital-intensive public health work: projects to improve water quality and accessibility; sanitation projects; reforestation programs; appropriate technology initiatives; and projects to improve the availability, quality, and safety of housing. Such projects cannot simply be imposed from the outside (see Pratt and Boyden 1985). If they are to be useful, they must be initiated, designed, and carried out by local residents, with international workers providing advice and guidance only when requested.

At the regional level, international workers can provide training and resources to the Ministry of Health clinics in the smaller cities. These clinics are severely understaffed and short on equipment. At the time of our visit, for example, the laboratory at the Suchitoto clinic contained only two microscopes and one centrifuge. This is clearly inadequate for the diagnostic tasks that a regional clinic is supposed to perform. International agencies should avoid sending just equipment, however, unless the clinic staff requests it and is trained in its use. Most clinic directors welcome such training, and can be quite candid about the areas in which they need more expertise. But international workers should be wary of becoming solely identified with the Ministry; doing so may cut off their access to the villages, which tend to support one or another of the FMLN factions.

Effective public health work depends on accurate information; such information is sparse in rural El Salvador. Some of this lack is due to the war, and some is due to the recent movement of people into and out of the rural areas. Some is common to other poor countries. Outside workers can help carry out baseline surveys of malnutrition, infant mortality, water- and insect-borne disease, and so on, which could greatly improve rural health in the long term. Again, close attention must be paid to political factionalism, and to the fact that accurate information about public health may be misused by a hostile government.

At the national level, El Salvador's major public hospitals and medical schools need much assistance. They lack equipment, physical plant, and training staff, all of which results in a lessened ability to serve the poor. Refurbishing these facilities is probably beyond the capabilities of all but the largest international agencies, though there is plenty of work for interested volunteers. Improvements here, however, would do little to improve the health of the rural population; they need health aid that is closer to home.

CONCLUDING REMARKS

This article presents a snapshot of the health care situation in rural El Salvador as of early 1994. Though the political situation in that country will undoubtedly change over the next months and years, we believe that the underlying obstacles to adequate rural health care will not change so quickly. No matter who wins the 1994 elections, land titles will not be quickly resolved, health budgets will not be greatly increased, and economic opportunities for the rural poor will not quickly expand. Even if a true peace is achieved, El Salvador's rural health problems will not vanish overnight.

We also believe that the Salvadoran case is typical of many countries, especially those in which access to health care has been used as a weapon of civil war (Cahill 1993). The details of rural socioeconomic structures in these countries will differ, as will the specific constellation of political forces. But the social inequality, the political factionalism, the imbalance of resources between urban and rural areas, and so on, will all be similar. So will the projects needed to improve rural health. And so will the constraints under which international health workers must operate. We present this analysis of the Salvadoran rural health care system as a case study of the situation in one country—in the hopes that by examining that country closely, we can learn more about bringing adequate health care to all parts of the world.

NOTE

[1] The authors wish to thank the Division of Higher Education of the Christian Church (Disciples of Christ), who helped support our research travel with a grant to the Office of the Chaplain at the University of Redlands. We wish to thank the Institute for Latin American Studies at the University of Texas at Austin for permission to use the Benson Collection and for administrative support of the senior author. We wish also to thank the representatives of many Salvadoran and international Non-Governmental Organizations (NGOs), whose names we cannot mention due to the still-tense political situation in which they must live.

REFERENCES

AIZENBERG, MOISES. 1968. *La Salud en el Proceso de Desarrollo de la Comunidad*. Patzcuaro, Mexico: Centro de Educación Fundamental para el Desarrollo de la Comunidad en América Latina.

ARIAS, SALVADOR. n.d. *Seguridad o Inseguridad Alimentaria: Un Reto Para la Región Centroamericana. Perspectives Para el Año 2000*. San Salvador: UCA Editores.

BARRY, TOM. 1987. *The Roots of Rebellion: Land and Hunger in Central America*. Albuquerque, NM: Interhemispheric Education Resource Center.

———. 1990. *El Salvador: A Country Guide*. Albuquerque, NM: Interhemispheric Education Resource Center.

CAHILL, KEVIN, editor. 1993. *A Framework for Survival: Health, Human Rights, and Humanitarian Assistance in Conflicts and Disasters*. New York: Basic Books.

CLEMENTS, CHARLES, M.D. 1984. *Witness to War*. New York: Bantam.

DAJER, ANTONIO. 1989. "The Complicated Path to Simple Medicine: Interview with Francisco Metzi." *Links* (Summer) (NCAHRN).

DONAHUE, JOHN. 1989. "Rural Health Efforts in the Urban-Dominated Political Economy: Three Third World Examples." *Medical Anthropology* 11:109-25.

Economist Intelligence Unit. 1993. *Country Profile: Guatemala and El Salvador: 1993/94*. London: The Economist.

GRIEG, KENNETH J. 1971. "The United States and the Rise of General Maximiliano Hernández Martínez," *Journal of Latin American Studies*. P. 152.

Instituto de Investigaciones Económicas. n.d. "Necesidades Básicas y Deterioro de las Condiciones de Vida," *Coyuntura Económica* Year 5, no. 28:17-19. San Salvador: Universidad de El Salvador.

Links. 1989. (NCAHRN). "A Ten-Year War on Health." (Spring.)

Los Angeles Times. 1993. "U.N. Truth Commission Reports Salvadoran Abuses." (March 15.)

LUNDGREN, REBECKA INGA, and ROBERT LANG. 1989. "'There Is No Sea, Only Fish': Effects of United States Policy on the Health of the Displaced in El Salvador," *Social Science and Medicine* 28/7:697-706.

METZI, FRANCISCO. 1988. *The People's Remedy: Health Care in El Salvador's War of Liberation*. Translated by Jean Carroll. New York: Monthly Review Press.

Ministerio de Salud Pública y Asistencia Social. 1991. *Salud Pública en Cifras 1991, Anuario No. 23*. San Salvador: Unidad de Estadística de Salud.

MONTES, SEGUNDO. 1988. *Estructura de Clases y Comportamiento de las Fuerzas Sociales*. San Salvador: IDHUCA.

MONTES, SEGUNDO, FLORENTÍN MELÉNDEZ, and EDGAR PALACIOS. 1988. *Los Derechos Económicos, Sociales, y Culturales en El Salvador*. San Salvador: IDHUCA.

MORÁN QUIJADA, HUGO. 1988. "El Salvador." Pp. 333-49 in *Políticas de Salud en América Latina: Aspetas Institucionales de Su Formulación, Implementación y Evaluación*. Edited by David Gómez Cova. Caracas, Venezuela: Centro Latinoamericano de Administración para el Desarrollo.

MULLER, FRITS. 1991. *Pobreza, Participación, y Salud: Casos Latinoamericanos*. Medellin, Colombia: Editorial Universidad de Antioquia.

MUÑNOZ, EDGAR P. 1985. *La Repercusion de la Crisis Centroamericana en La Salud*. San José, Costa Rica: CSUSA Cuadernos de Investigación.

MYERS, ALAN, and ADRIENNE EPSTEIN. 1988-1989. "Passage to Chalatenango," *Links* (NCAHRN). (Winter.)

National Labor Committee in Support of Democracy and Human Rights in El Salvador. 1989. *El Salvador: Critical Choices—A Special Report*.

New York Times. 1988. "US-AID Figures Show Salvador Decline." (October 16.)

PAHO (Pan American Health Organization). 1986. *Health Conditions in the Americas, 1981-1984*. Volume II. Washington, D.C.: PAHO.

———. 1988. *Los Servicios de Salud en Las Américas: Analysis*. Technical Report #14. Washington, D.C.: PAHO.

PRATT, BRIAN, and JO BOYDEN, editors. 1985. *The Field Directors' Handbook: An Oxfam Manual for Development Workers*. Oxford: Oxfam Publications.

Processo, 1989. (Article on the economic effects of the November uprising). San Salvador. (December 6.)

SMRF (Salvadoran Medical Relief Fund). n.d. *Healing the Wounds of War*. (Pamphlet)

US-AID (United States Agency for International Development). 1985. *Baseline Survey of the Displaced Population*, AID Project no. 519-0178-D-00-5237-00. San Salvador: USAID.

WILLIAMS, ROBERT G. 1991. "Land, Labor, and the Crisis in Central America." Pp. 23-43 in *Harvest of Want: Hunger and Food Security in Central America and Mexico*, edited by Scott Whiteford and Anne E. Fergusen. Boulder, CO: Westview Press.

PART V

COMPARATIVE STUDIES

CHAPTER 14

Medicine as a Profession: Lessons from Some Cross-National Case Studies

Frederic W. Hafferty[1]

Until recently, analyses of medicine's status as a profession have been drawn largely from observations based on the organization and delivery of medical care in the United States and Britain. One consequence of this restricted focus has been a preoccupation with factors that might constrain or otherwise dictate the work of physicians. Relatedly, the "professionalism debate" has focused on the issue of whether medicine is losing or, conversely, still maintaining its professional dominance. On one side stand those who conclude that there has been a diminution of professional powers and prestige, with medicine becoming "deprofessionalized" (Haug 1973, 1988), "proletarianized" (McKinlay 1982, 1988; Oppenheimer 1973), "corporatized" (Light and Levine 1988; McKinlay and Stoeckle 1988), or competitively diminished by a broad constellation of "countervailing forces" (Light 1991; Mechanic 1991).[2] Standing in contrast to these various arguments is the professional dominance perspective (Freidson 1970, 1989, 1990), with its central thesis that medicine continues to maintain its professional prerogatives. Seemingly missing from this debate about loss versus maintenance, however, is any formal recognition that we still might need to concern ourselves with issues of professional ascension and the expansion of medicine's status and powers—a theme to which we will return.

Over the past ten years, there have begun to emerge an impressive number of case studies analyzing medicine's status as a profession in countries other than the United States and Britain. Notable works include Andrew Abbott's analysis of intraprofessional competition and jurisdictional disputes in the United States, Britain, and France (Abbott 1988); David Wilsford's comparative study of France and the United States (Wilsford 1991); Anthony Jones' collection of essays on medicine in the former Soviet Union and Eastern Europe (Jones 1991); and Arnold Heidenheimer's comparative analysis of medicine in Britain, the United States, and Germany (Heidenheimer 1989). Works in progress include Eliot Krause's (1995) study of professions in five countries (United States, England, France, Italy, and Germany) and Eliot Freidson's (1994) analysis of five professions (medicine, law, engineering, the research sciences, and academics) in five countries (United States, Britain, Germany, France, and the former Soviet Union). In addition there have been several influential articles covering countries such as Germany (Light and Schuller 1986; Light, Liebfried, and Tennstedt 1986; Stone 1991).

In this chapter medicine's professional status will be examined under a cross-national lens using the case study approach and relying heavily on two previously published collections: a special issue of the *Milbank Quarterly* (Willis 1988) guest edited by John McKinlay, and the recently published *The Changing Medical Profession: An International Perspective* (Hafferty and McKinlay 1993). Within these two volumes, fifteen countries are reviewed: the United States (Light 1993), Britain (Larkin 1988, 1993), Canada (Coburn 1988; 1993a), Australia (Willis 1988, 1993), New Zealand (Fougere 1993), France (Wilsford 1991; 1993), Italy (Krause 1988a), Greece (Colombotos and Fakiolas 1993), Finland, Norway, Sweden, and Denmark (Riska 1988, 1993), the erstwhile Soviet Union (Field 1988, 1993), Czechoslovakia (Heitlinger 1993), and China (Henderson 1993). To this group were added a case study of Spain (Rodriguez 1992) and related work by some of the above authors (e.g., Coburn 1993b; Field 1990, 1991; Krause 1988b).

This chapter will argue that there is no *one* medical profession undergoing some universal and unidirectional process of professional ascension, maintenance, or decline. It will also argue against the proposition that the process of professionalization itself is unidimensional or linear in nature. Instead, there exist a host of medical professions that, when examined in terms of their own historical, political, economic, epidemiological, and cultural circumstances, document the process of professionalization as a multifaceted phenomenon allowing for circumstances of professional ascension as well as decline and maintenance. Overall, this chapter affirms what is becoming an increasingly accepted observation: that the United States, with its particular configuration of professional/state/market/cultural/disease etiological and epidemiological factors is a highly idiosyncratic entity, and as such, stands as virtually useless—and often misleading—for the purposes of developing a general theory of professional dynamics. As noted by Jones (1991), the United States not only represents a different set of conditions relative to, for example, socialist countries but also the differences between the United States and other western industrialized nations, particularly those in western Europe, is as large as those between the U.S. and socialist nations.

To best capture this diversity as well as to highlight the patterns that link individual case studies, this chapter has been organized into three sections: First, I present a list of abbreviated observations about the nature of professional dynamics drawn from the case studies listed above. Second, I take a slightly more extended look at some selected case studies in order to illustrate the diversity of players and processes contributing to the overall dynamics of professionalization. Third, and drawing upon the previous two sections, I offer some limited theoretical observations about the nature and dynamics of professionalization. I conclude with some brief recommendations for further work.

TEN OBSERVATIONS ON THE NATURE OF PROFESSIONALISM AND/OR THE NATURE OF PROFESSIONS

1. There is no one medical profession undergoing some universal process of deprofessionalization, proletarianization, or the maintenance of professional dominance. Instead, and depending on the country and time frame in question among other factors, there are numerous "medicines," the totality of which expands our understanding of the broad dynamics and structural influences that constitute the professionalization process.

2. The overall process of professionalization is influenced by the historical interplay of professional/state/market/cultural/etiological/epidemiological factors. At the present time, the bulk of analytical attention is focused on market forces and to a lesser extent on the nature of professional-state relations. Conversely, relatively little attention has been devoted to cultural factors, and virtually none to the role played by different stages and changing patterns in disease etiology and epidemiology (McKinlay 1993).

3. The process of professionalization can be viewed as occupying three different stages or phases—professional attainment, professional maintenance, and professional decline. Although related, they are analytically, structurally, and dynamically quite distinct (see section on theoretical considerations).

4. The maintenance of professional dominance is a contentious, decidedly problematic, enigmatic process. The loss of professional prerogatives is always contested by the profession and as such takes place in incremental stages. Conversely, the attainment of professional powers, while never a foregone conclusion, can appear swift and dramatic under certain circumstances.

5. The most difficult boundary to navigate analytically is the one between the maintenance of professional prerogatives and the loss of those powers. To date, we lack criteria for clearly distinguishing the advent of deprofessionalization or proletarianization from what might justifiably be claimed as the "routine swings" of "normal" maintenance activities. In other words, parties on opposite sides of the interpretive fence may agree that particular changes have taken place but differ on whether to interpret these changes as indicating the presence of deprofessionalization or as evidence of normal boundary maintenance and organizational homeostasis.

6. In drawing conclusions about losses, gains, or the retention of profession-al prerogatives, it is critical to differentiate among the *terms of work* (e.g., pay, hours), the *conditions of work* (e.g., organizational structure, employ-ment status), and the *content of that work* (e.g., the technical core) (Haf-ferty and McKinlay 1993). These are three different dimensions of work; gains or losses in one do not necessarily imply comparable and related gains or losses in the others. For example, presently there is broad con-sensus among the competing models that medicine in the United States has lost appreciable control over the terms and conditions of its work. There is less agreement as to whether control over the content of its work is similarly diminished.

7. Relatedly, insufficient attention has been devoted to the interdependent relationships among these factors—in particular to the mechanisms by which changes in the terms or the conditions of work may directly or indi-rectly impact on the content of work (Hafferty and McKinlay 1993). For example, it is not unreasonable to expect that certain changes in reim-bursement policies or the availability (or more literally, unavailability) of certain treatment options (e.g., being required to choose drugs from a pre-scribed list) may influence how physicians diagnose and treat patients and, thus, ultimately, their technical discretion. The Clinton health care plan's recommendation to link malpractice exposure to the use of clinical proto-cols (e.g., physicians who follow recommended protocols could not be held liable for negative patient outcomes[3]) is one example of where vari-ability in individual physician decision-making is reduced by the utilization of some predefined protocol.

8. The process of professionalization can appear quite different depending upon one's level of analysis. For example, a focus on medicine at the indi-vidual practitioner-patient level versus the organization level may result in different processes or variables being involved or different conclusions being drawn. Thus, to provide insight into health care, McKinlay (1977, 1988) has employed the analogy of professional athletic competition. He points out that one's view of the game, and thus one's understanding of what is going on, is extremely dependent upon whether one is viewing the situation from the position/perspective of spectator (patient), player (providers), referee (the state), or owner (financial and industrial capital).

9. In analyzing issues of professional dynamics, it is important to differentiate among *autonomy* (control over the content of one's work), *dominance* (authority over related health workers), and *sovereignty* (dominion over the matters of ill health) (see Willis 1988). These are three different sectors of influence, and once again, losses or gains in one do not necessarily imply losses or gains in another.

10. As efforts to contain cost and restructure service delivery have assumed greater viability and urgency in Western industrialized nations, the analytical focus on professionalization has gravitated toward examining the effect of external pressures on the professionalization process, particularly those brought to bear by state and corporate interests. However, this new empha-

sis ignores factors more indigenous/internal to the profession, including those of internal solidarity/fragmentation and stratification. While it is impossible to delineate unequivocally between these two spheres of influence (e.g., the rise of specialization, specialty organizations, and the concomitant loss of influence by national organizations such as the AMA clearly have been influenced by governmental subsidies to education and clinical-reimbursement policies), it remains critical that the processes of intraorganizational structure and dynamics not be ignored in any analysis.

CASE EXAMPLES

Case studies of Italy (Krause 1988a, 1988b) and Greece (Colombotos and Fakiolas 1993) show how critical party politics—as a factor distinct from state influence—can play a pivotal role in the process of professionalization. Modern Italy, built upon a political history of feuding principalities and a post-World-War-II distaste of a strong central state by both the Christian Democrats (CD) and the Communist Party, serves as an excellent example of government by political party (*partitocrazia* or party-ocracy). This form of political influence and organization has no parallel in the U.S., but shares similarities with countries such as China or the erstwhile Soviet Union in which one political party controls state functioning.

It Italy, the forces of *partitocrazia* traditionally have weakened not only the state but the solidarity of the medical profession. Professional groups are divided along party lines, often building upon specialist-generalist divisions (e.g., elite specialists voting CD and general practitioners voting socialist). The result is a system where patronage and sponsorship permeate all levels of medical decision-making. But with the advent of accelerating health care costs and a service delivery system biased towards expensive hospital-based care in the 1980s, the Italian government began to pass laws requiring medical groups to negotiate with local and regional governments for fees and payments. These laws effectively required organized medicine to function as a bargaining agent that combined the threat of price controls and served to unify a traditionally weak profession. Rather than controlling the profession by fragmenting it, these state-generated actions fostered an emergent awareness of common interests among long-time antagonists. The result has been a rise in organized medicine's solidarity and power. In sum, state efforts to cap costs and rationalize its health care system system do not *necessarily* result in greater external control of the medical profession nor a loss of its professional status. Similar conclusions have been noted for such politically disparate countries as New Zealand (Fougere 1993) and Spain (Rodriguez 1992).

The case of Greece (Colombotos and Fakiolas 1993) also illustrates how factors other than the technical control of work can exercise a decisive influence over the gain, loss, or maintenance of professional powers. Greece, too, has a turbulent political history, with party politics and party loyalty exercising a decisive influence over the content and the context of medical work. Correspondingly, there is an oversupply of physicians that has been unchecked by the medical profession.

One important difference between Greece and Italy is that Italy stands as an example of a weak state alongside a weak medical profession, while Greece is characterized by a state that is relatively stronger than the profession. Although there are many examples of state-dominated medical professions, what is of interest in the case of Greece are the particular points of influence. In addition to establishing its domain over the areas of licensing and the credentialling process, the Greek state extends that influence by its control over medical societies. In Greece, laws govern the composition, structure, governance, and even the internal functioning of professional societies. The result is that medical societies exist as subsidiaries of the state, performing many administrative functions on the state's behalf. There do exist a number of non-official organizations, often built around specialty or geographical interests, but they engage mainly in scientific discourse and have little political presence.

Reflecting the dominant cultural presence of a patronage system, the influence exerted by Greek physicians is personal and informal rather than organizationally based. Although most physicians are salaried employees (either by the National Health Service, the Social Insurance Institute, or one of the health insurance funds), virtually all operate a private practice on the side and neglect to report that income for tax purposes. Physicians also foster public dissatisfaction with the technical and personal quality of services in the public sector. By artificially limiting access to their public services, physicians seek to encourage patients to shift from the physician's salaried practice to his/her private practice. Finally, physicians, surgeons especially, illegally solicit and accept bribes—*fakelaki* (the "little envelope")—to ensure preferential treatment, or even any treatment at all.

In the case of Greece, then, we can follow the emergence of a reactionary, underground, "renegade capitalist" medical system that is at least partially driven by the conditions of a dominant state and a relatively weak profession. In this respect, Greece mirrors conditions in the Soviet Union, Czechoslovakia, Yugoslavia, and China, for example, where similar dissatisfactions with the state-controlled medical system have fostered a similar private, underground delivery system, similar manipulations of this dual system by physicians, and a similar practice of under-the-table payments to physicians for preferential treatment and access privileges. While acknowledging that there exist important cultural differences between the United States and countries such as those listed above, the presence of this "gray economy" raises critical questions about the ethical core of professions and medicine's alleged status as an altruistically motivated occupation.[4]

Soviet Union/Czechoslovakia/China

The unleashing of political, social, and economic turmoil, along with the weakening of state and party controls in countries such as Russia and Hungary (Field 1988, 1993), Czechoslovakia (Heitlinger 1993), Yugoslavia (Dill 1993), and China (Henderson 1993), offer researchers a natural experiment in the professionalization process. Each of these countries stand as an example of medicine stretching its professional wings after decades of external control.

This metamorphosis, however, is not restricted to those beginning their quests from ground zero. For example, Henderson (1993) characterizes the Chinese Cultural Revolution as the most extreme example of radical deprofessionalization ever undertaken. Nonetheless, she argues that, even during this period of extreme professional oppression, the cultural authority of physicians was "never entirely eroded." In this respect China may serve as an excellent example of how physicians in state-run medical organizations can maintain in a diminished form, and subsequently reassert, control over many aspects of their training, evaluation, and practice. Henderson's analysis also ties state control to geography, noting that the state and the party were much better able to control urban-based specialty physicians than rurally located primary care physicians. Finally, Henderson explicitly links gains in technical expertise to a rise in professional status. In this latter respect, we can contrast her observations with Krause's seminal observation (1988) that if power and control over work is derived from medical expertise, why did the Italian medical profession not dominate the workplace and the state prior to 1981? His answer—*partitocrazia*—reminds us that technical expertise need not be the pivotal factor in issues of professional dynamics.

The dismantling of the former Soviet Union and the political turmoil underlying change in Russia, Czechoslovakia, and other Eastern European countries offer opportunities to observe how a weakening of state and/or party control can foster the rise of professional power and influence. Observers such as Field (1988, 1991, 1993), Heitlinger (1993), and Dill (1993) concur that a weakening of domination by a centralized state may lay the groundwork for a surge in organized medicine's influence and an increase in individual physician autonomy. More specifically, this weakening has allowed for the formation and growth of independent medical associations. These organizations constitute an emergent corporate entity whose independence from state control facilitates its ability to represent the interests of its constituencies. It is not clear, however, that this increased political presence will result in increased administrative and economic independence. As has been evident in Spain, vestiges of bureaucratic power and influence die slowly. Field (1993), for example, questions whether the current emergence of organized medicine as a corporate group and private practice will translate into emancipation of medical practice from the control of medical bureaucrats. Related questions include whether increases in control over the terms and/or conditions of work will result in changes in medicine's control over the content of work.

In addition to the emerging presence of medicine as a corporate force, the study of medicine in these countries raises other important questions. For one, the routine practice of patients making under-the-table payments to physicians in order to ensure access and other forms of favorable treatment has implications beyond those of professional status and the identification of core attributes (an approach that has fallen on disfavor among sociologists of late).[5] The claim that medical services are delivered on the basis of patient need and not on the form, type, or amount of compensation offered has long been a central part of medicine's ideological core. How this face-to-face commingling of remuneration and professional services shapes the dynamics of the physician-patient relationship (including issues of trust) is a key question that in the end will be most clearly illuminated by cross-national research. On the one hand, one might invoke a corporate-commercialist argument and reason that the presence of a gray market represents another layer of patient disenfranchisement and exploitation. On the other hand, one might suggest, as does Field (1988) that such a practice affords patients a form of control over physician behavior that is otherwise unavailable. I believe the question remains open, but it is one that is particularly germane to the United States as services move more towards a managed care/gatekeeper system where rationing will become a more explicit and formally viable entity at the individual practitioner level.

THEORETICAL OBSERVATIONS

As noted above, the status and condition of medicine in countries other than the United States, as well as the dynamics of professionalism under different political, economic, social, epidemiologic, and cultural conditions, amply illustrate that it is overly simplistic to assume that there is a single medical profession undergoing some unidimensional gain, loss, or maintenance of professional dominance. At any given point in time, it is possible to identify examples of professions in ascension, decline, or immersed in maintenance activities.

Of these three phases, the process of professional *maintenance* has received the least analytical attention. Too often, efforts made by professional groups to consolidate their prerogatives, or respond to outside threats, are interpreted by social scientists either as evidence of professional *ascension* or professional *decline*. Neither interpretation is analytically satisfactory because they both ignore or misinterpret activities and dynamics that rightly should be characterized as activities of *maintenance*.

The growth of professional dominance follows a different dynamic than does the maintenance of professional powers, with professional decline constituting yet a third dynamic. For example, the attainment of professional prerogatives (to whatever degree) is always followed/accompanied by a "stage" in which the group in question seeks to solidify, protect, and simultaneously extend those prerogatives against encroachment from outside groups. This stage is best captured by the term "maintenance" and should not be interpreted as a byproduct of ascension or a harbinger of decline.

The presence of competing interests, threats, or countervailing forces (see Light 1991; Mechanic 1991) is a ubiquitous part of any maintenance stage. The rise of such forces may signal the shift from ascension to maintenance. These countervailing forces can be found in the actions of other groups who seek to establish their own "professional credentials"; in actions taken by the state to control, restrain, or otherwise recapture some of the autonomy it once ceded to the group in question; or in the perception of the dominant group that its interests are being threatened, regardless of whether they are or whether that is the intention of the "offending" group.

Turning to the dynamic of professional decline, the greatest roadblock to an adequate conceptualization of this process is in viewing it as the antithesis of professional ascension—and, as such, simply the reversal of the path and a mirroring of the tempo of the preceding rise. In fact, professional decline is not the inverse of professional ascension nor is it as decisive as professional ascension. As a slow historical process the diminution of medical prerogatives is something distinct from the rise of professional entitlements and protections. At minimum, the shift from dominance to decline is buffeted by a period marked by maintenance activities. Nonetheless, it would be analytically limiting to view maintenance activities simply as a transient way station en route to some more definitive set of dynamics.

What I am *not* proposing is a model of professional dynamics in which the processes of ascension, maintenance, and decline proceed in some stepwise fashion, whether that be linear (from ascension to maintenance to decline) or circular (from ascension to maintenance to decline, back to ascension, and so on). What I *do* claim is twofold. First, the attainment of professional prerogatives is always accompanied by some form of professional solidification and maintenance. Similarly, any claims of professional decline must differentiate between a "real" loss of professional prerogatives and what Freidson has so aptly characterized as "mere" skirmishes along the boundaries of professional powers. Activities directed towards consolidation and maintenance, whether they be proactive or reactive, cannot be taken as prima facie evidence of professional decline. Such actions and activities may extend over a considerable period of time and do not necessarily lead to the diminishment of professional prerogatives nor indicate the presence of imminent decline. In fact, maintenance activities may serve as a precursor to a subsequent period of professional ascendancy.

The second claim involves the relationship among these three dynamic entities. Although maintenance does not signal the arrival of either decline or ascendancy, it is a stage of transition. Even though activities intended to extend, sustain, and protect a profession's boundaries should be approached as a separate stage of organizational behavior and not as a subset or byproduct of some other dynamic, all such conflict cannot be subsumed under this banner. In spite of the fact that maintenance activities may stretch over a considerable time period and be accompanied by much buffeting and turmoil, at some point it is necessary to step back from the particular skirmishes under consideration and draw conclusions as to whether there has been some meaningful change in powers and prerogatives or whether these powers remain fundamentally intact. At this point, the interpretive key lies within the criteria being used to establish the presence and the meaningfulness of change. Addressing the differences among the terms, conditions, and content of work is one such device. Drawing distinctions among autonomy, dominance, and sovereignty is another (see above, "Ten Observations").

Although there is no strict timetable governing transitions among the three stages, it appears that ascension is the most rapid, maintenance the most incremental, and decline the most enigmatic. Part of the difficulty in delineating ascendancy or decline from maintenance is that claims to professional prerogatives and status are often infused with elements of rhetoric and ideology. For the dominant profession, a fundamental element in its maintenance efforts is the attempt to convince other parties—including pretenders, the state, the public at large, and its own rank and file—that its dominance justly continues and that the existence of conflict per se does not demonstrate a waning of its professional powers. Any dominant group will continue to claim control over critical domains, even if that control is no longer effective. Similarly, pretenders will issue their own claims, seeking to influence the same parties, but in this case to convince others that the dominant group no longer warrants the cultural authority and/or legislative protections previously established. Sociologists add to this collection of voices by their various announcements as to the death or the continued vigor of medicine as a profession. In sum, the process of maintenance is characterized by a plethora of conflicting and ideologically based claims emanating from rival interest groups. These difficulties in delineation notwithstanding, it is important to avoid misinterpreting actions that fall within the normal swings of homeostasis or within the course of routine maintenance activities as indicative of either ascendancy or decline.

CONCLUSIONS

The study of medicine—whether at the level of the individual physician-patient relationship or that of professional-state relations—is well served by focusing on the dynamics of medicine *as a profession*. By attempting to understand issues of autonomy and power along with those of trust and fiduciary orientation, and by emphasizing the broader environment in which occupations operate in contemporary societies, one can obtain a detailed picture of occupational culture and the nature of medical work in modern society. To this end, a cross-national focus based on case studies of particular nation-states or collectivities of states (for example, the European Common Market) further highlights the diversity and complexity of the professional form of organization, as well as reinforcing the fundamental message of flux and constant change.

Although it has been well over twenty years since the publication of Freidson's seminal *Profession of Medicine* (1970), our understanding of the diversity and complexity of medicine is in its infancy. In spite of the recent proliferation of case studies focusing on countries other than the United States and Britain, this expansion remains dominated by a focus on Europe, former British Commonwealth countries, Eastern Europe, the former Soviet Union, and China. Other countries (for example, Japan), continents (Africa), regions (Central and South America, Southeast Asia, and the Middle East), and developing and Third World countries, have barely been explored. In many cases, this neglect is not due to a lack of interest in these countries per se or to matters of health care, but rather a neglect of a particular perspective—the professionalization process and medicine's status as a profession.

The call, then, is for more case studies—but this time relying less on the traditionally favored beacons of Western industrialized nations. In addition, the economic, political, cultural, and epidemiological changes cascading through Eastern Europe and the former Soviet Bloc represent an exciting opportunity to explore, in vitro, the range of professional dynamics. There is much work to be done.

NOTES

[1] This chapter is based on a presentation given by Frederic W. Hafferty and John B. McKinlay at the 88th Annual Meeting of the American Sociological Association, Miami, August 13–17, 1993. Grateful appreciation is extended to John McKinlay for his comments on this chapter.

[2] We will not explore the differences or similarities of deprofessionalization, proletarianization, and corporatization in this paper. Let us simply note that of the three, proletarianization, with its roots in Marx's labor theory of value, is the most theoretically well grounded. In turn, those adopting a deprofessionalization perspective have focused more on identifying variable sets (e.g., advances in information technology, the growth of the self-help and women's movement) in their attempt to explain perceived changes in medicine's position and power. Corporatization, which McKinlay has labeled as "proletarianization beyond Marx," lacks the tradition and body of writings accompanying the other two schools of thought. Its focus on the interplay of state, corporate, and professional forces holds promise, particularly in integrating the respective strengths of deprofessionalization and proletarianization, but it remains an underexplored and underdeveloped analytical perspective.

[3] Whether this type of legal protection would distinguish among "mistakes" (often considered to be nonculpable), "malpractice" (clearly culpable), and outcomes classified as random or chance events (e.g., where outcomes and conditions cannot be causally linked) is unclear. See Hiatt (1990) for more on these distinctions.

[4] Discussions of underground economies and gray markets often focus on how these mechanisms help the poor. In contrast, it appears that, in this instance, the "privilege" of paying considerable amounts of money to gain access to services is a practice that benefits the rich.

[5] Jones (1991) posits a two-stage process in the sociological study of professions. The first stage is marked by attempts to describe and define professions by emphasizing definitions and typologies. In the second stage, this effort was abandoned as unworkable and attempts were made to understand the process by which an occupation became a profession. At this second stage there is more attention devoted to locating a profession within its environment—and thus to issues of boundary establishment/maintenance and territorial imperatives.

REFERENCES

ABBOTT, ANDREW. 1988. *The System of Professions. An Essay on the Division of Expert Labor*. Chicago: University of Chicago Press.

COBURN, DAVID. 1988. "Canadian Medicine: Dominance or Proletarianization?" *Milbank Quarterly* 66 (Suppl. 2):92–116.

———. 1993a. "Professional Powers in Decline: Medicine in a Changing Canada." Pp. 92–103 in *The Changing Medical Profession: An International Perspective*, edited by Frederic W. Hafferty and John B. McKinlay. New York: Oxford University Press.

———. 1993b. "State Authority, Medical Dominance, and Trends in the Regulation of the Health Professions: The Ontario Case." *Social Science & Medicine*. 37 (2):129–38.

COLOMBOTOS, JOHN, and NIKOS P. FAKIOLAS. 1993. "The Power of Organized Medicine in Greece." Pp. 138–49 in *The Changing Medical Profession: An International Perspective*, edited by Frederic W. Hafferty and John B. McKinlay. New York: Oxford University Press.

DILL, ANN. 1993. "Ideology and the Rationalization of Health Care: The Case of Former Yugoslavia." A paper presented at the 88th Annual Meeting of the American Sociological Association, Miami, August 13–17.

FIELD, MARK G. 1988. "The Position of the Soviet Physician: The Bureaucratic Professional." *Milbank Quarterly* 66:182–201.

———. 1990. "Noble Purpose, Grand Design, Flawed Execution, Mixed Results: Soviet Socialized Medicine after Seventy Years." *American Journal of Public Health* 80:144–45.

———. 1991. "The Hybrid Profession: Soviet Medicine." Pp. 43–62 in *Professions and the State: Expertise and Autonomy in the Soviet Union and Eastern Europe*, edited by Anthony T. Jones. Philadelphia: Temple University.

———. 1993. "The Physician in the Commonwealth of Independent States: The Difficult Passage from Bureaucrat to Professional." Pp. 162–71 in *The Changing Medical Profession: An International Perspective*, edited by Frederic W. Hafferty and John B. McKinlay. New York: Oxford University Press.

FOUGERE, GEOFF. 1993. "Struggling for Control: The State and the Medical Profession in New Zealand." Pp. 92–103 in *The Changing Medical Profession: An International Perspective*, edited by Frederic W. Hafferty and John B. McKinlay. New York: Oxford University Press.

FREIDSON, ELIOT. 1970. *Profession of Medicine: A Study of the Sociology of Applied Knowledge*. New York: Dodd & Mead.

———. 1989. *Medical Work in America*. New Haven: Yale University Press.

———. 1990. "The Centrality of Professionalism to Health Care." *Jurimetrics Journal of Law, Science and Technology* 30:431–45.

———. 1994. *The Fate of Knowledge*. Cambridge [England]: Polity Press.

HAFFERTY, FREDERIC W. 1988. "Theories at the Crossroads: A Discussion of Evolving Views of Medicine as a Profession." *The Milbank Quarterly* 66 (Suppl. 2):202–25.

———. 1991. "Trust, Ideology, and Professional Power." A paper presented at the American Sociological Association, 86th Annual Meeting, Cincinnati, August 23-27.

———, and DONALD W. LIGHT. 1989. "The Evolution of Eliot Freidson's Theory of Professional Dominance: A Twenty-year Retrospective." A paper presented at the 53rd Annual Meeting of the Midwest Sociological Society, St. Louis, April 6-9.

———, and JOHN B. MCKINLAY (eds.). 1993. *The Changing Medical Profession: An International Perspective.* New York: Oxford University Press.

———, and FREDRIC D. WOLINSKY. 1991. "Conflicting Characterizations of Professional Dominance." Pp. 225-49 in *Current Research on Occupations and Professions*, edited by Judith Levy. Greenwich, CT: JAI Press.

HAUG, MARIE. R. 1973. "Deprofessionalization: An Alternate Hypothesis for the Future." *Sociological Review Monograph* 20:195-211.

———. 1988. "A Re-examination of the Hypothesis of Physician Deprofessionalization." *Milbank Quarterly* 66 (Suppl. 2):48-56.

HEIDENHEIMER, ARNOLD J. 1989. "Professional knowledge and state policy in comparative historical perspective: law and medicine in Britain, Germany and the United States." *International Social Science Journal.* (41):529-53.

HEITLINGER, ALENA. 1991. "Hierarchy of Status and Prestige within the Medical Profession in Czechoslovakia." Pp. 207-32 in *Professions and the State: Expertise and Autonomy in the Soviet Union and Eastern Europe*, edited by A. T. Jones. Philadelphia: Temple University.

———. 1993. "The Medical Profession in Czechoslovakia: Legacies of State Socialism, Prospects for the Capitalist Future." Pp. 172-83 in *The Changing Medical Profession: An International Perspective*, edited by Frederic W. Hafferty and John B. McKinlay. New York: Oxford University Press.

HENDERSON, GAIL. 1993. "Physicians in China: Assessing the Impact of Organization and Ideology." Pp. 184-94 in *The Changing Medical Profession: An International Perspective*, edited by Frederic W. Hafferty and John B. McKinlay. New York: Oxford University Press.

HIATT, HOWARD. 1990. *Patients, Doctors, and Lawyers: Medical Injury, Malpractice Litigation and Patient Compensation in New York.* Cambridge, MA: Harvard Medical Practice Study.

JONES, ANTHONY T. (ed.). 1991. *Professions and the State: Expertise and Autonomy in the Soviet Union and Eastern Europe.* Philadelphia: Temple University Press.

KRAUSE, ELIOT A. 1988a. "Doctors, Partitocrazia, and the Italian State." *The Milbank Quarterly* 66 (Suppl. 2):148-66.

———. 1988b. "Doctors and the State: An Italian/American Comparison." *Research in the Sociology of Health Care* 7:227-45.

———. (In Press). *Death of the Guilds: Professions, States, and the Advance of Capitalism—1930 to the Present.* New Haven: Yale University Press.

LARKIN, GERALD V. 1988. "Medical Dominance in Britain: Image on Historical Reality." *The Milbank Quarterly* 66 (Suppl. 2):116-32.

———. 1993. "Continuity in Change: Medical Dominance in the United Kingdom." Pp. 81-91 in *The Changing Medical Profession: An International Perspective*, edited by Frederic W. Hafferty and John B. McKinlay. New York: Oxford University Press.

LARSON, MARGALI S. 1977. *The Rise of Professionalism: A Sociological Analysis.* Berkeley: University of California Press.

———. 1979. "Professionalism: Rise and Fall." *International Journal of Health Services* 9:607-27.

LIGHT, DONALD W. 1991. "Professionalism as a Countervailing Power." *Journal of Health Politics, Policy and Law* 16:499-506.

———. 1993. "Countervailing Power: The Changing Character of the Medical Profession in the United States." Pp. 69-80 in *The Changing Medical Profession: An International Perspective*, edited by Frederic W. Hafferty and John B. McKinlay. New York: Oxford University Press.

———, STEPHAN LIEBFRIED, and FLORIAN TENNSTEDT. 1986. "Social Medicine vs. Professional Dominance: The German Experience." *American Journal of Public Health* 76 (1):78-83.

———, and SOL LEVINE. 1988. "The Changing Character of the Medical Profession: A Theoretical Overview." *The Milbank Quarterly* 66 (Suppl. 2):10-32.

——— and ALEXANDER SCHULLER (eds.). 1986. *Political Values and Health Care: The German Experience.* Cambridge, MA: MIT Press.

MCKINLAY, JOHN B. 1977. "The Business of Good Doctoring or Doctoring as Good Business: Reflections on Freidson's View of the Medical Game." *International Journal of Health Services* 7 (30):459-87.

———. 1982. "Toward the Proletarianization of Physicians." Pp. 37-62 in *Professionals as Workers: Mental Labor in Advanced Capitalism*, edited by Charles Derber. Boston: G. K. Hall Publishers.

———. 1988. "Introduction." *The Milbank Quarterly* 66 (suppl. 2):1-9.

———. 1993. Personal Communication.

————, and JOHN D. STOECKLE. 1988. "Corporatization and the Social Transformation of Doctoring." *International Journal of Health Services* 18 (2):191–205.

MECHANIC, DAVID. 1991. "Sources of Countervailing Power in Medicine." *Journal of Health Politics, Policy and Law* 16:485–98.

OPPENHEIMER, MARTIN. 1973. "The Proletarianization of the Professional." *Sociological Review Monograph.* 20:213–27.

RISKA, ELIANNE. 1988. "The Professional Status of Physicians in the Nordic Countries." *The Milbank Quarterly* 66 (suppl. 2):133–47.

————. 1993. "The Medical Profession in the Nordic Countries." Pp. 150–61 in *The Changing Medical Profession: An International Perspective*, edited by Frederic W. Hafferty and John B. McKinlay. New York: Oxford University Press.

RODRIGUEZ, JOSEPH A. 1992. "Struggle and Revolt in the Spanish Health Policy Process: The Changing Role of the Medical Profession." *International Journal of Health Services.* 22 (1):19–44.

STONE, DEBORAH A. 1991. "German Unification: East Meets West in the Doctor's Office." *Journal of Health Politics, Policy and Law* 16 (2):401–12.

WILLIS, DAVID (ed.). 1988. "The Changing Character of the Medical Profession." *The Milbank Quarterly* 66 (Suppl. 2).

WILLIS, EVAN. 1988. "Doctoring in Australia: A View at the Bicentenary." *The Milbank Quarterly* 66 (Suppl. 2):167–81.

————. 1993. "The Medical Profession in Australia." Pp. 104–14 in *The Changing Medical Profession: An International Perspective*, edited by Frederic W. Hafferty and John B. McKinlay. New York: Oxford University Press.

WILSFORD, DAVID. 1991. *Doctors and the State. The Politics of Health Care in France and the United States.* Durham, NC: Duke University Press.

————. 1993. "The State and the Medical Profession in France." Pp. 124–37 in *The Changing Medical Profession: An International Perspective*, edited by Frederic W. Hafferty and John B. McKinlay. New York: Oxford University Press.

CHAPTER 15

Rationing Medical Resources: From Advocacy to Allocation in British and American Nurses

Donna V. Stevenson

Richard M. Levinson

Nancy J. Thompson

INTRODUCTION

Everyone can't have everything. All technologically advanced societies are contending with this truism as they debate how to balance access to health services with the quality of care and its cost.

Recognizing the soaring costs, growing demand, and large segments of the population with restricted access to services in the United States, debates about rationing health care are now found on the pages of prominent medical journals (for example, Relman 1990; Callahan 1990; Levinsky 1990). The majority of Americans, however, oppose programs that would limit or reduce health services (Blendon et al. 1993), and most believe that this affluent country can avoid rationing (Miller and Miller 1986). By comparison, Britain is portrayed as a society that has, within its National Health Service, engaged in rationing health care both at the level of policy and in the delivery of clinical services (Schwartz and Aaron 1984).

As Mechanic notes (1986), the rationing of health care actually occurs in all societies through three basic approaches. Services may be rationed by cost-sharing or the imposition of fees; by making explicit decisions on limitations in coverage, the provision of care, facilities, or technologies ("explicit rationing"); or by setting general budgetary limitations, allowing professionals to establish internal priorities or expenditure patterns ("implicit rationing"). Most societies use a combination of the three approaches, although they differ significantly in the relative weight given to each. Mechanic argues that as concerns about the cost of health services increase, providers may think more about conserving resources, acting like "allocators" in clinical decisions, rather than performing in the more traditional role of patient "advocate," calling for everything possible in patient care (Mechanic 1986).

Although the move "from advocacy to allocation" may be occurring in all technologically advanced societies, many perceive Britain as further along in this process. Aaron and Schwartz's popular study, *The Painful Prescription* (1984), left many with the impression that health care providers in Britain approach the delivery of services much as allocators of scarce resources, with rationing guiding their decisions. In contrast to this image, U.S. health providers have been portrayed as advocates for the delivery of all available services and technology, unrestrained by matters of cost (Reagan 1992).

This study postulates a more complex, paradoxical situation. We suggest that the structure and finance of health services in the U.S. will, in fact, produce clinicians who are more concerned about the allocation of care according to cost than their counterparts in Britain, where rationing is said to be commonplace. Conversely, we anticipate that the structure and financing of health services in Britain will lead their clinicians to advocate the provision of all health care needed by patients regardless of its cost, more than will Americans. A survey examines whether American nurses are more likely than British nurses to support rationing—limiting the allocation of health services because of their costs.

The United States: Structure of Explicit Rationing and Culture of Allocators

The U.S. rations health care largely through fees for service and explicit measures (Mechanic 1986). Most patients shop in a marketplace of services based on what they can afford, which is determined by employment-based health insurance coverage and personal income (Stoline and Weiner 1988). Private or public (Medicare or Medicaid) insurance programs have explicit restrictions on qualifications for coverage and its limitations. Although implicit rationing underlies the growing prepaid health programs or health maintenance organizations, explicit rationing and fee-based restrictions predominate.

At the clinical level, explicit and fee-based rationing can be very intrusive and undermine the autonomy of health professionals (Reagan 1992). Decisions about what should be done for patients must be made with deference to third parties who decide on what is to be covered. Physicians may be required to call insurance companies to obtain prior approval or "precertification" for hospitalization or diagnostic procedures, and managed care insurance plans guide patients to particular providers and dictate the conditions under which their services may be used.

Providers in the U.S. may deliver more services because fee-for-service payment encourages excessive care, concerns about malpractice litigation, a "technological imperative" learned in training, or because patients themselves request procedures and tests. Nevertheless, the pressures of explicit rationing associated with third parties should promote an atmosphere or culture in clinical settings in which matters of cost become salient in health care decisions. Physicians and nurses are likely to become sensitized to the financial constraints of care and explicit rationing should contribute to a "culture of allocators" among those delivering services.

Britain: Structure of Implicit Rationing and Culture of Advocates

Britain's National Health Service (NHS), which delivers approximately 90 percent of the health care, allocates resources primarily out of tax revenues through a central ministry of health. There is universal coverage. Even with the initiation of reforms attempting to create an internal market within the NHS (Light 1991), hospitals still operate largely on prospective budgets. Salaried physician specialists working within hospitals have clinical freedom, but face the necessity of making decisions within the limits of their resources. General practitioners, located in the community and paid by a complex capitation formula, are also free to make decisions about patient care without regard to personal income or financially burdening the patient.

We believe that aspects of cost should be less salient in clinical decision-making for British providers than their colleagues in the U.S. (Reagan 1992). Although community or hospital-based practitioners must allocate services and resources within operating budgets, clinicians can focus more on patient needs rather than financial matters. Providers might therefore approach patient care more like traditional advocates, recommending actions that are medically appropriate without regard for their cost.

Aaron and Schwartz's (1984) description of hospital-based care in Britain's National Health Service suggested that physicians were "rationing" on the basis of anticipated demand and the availability of resources. They noted, however, that physicians rarely justified their decisions as economic rationing but instead described how their decisions were in the best interests of their patients' well-being. Although physicians behaved as allocators of scarce resources, the values expressed in conversations with investigators reflected a culture of advocacy—doing what is best for clients without regard for costs.

Research Hypothesis

British nurses are part of a health care system featuring implicit rationing. Although the structure requires clinicians to act as allocators of services within limited resources or budgets, professionals have the autonomy to make decisions without intrusive third-party guidelines. Clinicians in America are likely to be more sensitive to matters of cost because of the increasingly pervasive explicit rationing restrictions.

British nurses within an implicit rationing system should reflect a culture of advocates for services, regardless of their cost to patients. American nurses, within an explicit rationing system, should reflect a culture of allocators with primary concerns about the cost of care. Paradoxically, nurses in Britain's National Health Service, often characterized as rationing health resources, may be less supportive of limiting care because of its cost than American nurses.

We therefore hypothesize that nurses in the U.K. will hold more favorable attitudes than American nurses about providing health services to all regardless of cost and that American nurses will hold more favorable attitudes than their British counterparts about rationing health care, i.e., restricting the delivery of health services because of cost.

METHODS

Sample

A convenience sample of nurses in Britain and the U.S. were given questionnaires to complete. All were qualified nurses, having been licensed or registered to practice by the state. Nurses were asked to complete the questionnaire at home or, if there was time, at work, and the questionnaires were collected in a manner that protected the respondents' identity.

In Britain, questionnaires were distributed and collected by contact persons (nurses) at hospitals and health centers in London, Oxford, Manchester, and Yorkshire. Of 108 questionnaires distributed, 77 (71 percent) were returned, but only 51 surveys (47 percent) were sufficiently completed to be used for the analysis. In the U.S., contact persons distributed questionnaires at hospitals, clinics, and other agencies in Atlanta, Georgia; Tucson and Phoenix, Arizona; Denver, Colorado; Amherst, Massachusetts; Urbana, Illinois; and San Francisco, California. Of 118 questionnaires distributed, 104 (88 percent) were returned, but only 71 (60 percent) were completed sufficiently for analysis.

Without the presence of an investigator and with the apparent absence of clear instructions, nurse respondents often left out responses to key items. We attribute the larger proportion of completed questionnaires in the U.S. to greater familiarity with surveys and Likert-type items among health personnel. Many of the British nurses wrote answers to questions in the margins rather than circle response alternatives.

Although the method of sample selection restricts any claims that the respondents are representative of all nurses in the U.S. or U.K., they are a diverse group from several cities and regions in both countries. Nurses were employed in various health service settings including specialties in surgery, geriatrics, hematology/oncology, emergency and accident, critical care, maternal and family planning, psychiatry, occupational health, public health, and community nursing.

Table 1 summarizes the nurses' characteristics. The bulk of respondents were women, 92 percent in Britain and 99 percent in the U.S., roughly corresponding to the preponderant number of women in nursing in each country. The ages of nurse respondents ranged 25–58 (mean = 38) in Britain and 26–64 (mean = 40) in the U.S.

In Britain, 77 percent were State Registered Nurses without higher degrees, 18 percent had a baccalaureate degree and 6 percent, a masters degree. In the U.S., 25 percent had a diploma, 13 percent an associate degree, 48 percent a baccalaureate degree and 14 percent a masters degree. The U.S. sample was better educated, on average, than all nurses in the U.S. (i.e., the sample had fewer di-

TABLE 1.   BACKGROUND OF NURSE RESPONDENTS FROM BRITAIN
AND THE UNITED STATES

	BRITAIN **(N = 51)**	**U.S.** **(N = 71)**
Gender		
Male	8 percent	1 percent
Female	92 percent	99 percent
Education		
SRN (Britain)	77 percent	—
Diploma (U.S.)	—	25 percent
Associate (U.S.)	—	13 percent
Baccalaureate	18 percent	48 percent
Masters	6 percent	14 percent
Work Site		
Hospital	52 percent	51 percent
Other	48 percent	49 percent
Mean Age	38	40
Mean Years of Experience	16	14

ploma- and associate-level nurses than the population of practicing nurses as a whole). Nurses in the U.S. were more likely than nurses in Britain to have bachelors and masters degrees, which parallels the differences in nursing education in each country.

Fifty-one percent of the American nurse respondents were employed in hospitals, lower than the 68 percent of all U.S. nurses working in hospitals. Fifty-two percent of nurses in Britain worked in hospitals, also lower than the overall proportion of British nurses employed by hospitals (85 percent). The mean number of years of work experience for American nurses was fourteen, whereas the mean number of years for British nurses was sixteen.

Measurement of Support for Rationing

We drew on the observations of British physicians by Aaron and Schwartz (1984) to develop some of the items for measuring attitudes about rationing of health care. Aaron and Schwartz did not use questionnaires to describe physician attitudes and behaviors, but reached conclusions based on their informal observations and interviews, which were not described in detail.

Attitudes about the rationing of health resources were indicated by responses to six items, one of which inquired about treatment for twelve different health problems. Questions tap whether nurses believe that cost should be considered in the provision of services or treatments. Each item comprised a Likert scale with five response options: agree strongly, agree somewhat, undecided, disagree somewhat, and disagree strongly. In this pilot study, we can rely only on the items' face validity as to whether they actually measure attitudes about rationing medical resources.

Analysis

Each of the five items and the twelve parts of the sixth—seventeen in all—served as dependent variables. We initially examined the differences between

British and American nurses on the mean scores (strongly agree to strongly disagree) for each item. Because differences between British and American nurses could be confounded by level of education or experience, multiple regression analysis was used. This tests whether country is associated with each of the rationing attitude items, independent of (controlling for) the level of nursing education and years of work experience. Education was treated as a 3-item index, with Americans ranging from 1 = diploma or associate degree, 2 = BSN, and 3 = masters. For British nurses, the range was 1 = SRN, 2 = bachelors degree, and 3 = higher education.

FINDINGS

Differences in Means

Table 2 compares the mean responses to each item on an agree to disagree continuum for nurses in the U.S. and Britain (5 = strongly agree to 1 = strongly disagree). For three of the first five items, American nurses appear more supportive of rationing, or considering cost in the provision of care, than British nurses.

American nurses scored significantly higher than British nurses on agreement with the statements, "Doctors should consider the needs of society to control health care costs," "Doctors should consider treating terminally ill patients less aggressively in order to conserve costs," and "It is proper for a doctor to decide not to resuscitate an elderly comatose patient in order to conserve costs." The differences were not statistically significant for the two remaining items, "Doctors and nurses have an obligation to preserve life at any cost" and "Newborns with congenital defects should be treated aggressively regardless of costs." Findings generally supported the research hypothesis.

The remaining item asked respondents whether they agreed that "If the following is medically needed, everyone in our society should receive it regardless of their ability to pay." Twelve health or medical services were listed, as indicated in Table 2. On each item, a lower score indicates greater agreement, i.e., the responses were coded so that 1 = agree strongly to 5 = disagree strongly. On each of the twelve services, British nurses were more likely to agree than American nurses. Except for hospital treatment for a heart attack, the differences were all statistically significant. The findings were again consistent with the research hypothesis.

Regression Analyses

To investigate whether the differences between American and British nurses were confounded by work experience or level of education, separate regression analyses were performed for each of the items. Responses to each item were regressed on country (1 = U.S., 2 = Britain), years of work experience as a nurse, and level of education (a 1-3 scale). Rather than presenting the full regression findings for seventeen separate analyses, the results are summarized in Table 3.

The regression findings generally support those from the differences of means. American nurses were more likely to agree that doctors should consider the need to control health costs and that doctors should consider costs in treating the terminally ill and in resuscitating elderly comatose patients. Americans

TABLE 2.   MEAN SCORES OF AGREEMENT OF NURSES ON RATIONING ITEMS
BY COUNTRY

ITEM	U.S. x (SD) $N = 71$	BRITAIN x (SD) $N = 51$	F $(1,120)$	p value
Doctors should consider the need of society to control costs*	3.8 (1.8)	2.8 (1.4)	15.5	.000
Doctors and nurses have an obligation to preserve life at any cost*	4.3 (1.1)	4.5 (0.9)	NS	
Newborns with congenital defects should be treated aggressively regardless of costs*	3.9 (1.2)	3.5 (1.2)	NS	
Doctors should consider treating terminally ill patients less aggressively in order to conserve costs*	3.3 (1.3)	2.0 (1.2)	30.2	.000
It is proper for a doctor to decide not to resuscitate an elderly comatose patient in order to conserve costs*	3.0 (1.4)	2.1 (1.3)	10.6	.002
If the following is medically needed, everyone in our society should receive it regardless of their ability to pay:**				
basic primary care	1.4 (1.0)	1.0 (0.2)	7.98	.005
prenatal care	1.3 (0.8)	1.0 (0.2)	4.91	.026
hospital treatment for cancer	1.7 (1.0)	1.0 (0.3)	18.20	.000
hospital treatment for heart attack	1.2 (0.7)	1.0 (0.3)	NS	
abortion, for reasons other than saving mother's life	2.8 (1.6)	2.0 (1.3)	7.76	.006
cosmetic surgery to remove facial wrinkles	4.7 (0.8)	4.2 (1.1)	7.64	.006
hip replacement	1.7 (0.9)	1.0 (0.2)	21.70	.000
surgery for hernia repair	1.9 (1.0)	1.0 (0.2)	27.80	.000
hysterectomy	1.8 (1.0)	1.0 (0.2)	26.80	.000
heart transplant	2.9 (1.4)	1.7 (0.9)	26.30	.000
dialysis for end-stage renal failure under age 50	2.0 (1.0)	1.6 (0.9)	6.26	.013
dialysis for end-stage renal failure over age 60	2.7 (1.3)	1.8 (1.1)	12.80	.000

*based on a scale ranging from 1 (strongly disagree) to 5 (strongly agree)

**based on a scale ranging from 1 (strongly agree) to 5 (strongly disagree)

TABLE 3. SUMMARY OF REGRESSIONS OF EACH RATIONING ITEM ON COUNTRY, EDUCATIONAL LEVEL, AND YEARS OF EXPERIENCE

ITEM	F (3,118)	P VALUE	INDEPENDENT VARIABLES* COUNTRY/EDUC./YEAR		
Doctors should consider the needs of society to control costs	5.39	<.005	−		
Doctors and nurses have an obligation to preserve life at any cost	1.34	NS			
Newborns with congenital defects should be treated aggressively regardless of costs	2.65	NS			
Doctors should consider treating terminally ill patients less aggressively in order to conserve costs	10.51	<.001	−		
It is proper for a doctor to decide not to resuscitate an elderly comatose patient in order to conserve costs	5.02	<.005	−	+	
If the following is medically needed everyone in our society should receive it regardless of their ability to pay:					
basic primary care	4.06	<.01	−		
prenatal care	2.88	NS			
hospital treatment for cancer	6.51	<.001	−		
hospital treatment for heart attack	1.66	NS			
abortion for reasons other than saving the mother's life	6.41	<.001	−	−	
cosmetic surgery to remove facial wrinkles	2.65	NS			
hip replacement	7.96	<.001	−		
surgery for hernia repair	10.95	<.001	−		
hysterectomy	11.37	<.001	−	−	
heart transplant	12.00	<.001	−		+
dialysis for end-stage renal failure under age 50	2.16	NS			
dialysis for end-stage renal failure over age 60	5.66	<.005	−		+

*for country: + = significantly greater agreement by British than American nurses on 5 attitudinal items; significantly greater agreement by American than British nurses on 12 treatments

for education: + = higher education significantly associated with greater agreement on 5 attitudinal items; higher education significantly associated with less agreement on 12 treatments

for years of experience: + = longer experience significantly associated with greater agreement on 5 attitudinal items; longer experience significantly associated with less agreement on 12 treatments were less likely to agree that most medically needed services should be provided to a population regardless of an ability to pay. As with the difference of means, heart attack was not statistically significant but previously significant associations did not remain so for prenatal care, cosmetic surgery, and dialysis for patients under age 50.

In a few instances, the experience and education control variables were significantly associated with agreement on some of the attitudinal items. Level of education was significantly and positively associated with agreement that physicians should not resuscitate elderly comatose patients because of cost considerations and that elective abortions and hysterectomies should be provided to all who desire them regardless of their capacity to pay. Years of experience was significantly associated with two attitudinal variables, more experienced nurses showing less agreement that heart transplants should be provided to all in need and providing dialysis to all persons over age 60 and in need.

DISCUSSION

We hypothesized that the structure of health systems would result in clinical cultures where cost of services is of less concern among British than American nurses. The findings generally supported this hypothesis. Although American nurses may participate in a more unrestrained system of service delivery, matters of cost were intrusive, as reflected in nurses' beliefs that expenditures on health services should be limited because of their cost. British nurses, working in a system providing budgets and depending on clinicians to work within the limits, were less likely than their American counterparts to believe that cost should be considered in caregiving.

Americans maintain a "myth" that they do not ration health services while adopting explicit rationing methods in national and state policies (Miller and Miller 1986). For the last two decades, American health policy has been driven by concerns about a "crisis" in health care costs (Starr 1982). Americans experience the impact of cost-containment programs in clinical settings, as they affect the autonomy of physician decisions and hospital policy (Reagan 1992). Many Americans are also experiencing anxieties about insurance coverage, as benefits are cut, premiums increased, and private carriers look for ways to avoid chronically ill patients who are most in need of coverage (Blendon et al. 1993). Thus, it may not be surprising that American nurses are concerned about cost matters and receptive to acting as resource allocators in clinical decisions.

On three of the first five items, American nurses indicated that they, more than British nurses, believed that doctors should consider the allocation of resources in treatment decisions. The meaning of responses to the last series of items, however, is more problematic. Here we asked if all should receive a list of twelve services "regardless of their ability to pay." This is, perhaps, a double-barrelled question, asking both whether the services should be available to all in need and whether society has an obligation to provide them to patients without a capacity to pay. Agreement signified whether citizens are entitled to services, not necessarily a position on rationing. Perhaps it should be expected that nurses working in a system with universal access would agree that all health services should be provided to all patients in need without regard for their ability to pay. Although the last set of questions may be ambiguous indicators of attitudes on rationing medical services, responses consistently showed that British nurses would not want cost issues to influence the provision of services.

An alternative explanation for the same findings may be that nurses' attitudes are reactions to the extremes in patient treatment characteristic of each setting. Nurses in the U.S. may have participated in, or witnessed, excessive medical interventions that were essentially futile. A more conservative demeanor about medical interventions could be a reaction to seemingly wasteful applications of medical technology. Conversely, British nurses may be reacting to cases that received less than an optimal level of care in the context of limited resources. Their attitudes could reflect a sense that patients should not be deprived of any interventions from which they might benefit.

Responses may have differed if we had been comparing physicians in each country. Physicians make most of the patient treatment decisions, although they sometimes consider the input of nurses in the process. Nurses may be more removed from the financial incentives associated with treatment decisions. Nevertheless, the responses of British nurses appear consistent with the responses Aaron and Schwartz (1984) received from British physicians. Doctors limited the use of some expensive services or procedures to conserve resources but justified their decisions according to what was medically appropriate for their patients. The structure encouraged allocative decisions but the culture remained one of advocacy dominated by the patients' needs.

Although some of the differences between British and American nurses were statistically significant, they were small in magnitude and generally reflect similar attitudes. For example, both British and American nurses believed that all people should receive necessary medical services required by their health status. Nurses from both countries generally agreed that doctors and nurses have an obligation to preserve life at any cost but were more ambivalent about the aggressive treatment of congenitally deformed newborns. In health care, there may be a convergence of values and attitudes among providers, and perhaps populations, in all technologically developed societies (Colombotos et al. 1977; Mechanic 1976).

Survey results should be considered as tentative because of the sampling design; we cannot be confident that the respondents comprise a representative sample of nurses in Britain and the U.S. The convenience sample method, relying on contacts in British and American facilities to distribute questionnaires to their colleagues, could have biased the selection of respondents. For example, in both countries we may have included more sophisticated or cosmopolitan nurses who may be more similar across countries than less educated nurses or those not practicing in major metropolitan areas. Perhaps some of those biases were partially accounted for by controlling for the level of education and experience in the regression analyses.

CONCLUSIONS

We expected that Britain's National Health Service, characterized by implicit rationing, would result in a culture of advocacy favoring the provision of all available services to patients in need, regardless of cost. Conversely, we anticipated that explicit rationing methods typical of the U.S. would be associated with expressions of concern about cost among American nurses. We hypothesized and found that American nurses would be more amenable to rationing, or decisions based on cost (an "allocation" perspective), than nurses in Britain.

Many share the belief that Britain rations its health resources whereas the Americans do not. In reality, both countries ration but they use different methods of rationing. Indeed, the methods of explicit fee-based rationing in the U.S. are more intrusive in clinical decision-making and professional autonomy than those used in Britain. This study suggests that American nurses are more concerned about the cost consequences of care than nurses in Britain. A conscious rationing of health care on the basis of cost may actually be more pervasive in the U.S. than in Britain.

REFERENCES

AARON, HENRY J., and WILLIAM B. SCHWARTZ. 1984. *The Painful Prescription: Rationing Hospital Care.* Washington, D.C.: The Brookings Institution.

BLENDON, ROBERT J., TRACEY S. HYAMS, and JOHN M. BENSON. 1993. "Bridging the Gap Between Expert and Public Views on Health Care Reform." *Journal of the American Medical Association* 269:2573–78.

CALLAHAN, DANIEL. 1990. "Rationing Medical Progress: The Way to Affordable Health Care." *New England Journal of Medicine* 322:1810–13.

COLOMBOTOS, JOHN, KATHERINE A. CHARLES, and CORINNE KIRCHNER. 1977. "Physicians' Attitudes Toward Political and Health Policy Issues in Cross-National Perspective: A Comparison of FMGs and USMGs." *Social Science and Medicine* 11:603–09.

LEVINSKY, NORMAN G. 1990. "Age as a Criterion for Rationing Health Care." *New England Journal of Medicine* 322:1813–16.

LIGHT, DONALD W. 1991. "Observations on the NHS Reforms: An American Perspective." *British Medical Journal* 303:568–70.

MECHANIC, DAVID. 1976. *The Growth of Bureaucratic Medicine.* New York: John Wiley.

———. 1986. *From Advocacy to Allocation: The Evolving American Health Care System.* New York: The Free Press.

MILLER, FRANCES H., and GRAHAM A. H. MILLER. 1986. "The Painful Prescription: A Procrustean Perspective?" *New England Journal of Medicine* 314:1383–85.

REAGAN, MICHAEL D. 1992. *Curing the Crisis: Options for America's Health Care.* Boulder, CO: Westview Press.

RELMAN, ARNOLD S. 1990. "Is Rationing Inevitable?" *New England Journal of Medicine* 322:1809–10.

SCHWARTZ, WILLIAM B., and HENRY J. AARON. 1984. "Rationing Hospital Care: Lessons from Britain." *New England Journal of Medicine* 310:52–56.

STARR, PAUL E. 1982. *The Social Transformation of American Medicine.* New York: Basic Books.

STOLINE, ANNE, and WEINER, JONATHAN P. 1988. *The New Medical Marketplace.* Baltimore: The Johns Hopkins University Press.

CHAPTER 16

Major Orientations in Japanese Health Care[1]

T. Neal Garland

INTRODUCTION

It is somewhat ironic that in the United States, where the cultural emphasis is on diversity, multiculturalism, and heterogeneity, a relatively monolithic biomedically based health care system has evolved (Starr 1982). Japan, on the other hand, is widely regarded as a highly homogeneous and tightly integrated society exemplified by the concept of "Japan, Incorporated." However, as Long has pointed out,

> Japanese patients have a wide range of options for obtaining treatment for illness. They may consult a religious specialist or participate in the group therapy of the "new religions." If they prefer a secular cure, they may turn to an herbalist or other folk healer, a specialist in moxibustion or acupuncture, a physician, nurse, or pharmacist. They may elect to treat themselves with home remedies or with over-the-counter medications of natural or synthetic varieties; or, they may do nothing at all. (Long, 1987:66)

It is true, of course, that a variety of comparable options are also available to the citizen of the United States who is feeling out of sorts. The difference is that in the United States there is only one medical system that is legitimated and institutionalized in the sense that it systematically receives the legal and financial backing of federal and state governments through such things as licensure of practitioners and receipt of funds generated through taxation. Legitimate health care in the United States basically means "biomedicine"—the system of health care based on the assumptions of what is commonly referred to as "germ theory." Other approaches to healing, such as faith healing, are regarded as "marginal" forms of health care at best (Wardwell 1979), although this view may be changing (Poloma 1991; Shupe and Hadden 1989).

While it is true that biomedicine is clearly the dominant institutionalized approach to health care in Japan, it also is true that a number of alternative approaches to healing enjoy a high level of legitimacy in the eyes of the public and, to some extent, in the laws of the land. In this sense, the Japanese citizen has a much wider range of alternatives for dealing with health problems than does the American. In this chapter, two of the most important orientations regarding health care in Japan will be discussed. These are the biomedical orientation and the Chinese-based *kanpo* orientation. There are others, such as religious healing and folk medicine, which also are quite important but which cannot be examined here because of limitations of space. The word *orientation* is used here to indicate a set of assumptions about the causes of illness and the appropriate approaches to preventing and/or curing them.

THE BIOMEDICAL ORIENTATION

The term *biomedicine*, as used in this chapter, refers to the system of medicine based on "germ theory," which grew out of classical Greek medicine and which developed into its present form in Europe and the United States during the nineteenth and twentieth centuries. Other writers have used such terms as *cosmopolitan medicine, Western medicine*, or *modern medicine* to refer to the same medical system.

Biomedicine has been known in Japan since the early days of contact with Europeans in the sixteenth century (Bowers 1970). Its popularity rose and fell as various Japanese leaders accepted or rejected it. By the time of the Meiji Restoration in 1868, however, it had become firmly established. The Meiji leaders endorsed it and took steps to promote biomedicine at the expense of traditional Chinese medicine. Biomedicine clearly is the major health care orientation in Japan today, where it exhibits many of the same characteristics as it does in the United States and other Western nations. For example, it is strongly based in biomedical science; practitioners are criticized for treating patients impersonally and for paying more attention to the disease than to the person; there is a geographic maldistribution of doctors; and it is expensive. However, as with nearly everything Japan has adopted from other cultures, biomedicine as it is currently practiced in Japan has developed certain features that give it a distinctly Japanese character. It is to these features that the present discussion will be directed.

Training of Physicians

While biomedicine in Japan following the Meiji Restoration was patterned after the German model, the American influence following World War II played a strong role in shaping current programs for the training of physicians. New educational laws instituted in 1947 as a result of American pressure led to the creation of a system of medical education in which students graduate from high school and then take a rigorous entrance examination for medical school. After passing the examination, the student must complete two years of premedical education, followed by four years of medical school. Graduation from medical school is followed by a national medical examination administered by the Ministry of Health and Welfare. The national examination is quite demanding and a substantial proportion of those who attempt it each year do not pass (Hashimoto 1984).

Prior to 1968, a one-year internship was required of those who had passed the national examination before they were allowed to begin practice. In 1968, however, this requirement was removed. It is now recommended that new doctors undergo a residency of two or more years before entering practice. A large majority of all new doctors do so, most often in a hospital affiliated with a medical school. Typically, a medical school graduate who has passed the national examination spends five or more additional years at a medical school or university to earn a "Doctor of Medical Science" degree, which is somewhat equivalent to a Ph.D. in the American educational system. The Doctor of Medical Science degree is a status symbol that is important to the success of the physician's practice (Hashimoto 1984).

Although it has been strongly affected by American influences, in certain ways the Japanese system of medical education is more similar to the system of some European countries than it is to that of the United States. Only a small percentage of American physicians are trained in six-year or accelerated programs; by far the majority of them complete four years of undergraduate college and then four years of medical school before entering a residency program. Most American physicians have thus received two more years of schooling than have Japanese physicians, although it must be pointed out that the typical Japanese school year is longer (a minimum of 210 days) than it is in the United States (180 days). This means that the average Japanese student who graduates from high school has spent as much time in the classroom as the average American college sophomore.

Medical Practice

Private practice and hospital practice are clearly divided in Japan. Private practice physicians are not allowed to continue to care for their patients once the patients have been admitted to a public hospital because public hospitals maintain their own staffs of physicians. A slight majority of physicians are hospital-based, although the private practice physicians control the very powerful Japan Medical Association.

As in some European nations that utilize the same type of division, this situation has given rise to two important criticisms of health care in Japan: (1) continuity of care is affected, and (2) private practitioners are sometimes reluctant to send their patients to the hospital out of fear of losing the patient to hospital-based physicians, some of whom do provide primary care (Yamamoto 1983). This fear has been cited as one reason why Japan has the lowest rate of hospital admissions of any modern nation—7.5 admissions per 100 persons per year. The rate for the United States is roughly twice this figure (Phelps 1992).

Group practice is not popular in Japan. Most physicians are engaged in solo practice. This appears to be changing, however, for the group setting appears to be more appealing to younger physicians.

While the rate of hospitalization is exceptionally low in Japan compared to that of other nations, the rate of visits to physicians is exceptionally high. In the United States, the average patient makes about five office visits per year, with each visit lasting from 12 to 15 minutes. In Japan the average number of visits is fifteen, with each visit lasting from 3.5 to 4.5 minutes (Ohnuki-Tierney 1984). There would appear to be at least two reasons for this visitation pattern in Japan.

First is the fact that under the Japanese insurance system, the doctor is paid on the basis of a point system. Each procedure that the doctor performs is assigned a point value by the government. The monetary value of the points is decided by negotiations between the Japan Medical Association, the Japan Hospital Association, the Japan Pharmaceutical Association, and the Japan Ministry of Health and Welfare (Levin and Wolfson 1989; Hashimoto 1984). Physicians complain that the monetary value assigned to the points is so low that they must see large numbers of patients—in some cases as many as one hundred per day—in order to maintain a middle-class income (Lock 1980). The structure of the payment system therefore contributes directly to the fact that Japanese physicians work long hours, see large numbers of patients, and spend relatively little time with each patient. This pattern is highly detrimental to the image of biomedicine in Japan, for Japanese culture emphasizes the importance of personal acquaintance and harmonious interpersonal relationships, even in practitioner-client situations.

A second factor contributing to the high number of visits to physicians is quite controversial: Physicians not only prescribe medications for their patients—they are also the ones who sell the medications to those patients. In fact, a major portion of the incomes of most physicians comes from the sale of medications. It is typical for a doctor to provide the patient with only small amounts of medicine at a time and to request that the patient return to the doctor's office often to receive further examination and additional amounts of medication. This has led to the widespread belief that doctors routinely require return visits and overprescribe in order to increase their income and that the result is a high level of drug-induced iatrogenic illness.

Lock (1980) points out that the physicians' side of this second factor is understandable, given the historical development of medical practice in Japan. When biomedicine was first introduced—and for a considerable period after its introduction—the predominant medical system was *kanpo*, which is based on traditional Chinese medicine. An essential element of *kanpo* is frequent—perhaps even daily—examination of the patient by the doctor so that the specific formulation of herbal medicine can be adjusted to suit the patient's changing condition. While biomedicine grew in popularity, the practitioners were still very much immersed in the culture of *kanpo* and naturally continued to utilize many of the same modes of thought that were part of *kanpo* practice. Even though biomedicine has been the major medical system for quite some time, the influences of *kanpo* remain strong. Biomedical doctors claim that, without seeing their patients often and without the right to sell medication to their patients, their ability to meet patients' changing needs would be seriously affected.

It is worth noting that Japanese patients *expect* to receive medications when they visit the doctor and that they do not object to the doctor's selling medicine to them. What they do object to is that sometimes the synthetic drugs are too strong and may produce negative side effects. They do not seem to object to the amount of drugs they receive, for they feel that the doctor must make a living and must sell drugs in order to do so. Frequently patients accept the medication—which is paid for by the national insurance system—and simply throw away what they do not want to use. The patient considers it rude to tell the doctor that he or she is overprescribing (Lock 1980).

Attitudes Toward Biomedicine

Certain aspects of Japanese culture promoted a rapid acceptance of the biomedical model of health care (Lock 1980). At the time when Japan was making major efforts to modernize in the nineteenth century, biomedicine was beginning to make rapid technological advances, which would lead to the conquering of many of the acute infectious disorders that were major causes of death at the time. The rapid and dramatic cures that biomedicine could offer for these acute disorders caught the imagination of the Japanese, as it did of other peoples, and contributed to a decline of interest in traditional Chinese medicine, the treatments in which tended to require time to be effective.

Another factor was that the extremely strong work ethic and group orientation in Japanese culture promoted acceptance of fast-acting biomedical cures. To be unable to do one's work is to be unable to meet one's obligations to family, peers, and society in Japan. Illness that prevents one from working, or that reduces one's efficiency at work, must be dealt with in the most effective way possible. Biomedicine appeared to offer a clear advantage over other forms of health care in this regard.

Finally, Lock (1980) suggests that fear of the stigma and potential ostracism that accompanies such diseases as tuberculosis, schizophrenia, or certain types of cancer in Japan contributed to a rapid embrace of health care that had been so effective in dealing with serious health menaces in the past. If biomedicine could practically eliminate acute disorders, why could it not do the same for chronic illnesses?

On the other hand, certain factors also are working against continued unquestioning acceptance of the biomedical orientation. Biomedicine has not been able to eliminate chronic illnesses. As these types of illnesses have become increasingly important in Japan, doubts have arisen about biomedicine. Fear of negative side effects of synthetic drugs has already been mentioned as a factor leading people to question biomedical treatments. Factors such as these have led to a renewed interest in *kanpo*, the Japanese version of traditional Chinese medicine.

THE *KANPO* ORIENTATION

Kanpo is the medical system that was introduced to Japan from China, probably somewhere around the sixth century (Long 1987). It is strongly based upon traditional Chinese medicine, although over the centuries it has undergone extensive changes that have given it a uniquely Japanese character.

The national government's attitude toward *kanpo* has varied over time. There have been two major attempts by the government to eliminate *kanpo* altogether (Ohnuki-Tierney 1984). The first took place shortly after the Meiji Restoration of 1868. The new national leaders saw *kanpo* as a vestige of the nation's feudal past and tried to eradicate it as part of their drive toward modernization. A proclamation was issued in 1875 that prohibited practitioners of *kanpo* from pursuing their practices until they had passed examinations in seven subjects in Western medicine. This was a clear attempt to discourage the practice of *kanpo*.

The second major attempt to put an end to *kanpo* occurred as a result of pressure from the Allied Forces in Japan during the early years of their occupation of the country after World War II. *Kanpo* was seen by the Westerners as too "barbaric" to be allowed to continue. The healing practices followed by *kanpo* doctors were prohibited by the new government.

Neither of these attempts to stamp out *kanpo* was successful, however, because the basic assumptions and techniques of this health care orientation are deeply ingrained in Japanese culture (Ohnuki-Tierney 1984). An examination of some of the major characteristics of this approach to health care will illustrate this claim.

BASIC CHARACTERISTICS OF *KANPO*

The Cause of Illness

Views regarding causes of health and illness are fundamentally different in *kanpo* and biomedicine. Traditional Chinese medicine, out of which Japanese *kanpo* has grown, is based on the belief that all nature, including humans, is guided by Tao, a force that was responsible for creating an ordered world out of a state of chaos (Tan, Tan, and Veith 1973). Tao is composed of two opposing forces, which, in a vastly oversimplified view, can be summarized as yin (the negative element) and yang (the positive element). There is a continual struggle to maintain a proper balance between yin and yang in all things. This is what causes the seasonal changes, the cycle of light and darkness that we call day and night; tidal waves; and all other things—including health and illness.

The struggle between yin and yang within the living body is manifested through *ch'i*, which is a harmonious mixture of these two forces. *Ch'i* is conveyed through the body via twelve pairs of main ducts and two trunk ducts running along the front and back midlines of the body. In Western terminology, these ducts are known as "meridians." The points at which the meridians come to the surface of the body are called acupuncture points, of which there are 365. These points provide the sites for certain of the *kanpo* treatments, which will be discussed below.

In the ancient Chinese medical tradition, diseases were not specifically identified. There was only *disease*, as opposed to health, and there was only one cause—an imbalance of yin and yang within the body. The task of the physician was to identify the cause of the imbalance and to take appropriate measures to help restore a proper balance.

Diagnosis

The process of diagnosis in biomedicine consists of the physician searching for a pathogen that has caused the disease from which the patient is suffering (Ohnuki-Tierney 1984). The physician looks for symptoms that help to identify the specific disease afflicting the patient, for this helps to identify the pathogen that must be eradicated. The patient's symptoms are important only insofar as they help the physician to track down the correct pathogen. The patient's subjectively perceived symptoms are significant in the diagnostic process only to the extent that they are judged as biomedically relevant by the physician, who is likely to rely heavily on "objective" tests such as x-rays or analysis of the blood in order to arrive at a diagnosis. In other words, the focus of the diagnostic procedure will be—as much as possible—on objectively determined biomedical facts.

In contrast, in *kanpo* the primary emphasis is on symptoms, rather than on what biomedicine would identify as the underlying cause of the symptoms. Ohnuki-Tierney points out that:

> An important term in *kanpo* is *shokogun.* Although *shokogun* literally means a cluster (*gun*) of symptoms (*sho*) and prodromes (signs forecasting the onset of an illness, *ko*), the concept is quite different from the notion of syndromes in biomedicine. In dictionary definitions, a *syndrome* is "the pattern of symptoms in a disease"; in biomedicine, a syndrome thus defines a disease. *Shokogun* includes any number of symptoms, which may or may not define a particular disease. These symptoms include those consciously perceived by the patient as well as those detected by the *kanpo* doctor. (Ohnuki-Tierney 1984:93)

While symptoms thus play a role in both systems of medicine, the term *symptom* has a quite different meaning in *kanpo* than it does in biomedicine. To the *kanpo* doctor, anything that the patient chooses to describe as a symptom *is* a symptom and becomes a relevant part of the *shokogun* of the patient. Biomedical tests are not necessary in order to make the patient-identified symptoms relevant to his or her problem. In fact, *kanpo* doctors depend on their senses of sight, hearing, touch, and smell rather than on biomedical tests and internal examinations of the patient to arrive at a diagnosis. Evidence from these senses is added to the symptoms perceived by the patient in order to make a decision about the patient's problem.

The *kanpo* doctor makes use of four major techniques in arriving at a diagnosis. These are (Ohnuki-Tierney 1984):

1. *Observation Diagnosis (booshin):* The doctor makes a close visual examination of the patient, paying special attention to such things as the color and texture of the skin, eyes, ears, lips, tongue, and all other external bodily surfaces. Attention is also given to visual inspection of excreta.

2. *Listening Diagnosis (bunshin):* Attention is focused on the qualities of the patient's voice, the sound of his or her breathing and coughing, and the smell of the excreta and of the body odor in general.

3. *Questioning Diagnosis (monshin):* The doctor questions the patient about the history of the illness and about numerous bodily characteristics, such as the amount of sweating and other excretory patterns. The patient is also

asked about sleep habits, preferences in taste (sweet, salty, hot, mild, and so on), and about his or her inborn constitution. The concept of inborn constitution is quite important in Japanese culture in general, with some people being identified as having a weak constitution and others as having a strong constitution. It is believed that a medication that will be effective for a person with a strong constitution will not be effective for a person who has the same medical problem but who has a weak constitution, and vice versa.

4. *Touching Diagnosis (sesshin)*: There are two parts to the touching diagnosis. The first is the taking of the pulse, which is a considerably more complex process than it is in biomedicine because the patient is considered to have several pulses, each of which reflects the condition of various body systems. The second is touching of the stomach (which has special significance in Japanese culture) and other parts of the body in order to analyze their condition.

What is apparent in all four of these methods of diagnosis is the fact that the *kanpo* doctor must pay extremely close attention to the patient *as an individual*. To the symptoms identified by the patient and the results of the four types of diagnoses the *kanpo* doctor will add information provided by certain inherent characteristics of the patient, such as age and sex, in order to decide the cause of the imbalance in the patient's body. This decision will guide the choice of treatment or treatments, which also will be affected by such things as the climate of the area in which the patient lives.

Treatment

The basic treatment in *kanpo* is regulation of daily habits, of which the diet is of greatest importance (Ohnuki-Tierney 1984). In terms of specific treatments, natural medications derived from plants and, to a much lesser extent, animals, are used. Most *kanpo* medications are made from a complex mixture of dried herbs, the exact blend and dosage of which depends on the diagnosis made by the doctor. Since the medication is tailored specifically to the needs of the individual patient and since the patient's condition may change from day to day, frequent visits to the doctor are necessary. At each visit, the patient typically receives sufficient medication to last for only a short period of time.

Herbal medications used by *kanpo* doctors differ from the synthetic medications used by biomedical doctors in several important respects. These include (Ohnuki-Tierney 1984):

1. The *kanpo* medications tend to be multipurpose rather than single purpose. The medications are not aimed at specific pathogens, but rather are intended to restore a proper balance to the body's overall functioning.

2. Most of the *kanpo* medications exert their effects slowly, so that the patient may be required to take them for an extended period before benefits become apparent. This is so because the medication works on the entire body system rather than on one isolated part or problem.

3. *Kanpo* medications are much less likely to produce negative side effects than are synthetic drugs.

4. *Kanpo* medications are much easier for the body to digest and absorb than are synthetic drugs.

These "natural" medications may be combined with acupuncture and/or moxibustion and/or massage. Acupuncture consists of inserting needles into the body at specific acupuncture points, which exist in places where the meridians that convey the *ch'i* through the body reach the body's surface. Moxibustion consists of placing small cones (moxa) made from the dried leaves of the mugwort or wormwood plant (*Artemisia vulgaris*) on the appropriate acupuncture points and igniting them (Tan, Tan, and Veith 1973). The resulting heat stimulates the acupuncture points and helps to restore the balance of the yin and yang forces within the body. Sometimes a thin slice of garlic is placed between the skin and the burning cone. Moxibustion appears to be more popular than acupuncture, perhaps because it is perceived as less threatening than being pierced by needles.

Sometimes the two techniques are combined. A needle is inserted at the acupuncture point and a moxa is placed in such a manner that, when it is ignited, the heat will warm the needle and promote a deeper stimulation of the acupuncture point.

Kanpo Practitioners

Kanpo doctors are allowed to practice *kanpo* only after they have completed regular training in biomedicine. This restriction was established in 1875 and remains in effect today. As a result, there are three types of licensed physicians in Japan: those who practice biomedicine only, those who practice *kanpo* only, and those who combine the two approaches. A large majority of physicians are in the first category, while only a very small proportion (an estimated 100 to 150 in the mid-1980s) are in the second. Physicians who wish to provide *kanpo* treatments for their patients can do so in one of three ways (Ohnuki-Tierney 1984:111–112):

1. Doctors who do not practice *kanpo* themselves regularly refer patients to *kanpo* doctors when the biomedical treatments do not work. Doctors who work in large hospitals and who are well informed on recent biomedical advances appear to be more likely to refer patients for *kanpo* treatments than are doctors who work in smaller hospitals or who are in private practice.

2. At some clinics biomedical doctors and paramedics who perform acupuncture and moxibustion work together.

3. Some doctors practice both biomedicine and *kanpo* themselves. The number of such doctors appears to be increasing.

In the eyes of many Japanese, acupuncture and moxibustion are not particularly associated with *kanpo* medicine, for these treatments most often are provided by trained religious specialists or paramedics who are not doctors. The number of doctors who are licensed to provide acupuncture and moxibustion treatments is insignificant in comparison to the number of licensed paramedics and religious personnel.

Effectiveness

Kanpo is based on an entirely different set of assumptions than is biomedicine. This fact leads many Western followers of biomedicine to view *kanpo* with skepticism in spite of the fact that it has been in existence for literally thousands of years and has millions of adherents in Asian nations. Countless stories of cures brought about through *kanpo* exist, although most of them tend to be anecdotal.

Ohnuki-Tierney (1984) points out that in Japan *kanpo* has been most successful in dealing with disorders that have not responded well to the efforts of biomedicine, such as chronic pain, obesity, and a number of chronic illnesses in general. Biomedicine tends to have had greater success in dealing with acute disorders.

Western researchers persist in attempting to explain the efficacy of *kanpo* techniques in terms understandable in the biomedical perspective. For example, Stux and Pomeranz (1988) cite numerous attempts to explain the effectiveness of acupuncture by investigating the extent to which it promotes biochemical changes in the body. Ohnuki-Tierney (1984) notes that considerable effort has been expended on attempts to isolate the pharmacologically active ingredients in *kanpo* herbal medicines. Such efforts have yielded some "successes,"—as defined in biomedical terms—but much of the efficacy of *kanpo* remains unexplained in "scientific" terms.

What can be said about *kanpo* is that it does appear to be effective in many cases, and it thus makes a positive contribution to health care in Japan. It also plays an important role in encouraging a preventive orientation toward illness due to its emphasis on proper diet and other health-promoting habits (Ohnuki-Tierney 1984).

Popularity of Kanpo

While biomedicine is the dominant approach to health care in Japan, *kanpo* has enjoyed a strong growth in popularity that began in the 1970s. Ohnuki-Tierney (1984) suggests two major categories of reasons for this fact. They are:

1. The first category includes factors pertaining to the nature of the two systems of medicine, their practices, and their practitioners. Within this general category she identifies the following specific points:
   a. An increasing realization on the part of the public that biomedicine does not have all the answers to their health problems.
   b. An increasing public recognition of the potential for negative side effects of many synthetic drugs used in biomedicine.

c. The fact that the Japanese insurance system encourages the overuse of synthetic drugs. Since biomedical drugs are covered by the insurance system and the doctor is the one who sells drugs as well as prescribes them, there is a financial incentive for doctors to overmedicate their patients. This increases the probability that a patient will, sooner or later, experience negative side effects from biomedical medications. Most *kanpo* drugs are not covered by insurance.

d. An awareness that the negative side effects of *kanpo* medicines tend to be minimal to nonexistent.

e. The compartmentalized approach to health care that characterizes biomedicine has been highlighted by the negative side effects of drugs. Biomedical drugs tend to be used to treat a specific problem, regardless of what they might do to the rest of the patient's body. This has made the holistic approach of *kanpo* more attractive to Japanese patients.

f. The impersonal way in which biomedicine tends to be delivered is not compatible with the emphasis that Japanese culture places on interpersonal relations. In contrast, the interpersonal skills of the *kanpo* doctors are a very important part of the doctor's ability to make an appropriate diagnosis and to prescribe an appropriate treatment. Further, the treatment is likely to require an ongoing interpersonal relationship between the doctor and the patient and this is highly compatible with Japanese cultural values.

2. The second category includes factors pertaining to changing patterns of disease, demography, and politics in Japan. These include:

a. The importance of chronic illnesses is increasing and the importance of acute illnesses is decreasing. *Kanpo* medicine has enjoyed its greatest successes in dealing with chronic illness, while biomedicine has been more successful in dealing with acute illnesses.

b. The aging of the Japanese population has led to an increase in the need for effective treatment of chronic illnesses.

c. Obesity is increasing in Japan. In the past, obesity seldom was regarded as a problem because few Japanese were obese. Also, thinness was regarded as unattractive so obesity was looked upon with some degree of favor. However, Japanese today have adopted the Western attitude toward obesity as being undesirable and, at the same time, more Japanese—especially of the younger generation—are obese. *Kanpo* has been relatively successful in treating obesity.

d. In 1954 a pharmaceutical company developed a process for making granular extractions of a number of *kanpo* herbs. This made it possible to market *kanpo* medications that fit in with the increasing pace of Japanese life. Traditional herbal preparations may require hours for proper brewing. The 1954 development made many *kanpo* herbs available in an "instant" form, much like the "instant" coffee favored by Amer-

icans who do not want to take the time to brew an entire pot of fresh-
ly ground coffee.

e. Improved communication and trade with mainland China has led to a
renewal of interest in things of Chinese origin, and this includes *kanpo*
medicine.

In summary, *kanpo* has increased in popularity in Japan because of a growing dissatisfaction with biomedicine and the way in which it typically is delivered. Even though *kanpo* treatment is more expensive because it is not covered
by the health insurance system, many Japanese find it to be an attractive alternative to biomedicine.

CONCLUSION

Health care in Japan includes two major orientations, which are based on drastically different sets of assumptions about the causes of illness and the appropriate ways to bring about cures. In addition to these two major orientations—
biomedicine and *kanpo*—there are many others (such as religious healing and
folk medicine) that have not been included in this chapter but that also play
important roles in the efforts of Japanese to deal with illness. This multifaceted
approach to health care is interesting in light of the emphasis on conformity and
lack of tolerance of diversity that characterizes Japan in the thoughts of many
Westerners. At the same time, in the United States—where diversity is highly valued—only one orientation toward health care receives official legitimation. Reasons for this apparent irony must be sought in the historical backgrounds of the
two countries and in the roles—both medical and nonmedical—played by their
health care systems.

NOTE

[1] This chapter is a revised version of a paper originally presented at the Annual Meeting of the Midwest Sociological Society, Chicago, Illinois, April 7–10, 1993.

REFERENCES

BOWERS, JOHN Z. 1970. *Western Medical Pioneers in Feudal Japan.* Baltimore: The Johns Hopkins University Press.

HASHIMOTO, MASAMI. 1984. "Health Services in Japan." Pp. 335–70 in *Comparative Health Systems:
Descriptive Analyses of Fourteen National Health Systems,* edited by Marshall W. Raffel. University Park, PA: University of Pennsylvania Press.

LEVIN, PETER J., and JAY WOLFSON. 1989. "Health Care in the Balance: Japanese Eurythmy." *Hospital and
Health Services Administration* 34:311–23.

LOCK, MARGARET M. 1980. *East Asian Medicine in Urban Japan.* Berkeley: University of California
Press.

LONG, SUSAN ORPETT. 1987. "Health Care Providers: Technology, Policy, and Professional Dominance." Pp.
66–88 in *Health, Illness, and Medical Care in Japan,* edited by Edward Norbeck and Margaret
Lock. Honolulu: University of Hawaii Press.

OHNUKI-TIERNEY, EMIKO. 1984. *Illness and Culture in Contemporary Japan: An Anthropological View.*
Cambridge: Cambridge University Press.

PHELPS, CHARLES E. 1992. *Health Economics.* New York: Harper Collins.

POLOMA, MARGARET M. 1991. "A Comparison of Christian Science and Mainline Christian Healing Ideologies and Practices." *Review of Religious Research* 32:337–50.

SHUPE, ANSON, and JEFFREY K. HADDEN. 1989. "Symbolic Healing." *Second Opinion: Health, Faith, and Ethics* 12:75–97.

STARR, PAUL E. 1982. *The Social Transformation of American Medicine*. New York: Basic Books, Inc.

STUX, GABRIEL and BRUCE POMERANZ. 1988. *Basics of Acupuncture*. Berlin: Springer-Verlag.

TAN, LEONG T., MARGARET Y. C. TAN, and ILZA VEITH. 1973. *Acupuncture Therapy: Current Chinese Practice*. Philadelphia: Temple University Press.

WARDWELL, WALTER I. 1979. "Limited and Marginal Practitioners." Pp. 230–50 in *Handbook of Medical Sociology*, Third Edition, edited by Howard E. Freeman, Sol Levine, and Leo G. Reeder. Englewood Cliffs, NJ: Prentice-Hall, Inc.

YAMAMOTO, MIKIO. 1983. "Primary Health Care and Health Education in Japan." *Social Science and Medicine* 17:1419–31.

CHAPTER 17

Society and Indigenous Health Care: The Cases of Nepal and Alaska

Janardan Subedi
Nancy Andes
Sree Subedi

Medical pluralism exists in societies where indigenous (folk and traditional) health care systems exist parallel to the modern (Western) health care system. While modern health care services have expanded into most countries of the world, folk and traditional health care continue to be used mostly in developing countries, as well as in European and North American countries. Nepal in Asia and Alaska in the United States have pluralistic systems built upon the economic, ethnic, and cultural diversity extant in their societies. Various sociological and anthropological studies conducted in Nepal and Alaska (among Alaska natives) suggest the persisting wide use of indigenous health care systems in spite of the availability of modern health care services (e.g., Cordes 1986; Fortuine 1988; Subedi 1989a, 1989b; Justice 1981). The basic question we explore in this paper is: Why do the indigenous health care systems flourish and why do people turn to them even when modern health care services are readily available? In trying to address the above issue, sociocultural (in Nepal) and socio-organizational (in Alaska) factors are examined. The conclusions derived from these two societies may have relevance for indigenous medicine in general and offer a guide for the development of health policy in medically pluralistic societies.

MEDICAL PLURALISM

Pluralistic health care systems evolved largely because of European and North American expansion during colonialism (Bhardwaj and Paul 1986; Jingfeng 1987; Pedersen and Baruffati 1989). Rather than supplanting the indigenous health care systems, modern medicine became one of several symbolic systems for coping with illness (Fox 1976; Payer 1988). While folk medicine is not organized or taught formally, modern medicine has become formalized into medical schools with practitioners receiving professional licenses to practice it. Several Asian countries (India, Bangladesh, Pakistan, Sri Lanka, and Burma) have also legally recognized traditional medicine (there are various schools of traditions within the traditional medical system). Some of these specific types of traditional medicine are being taught in traditional medical schools with state support. Others (China, Democratic Korea, U.K., and Germany) combine alternative technologies, for example, traditional and modern medicine, in their formal medical systems. In most countries (for example, the United States), however, indigenous medicine coexists informally with modern medicine to form a pluralistic and diversified health care system. Overall, folk practitioners typically include witch doctors, religious healers, and spiritualists while traditional medical practitioners are trained in the use of herbal, animal, and/or natural products. Thus, each health care system (folk, traditional, and modern) has its own distinctive and more or less organized set of ideas, practices, and methods of treatment. In other words, pluralistic health care includes "multiple systems of knowledge and action, phenomena and interaction, that characterize [health and illness] as well as . . . the medical treatises and institutions that formalize them" (Nordstrom 1988).

HEALTH CARE IN NEPAL AND ALASKA

In Nepal, health care consists of the folk, traditional, and modern health care systems (See Table 1). The most prevalent form of treatment in Nepal, especially in rural areas, has a spiritual (folk medicine) base, and its practitioners are Nepali shamans or *dhamis* and *jhankris*. Since these practitioners are apprenticed within villages, no codification of knowledge exists. This medicine is extremely decentralized and draws on local traditions, family networks, and spiritual beliefs for treatment. Orthodox Buddhist practitioners (*amchis*) also practice this type of medicine, though this is largely restricted to the Tibetan refugees in Nepal (Adams 1988).

The traditional medical system essentially consists of three types of traditions—*Ayurveda, Unani*, and homeopathy. Ayurveda, literally meaning the knowledge of life, draws from ancient Hindu literature concerned with health and disease, and the Unani tradition derives from Greco-Arabic medicine. Both of these traditions use herbal, animal, and/or natural products and came to Nepal from India. Further, both are currently being formally taught in three-year courses in traditional medical schools. Two hospitals and approximately two thousand Ayurvedic and Unani physicians are available to treat illness (Streefland 1985).

Homeopathy is a system of healing developed by Samuel Hahnemann, a German physician in the eighteenth century. The approximately two hundred homeopathic practitioners in Nepal received training in India (Streefland 1985; Bhardwaj 1980). Homeopathy is grounded on the law of similar: let likes be cured by likes. Treatment involves the use of natural, chemical, and/or mineral salts. Homeopathy is found in larger Nepali towns; all of its medicines and raw materials are imported from India.

Besides Ayurvedic and homeopathic practitioners (commonly referred to as *baidya* and *kaviraj*), Unani practitioners (*hakim*), traditional practitioners such as midwives (*camain*) and rustic doctors (*dehati dakdar*) draw from long-standing cultural beliefs and practices. Most of traditional healing, however, relies on knowledge of the values and beliefs that guide people's lives and synthesizes professional/nonprofessional practices into a range of rituals and treatments (Nordstrom 1988; Reissland and Burghart 1989). This approach can be characterized as having a holistic, flexible viewpoint in which the treatment of a patient should vary according to differing conditions of place, time (season), and person. It may vary even in the same patient according to the different stages of the same case, both in its treatment and concrete prescription (Jingfeng 1987).

Modern medicine in Nepal is commonly referred to as "allopathic" medicine or the *angrezi* (English) system of medicine. A medical school and several public and private hospitals are found in Kathmandu, the capital city. Similarly, modern hospitals and clinics are found in larger cities and towns throughout the country. Rural areas are served mainly by modern health centers and health posts.

In Alaska, the health care system is totally dominated in the professional sector by modern medicine. (Refer to Table 1.) One source of this difference may derive from the four sources of formal health care responsible for delivering medical care to all in Alaska. The first source is the private sector, and a second is the state: private and public health care sources common to other states in the United States. The third source is the federal Indian Health Service, which provides health care to eligible Alaska Natives. A fourth system, which is provided by the Native regional health corporations, derives from the 1971 Alaska Native Claims Settlement Act concerning the creation of profit-making corporations from the lands the federal and state government appropriated. Part of the responsibility of the Native regional health corporations is to provide health and human services to its members (Cordes 1986, DeGross 1991).

Within Alaska's intersection of private, public, federal and Alaska Native systems, several innovative programs have developed. One is a Community Health Aide program—similar to primary health care programs in developing countries—where village members are trained in acute care, health surveillance, preventive care, and administrative and community services. Because of large distances between villages and the many locations accessible only by air travel, the community health aide is typically the only formally trained health practitioner in a village. While community health aides remain in telephone contact with physicians at regional hospitals, a range of pharmaceutical drugs are available for dispensing (Cordes 1986).

Since health strategies that are successful in other states and in other industrialized areas are not viable in sparsely-settled rural Alaska, new strategies must

TABLE 1.   HEALTH CARE SYSTEMS IN NEPAL AND ALASKA

HEALING TECHNIQUE	NEPAL	ALASKA
Modern	Allopathy (*angrezi*)	Allopathy Including Community Health Aide, Village Health Educator
Folk	*Dhamis, Jhankris,* Orthodox Buddhist Practitioners	Diviners
Traditional	*Ayurveda Unani* Homeopathy Midwives	Tribal Doctors Midwives

be devised. Thus, a Native Health Corporation has instituted a Village Health Educator Project. This community-based, grassroots approach to disseminating health information uses a village promoter to advise, inform, and facilitate health promotion activities. These health promoters act as liaisons between youth, parents, elders, professionals, school staff, public safety, and the village council. Village health educators are the first-level professionals within the modern medical configuration, but their primary orientation is toward the village, their values, and networks (Larson 1991).

In indigenous medicine, the process of defining the affliction and determining its causation often involves procedures where the practitioner, patient, and family members participate. The naming of the illness has significant therapeutic effects and may lead to symptom relief. Once the offending circumstance act or agent is identified, the patient and his or her network can take remedial procedures within a culturally sanctioned framework (Jilek 1982).

In Alaska, the folk sector is comprised of diviners who diagnose causes of illnesses and advise patients and their families through interpretation using special diagnostic objects. They also communicate with supernatural, ancestral, guardian, or other spirits by revelation in visions or dreams.

The most prevalent procedures used by traditional practitioners in Alaska are herbal or animal treatments for illnesses (Fortuine 1988). Tribal doctors and village midwives use herbal or animal products such as seal oil and whale fat for therapeutic uses. Massage or holding therapy is also widely used. Massage may be employed during labor, for manipulating broken bones, and/or in the treatment of internal organs. Further, poking the skin (*kapi*) with a sharp knife or razor to release blood or fluids is common. For example, this practice is prevalent among the Inupiat, Yup'ik, and Athabascans (Lantis 1954; 1963; Cordes 1986; Fortuine 1988).

Sociocultural Determinants of Indigenous Health Care in Nepal

Durkin-Longley (1982) states that in Nepal popular Hindu and Buddhist ideologies legitimize five categories or sources of power: namely, supernatural beings, divinities, fate resulting from past actions (Karma), humoral states of the body, and foreign scientific technology. Nepali people explain and respond to misfortune and illness with reference to these five types of power. These beliefs/ideologies, in turn, determine which type of treatment will be chosen as suitable.

According to studies (Justice 1981; Subedi 1989a, 1989b) conducted in Nepal, most individuals relied on folk and/or traditional health care either in home-remedies or professional health care services. Modern health care services were only sought as a last resort and usually for serious and/or persistent problems. However, interestingly, Justice (1981) found that when modern health care failed, the patients frequently returned to the use of indigenous health care.

Similarly, in a survey conducted in two Kathmandu government hospitals where services are nominally free of charge, Subedi (1989a) interviewed 760 patients who were currently using the modern hospital services about their health-seeking behavior. Individuals were asked about beliefs and behaviors that affected their choice of a particular health care system. The sequence of treatments was captured in a health care history. Table 2 summarizes patients' use of, and satisfaction with, indigenous medicine.

In spite of the fact that all individuals interviewed were currently seeking treatment from a modern hospital, 87 percent had first sought help from indigenous practitioners. In other words, only 13 percent of the patients had turned directly to modern health care services without first seeking indigenous health care. The authors feel that these estimates must be below the actual prevalence in the Nepali population, since predominantly urban people with access to the modern health care system were included in this sample, and, even then, the study found that most people did not seek modern health care services.

According to social researchers (Kroeger and Franken 1981; Gesler 1984; Durkin 1988; Christie and Halpern 1990; Boessen 1991), indigenous health care services continue to flourish and be sought because they are not only socially and culturally closer to the beliefs/culture of the local people and hence more acceptable, but also provide more satisfaction. Hence, although modern medicine can effectively treat a problem, indigenous medicine can not only treat a problem but also offer a culturally defined meaning (leading to satisfaction) for it.

Overall, modern medicine has to compete with the indigenous health care systems because it is an exogenous and culturally foreign institution premised on a significantly different cultural belief system that is not legitimated by the dominant values of Nepali society.

TABLE 2.   USE AND SATISFACTION OF NEPALI POPULATION WITH INDIGENOUS MEDICAL PRACTITIONERS (N = 760)

Sought help first from indigenous practitioner	87%
Used home remedies for current illness	31%
Indigenous practitioner advised patient to go to modern medical hospital	13%
Indigenous practitioner made decision that patient must go to modern medical hospital	8%
Dissatisfaction with indigenous consultation led patient to turn to modern medicine	29%

Social Organizational Determinants of Indigenous Health Care in Alaska

The social organizational context plays a primary role in determining how outside forces of social and economic structure influence the continued use of indigenous medicine. The importance of social factors was first noted in studies of morbidity and mortality (Dubos 1968; McKeown 1976; Illich 1976). Macro-level ecological, social, and cultural contexts constrain the behavior and opportunities of individuals living within them. Societies in transition—due to modernization pressures, cultural trauma, or dependency relations—face poverty, social disorganization, breakdown of traditional support systems, and confusion about available services and care. Social inequality creates circumstances that predispose individuals to underutilize formal medical care.

Alaska Natives live in small villages scattered across 570,000 square miles. The economies in rural Alaska are built upon extraction of natural resources and a large portion of food is gathered from the land and oceans. Simple commodity production (commercial fishing, trapping, and craft production) is the largest, single source of income for the community, providing the primary source of income for one-third of Alaska natives. Wage employment is the other source of monetary income, while many natives derive income from a combination of wage work and simple commodity production.

Most Alaskan villages are not accessible by road primarily because of distance, island location, or arctic climate. Transportation between villages and regional centers occurs primarily using airplanes or boats. Some cities can be reached by snow machines or dog sled. While the remoteness and isolation limit Alaska Natives' access to economic, political, and social institutions including a modern health care system, there is improved internal cohesion as well as increased linkages to indigenous cultural foundations such as folk and traditional medicine.

The ability of Alaska Natives to continue their cultural and economic lifestyle depends upon political and economic sovereignty (Berger 1985). Tribal sovereignty has been legally recognized with the creation of Alaska Native Regional Corporations in 1971 and village councils and judicial boards based on Native political structures within each region. Loss of control over local actions that affect the Natives' livelihoods and indigenous lifestyles results in social pathologies such as alcohol and substance abuse, suicide, and other injurious practices (Cordes 1986). The economic dependence on external institutions including outside business interests, public schools, public communications, transportation, stores, and health services strengthens dependency relations. Introducing non-Native concepts into the village life creates cultural conflicts and undermines the capacity of the community to direct its affairs. Research in Alaska suggests that there is a relationship between economic and cultural dependency and poor health (Lantis 1963; Alaskan Federation of Natives 1989; Christie and Halpern 1990).

Discussion and Social Policy Implications

This study elucidates the indigenous health care systems prevalent in Nepal and Alaska. Since these regions represent only two case studies, one must be careful in generalizing findings. The two examples, which are disparate in many economic, political, and social traditions, nevertheless illustrate the persistence of diversity in health care systems. These cases also suggest that medical pluralism reflects inherent characteristics of indigenous cultures.

Pluralistic health care systems are manifestations of the social and economic organization of societies, health behaviors of people, and availability of health care services. Combinations of biomedical, preventive, and indigenous approaches for the treatment of illness and disease form an empirical range of options available for people's choice in most localities. Indigenous health care draws its legitimacy from the social organization of the society interacting with personalized individual, family, and village networks, and with world views. The continuation of indigenous health care is assured in large measure because it draws from people's knowledge of what works, and it is locally accessible at a reasonable cost.

Further, distributional inequity in health outcomes exists in part because people differ in their choice of health care systems. Some component of choice has to do with physical availability or distance to treatment. Low-income, rural, or indigenous people tend to use the smaller, more decentralized modes of service delivery. It is interesting to note that in Alaska modern health care is, by and large, freely available to Alaska Natives. Nevertheless, an indigenous health care system continues to exist.

We argue that the reason why indigenous medicine continues to flourish in Alaska and Nepal is that indigenous medicine rises out of local cultural and traditional values. When individuals, families, communities, and service providers together identify health problems and formulate solutions, then humane sensitivities, community involvement, and cultural integrity are strengthened and honored (Airhihenbuwa and Harrison 1993).

Pluralistic systems represent cultural strategies necessary for people's survival and well-being (Pedersen and Baruffati 1989). One value of knowing more about indigenous medical systems is that it offers advantages for understanding the entire health care system. Indigenous practitioners can offer health care relevant to the expressed needs of people by healing and caring in a more integral and comprehensive sense. Knowledge of indigenous medicine can also serve to develop new models of medical practice. For example, while there are few studies of the effectiveness of indigenous medicines' treatment compared to modern medicine, Wheatley (1991) suggests that native healing approaches to psychiatric or psychological syndromes such as drug or alcohol abuse are more effective. Since illnesses such as alcoholism and symptoms such as pain can vary within ethnicities, treatment and control of these illnesses and symptoms can be done according to the cultural explanatory model for these syndromes. Understanding cultural meanings contributes toward an adequate diagnosis and choice of treatment that will be more effective in the curing of disease and healing of illness.

Knowledge of indigenous medicine can also contribute to the extension of social science health care models by obtaining better information about illnesses and by understanding how historical, social, and economic conditions determine the appearance and distribution of illness and disease. Development of health policies and the construction of new health care systems can be reoriented to include a criterion of equity in the distribution of health resources if underlying forces for the existence of pluralistic medical systems are fully understood.

This chapter has argued that medical pluralism persists because of its social organizational structural supports and cultural authority among the ethnic, economic, and socially diverse populations within a nation. Future work should address three points. First, research should be conducted to investigate how pluralistic health care systems coexist. Young (1983) suggests that modern and indigenous health care systems may integrate, serve supplementary roles, or intercalate. Additional questions however, remain concerning modes of education and subsequent professionalization of indigenous health practitioners, integration of pharmaceutical or indigenous drugs into treatment protocols, and the autonomy of practice from other treatment. Research should focus on specific policy issues to promote equity in health. Utilization research should incorporate cultural, socioeconomic, and service delivery factors for all health care options available. Structural sources of differentiation in health care behavior can identify cultural, economic, and political factors amenable to necessary and meaningful change.

REFERENCES

ADAMS, VINCANNE. 1988. "Modes of Production and Medicine: An Examination of the Theory in Light of Sherpa Medical Traditionalism." *Social Science and Medicine* 27:505–13.

AIRHIHENBUWA, COLLINS O., and IRA E. HARRISON. 1993. "Traditional Medicine in Africa: Past, Present, and Future." Pp. 122–34 in *Health and Health Care in Developing Countries: Sociological Perspectives*, edited by Peter Conrad and Eugene B. Gallagher. Philadelphia: Temple University Press.

Alaskan Federation of Natives. 1989. *The AFN Report of the Status of Alaska Natives: A Call for Action*. Anchorage, Alaska: Alaskan Federation of Natives.

BERGER, THOMAS R. 1985. *Village Journey: Report of the Alaska Native Review Committee*. New York: Hill & Wang.

BHARDWAJ, SURINDER MOHAN. 1980. "Medical Pluralism and Homeopathy: A Geographic Perspective." *Social Science and Medicine* 14B:209–16.

———— and BIMAL KANTI PAUL. 1986. "Medical Pluralism and Infant Mortality in a Rural Area of Bangladesh." *Social Science and Medicine* 23:1003–10.

BOESSEN, E. M. 1991. "Training/Education of Local People for Posts in the Health Service—Neocolonialism?" Pp. 149–50 in *Circumpolar Health 90: Proceedings of the 8th International Congress on Circumpolar Health, Whitehorse, Yukon, May 20-25, 1990*, edited by Brian D. Postl, Penny Gilbert, Jean Goodwill, Michael E. K. Moffatt, John D. O'Neil, Peter A. Sarsfield, and T. Kue Young. Winnipeg: University of Manitoba Press.

CHRISTIE, LAIRD, and JOEL M. HALPERN. 1990. "Temporal Constructs and Inuit Mental Health." *Social Science and Medicine* 30:739–49.

CORDES, PENELOPE M. 1986. Alaskan Community Health Aides: An Alternative Approach to Rural Health Care, Volumes I and II. *Doctoral Dissertation*. Palo Alto, CA: Stanford University.

DEGROSS, DENNIS P. 1991. "A Brief Discussion of the Development of Native-Owned Health Provider Agencies in Alaska within the Context of Anticipated Health and Systems Issues." Pp. 101–05 in *Circumpolar Health 90: Proceedings of the 8th International Congress on Circumpolar Health, Whitehorse, Yukon, May 20-25, 1990*, edited by Brian D. Postl, Penny Gilbert, Jean Goodwill, Michael E. K. Moffatt, John D. O'Neil, Peter A. Sarsfield, and T. Kue Young. Winnipeg: University of Manitoba Press.

DUBOS, RENÉ. 1968. *Man, Medicine, and Environment*. New York: Praeger.

DURKIN, MAUREEN S. 1988. "Ayurvedic Treatment for Jaundice in Nepal." *Social Science and Medicine* 27:491–95.

DURKIN-LONGLEY, MAUREEN S. 1982. "Ayurveda in Nepal: A Medical Belief System in Action." *Doctoral Dissertation*. Madison, WI: University of Wisconsin-Madison.

FORTUINE, ROBERT. 1988. "Empirical Healing Among the Alaska Natives: An Historical Perspective." *Arctic Medical Research* 47 (Supplement):296–302.

Fox, Renee C. 1976. "The Sociology of Modern Medical Research." Pp. 102-14 in *Asian Medical Systems: A Comparative Study*, edited by Charles M. Leslie. Berkeley, CA: University of California Press.

Gesler, Wilbert M. 1984. "Health Care in Developing Countries." *Association of American Geographers*. State College, PA: Commercial Printing Inc.

Illich, Ivan. 1976. *Medical Nemesis: The Expropriation of Health*. New York: Random House.

Jilek, Wolfgang G. 1982. *Indian Healing: Shamanic Ceremonialism in the Pacific Northwest Today*. Surrey, British Columbia: Hancock House.

Jingfeng, Cai. 1987. "Toward a Comprehensive Evaluation of Alternative Medicine." *Social Science and Medicine* 25:659-97.

Justice, Judith. 1981. "International Planning and Health: An Anthropological Case Study of Nepal." *Doctoral Dissertation*. Berkeley, CA: The University of California Press.

Kroeger, A., and H. P. Franken. 1981. "The Educational Value of Evaluation of Primary Health Care Programs: An Experience with Four Indigenous Populations in Ecuador." *Social Science and Medicine* 15B:535-39.

Lantis, Margaret. (1954) 1963. "Acculturation and Health." Revision in *Alaska's Health: A Survey Report*. Pittsburgh, PA: University of Pittsburgh.

Larson, Kristina. 1991. "The Evolution of a Village-based Health Education Project." Pp. 153-56 in *Circumpolar Health 90: Proceedings of the 8th International Congress on Circumpolar Health, Whitehorse, Yukon, May 20-25, 1990*, edited by Brian D. Postl, Penny Gilbert, Jean Goodwill, Michael E. K. Moffatt, John D. O'Neil, Peter A. Sarsfield, and T. Kue Young. Winnipeg: University of Manitoba Press.

McKeown, Thomas. 1976. *The Modern Rise of Population*. New York: Academic Press.

Nordstrom, Carolyn R. 1988. "Exploring Pluralism—The Many Faces of Ayurveda." *Social Science and Medicine* 27:479-89.

Payer, Lynn. 1988. *Medicine and Culture: Varieties of Treatment in the United States, England, West Germany, and France*. New York: Henry Holt.

Pedersen, Duncan, and Veronica Baruffati. 1989. "Healers, Deities, Saints and Doctors: Elements for the Analysis of Medical Systems." *Social Science and Medicine* 29:487-96.

Reissland, Nadja, and Richard Burghart. 1989. "Active Patients: The Integration of Modern and Traditional Obstetric Practices in Nepal." *Social Science and Medicine* 29:43-52.

Streefland, Pieter. 1985. "The Frontier of Modern Western Medicine in Nepal." *Social Science and Medicine* 20:1151-59.

Subedi, Janardan. 1989a. "Factors Affecting the Use of Modern Medicine in a Pluralistic Health Care System: The Case of Nepal." *Doctoral Dissertation*. Akron, OH: University of Akron.

————. 1989b. "Modern Health Services and Health Care Behavior: A Survey in Kathmandu, Nepal." *Journal of Health and Social Behavior* 30:412-20.

Wheatley, Margaret A. 1990. "Developing an Integrated Traditional/Clinical Health System in the Yukon." Pp. 217-19 in *Circumpolar Health 90: Proceedings of the 8th International Congress on Circumpolar Health, Whitehorse, Yukon, May 20-25, 1990*, edited by Brian D. Postl, Penny Gilbert, Jean Goodwill, Michael E. K. Moffatt, John D. O'Neil, Peter A. Sarsfield, and T. Kue Young. Winnipeg: University of Manitoba Press.

Young, Allan. 1983. "The Relevance of Traditional Medicine Cultures to Modern Primary Health Care." *Social Science and Medicine* 17:1205-11.

CHAPTER 18

A Comparison of Nurse Assistants in Nursing Homes in the United States and Ward Assistants for the Elderly in Ghana

Dorothy J. Blackmon

Lawrence A. Kannae

T. Neal Garland

INTRODUCTION

The elderly population of the United States is growing both larger and older (Bye and Iannone 1987). The individuals who provide a large share of the care for these elderly are nurse assistants. These individuals are the ones who have the largest amount of close daily contact with the elderly residents in nursing homes. In fact, it has been estimated that nurse assistants provide from 80 to 90 percent of the actual hands-on care given to the institutionalized elderly in the United States (Institute of Medicine 1986).

The nurse assistant's occupation is a demanding one that requires lifting, feeding, bathing, and performing all of the other activities that are required for the elderly patient's personal comfort and hygiene. Since these activities require daily interaction with the elderly, the nurse assistants get to know the elderly on a personal basis and experience the emotions of working with them day in and day out. The large amount of personal contact between nurse assistants and their elderly patients means that the nurse assistants play an extremely important part in determining the quality of life of nursing home residents. Therefore, there is a need to examine the characteristics and the attitudes and levels of job satisfaction of nurse assistants in order to get a better understanding of these important health care workers.

Most studies of nurse assistants have been conducted in the United States. Very little is known about the perceptions and attitudes toward the elderly held by nurse assistants or comparable workers in other cultures. In fact, very little is known even about the demographic characteristics of such workers. The result is that even the little that is known about nurse assistants is limited by culture-bound interpretations (Kohn 1989). A number of important questions about nurse assistants and their work remain unanswered due to the lack of a cross-cultural perspective in the research. For example, in what ways do the perceptions and attitudes toward the elderly held by nurse assistants reflect larger cultural value systems? To what extent are levels of job satisfaction or dissatisfaction among nurse assistants influenced by a nation's internal economic conditions? Is the demographic profile of nurse assistants similar in different parts of the world? How are demographic similarities or differences to be explained? The research reported here is an attempt to begin the exploration of such issues.

This chapter presents the results of a comparative study of demographic characteristics, levels of job satisfaction, and attitudes toward the elderly found among samples of nurse assistants in the United States and their counterparts in Ghana. Because the samples were not randomly selected, no claims can be made that they are representative of these occupational groups in the two nations. However, the data presented in this report serve the important function of providing an empirical basis that can serve as a starting point for more rigorous explorations.

WHY COMPARE GHANA AND THE UNITED STATES?

Ghana and the United States were chosen for this study because they represent, in many ways, two quite different types of societies. In terms of population, Ghana is one of the fastest growing countries in the world, with an estimated annual growth rate of 3.1 percent (Population Reference Bureau 1993). The population increased more than five-fold between 1921 and 1984 (World Population News Service 1992). The current population of 16.4 million is projected to double in only 23 years unless the growth rate is curbed. Over 45 percent of the population is under 15 years of age and 70 percent is under the age of 25. This youthfulness suggests that a decline in the growth rate is unlikely in the near future (Population Reference Bureau 1989). The economy is based predominantly on subsistence farming, with approximately 70 percent of the labor force engaged in the agricultural sector. The literacy rate is estimated at 25 to 30 percent.

On the other hand, the United States is a large, modern nation with a population of approximately 254 million and an annual growth rate of 1.1 percent (United States Department of Commerce 1993). The estimated middle-range projection for population growth is that there will be a 50 percent increase by the year 2050.

In contrast to Ghana, the United States has an aging population. Over 51 percent of Americans are between the ages of 25 and 64 and 12.6 percent are 65 years of age or older. In 1991 the median age in the United States was 32.8 years. It is estimated that this figure will increase to 39.3 years by 2050 (United States Department of Commerce 1993). These figures suggest that the population growth rate of the United States will remain low into the foreseeable future. The economy is usually described as postindustrial, with 74 percent of the labor force engaged in the tertiary or service sector. The literacy rate is high, with 78.4 percent of all Americans being high school graduates.

A comparison of Ghana and the United States thus makes it possible to examine certain assumptions that are rooted in modernization theory (Rostow 1960; Deane 1969). According to Goode (1963), before industrialization and modernization, the elderly were respected in all cultures. The elderly were seen as custodians of wisdom and authority. They were respected, loved (and/or feared), obeyed, and honored. However, many writers argue that with the advent of industrialization and scientific development that respect has faded away and the elderly are no longer seen as very important or valuable to society. Cowgill (1974) has noted that the status of the elderly declines with increasing modernization. Similarly, Bengtson, Dowd, Smith, and Inkeles (1975) reported negative perceptions of aging with increasing modernization in six developing countries.

An empirical examination of nurse assistants in Ghana and the United States makes it possible to compare groups of workers who serve the elderly in settings where the levels of modernization are quite different. It therefore can be expected that attitudes toward the elderly in the two nations will be quite different. This, in turn, can be expected to result in different demographic profiles, attitudes toward the elderly, and levels of job satisfaction among health care workers who provide care for the elderly.

COMPARABLE WORKERS: NURSE ASSISTANTS IN THE UNITED STATES AND WARD ASSISTANTS IN GHANA

The focus of this study is on health care workers who perform similar types of work in the United States and Ghana. The title given to these workers in the United States is *nurse assistants* (although the term *nurse aide* also often is used). Comparable workers in Ghana are known as *ward assistants*. A brief description of each group will help put this comparative study into perspective.

Nurse Assistants in the United States

Nurse assistants occupy the lowest level in the hierarchy of health care providers in the United States. They may be employed in hospitals, nursing homes, or other long-term care facilities. Those who work in nursing homes are the focus of this study. In spite of their low status in the nursing home, nurse assistants perform an important and demanding job. They are highly likely to be women in their middle years and to have completed twelve or fewer years of formal education. Minority groups are overrepresented and pay tends to be at or near the minimum-wage level (Blackmon 1993; Oyabu 1989; Bye and Iannone 1987; Day 1971).

Although the work performed by nurse assistants has a strong impact on the well-being of nursing home residents, until recently no formal training was required for this job. The importance of nurse assistants was recognized by Congress when it passed the Omnibus Budget Reconciliation Act (OBRA) in 1987. OBRA mandated a minimum level of training for nurse assistants and instituted requirements that they pass a competency examination and be registered with the state in which they are employed (Congressional Quarterly Almanac 1987; Reublinger 1989; Heiselman, Oyabu, and Gipson 1989). Recent amendments have added requirements for twelve hours annually of in-service education and the learning of certain specific techniques of care.

Ward Assistants in Ghana

The comparable category of care providers in Ghana is known as *ward assistants*. Like nurse assistants in the United States, ward assistants in Ghana occupy the lowest level in their nation's hierarchy of health care providers. They are generally women. Although their level of formal education is higher than that of the population as a whole, a majority of the ward assistants have obtained only the middle school leaving certificate, which is the lowest level of certified education in Ghana. The basic function of the ward assistants in the health care system of Ghana is to assist patients in the performance of the activities of daily living (ADLs) and the instrumental activities of daily living (IADLs). Unlike nurse assistants employed in nursing homes in the United States, ward assistants in Ghana provide care to a broad range of people that includes all age categories. Another significant difference is that ward assistants work in hospitals and health care clinics/centers rather than in nursing homes. Ghana does not have nursing homes for the elderly, as such, for they are generally taken care of by family members unless they are sufficiently ill to warrant admission to a hospital.

ISSUES INVESTIGATED IN THIS STUDY

Based on the arguments of modernization theory, three issues served as the focus of this study. These issues were: (1) A comparison of the demographic profiles of nurse assistants in the United States and ward assistants in Ghana; (2) a comparison of attitudes toward the elderly held by members of the two groups; and (3) a comparison of levels of job satisfaction of the two groups of health care workers. These issues are all related to the claim that the elderly have higher status in developing societies than in modern ones. If this claim is true, then nurse assistants in the United States should have lower social status characteristics and relatively negative attitudes toward the elderly compared to those of nurse assistants in Ghana. On the other hand, nurse assistants in Ghana should obtain greater job satisfaction from working with elderly clients because the higher status of the elderly in Ghana should convey higher status on those who take care of them than is the case in the United States.

RESEARCH METHODS

Samples for the Study

The United States sample for this study consisted of 188 nurse assistants who comprised the first class to complete the Ohio Teaching Network Program (in 1987). The Ohio Teaching Network Program was a training program devoted to teaching trainers and clinical supervisors in the state of Ohio how to teach nurse assistants the skills and attitudes needed for successful performance of their jobs (for descriptions of the Ohio Teaching Network Program, see Blackmon 1993; Gipson, Garland, and Oyabu-Mathis 1994; Blackmon, Gipson, Oyabu-Mathis, and Garland 1993). Nurse assistants were selected to participate in this training program by the administrators of the facilities in which they were employed.

In the summer of 1992 the second author of this chapter, Lawrence Kannae, traveled to Ghana, where he organized the sampling procedure and the collection of data in Ghana for this study. From a current list of hospitals and health care centers, seven were randomly selected. At each of these sites, the highest-ranking member of the nursing staff was asked to distribute questionnaires to all ward assistants who reported for work on the day of the survey. Completed questionnaires were returned to the responsible member of the nursing staff, who mailed them to a nursing official who had agreed to act as coordinator for the study. This individual mailed the questionnaires to the investigators in the United States because the second author was not able to remain in Ghana long enough to collect all of them himself. This procedure resulted in a total of fifty-three useable questionnaires from Ghana.

Data Collection Technique

The data for the two samples were collected using self-administered questionnaires. In the United States, the questionnaires were completed in the classroom on the last day of the Ohio Teaching Network Program training session. In Ghana, ward assistants completed their questionnaires at the workplace during working hours.

Measurement of Variables

Comparable measurement of variables is a major problem in any cross-national research. Because English is the language of instruction in the educational system of Ghana, the authors chose to use English versions of the questionnaire in both countries. Some changes in wording were made in the version of the questionnaire used in Ghana to make the items fit better with conditions in Ghana. For example, the occupational category is called "nurse assistants" in the United States, but "ward assistants" in Ghana in order to correspond to local useage.

Demographic characteristics were measured by collecting information on age, sex, education, length of employment as a nurse assistant, length of employment with current employer, shift, religion, and degree of religiosity. The variables of *attitudes toward the elderly* and *job satisfaction* were measured by using modified versions of existing instruments. These modified instruments are described briefly below.

Attitudes Toward the Elderly

The instrument used to measure attitudes toward the elderly was a shortened (six-item) version of the Old People scale developed by Kogan (1961). Kogan's original scale contained seventeen items that express positive views of the elderly and seventeen items that express negative views. These items thus formed two separate scales: the Old People Positive scale and the Old People Negative scale. Kogan asked his respondents to indicate the extent to which they agreed or disagreed with each item (using a five-point Likert format).

Five of the items used in the present study were taken from the Old People Negative scale because it has been found to have a higher reliability than the Old People Positive scale (Kogan 1961). One item (number two in the questionnaire used in this study) was taken from the Old People Positive scale because it seemed especially appropriate for this cross-cultural comparison.

The shortened scale consisted of six statements to which respondents were asked to respond in a Likert fashion (from strongly agree to strongly disagree). The nurse assistants were asked to indicate their feelings about the following statements concerning the elderly:

1. If old people expect to be liked, their first step is to try to get rid of their irritating faults.
2. One of the most interesting qualities of old people is their accounts of their past experiences.
3. Most old people make one feel ill at ease.
4. Most old people are irritable, grouchy, and unpleasant.
5. Most old people make excessive demands for love and reassurance.
6. Most old people are set in their ways and are unable to change.

Job Satisfaction

Three areas of job satisfaction were examined: satisfaction with doing the work; satisfaction with the staff; and satisfaction with the place of work. These job satisfaction indicators were borrowed from the job satisfaction scale developed by Kahn, Wolfe, Quinn, Snoek, and Rosenthal (1964). The items used in the present study were:

1. I feel a great deal of satisfaction from doing my job as a nurse assistant.
2. I feel a great deal of satisfaction from doing my job as a member of the staff.
3. How do you like working for this facility/hospital or health care center?

Response choices to the first two items were in the form of a five-point Likert scale (from strongly disagree to strongly agree). Responses to item number three were in the form of a five-point Likert scale that ranged from "It's not a very good place" to "It's a very good place."

RESULTS

Demographic Characteristics

Table 1 shows the demographic characteristics of the two samples. The data shown in this table do not include missing cases, so the number of respondents for each variable may not add up to the original sample size (N = 188 for the United States and N = 53 for Ghana).

In examining the sex ratios of the samples, it is apparent that females predominate in both countries. Data regarding the gender of nurse assistants in the sample from the United States are consistent with previous studies in this area (e.g., Oyabu 1989; Bye and Iannone 1987; Day 1971)—most are females. It appears that this is also the case in Ghana. This may reflect cultural values that seem to be similar in both a modern and a developing nation: caring for the

TABLE 1.   DEMOGRAPHIC CHARACTERISTICS OF THE SAMPLE

VARIABLE	U.S. (N = 188)		GHANA (N = 53)	
	FREQUENCY	PERCENTAGE	FREQUENCY	PERCENTAGE
Sex				
Male	4	2.2	1	1.9
Female	182	97.8	52	98.1
Age				
16-19	3	1.6	2	3.8
20-29	47	25.5	17	32.0
30-39	65	35.3	17	32.0
40-49	41	22.3	17	32.0
50-59	25	13.6	0	0.0
60 +	3	1.6	0	0.0
*Educational Attainment**				
Elementary	6	3.3	—	—
Middle school	—	—	37	78.7
Some high school	46	25.0	—	—
High school	123	66.8	10	21.3
Some college	6	3.3	—	—
College graduate	3	1.6	—	—
Length of Employment with Current Employer				
0-2 years	63	38.0	1	1.9
3-5 years	37	22.3	12	22.6
6-10 years	43	25.9	22	41.5
11 + years	23	13.9	18	34.0
Shift				
Morning	83	50.9	48	90.6
Afternoon	55	33.7	5	9.4
Evening	25	15.3	0	0.0
Length of Employment as a Nurse Assistant				
0-2 years	37	23.9	1	1.9
3-5 years	33	21.3	12	22.6
6-10 years	45	29.0	22	41.5
11 + years	40	25.8	18	34.0
Plan to Work at Present Nursing Home/Facility Two Years from Now?				
Definitely no	3	1.7	0	0.0
Probably no	9	5.2	2	3.8
Probably yes	95	54.9	9	17.0
Definitely yes	65	37.6	42	79.2
Religious Affiliation				
Protestant	121	65.1	8	16.3
Catholic	26	14.0	13	26.5
Jewish	1	0.5	0	0.0
Jehovah's Witness	1	0.5	0	0.0
Muslim	0	0.0	7	14.3
Traditional	9	4.8	21	42.9
Other	2	1.1	0	0.0
None	6	3.2	0	0.0
Degree of Religiosity				
Not important at all	13	7.3	0	0.0
Somewhat unimportant	7	4.0	0	0.0
Undecided	29	16.4	0	0.0
Somewhat important	43	24.3	5	9.4
Very important	85	48.0	48	90.6

Note: U.S. sample size may not total to 188 due to missing data; Ghana sample size may not total to 53 due to missing data.

*Educational categories were not identical for the two countries.

elderly (and for the infirm in general) is viewed as women's work. It also may reflect the view that, in both modern and developing nations, such work is regarded as being of relatively low status and therefore to be avoided by males (who can more easily obtain higher-status positions). The latter view is a question that should be subjected to empirical investigation, for if this interpretation is accurate, it raises questions about the actual (as opposed to the *ideal*) status of the elderly in developing nations. If the elderly truly are held in high regard, then it would be reasonable to assume that working with them would convey high status upon the workers. If this is not the case, then it may be that the *actual* status of the elderly in such societies is different from their *ideal* status.

The mean age for nurse assistants in the United States was 36.6 years and the mean age for the Ghanaian sample was 33.7 years. While the average nurse assistant in the United States was about three years older, the age difference was not large. In both countries, the picture of nurse assistants/ward assistants that emerges is that they are likely to be middle-aged females.

The mean level of education for nurse assistants in the United States was twelve years and 66 percent of the nurse assistants had completed high school. Their educational level thus was lower than the national average. However, in Ghana the majority (78.8 percent) of the nurse assistants had completed middle school, with only a little more than 21 percent having completed high school. This suggests that when compared to the population as a whole, the ward assistants in Ghana have above average educational attainment. However, when compared to other health care providers such as physicians and nurses, their educational level places them in the lower level of the health care hierarchy.

A review of the literature indicates that there is a high turnover rate for nurse assistants in the United States (e.g., Wagnild and Manning 1986; Winston 1981; Ross 1972). The results of the present study indicate that approximately 38 percent of the nurse assistants in the United States sample were new employees with a tenure of two years or less at their current place of employment, while only 1.9 percent of the Ghanaian sample were in the same category. On the other hand, 39.8 percent of the nurse assistants in the United States had been with their current employer for six or more years. A much larger proportion—75 percent—of the nurse assistants in Ghana had been with their current employer for six years or more.

With regard to the total number of years employed as a nurse assistant (in the current and/or other places of employment), 23.9 percent of the nurse assistants in the United States had worked as nurse assistants for two years or less, while those with six years or more constituted 54.8 percent.

Both in terms of the number of years in the occupation of nurse assistant and in terms of the number of years with the current employer, the nurse assistants from the United States in this sample do not fit the image of the nurse assistant as a short-term employee who is highly prone to leave her job. Nearly half of these respondents had been with their current employers for six or more years, and more than half had been in the same line of work for a similar number of years. Two potential explanations for these anomalies are possible. The first is that the figures on job turnover among nurse assistants in nursing homes in the United States typically have been based on a very gross measure—

the number of new nurse assistants hired per year divided by the total number of nurse assistant staff positions available during that year. This measure misses the fact that a significant proportion of nurse assistants remain in their jobs for considerable lengths of time, while others exhibit very volatile employment histories (see Garland, Oyabu, and Gipson 1988). It is possible that existing figures on job turnover among nurse assistants present an inaccurate picture of the situation.

A second possible explanation for the current finding is that nurse assistants with more stable employment records were more likely to show up in the sample from the United States because they had been selected by the administrator of their nursing home to receive special training. Since this training involved an expenditure on the part of the nursing home, it is likely that the administrators selected their more stable employees to participate.

The results also seem to suggest that, once ward assistants have been hired in Ghana, they tend to remain in employment with the same organization for an extended period. The length of employment in this line of work and the length of employment with the current employer both indicate a high degree of employment stability—even more so than in the United States. Possible explanations for this high degree of stability may include: (1) a limited number of job opportunities for females in Ghana; and (2) the existence of strong, extended-family ties that limit seeking jobs outside the woman's home area.

Over 92 percent of the nurse assistants in the United States and over 96 percent of Ghanaian ward assistants planned to be at the same job two years from now. This further supports the contention that some nurse assistants/ward assistants tend to be quite stable in their employment. The ratio of stable-to-unstable lower-level health care employees in general remains to be determined in both countries. It may be that the proportion that is stable is more significant than is commonly assumed.

Distribution of religious affiliation reflected the cultural settings of the two samples. The vast majority of nurse assistants from the United States claimed affiliation with a Christian belief system, as did slightly more than two-fifths (16.3 percent Protestant plus 26.5 percent Catholic) of the ward assistants in Ghana. Further, 42.9 percent of the ward assistants claimed affiliation with various traditional local religions. The number of respondents in both countries who claimed no religious affiliation was very small (none in Ghana and 4.3 percent in the United States). This may suggest that belief in a body of religious values is characteristic of those who care for the elderly, regardless of cultural setting. This is an empirical question that would be interesting to investigate in future research. A related and also important question is the extent to which the various religious belief systems emphasize care of the elderly as a duty or as something that brings rewards of various kinds to the care provider.

The suggestion that religious beliefs may be an important variable for future examination receives further support from the fact that approximately 72 percent of the American nurse assistants thought religion was either very important or somewhat important in guiding their everyday life. National public opinion polls in the United States suggest that approximately 55 percent of all respondents claim religion is "very important" in their daily lives (The Gallup

Report, cited in Brinkerhoff and White 1991). The nurse assistants from the United States sample are thus more likely than the "average American" to rate religion as being very important to them.

A larger proportion—90.6 percent—of the Ghanaian ward assistants reported that religion was very important in their daily life. This may suggest that religion is a significantly more important factor in the lives of the ward assistants in Ghana compared to their counterparts in the United States. Data on the religiousness of the "average Ghanian" are not readily available.

Over half of the United States sample came from the morning shift, 33.7 percent came from the afternoon shift, and over 15 percent of the sample came from the evening shift. For the Ghanaian sample over 90 percent came from the morning shift, 9.4 percent came from the afternoon shift, and none came from the evening shift. It is not clear why the distribution was so skewed among the Ghanaian respondents. This uneven distribution should be kept in mind when considering the results of this study.

Attitudes Toward the Elderly

Table 2 presents the results of the measurement of attitudes toward the elderly among respondents in the two countries. Contrary to expectations, nurse assistants from the United States held more positive attitudes toward the elderly than did the ward assistants from Ghana—at least, as measured by these questions. For example, 71.2 percent of American nurse assistants disagreed or strongly disagreed with the statement "If old people expect to be liked, their first step is to try to get rid of their irritating faults." However, 77.2 percent of nurse assistants in the Ghana study agreed or strongly agreed with this statement. The statement makes the assumption that all old people do have irritating faults, so to agree with this statement is to indicate a negative attitude toward the elderly.

The second statement in the attitude measurement instrument ("One of the most interesting qualities of old people is their accounts of their past experiences.") can be interpreted in either a positive or a negative sense. From a negative perspective, it suggests that the elderly have a tendency to dwell on the past rather than to live in the present. Conversely, it can be taken to indicate that a wealth of past experiences is something the elderly possess and younger people do not, thus making the elderly more interesting. Kogan (1961) apparently took the second point of view, for he included this item in the positive dimension of his Old People scale.

The vast majority (93 percent) of nurse assistants from the United States disagreed or strongly disagreed with this statement, while 84.6 percent of the Ghanaians agreed or strongly agreed. One possible interpretation of this finding is that tradition and the past are more highly regarded in Ghana and that the elderly are seen as important links with the nation's cultural heritage. If this is the case, then the attitudes of the ward assistants may reflect traditional values in Ghana, while the attitudes of the nurse assistants in the United States may reflect that country's emphasis on modernity and a more positive value on the future.

Over 75 percent of American nurse assistants disagreed or strongly disagreed with the statement that "Most old people make one feel ill at ease." How-

TABLE 2.   ATTITUDES TOWARD THE ELDERLY

VARIABLE	U.S. (N = 188)		GHANA (N = 53)	
	FREQUENCY	PERCENTAGE	FREQUENCY	PERCENTAGE
If old people expect to be liked, their first step is to try to get rid of their irritating faults.				
Strongly agree	12	6.5	25	47.2
Agree	29	15.8	16	30.2
Undecided	12	6.5	6	11.3
Disagree	87	47.3	5	9.4
Strongly disagree	44	23.9	1	1.9
One of the most interesting qualities of old people is their account of their past experiences.				
Strongly agree	3	1.6	25	48.1
Agree	6	3.2	19	36.5
Undecided	4	2.2	2	3.8
Disagree	100	54.1	3	5.8
Strongly disagree	72	38.9	3	5.8
Most old people make one feel ill at ease.				
Strongly agree	4	2.2	18	35.3
Agree	25	13.4	19	37.3
Undecided	16	8.6	7	13.7
Disagree	102	54.8	5	9.8
Strongly disagree	39	21.0	2	3.9
Most old people are irritable, grouchy, and unpleasant.				
Strongly agree	6	3.2	20	38.5
Agree	14	7.5	17	32.7
Undecided	10	5.3	5	9.6
Disagree	102	54.5	6	11.5
Strongly disagree	55	29.4	4	7.7
Most old people make excessive demands for love and reassurance.				
Strongly agree	18	9.7	21	41.2
Agree	78	41.9	23	45.1
Undecided	17	9.1	3	5.9
Disagree	60	32.3	4	7.8
Strongly disagree	13	7.0	0	0.0
Most old people are set in their ways and are unable to change.				
Strongly agree	34	18.4	20	37.7
Agree	87	47.0	24	45.3
Undecided	17	9.2	7	13.2
Disagree	40	21.6	1	1.9
Strongly disagree	7	3.8	1	1.9

ever, 72.6 percent of Ghanaian ward assistants agreed or strongly agreed with this statement. The response in Ghana can be interpreted in two ways. One interpretation is that the ward assistants have a strongly negative attitude toward the elderly and are therefore uncomfortable when dealing with them. An alternative interpretation is equally, if not more, plausible. Ghanaian culture discourages casual or informal interaction between generations. This would lead ward assistants to be "ill at ease" when working with elderly patients regardless of their attitude toward the elderly as individuals. Further research is needed to clarify this finding. Values in the United States emphasize (ideally) the equal treatment of all individuals regardless of personal demographic characteristics, so nurse assistants in the United States would feel they should not differentiate on the basis of age.

Item number four states: "Most old people are irritable, grouchy and unpleasant." A large majority (83.9 percent) of nurse assistants in the United States disagreed or strongly disagreed with this negative attitude, but 71.2 percent of Ghanaians agreed or strongly agreed. This may indicate a more negative attitude toward the elderly among the ward assistants. An alternative interpretation is that the elderly who receive care from ward attendants are quite likely to be seriously ill or to have no family members who are willing or able to take care of them. Thus, they may in fact be more irritable and unpleasant than the older people receiving care from nurse assistants in the United States. Many of the older Americans in nursing homes are likely to be in relatively good health compared to those in hospitals in Ghana. Differences in the responses of nurse assistants and ward assistants to this question may therefore reflect realistic appraisals of their respective clients.

Question five states: "Most old people make excessive demands for love and reassurance." A slight majority (51.6 percent) of the American nurse assistants agreed or strongly agreed with this premise. A significantly larger proportion (86.3 percent) of the Ghanaians agreed or strongly agreed. Again, it is possible that this difference in responses reflects a true difference in attitudes toward the elderly. However, it is also possible that the responses are due to differences in the conditions and situations of the elderly persons being cared for by the two groups of health care workers. This latter possiblity should be controlled in future studies.

The last attitude measure states: "Most old people are set in their ways and are unable to change." About two-thirds (65.4 percent) of the nurse assistants agreed or strongly agreed with this idea, while more than four-fifths (83.0 percent) of the ward assistants did so. Interpretation of this finding is problematic and requires an understanding of the degrees of importance assigned to traditionalism and stability versus modernism and change in the two cultures. The ward assistants were more likely to see elderly people as resistant to change, but it is not clear from the present data whether they saw this as a positive or a negative factor.

In summary, the American sample appears to have more positive attitudes toward the elderly than do the Ghanian respondents. However, it is not clear whether the attitudinal questions had the same meaning in both cultures. For instance, statements such as "Most old people make me feel ill at ease" may elicit an affirmative response from the respondents in Ghana, but this may not necessarily indicate negative feelings about the elderly. What is clear from the responses to the attitudinal measures in this study is that cross-cultural researchers must measure not only attitudes, but *reasons* for those attitudes as well.

Job Satisfaction

Members of both samples reported receiving a great deal of satisfaction from the work that they do and from the colleagues with whom they work. Table 3 indicates that 95.6 percent of the American nurse assistants agreed or

TABLE 3.   JOB SATISFACTION

VARIABLE	U.S. (N = 188)		GHANA (N = 53)	
	FREQUENCY	PERCENTAGE	FREQUENCY	PERCENTAGE
I feel a great deal of satisfaction from doing my job as a nurse assistant.				
Strongly disagree	0	0.0	1	0.9
Disagree	1	0.5	4	7.5
Undecided	7	3.8	2	3.8
Agree	80	43.7	16	30.2
Strongly agree	95	51.9	30	56.6
I feel a great deal of satisfaction from doing my job as a member of the staff.				
Strongly disagree	1	0.5	2	3.8
Disagree	3	1.6	2	3.8
Undecided	13	7.1	6	11.3
Agree	89	48.9	22	41.5
Strongly agree	76	41.8	21	39.6
How do you like working for this facility/hospital or health care center?				
It's not a very good place	6	3.5	29	54.7
It's all right	25	14.5	13	24.5
It's a fairly good place	76	44.2	2	3.8
It's a good place	0	0.0	5	9.4
It's a very good place	60	31.9	4	7.5

strongly agreed that they received satisfaction from doing their job and 86.8 percent of the Ghanaians felt the same way. A very high proportion (90.7 percent) of American nurse assistants and 81.1 percent of Ghanaian ward assistants also indicated that they were satisfied with being a member of the staff at their place of employment. Levels of satisfaction with the place of employment were lower in both countries, with the Americans generally having more positive feelings. About three-fourths (76.1 percent) of the nurse assistants said that the nursing home in which they worked was either a "good place" or a "very good place" to work, but only 16.9 percent of the ward assistants' responses fell into these categories. This may reflect objective differences in working conditions in the two countries. Many nursing homes in the United States make a considerable effort to provide pleasant surroundings for their residents, and it is likely that these efforts affect the attitudes of the nurse assistants as well as the comfort of the clients. Facilities in a developing nation may not be as adequate and this may be reflected in lower levels of satisfaction among employees, particularly at the lower levels of the health care hierarchy. Another factor that may affect the level of satisfaction with a place of employment is the quality of the relationship between supervisors and staff members. At this point, there is no empirical basis for making a comparison on this issue between nurse assistants in the United States and ward assistants in Ghana.

CONCLUSION

The purpose of this research was to compare the health care providers who are most directly responsible for hands-on care of the elderly in a modern and in a developing nation in terms of their demographic characteristics, their attitudes toward the elderly, and their levels of job satisfaction. Underlying this comparison was the premise that the elderly hold a higher status in developing nations and that this higher status influences such things as the types of individuals who enter occupations related to care of the elderly, attitudes toward the elderly held by these workers, and the levels of job satisfaction the workers experience. The findings contain a number of unexpected results.

In both nations the respondents tended to be middle-aged women who had relatively low levels of formal education. Attitudes toward the elderly were more positive among the American sample, even though modernization theory suggests that the elderly are held in higher regard in more traditional societies. The level of job satisfaction obtained from working with the elderly was slightly higher among the American respondents, as was the level of satisfaction with colleagues. Satisfaction with the place of employment was significantly higher among the American respondents.

Interpretation of these findings is difficult. While the results indicate a more negative attitude toward the elderly in Ghana, these results cannot simply be taken at face value. A more thorough analysis of cultural values, economic opportunities, and objective conditions in both countries is required before truly meaningful comparisons can be made. However, this study takes a first step.

REFERENCES

BENGTSON, VERN L., JAMES J. DOWD, DAVID H. SMITH, and ALEX INKELES. 1975. "Modernization, Modernity, and Perceptions of Aging: A Cross-Cultural Study." *Journal of Gerontology* 30:688–95.

BLACKMON, DOROTHY J., 1993. *Nurse Assistants in Nursing Homes: The Impact of Training on Attitudes, Knowledge, and Job Satisfaction*. Ph.D. dissertation. Department of Sociology, University of Akron, Akron, Ohio.

BLACKMON, DOROTHY J., GENEVIEVE A. GIPSON, NAOKO OYABU-MATHIS, and T. NEAL GARLAND. 1993. "The Ohio Teaching Network: A Training Program for Nurse Assistants Employed in Nursing Homes." Paper presented at the Seventeenth Annual Professional and Scientific Conference on Aging, sponsored by the Ohio Network of Educational Consultants in the Field of Aging (ONECA), March 26, Mansfield, Ohio.

BRINKERHOFF, DAVID B., and LYNN K. WHITE. 1991. *Sociology*. 3rd edition. St. Paul, MN: West Publishing Company.

BYE, MARGARET G., and JOAN IANNONE. 1987. "Excellent Care-Givers (Nursing Assistants) of the Elderly: What Satisfies Them About Their Work." *Nursing Homes* 35 (6):36–39.

Congressional Quarterly Almanac. 1987. "Congress Stiffens Nursing Home Regulation." 100th Congress, 1st Session. *Congressional Quarterly Almanac* XLIII. Washington, D.C.: Congressional Quarterly, Inc.

COWGILL, DONALD. 1974. "Aging and Modernization: A Revision of the Theory." Pp. 123–46 in *Late Life: Communities and Environmental Policies*, edited by Jaber F. Gubrium. Springfield, IL: Charles C. Thomas.

DAY, WILLIAM V. 1971. "How to Reduce Employee Turnover." *Nursing Homes* 20:16–17.

DEANE, PHYLLIS. 1969. *The First Industrial Revolution*. Cambridge: Cambridge University Press.

GARLAND, NEAL T., NAOKO OYABU, and GENEVIEVE A. GIPSON. 1988. "Stayers and Leavers: A Comparison of Nurse Assistants Employed in Nursing Homes." *Journal of Long-Term Care Administration* 16:23–29.

GIPSON, GENEVIEVE A., T. NEAL GARLAND, and NAOKO OYABU-MATHIS. 1994. "Ohio Teaching Network: Model for Training and Research in Long Term Care." Paper presented at the Twelfth Annual Meeting of the Association for Gerontology in Higher Education (AGHE), Cleveland, OH.

GOODE, WILLIAM J. 1963. *World Revolution and Family Patterns*. New York: Free Press.

HEISELMAN, TERRY, NAOKO OYABU, and GENEVIEVE A. GIPSON. 1989. "Evaluation of a Training Program for Trainers of Nursing Home Assistants." Paper presented at the Thirteenth Annual Professional and Scientific Conference on Aging and the Twelfth Annual Ohio Student Conference on Aging, sponsored by the Ohio Network of Educational Consultants in the Field of Aging (ONECA), April 7, Miami University, Oxford, OH.

Institute of Medicine. 1986. *Improving the Quality of Care in Nursing Homes.* Washington, D.C.: National Academy Press.

Kahn, Robert, Donald Wolfe, Robert, Quinn, J. Diedrick Snoek, and Robert Rosenthal. 1964. *Organizational Stress: Studies in Role Conflict and Ambiguity.* New York: Wiley.

Kogan, Nathan. 1961. "Attitudes Toward Old People: The Development of a Scale and an Examination of Correlates." *Journal of Abnormal and Social Psychology* 62:44–54.

Kohn, Melvin L. (ed.) 1989. *Cross-National Research in Sociology.* Newbury Park, CA: SAGE Publications, Inc.

Oyabu, Naoko. 1989. *Influences on Satisfaction and Self-Esteem Among Nurse Assistants Employed at Nursing Homes.* Ph.D. dissertation. Department of Sociology, University of Akron, Akron, OH.

Population Reference Bureau. 1993. *World Population Data Sheet.* Washington, D.C.: Population Reference Bureau.

———. 1989. *Population Pressures: Threat to Democracy.* Washington, D.C.: Population Reference Bureau.

Reublinger, Vera. 1989. "OBRA Sets New Threshold for Nursing Assistant Training." *Provider* 15:43–44.

Ross, Barbara. 1972. "Competent Aides: A Problem?" *Nursing Homes* 22:38 and 45.

Rostow, Walt W. 1960. *The Stages of Economic Growth: A Non-Communist Manifesto.* Cambridge: Cambridge University Press.

United States Department of Commerce. 1993. *Population Profile of the United States: 1993.* Washington, D.C.: United States Department of Commerce.

Wagnild, Gail, and Roger W. Manning. 1986. "The High-Turnover Profile: Screening and Selecting Applicants for Nurse's Aide." *The Journal of Long-Term Care Administration* 14 (2):2–4.

Winston, Carmen T. 1981. "Non-Professional Employee Turnover in Nursing Homes." *Nursing Homes* 30:37–42.

World Population News Service. 1992. *Popline* 14:4. Washington, D.C.: Population Crisis Committee.

CHAPTER 19

International Dependency and Health: A Comparative Case Study of Cuba and the Dominican Republic

Annette M. Schwabe

There is a wealth of literature comparing health care systems internationally (Burns and Li 1992; Schieber, Poullier, and Greenwald 1991; Waitzkin 1983). These studies examine many influential factors in health and health care, including cultural norms and values, economic structures, internal power relations within nations, and technological development. Also, many studies describe health care statuses of countries and provide useful statistics on several aspects of health and health care (Schieber et al. 1991), but do not frame their descriptions in any particular body of theory. Those that do account for the effects of economic standing or for the influence of social structures and culture on medical care and health are often politically benign (Krasny and Ferrier 1991). They ignore the global power relations that influence economic, political, and social well-being, or structures of health care and health outcomes. Further, many studies that assess health care structures in a given country in light of its global position and its social and political structures (for example, Elling 1978; Waitzkin 1983; Waitzkin and Britt 1989) do not directly address how international social relations influence internal stratification and, in turn, how international social relations affect the structure of health care and health outcomes.

This study uses dependency theory as a framework to examine differences in the health systems and health outcomes of two countries in the Caribbean—

Cuba and the Dominican Republic—according to their radically diverging positions in the scale of dependency on developed countries. Broadly, dependency theory shows that global relations are reproduced internally within a nation's economic, political, and social relations. Dependency theory seeks to explain health stratification within nations and to provide a theoretical position from which to compare health care internationally. It facilitates an explicit analysis of the linkages between global and local power relations, and between political and economic factors that are important for understanding cross-national differences in medical care and health.

The main features of dependency theory are as follows. First, it suggests that external stratification (inequalities across nations) leads to internal stratification (inequalities within a given nation-state), which has implications for health. Specifically, dependency theory asserts that basic resources (food, water, shelter) and access to social services such as health care are stratified cross-nationally as well as within nations because of a country's position in the world economy (Cardoso and Faletto 1979; So 1990). Second, dependency theory addresses how global power relations affect economic development internally (Hendricks 1991), which, in turn, is likely to affect health. A country's level of economic development affects the amount of health resources available to it relative to other countries in the world system. Third, dependency theory seeks to explain how a country's degree of political autonomy enables it to construct a health care system that meets the needs of its people. Since health care is a social resource, one may infer from dependency theory that the degree of dependency would affect the structure and quality of health care and health status itself. Thus, dependency theory reveals how structural factors—on both the global and local levels—determine one's life chances, including personal experiences of health.

The purpose of this chapter is to examine how dependency affects health—in particular, how the economic and political aspects of dependency shape health care structures and health itself. A cross-national comparison is used in order to contrast structural differences while "holding constant" several other variables that may influence a nation's economic robustness and political situations. I selected Cuba and the Dominican Republic because these countries share a common language, religion, geographical location, size, and agricultural potential (types of natural resources). They are both influenced by the capitalist world economically and, until the revolution in Cuba, had similar political, social, and economic histories. Further, although these two countries have roughly similar levels of development, their situations of dependency are different.

The questions that this chapter seeks to answer are:

1. How do the Dominican Republic and Cuba differ in their dependency situations?
2. How do they compare in economic development and inequality?
3. In what ways do their health structures vary?
4. Do they differ in health outcomes? and
5. What appear to be the specific factors of dependency that affect health?

DEFINITIONS OF DEPENDENCY

Before assessing differences and similarities between Cuba and the Dominican Republic, I wish to define dependency further to illuminate the aspects of this phenomenon that are critical to the study of health.

Conceptions of dependency vary among theorists (Bornschier, Chase-Dunn, and Rubinson 1978; Cardoso and Faletto 1979; dos Santos 1971; Frank 1971; Hammer and Gartrell 1986), who disagree whether it is economic or political factors that are paramount—and or whether these factors are mutually reciprocal.

Chase-Dunn (1975) pinpoints three main issues that dependency theory addresses: (1) global relations, including exploitation, (2) structural distortion of global and local economies related to a highly specified division of labor within and across nations; and (3) suppression of autonomy of the dependent state to make local policy decisions concerning economic structures and distribution of social resources. Dependency is characterized by an inherent imbalance of power that is present between two (or more) countries, indicated by quantitative factors such as trade patterns and debt, as well as by qualitative factors, including the role of the local state *vis a vis* foreign investors, with dependent countries having less autonomous control over internal decisions than core nations have (Gereffi and Fonda 1992). These features of dependency have important consequences for the internal well-being of the dependent nation, the primary outcomes being inequality and underdevelopment.

Many theorists have not clearly differentiated "dependency" from "development." Most commonly, *dependency* connotes a cluster of economic and political *relationships* between a core (developed) country and the dependent peripheral country whereby core countries in the worldwide capitalist system develop at the expense of underdeveloped countries, and dependent countries lose autonomy over political decisions in order to remain attractive or palatable to foreign investors (Cardoso and Faletto 1979; Chase-Dunn 1975; Evans 1979; Hendricks 1991). In contrast, *development* has most often been defined as a series of concrete economic *outcomes* (for example, growth in GNP) of structurally dependent relationships.[1] In this chapter, I distinguish dependency from development in the context of the two countries under study. In the following sections, I provide a model that specifies the relationships between dependency, development, inequality, and health, and then I compare Cuba and the Dominican Republic to reveal the relationships between dependency and health in these countries.

THE IMPACT OF DEPENDENCY ON HEALTH: A CONCEPTUAL MODEL

The chain of events connecting dependency and health proposed in this study is as follows (see Figure 1). First, dependency is predicted to have a direct, negative impact on economic development. In turn, level of development is expected to be positively related to health outcomes via its effect on health resources and infrastructure. For example, poverty would limit a nation's ability to supply basic needs such as food, housing (Klak 1993), and clean water (Burns and Li 1992). Quality of education is included here as a health resource, since a well-

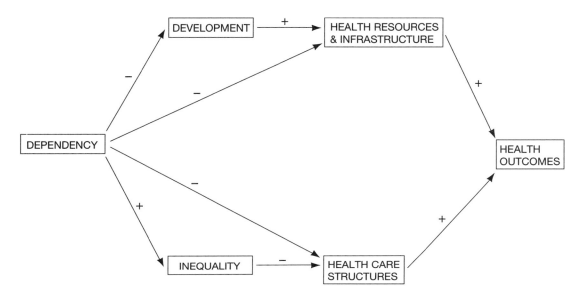

FIGURE 1: The Impact of Dependency on Health

educated populace is likely to be more able to be informed about health issues. Poverty would also limit funds available for investing in public health infrastructure, including medical goods, medical facilities, and health care personnel. Since the presence of health resources is positively related to health (Turshen 1989), dependency is expected to have an indirect negative impact on health outcomes via its influence on economic development and health resources.

Second, dependency is predicted to have a direct, negative impact on health resources and infrastructure because resources are likely to be directed externally for exports to appease foreign investors (in other words, to attract capital) rather than being directed to internal social needs and services (for example, food and medical facilities). A good health infrastructure is expected to be positively related to health outcomes, especially for infectious disease, which rises with poverty and poor access to care (Turshen 1989). Therefore, dependency is again predicted to be negatively related to health outcomes via a nation's health infrastructure.

Third, because of the lack of autonomy in public policy-making, dependency is predicted to have a direct negative effect on the structure of health care, since, in dependent nations, economic resources are frequently channelled to export production rather than to internal social needs, including health care.

Fourth, because of heightened inequality in access to resources, dependency is predicted to have a negative effect on health outcomes via its impact on degree of inequality of access to health resources, which is mitigated by the health care structure.[2]

Thus, just as dependency theorists assert that dependency relationships penetrate and are maintained by economic, political, and social structures, I argue that the negative social, economic, and political arrangements of dependency lead to poor health for the majority of the people in a dependent nation.

In particular, I assert that by increasing its autonomy from the world system, the Cuban state has increased the degree to which resources have been directed internally, enabling improvements in health care and health. In contrast, the Dominican Republic's dependency on the world system has had adverse effects on its social infrastructure, including the quality of health. Next, I present evidence regarding the impact of dependency on health in Cuba and in the Dominican Republic.

INDICATORS OF DEPENDENCY

The degree of autonomy of a nation to make decisions internally, based on local needs, is a key defining feature of dependency. Specifically, dependency is negatively associated with the degree of autonomy a nation has over internal affairs. I will compare degree of autonomy to identify differences in the dependency situations of Cuba and the Dominican Republic. Other features by which dependency will be measured here include degree of direct foreign investment and ownership, debt per capita, and the degree to which the economy is export-oriented. Each of these indicators has been found to be positively associated with dependency. Since structuring the local labor market to produce for export rather than for internal consumption is frequently marked by a concentration of the labor force in mining and agriculture (Chase-Dunn 1975), these two indicators will also be used to compare levels of dependency.

UNDERDEVELOPMENT AND INEQUALITY AS OUTCOMES OF DEPENDENCY

Underdevelopment

Underdevelopment has been found to be an outcome of dependency in several studies, especially in the long run (Hammer and Gartrell 1986; So 1990). According to these studies, dependency promotes underdevelopment because developed countries impose an international division of labor in order to extract surplus value from workers in underdeveloped countries. In this way, dependency is found to heighten poverty in peripheral countries, which limits their autonomy politically and economically and devastates social resources. Also, poor terms of trade result in debt, the repayment of which further increases poverty (Chase-Dunn 1975; Evans 1979; Shrestha and Patterson 1990). Although the overwhelming majority of the literature supports the idea that dependency promotes underdevelopment, this appears to vary across nations, and may depend on the time frame in which development is measured (Gereffi 1983; Smith and White 1992).

Inequality

The global division of labor characteristic of dependency is manifested in a local labor force that is sharply bifurcated into two main groups: a small, skilled clique of owners and managers, and a large reserve pool of unskilled laborers who supply cheap labor and who are economically and politically marginalized (Marcotte and Coughenour 1987). Thus, with greater dependency, social inequality increases between the local elite, who cater to the demands of core countries and are given personal rewards for their complicity, and laborers, who are exploited to produce for core countries rather than for themselves. Dependency theory asserts, then, that core countries directly derive and maintain their hegemony by exploiting peripheral countries, which suffer a consequent loss of power in the world system, worsened economic conditions, and increased internal inequality, conditions that are likely to affect health.

The data used to measure all concepts and variables under study are derived from multiple sources, including case studies presented in the literature as well as descriptive statistics presented in articles and statistical abstracts. In addition, there is a dearth of comparable and detailed data for these two countries, especially using the same sources and years. With these caveats in mind, I examine dependency and health in the Dominican Republic and Cuba.

EVIDENCE FOR DIFFERENCES IN LEVELS OF DEPENDENCY BETWEEN CUBA AND THE DOMINICAN REPUBLIC

The Cuban Revolution: Decreased Dependency

The broad goal of the Cuban revolution in 1959 was emancipation from foreign capitalist control, with specific plans to increase self-sufficiency and improve development while redistributing resources such as land, education, and health care. Since the revolution, there has been a general increase in autonomy over internal decisions, including increased investment in public sector industries and services (Waitzkin and Britt 1989). Cuba has not strictly conformed to the political policy of the Soviet Union[3] (Zimbalist and Eckstein 1987), has had a fair amount of leverage in negotiating with it over issues of trade, and has been able to direct resources locally (Cripps 1979; deBrun and Elling 1987; Fitzgerald 1988; Tsokhas 1980).

Cuba is subject to capricious market fluctuations in the capitalist world-system. It also relies heavily on the USSR for critical staples such as oil (Eckstein 1982). Nevertheless its ties to the Soviet Union are less exploitative than the relationships between the U.S. and Cuba prior to 1959, or between the U.S. and the Dominican Republic currently. For example, trade and aid between the USSR and Cuba differs from trade and aid between the U.S. and the Dominican Republic in several ways. First, much of trade and aid between the USSR and Cuba is based on barter, sugar is subsidized to exceed world market prices, and loans to Cuba are mostly interest-free, thereby buffering Cuba from the vicissitudes of market rates (Eckstein 1982; Fitzgerald 1988; Tsokhas 1980).

In Cuba, as in the Dominican Republic, sugar production constitutes a large portion of the agricultural sector. However, unlike the Dominican Republic, Cuba has had flexibility in contracting or expanding sugar production when world market demands changed: sugar production increased when the world market demand and prices were high, but was reduced when the market price plummeted in the 1970s (Eckstein 1982; Fitzgerald 1988). Second, price arrangements are long-term and are agreed upon before implementation, which allows Cuba to predict costs. These two features of trade and aid enable planning by Cuba and reduce interest debt. Although Cuba's reliance on the USSR for fuel, and the increasing political and economic instability of the USSR renders Cuba's well-being precarious, the benefits of autonomy for Cuba seem to outweigh the costs, as will become apparent in the discussion of health.

The Dominican Republic: Increased Dependency and Foreign Domination

The period of time from 1960 to the present marked an era of "neocolonialism" (Marcotte and Coughenour 1987) typified by an extension and deepening of exploitation and political control over the Dominican Republic by the developed world—especially the United States. Production in the Dominican Republic has become increasingly more export-oriented and less oriented to internal consumption needs, and production sectors have become increasingly structured around the interests of developed countries rather than internal needs.

While the Dominican Republic is ostensibly independent politically, the United States, in particular, has influenced Dominican politics to its advantage, lowering barriers to foreign investment and control (Black 1986; Griffin 1982; Wiarda and Kryzanek 1982). For example, many of the benefits of aid were channelled to oligarchists in the Dominican Republic who, in turn, supplied the U.S. with access to natural resources, cheap local labor, and numerous import and export privileges such as free trade zones, which are tax free to multinationals, have few restrictions on wages, and have a better infrastructure than most other parts of the country (Moreno 1986).

In contrast to Cuba, the Dominican Republic is heavily dependent on the capitalist world system, particularly the U.S. Aid from the U.S. is contingent on economic and political conformity (Chomsky and Herman 1977; Cripps 1979; Moreno 1975 and 1986). Trade ties between the Dominican Republic and the U.S. are highly subject to fluctuating demand and price on the world market, decreasing the stability of exported products—especially sugar—as a source of foreign revenues. Further evidence of the Dominican Republic's extensive dependency on the U.S. is that after the election of Balaguer, a president highly loyal to the U.S., per capita economic and military aid from the U.S. to the Dominican Republic was greater than to any other country in Latin America (Kryzanek and Wiarda 1988). Economic assistance from the U.S. (primarily) such as the Alliance for Progress, was frequently tied to military occupation by American forces, especially when leftist leaders unsympathetic to capitalism, such as Juan Bosch, rose to power (Chomsky and Herman 1977; Griffin 1982). According to Chomsky and Herman (1997), aid from the U.S. to the Dominican Republic necessitated the support of repressive regimes opposed to human rights within the country, underscoring the linkages between dependency and political repression.

Comparison of Foreign Ownership, Debt, Mining, and Agriculture

U.S. ownership of production and land in the Dominican Republic has increased since the 1960s. Investments by American companies and government have doubled since the overthrow of Juan Bosch in 1965, and more than 50 percent of the nation's assets are controlled by the U.S. (Moreno 1975). In contrast, the Soviet Union does not own production or land in Cuba and does not directly reap profits from its assistance to Cuba (Eckstein 1982).

Absolute debt and debt as a percentage of GNP in the Dominican Republic has increased substantially since 1970 (see Table 1). This increase is consistent with being dependent, and affects and reflects the level of development in the Dominican Republic. Debt as a percentage of GNP was 52.5 percent in 1986, again supporting the idea that a growing debt reduces available economic resources within a dependent country. Cuba's foreign debt is only slightly less than that of the Dominican Republic. However, Cuba's debt as a percentage of exports is lower, and, as noted above, Cuba has some power and flexibility in negotiating prices and in directing resources internally to meet local needs. Examination of mining activity and concentration in agriculture further illustrates the Dominican Republic's greater dependency relative to Cuba. Although both countries have rich mineral reserves, specialization in mining is about four-and-one-half times greater in the Dominican Republic than in Cuba, and agricultural concentration is about two times higher (see Table 1).

Looking at differences between Cuba and the Dominican Republic in terms of the indicators of dependency examined above, it is evident that the Dominican Republic is more reliant on more developed countries economically and socially than is Cuba, especially when examining the nature of trade and aid ties, and degree of internal political control. Since Cuba and the Dominican Republic appear to occupy different locations on a continuum of dependency, one would expect there to be different health care structures in each, as well as different levels of health.

TABLE 1.   INDICATORS OF DEPENDENCY

SOURCE	INDICATOR	CUBA	DOMINICAN REPUBLIC
Zimbalist and Eckstein[1] Marcotte and Coughenour[2]	Debt (1985–86, $U.S. billions)	2.86	3.0
Zimbalist and Eckstein[1] Marcotte and Coughenour[2]	Debt repayment as percentage of exports, 1986–87	18.7	25.0
World Bank[2]	Debt as percentage of GNP		
	1970	NA	15.7
	1986	16[3]	52.5
Diagram Group	Mining as percentage of Exports, 1983	7.6	32.2
Wilkie	Percentage Labor Force in Agriculture, 1981	23	49

[1]Cuba
[2]Dominican Republic
[3]Estimated based on GNP in 1987 and debt figure above.

SEQUELAE OF DEPENDENCY: COMPARISON OF CUBA AND THE DOMINICAN REPUBLIC

Development

Several indicators of development are well established in the literature as reflecting a country's situation of dependency (Cardoso 1977; Chase-Dunn 1975; Hammer and Gartrell 1986; Smith and White 1992; Stevenson 1972) and examination of these studies shows that the different situations of dependency in Cuba and the Dominican Republic are manifested in divergent levels of economic development. The economic indicators and their relation to dependency selected for this study include per capita Gross National Product (GNP), per capita income, annual consumption of kilowatts per hour (KWH) per capita, and economic growth (percent change in GNP), which are all negatively related to dependency.

Comparing the two countries on all indicators of economic development, Cuba clearly has a more robust economy (see Table 2). Economic growth rates in the Dominican Republic and Cuba as measured by GNP (including value of exports) underscore the extent and effects of dependency in these two countries. From 1964 to 1980, an era of heavy investment in the Dominican Republic by the U.S., GNP grew 7.5 percent (World Bank 1988), but economic stagnation occurred in the long run. From 1980 to 1986, the Gross National Product grew 1.1 percent. In contrast, Cuba's GSP[4] grew slightly less between 1965 and 1980 but economic growth was more stable than that of the Dominican Republic over time. Based on these data, the Dominican Republic's greater dependency is associated with economic robustness in the short run but it has a negative effect in the long run, as predicted by several dependency theorists (Evans 1979; Hammer and Gartrell 1986; Smith and White 1992).

Inequality

In the same period that Cuba gained increased political autonomy, social inequality decreased. In the first half of the twentieth century, two-thirds of the agricultural land in Cuba was held by U.S. companies and less than 10 percent of the population owned 90 percent of the arable land (Griffin 1982). Currently, land in Cuba is owned by the state or by small farmers (see Table 2). As dependency increased for the Dominican Republic, poverty and inequalities increased, along with growing disparities in access to a range of social resources (Cripps 1979). Farmland was, and still is, highly concentrated in the hands of a few large-scale owners in the Dominican Republic (see Table 2). Further, over the past few decades, economic disparities between the elite supporters of multinationals and the populace increased (Cripps 1979; Marcotte and Coughenour 1987). Using another index of stratification—gender equity—Cuba's rank is comparable to Austria, Belgium, and Denmark; its equity score is about 50 percent higher than the Dominican Republic on gender equity in the economic sphere.

Consistent with the dependency literature, the data provided here support the hypotheses that the Dominican Republic is more dependent than Cuba on the world system and that these differences in dependency have resulted in greater underdevelopment and inequality in the Dominican Republic relative to Cuba. While there is less disparity in the economic strength between these two coun-

TABLE 2. SEQUELAE OF DEPENDENCY: DEVELOPMENT AND INEQUALITY

SOURCE	INDICATOR	CUBA	DOMINICAN REPUBLIC
	Economic Development		
Sivard	GNP (1986, $U.S. Millions)	20,000	5,361
Sivard	GNP Per Capita (1986, $U.S.)	1,999	816
World Almanac	Per Capita Income ($U.S.; Cuba, 1983; D.R., 1980)	1,590	1,221
Wilkie	Kilowatt Hours Consumed Per Capita (1986)	1,301	723
United Nations	Percentage of Growth in GDP (1980–85)	+7.7	+1.8
Zimbalist and Eckstein[1] World Bank[2]	Percentage of Growth in GSP/GNP (1970s)[a]	+4.0	+7.3
Zimbalist and Eckstein[1] World Bank[2]	Percentage of Growth in GSP/GNP (1980s)[b]	+7.3	+1.1
	Inequality		
Diagram Group[1] Kryzanek and Wiarda[2]	Land Distribution	88 percent arable land publicly owned; 12 percent owned by small farmers	10 percent of population owns 63 percent of arable land
Population Crisis Committee	Economic Equality by Gender[c]	3.5	2
Population Crisis Committee	Total Social and Economic Equality by Gender[c]	4.5	3.5

[1]Cuba
[2]Dominican Republic
[a]Figures are for years 1964-1980 for Dominican Republic, and for 1976-1980 for Cuba.
[b]Figures are for years 1980-1986 for Dominican Republic, and for 1981-1985 for Cuba.
[c]Index ranges from 1 (unequal) to 5 (high equality). Total equality figure includes economic figure above it.

tries relative to highly developed countries, on a continuum of dependency, Cuba is more autonomous than the Dominican Republic and this appears to have had positive long-term effects for stabilizing the economy and fostering social equality.

VARIABLES FOR COMPARING HEALTH CARE AND HEALTH

The variables I use to assess the differences in health in the Dominican Republic and Cuba include health structures (socialized versus private, and degree of access to care), health resources and infrastructure, and health outcomes. The two structures of health care are compared using descriptive information, focusing on whether the system is socialized or private, and by addressing issues of access, especially rural/urban disparities. Health resources are ascertained by comparing availability of basic nutrition, clean water, and sanitation. Health care infrastructure indices include number of hospital beds, physicians, and nurses per capita. Indices of the potential for the populace to be educated about health were examined using literacy rates, school attendance, and percent of GNP spent on education.

The health outcome indicators used in this analysis are used commonly in the comparative health care literature to compare the quality of health across nations (Khan and Zerby 1982; Schieber et al. 1991). They include infant mortality; life expectancy; rates of preventable disease; mortality from causes indicative of poor economic standing and poor health infrastructure; and rates of chronic disease. Life expectancy and infant mortality are good general indicators of a nation's health status and well-being (Burns and Li 1992; Rowland 1991). Similarly, a high rate of tuberculosis is a clear indicator of social inequality, a low standard of living, and a lack of emphasis on primary health care (Turshen 1989). I compared chronic disease rates under the assumption that chronic disease is likely to be higher in Cuba than in the Dominican Republic because of the epidemiological transition—a situation where chronic disease rates increase relative to acute disease when a number of acute diseases have been eradicated following economic development. As with the data used to compare dependency, the health statistics are difficult to disentangle from other aspects of social well-being.

COMPARISON OF HEALTH CARE STRUCTURES

Cuba

Paralleling the broad changes wrought by the Cuban revolution, health care was restructured to direct large amounts of government funds into health care and to improve knowledge of good health practices by the populace, with an emphasis on preventative medicine (Navarro 1972a; Ubell 1983; Waitzkin 1983). Health care is socialized and is provided regardless of the ability to pay (see Table 3). Health policy is centrally planned by the Office of Planning and Evaluation and by the Ministry of Public Health, with much input given by physicians and the public (Guttmacher and Danielson; 1977; Navarro 1972a; Santana 1987). However, the administration of these plans in local areas is decentralized and is structured to respond to the needs of different communities.

Guttmacher and Danielson (1977), Navarro (1972a), and Santana (1987) have outlined the ways in which the Cuban health care system developed following the revolution. Although health reform paralleled other social, political, and economic changes, health care reform was, in itself, one of the primary goals of the revolution. Reform was particularly focused on the abolition of the pre-revolutionary system, which was highly stratified by race-ethnicity (for example, it gave nationals of Spanish ethnic background clear advantages in terms of access; most people able to belong to a managed-care plan were white), class, and geographical location. By closing small, private, urban hospitals and constructing larger facilities in urban areas and more facilities in rural areas, access to care improved generally, especially for residents of rural areas. For example, in 1959 Havana (22 percent of Cuba's population) had 54.7 percent of all beds while a rural province with 35 percent of the population had only 15.5 percent of beds. By 1970, Havana had 40 percent of all beds and the aforementioned

TABLE 3.   HEALTH CARE STRUCTURE DIFFERENCES

Cuba

* Socialized health care: provided regardless of ability to pay.
* Centralized planning, sensitive to local needs.
* Emphasis on equitable distribution of care between rural and urban areas.
* Emphasis on preventive and primary care, and on public health.

The Dominican Republic

* Health services are privatized, highly stratified: for those at the most marginal economic level; access is very poor and care is of low quality.
* Little coordination of services: practitioners keep irregular schedules, which reduces access to care.
* Poor distribution of care to rural areas, coupled with poor access by rural residents to reliable and affordable transportation to get to medical facilities; health services for poor are substandard.
* Emphasis on curative care, not preventive care.

rural province had 23 percent of beds (Navarro 1972a). After these concrete steps were taken to increase access—especially for the rural population—to health personnel, clinics, immunizations, and prenatal care in the early 1960s, morbidity and mortality declined dramatically (Cripps 1979; Guttmacher and Danielson 1977; Santana 1987).

Once a solid mechanism was in place to eradicate the majority of infectious and acute disease and the initial "crisis" of health care had been dealt with, the Cuban government was able to focus on coordinating primary and preventive care with secondary, tertiary, and "curative" care. This was done by developing a referral mechanism based on geographical location, with three levels of medical care. First, the polyclinics serve a relatively small community and provide primary care. Physicians from these centers refer patients to a second level, consisting of regional hospitals, which serve a larger population and provide specialty or secondary care (for example, otolaryngology, urology, psychiatry). The third level is made up of provincial hospitals, which serve populations of about one million and provide tertiary, "superspecialty" care such as plastic surgery, allergy, and rehabilitation medicine (Navarro 1972a; Navarro 1972b; Santana 1987; Ubell 1983).

The structure and orientation of the polyclinics presented the populace with opportunities to critique the system and to address their needs as health care recipients. This increased the ability of regional caregivers to tailor services to the needs and cultural dictates of locals, thereby reducing social distance, and led to further changes in the health care system in the mid-1970s (Santana 1987). These changes entailed improved coordination between primary, secondary, and tertiary caregivers, with specialists practicing according to guidelines mutually established with health team members, and an emphasis on community health education and participation. Also, committees representing groups of workers, women, small farmers and other community groups were formed and gave input into local health care through elections of political representatives and by direct participation in deciding how health care would be implemented regionally (Navarro 1972a; Waitzkin and Britt 1989). Despite these attempts to structure health care around local needs, continuity of care was difficult to maintain, which affected the perception of quality of care negatively. The care given by primary care groups practicing at polyclinics—internists, obstetrician-gynecologists, and pediatricians—did not overlap sufficiently, and was often redistributed to other nearby areas because of a shortage of professionals.

In the mid-1980s, the government responded to this problem by recruiting an increased number of physicians and nurses, streamlining several bureaucratic procedures, and initiating a family practice program. The family practice program was geared to coordinate care, survey the local population about their health status, and gather basic epidemiological information. Unlike the rural outreach in the USSR or China, greater provision of health care revolved around providing medical professionals (based on the Western model of care), rather than *feldshers*, or barefoot doctors. However, the emphasis on increasing the quality of care in rural areas has also been centered around teaching the citizens basic medical care, as well as being informed about preventative strategies (Cripps 1979; Navarro 1972b; Waitzkin and Britt 1989).

The Dominican Republic

In stark contrast to the Cuban case, health care in the Dominican Republic, like many other resources, remains highly stratified and of poor quality for the majority of society (see Table 3). Ugalde (1984) conducted extensive fieldwork assessing the Dominican health care system, focusing on rural care. Because of infusions of aid targeted for health care by the United States Agency for International Development (USAID) in 1976, Ugalde expected health care to be fairly accessible and of good quality. However, this was not the case. Although health services are free for indigent persons, their care is of low quality, and is poorly utilized. For persons above the most marginal economic level, out-of-pocket health care expenditures are high. At the same time, many medicines are free (despite shortages) on a first come, first served basis and there is an inappropriately high use of unnecessary medication. Vaccinations are also in short supply and are expensive. Coupled with low levels of education of health providers and users, and an orientation toward "remedial" medicine rather than preventive care, much of the medical care for the poor is ineffective.

Unlike the community orientation in Cuba, health care delivery in the Dominican Republic is not tailored to regional-cultural differences in the population. The *pasantes* (new physicians serving a year of compulsory service in rural areas) are inadequately trained in disease prevention, and receive virtually no education about rural health care (Library of Congress 1991; Ugalde 1984). Further, rural health centers are not ideally situated for the community to access them, especially in light of a poor transportation system and few private automobiles. Much of the rural population distrusts the *pasantes* who hold irregular, unannounced schedules, and again have little understanding of their patient population. Low quality of rural care related to poor physician education and coordination is also evident in short lengths of visit—slightly under three minutes on average—even though the medical staff was finished with their work by midmorning (Ugalde 1984). In short, in striking contrast to Cuba, the privatized Dominican health care system is highly stratified; out-of-pocket expenses are high; there is an emphasis on curative care rather than on preventive care (and these two domains are poorly integrated. Medical professionals are in short supply and are not well-trained). Finally, there is little public awareness of health and virtually no public participation in health care planning or administration.

HEALTH RESOURCES AND INFRASTRUCTURE

Cuba's health resource base and infrastructure far surpass those of the Dominican Republic, as is evident in the differences between these two nations on all indicators examined here (see Table 4). Both countries showed an increase in per capita calorie consumption from 1965 to 1986, but Cuba's remained much higher (World Bank 1988). In addition to having more food resources, food distribution in Cuba is equitable (Cripps 1979). Rates of electricity consumption (see Table 2), and availability of clean water are higher in Cuba than in the Dominican Republic. Cuba has a solid educational infrastructure for developing a health-educated populace, increasing the potential supply of providers as well as educated consumers of care. Literacy rates in Cuba and the Dominican Republic are widely discrepant and reflect Cuba's higher commitment to education along with a more solid economic base with which to fund it. Long-term trends indicate major improvements in potential access to health care in Cuba but little in the Dominican Republic (see Table 4). At the same time that there is a greater physician saturation in Cuba than in the Dominican Republic, there is a also a greater emphasis on basic, preventative care and equal distribution of services in Cuba.

Contrasting the two countries, it is evident that in the Dominican Republic there is little investment internally, and basic resources for promoting good health are scarce because of poverty and unequal distribution of resources

TABLE 4. HEALTH RESOURCES AND INFRASTRUCTURE

SOURCE	INDICATOR	CUBA	DOMINICAN REPUBLIC
Wilkie	Per Capita Daily Calories (1986)	3,107	2,464
Wilkie	Per Capita Daily Grams Protein (1986)	78.9	52.5
	Percent Population with Potable Water (1975):		
Wilkie	Urban	91	66
Wilkie	Rural	10	12
Sivard	Total	82	62
Sivard	Population per Hospital Bed (1986)	190	640
Sivard	Population per Physician (1986)	455	1,728
World Bank[1] UNESCO[2]	Population per Nurse (Mid-1980s)	370	1,200
Sivard	Percent of GNP Spent on Education (1986)	6.2	1.6
World Almanac[3]	Percent of Population that Is Literate	98	68
World Almanac[3]	Percent of Population that Attends School (between ages 6–14 years)	92	60

[1]Cuba

[2]Dominican Republic

[3]Figures are for 1989 for Cuba and for 1987 for the Dominican Republic.

among its citizens. These problems are evident in the fact that many of the life-threatening diseases in the Dominican Republic result directly or indirectly from unsanitary living conditions (Bell 1981). In comparison, Cuba has more health resources available, and has distributed these more equitably across the population. The effect of these efforts to improve basic living conditions and the public infrastructure will be apparent in the statistical figures presented in the following sections.

HEALTH OUTCOMES IN CUBA AND THE DOMINICAN REPUBLIC

The health outcomes associated with health care and development are far worse in the Dominican Republic than in Cuba, as indicated in Table 5. Life expectancy and infant mortality figures, indications of the general health of a nation, indicate that, on the whole, Cuba is superior to the Dominican Republic in terms of health. Infectious and parasitic disease death rates, often associated with a lack of immunizations and clean water, are over twice as high in the Dominican Republic as in Cuba. Nutritional marasmus is a protein-calorie deficiency related to unhygienic bottle feeding of children, repeated gastroenteritis and other infectious disease, and undernourishment. In Cuba, there was one death from marasmus in 1988; in that year, rates of marasmus were lower in Cuba than in the U.S. In the Dominican Republic there were nine deaths related to marasmus, even though the Dominican Republic has a smaller population than Cuba.

Hypertension and diabetes mellitus have several underlying etiologies (including genetic predisposition and diet). Rates of hypertension are similar between the two countries, and rates of diabetes are higher in Cuba than in the Dominican Republic (see Table 5). These findings indicate that an epidemiological transition is occurring in Cuba, as development has increased there.

Finally, although I am not aware of an association between indicators of dependency (low income, inequality, etc.) and pneumonia, it was notable that pneumonia deaths per 100,000 were about 50 percent higher in Cuba than in the Dominican Republic (United Nations 1992). U.S. death rates from pneumonia were similar to those in Cuba: 30.9/100,000. This relatively high rate of pneu-

TABLE 5.   HEALTH OUTCOMES IN CUBA AND THE DOMINICAN REPUBLIC

SOURCE	INDICATOR	CUBA	DOMINICAN REPUBLIC
Sivard	Life Expectancy (1986, in years)	73	65
Population Reference Bureau	Infant Mortality (1991, per thousand births)	11	61
Sivard	Percent of Babies with Low Birthweight (1986)	8	16
United Nations	Death Rates from Tuberculosis[a]	0.5	8.5
United Nations	Death Rates from Infectious and Parasitic Disease[a]	2.1	4.7
United Nations	Death Rates from Hypertension[a]	8.0	9.5
United Nations	Death Rates from Diabetes Mellitus[a]	20.8	8.9

[a]Deaths by cause per 100,000 population. UN data are for Cuba in 1988 and for the Dominican Republic in 1985.

monia in Cuba might also be a result of an epidemiological transition, having a larger aging population than the Dominican Republic, or a weakness in some aspect of the health care system among other possible reasons. However, a weakness in Cuba's health care system *relative to* that in the Dominican Republic is not the most likely factor in these differentials, given all of the evidence above. In summary, all of the areas of health and health care compared above indicate that Cuba's base resources for health, the structure and quality of its medical system, and equality of access are far superior to those in the Dominican Republic. In addition, the level of health of the population reflects the relative integrity of health care in these two countries.

CONCLUSIONS

While Cuba and the Dominican Republic have a great deal in common, the revolution in Cuba clearly increased Cuba's autonomy from the capitalist world system while the Dominican Republic became increasingly more dependent, with negative long-term effects on its economy. Reviewing the evidence presented here in light of the hypotheses outlined earlier, it is evident that the different degrees of dependency in these two countries have had a strong impact on the health care systems as well as on health outcomes per se. These data suggest that a country's level of economic dependency affects the quality of its health care, equality of access, and health outcomes.

These data indicate three positive effects that autonomy seems to have had on health care and health. First, having a larger measure of autonomy enables the local state to tailor the health care system to meet internal needs and to broaden access to care. Second, there are more resources for promoting health and these are available to more of the people because of a political and social orientation to mobilize resources internally and because increased economic growth and social equality are outcomes of autonomy. Third, the abundance of health resources and a well-planned, accessible health care system are vital for good health. Specifically, degree of infant mortality and infectious disease are much lower and life expectancy is higher in Cuba, which has better health resources and health care structures than the Dominican Republic. In looking at the patterns of the data presented here, dependency appears to affect health outcomes indirectly through its effects on the organization of health care, economic development, and the extent to which an economy can sustain health resources.

Gereffi (1983) and other dependency theorists suggest that, because of the extent of penetration of the capitalist world-system into virtually all economies on the planet, the "fundamental contradictions" of dependency will limit the extent to which political changes may release a given country from dependency. Specifically, a social revolution may moderate or mitigate the worst aspects of dependency but will not completely abolish global and local power relations ties and oppression. Thus I assert that, while Cuba has become less dependent on the capitalist world-system and its related political control or impositions, Cuba's legacy of underdevelopment and past control by capitalist superpowers will continue to restrict its full potential as an autonomous nation. Accordingly, Cuba's well-developed health care system and high level of health may be dismantled if international pressures to conform to the demands of the world system increase under the tightening rein of capitalism. Conversely, given the heightening contradictions between rich and poor and increased poverty within the Dominican Republic predicted by dependency and world-systems theorists, it is possible, too, that a revolution or widely supported social movement responding to these changes will lead to a better standard of living, including improved health.

One final question raised both by dependency theory and by recent changes in the global economy and international relations is: what are Cuba's prospects for the future given the collapse of the Soviet Union, Cuba's primary ally, source of economic support (e.g., sugar subsidies), and trading partner? There is growing evidence that Cuba's economy has become noticeably weaker since 1991, when the USSR dissolved. For example, there are major oil and food shortages, and an overall decreased standard of living. This economic downturn in Cuba appears to have forced Castro to seek out sources of foreign revenue from capitalist nations. Hence, I predict that Cuba will be increasingly drawn into the capitalist world system; recent evidence indicates that this is already beginning to occur. For example, the Cuban tourism industry has flourished with the active encouragement of the Castro government, with heavy participation by Canadian firms.

Another possibility for changes in Cuba's foreign relations is that there may be a rapprochement with the United States. If Cuba's market appears to be a potentially lucrative site of investment for U.S. businesses, and/or if leadership changes occur in Cuba so that a post-Castro government that is more amenable to U.S. demands and relations arises, there is a strong possibility that the U.S. trade embargo against Cuba would be lifted, leading to increased trade ties between Cuba and the United States. Dependency theory predicts that these ties would diminish Cuba's autonomy and there would follow a further decline in Cuba's economic standards, decreased control over the production of goods and allocation of resources, and increased stratification internally. Thus, it is likely that there would be fewer health resources available generally, the health care structure would likely become more stratified, and health outcomes would decline overall. However, under socialism, Cuba has had a long-standing tradition of attempting to equalize resource distribution and maintain local control over production and resources, which has the potential to moderate the effects of dependency on health and health care that may be wrought by renewed ties with the United States.

NOTES

[1] Countries that are underdeveloped initially are vulnerable to becoming dependent on core nations that have greater initial economic advantage. However, dependency refers to the ongoing *nature* of the relationship between the periphery and the core. It deepens the dependency of the periphery on the core and results in heightened, more entrenched underdevelopment in the long run (Gereffi 1983, Hammer and Gartrell 1986).

[2] In addition to fostering greater autonomy, the Cuban revolution entailed a commitment to socialism, which has had clear effects on the structure and distribution of care as well as the degree of commitment to directing economic resources into health (Waitzkin and Britt 1989). However, I argue that the broader relations of dependency may be examined in their effects on health, while recog-

nizing the importance of the influence of a socialist ideology in facilitating autonomy and that it has effects on the economic and social structure similar to those of dependency.

[3] Although the Soviet Union no longer exists, I will refer to it as the USSR or Soviet Union since I am considering the relationship between it and Cuba prior to its breakup in 1991.

[4] Gross Social Product (GSP) is a measure of economic activity or robustness for socialist economies. It includes output in the productive sector and does not include services such as health, transportation, or defense (Perez-Lopez 1987). As an index of economic activity, I am using growth in GSP to depict general trends in economic growth. Gross Domestic Product is a more comparable measure of economic strength; because GDP for both countries is difficult to obtain for comparable consecutive time periods, I provide data on GSP and GNP to look at trends across time segments and compare GDP growth for one time period.

REFERENCES

BELL, IAN. 1981. *The Dominican Republic*. Boulder, CO: Westview Press.

BLACK, JAN KNIPPERS. 1986. *The Dominican Republic: Politics and Development in an Unsovereign State*. Boston: Allen and Unwin.

BORNSCHIER, VOLKER, CHRISTOPHER CHASE-DUNN, and RICHARD RUBINSON. 1978. "Cross-National Evidence of the Effects of Foreign Investment and Aid on Economic Growth and Inequality: A Survey of Findings and a Reanalysis." *American Journal of Sociology* 84:651-83.

BURNS, THOMAS J., and LI-YING LI. 1992. "Infant Mortality in a Cross-National Perspective." Paper presented at the 87th Annual Meeting of the American Sociological Association. August 20-24, Pittsburgh, PA.

CARDOSO, FERNANDO H. 1977. "The Consumption of Dependency Theory in the United States." *Latin American Research Review* 12:7-24.

CARDOSO, FERNANDO H., and ENZO FALETTO. 1979. *Dependency and Development in Latin America*. Berkeley: University of California Press.

CHASE-DUNN, CHRISTOPHER. 1975. "The Effects of International Economic Dependence on Development and Inequality: A Cross-National Study." *American Sociological Review* 40:720-38.

CHOMSKY, NOAM, and EDWARD HERMAN. 1977. "The United States versus Human Rights in the Third World." *Monthly Review* 29:22-45.

CRIPPS, LOUISE L. 1979. *The Spanish Caribbean: From Columbus to Castro*. Boston: G.K. Hall and Co.

DEBRUN, SUZANNE, and RAY H. ELLING. 1987. "Cuba and the Philippines: Contrasting Cases in World-System Analysis." *International Journal of Health Services* 17:681-701.

Diagram Group, The. 1985. *The Atlas of Central America and The Caribbean*. New York: Macmillan Publishing Company.

DOS SANTOS, THEOTONIO. 1971. "The Structure of Dependence." Pp. 225-36 in *Readings in United States Imperialism*, edited by K. T. Fann and Donald Hodges, Boston: Porter Sargent.

ECKSTEIN, SUSAN. 1982. "Cuba and the Capitalist World-Economy." Pp. 203-17 in *Socialist States in the World System*, edited by Christopher Chase-Dunn. Beverly Hills: Sage Publications.

ELLING, RAY. 1978. "Medical Systems as Changing Social Systems." *Social Science and Medicine* 12:107-15.

EVANS, PETER. 1979. *Dependent Development: The Alliance of Multinational, State, and Local Capital in Brazil*. Princeton, NJ: Princeton University Press.

FITZGERALD, FRANK T. 1988. "The 'Sovietization of Cuba Thesis' Revisited." *Science and Society* 51:439-57.

FRANK, ANDRE GUNDER. 1971. "On the Mechanisms of Imperialism: The Case of Brazil." Pp. 237-48 in *Readings in United States Imperialism*, edited by K. T. Fann and Donald Hodges. Boston: Porter Sargent.

GEREFFI, GARY. 1983. *The Pharmaceutical Industry and Dependency in the Third World*. Princeton, NJ: Princeton University Press.

GEREFFI, GARY, and STEPHANIE FONDA. 1992. "Regional Paths of Development." *Annual Review of Sociology* 18:419-48.

GRIFFIN, ERNEST C. 1982. "Latin America: How Much Progress 20 Years after the Alliance for Progress?" Pp. 307-25 in *Tension Areas of the World*, edited by David Gordon Bennett. Delray Beach, FL: Park Press.

GUTTMACHER, SALLY, and ROSS DANIELSON. 1977. "Changes in Cuban Health Care: An Argument Against Technological Pessimism." *International Journal of Health Services* 17:383-400.

HAMMER, HEATHER-JO, and JOHN GARTRELL. 1986. "American Penetration and Canadian Development: A Case Study of Mature Dependency." *American Sociological Review* 51:201-13.

HENDRICKS, JON. 1991. "Dependency Theory." Pp. 458-66 in *Encyclopedia of Sociology*, Vol. 1, edited by Edward F. Borgatta and Marie Borgatta. New York: Macmillan Publishing Company.

KHAN, M. H., and J. A. ZERBY. 1982. "A Comparative Study of Socioeconomic Development in Latin America." *Social and Economic Studies* 31:129-54.

KLAK, THOMAS. 1993. "Contextualizing State Housing Programs in Latin America: Evidence from Leading Housing Agencies in Brazil, Ecuador, and Jamaica." *Environment and Planning A* 25:653-76.

KRASNY, JACQUES, and IAN R. FERRIER. 1991. "A Closer Look at Health Care in Canada." *Health Affairs*, Summer:152-72.

KRYZANEK, MICHAEL J., and HOWARD J. WIARDA. 1988. *The Politics of External Influence on the Dominican Republic.* New York: Praeger.

Library of Congress. 1991. *Area Handbook Series: Dominican Republic and Haiti, Country Studies.* Washington, D.C.

MARCOTTE, PAUL, and C. MILTON COUGHENOUR. 1987. "The Dominican Republic: A Case of Colonial Underdevelopment and the Present Socio-Political Crisis." *International Journal of Contemporary Sociology* 24:69-84.

MORENO, JOSE A. 1975. "Intervention and Economic Penetration: The Case of the Dominican Republic." *Summation* 5:65-85.

———. 1986. "Economic Crisis in the Caribbean: From Traditional to Modern Dependency. Case of the Dominican Republic." *Contemporary Marxism* 14:97-114.

NAVARRO, VICENTE. 1972a. "Health Services in Cuba: An Initial Appraisal." *The New England Journal of Medicine* November 9:954-59.

———. 1972b. "Health, Health Services, and Health Planning in Cuba." *International Journal of Health Services* 2:397-432.

PEREZ-LOPEZ, JORGE. 1987. *Measuring Cuban Economic Performance.* Austin, TX: University of Texas Press.

Population Crisis Committee. 1988. *Country Rankings of the Status of Women.* Washington, D.C.

Population Reference Bureau. 1991. *World Population Data Sheet.* Washington, D.C.

ROWLAND, DIANE. 1991. "Health Status in East European Countries." *Health Affairs* Fall: 202-15.

SANTANA, SARAH M. 1987. "The Cuban Health Care System: Responsiveness to Changing Population Needs and Demands." *World Development* 15:113-25.

SCHIEBER, GEORGE J., JEAN-PIERRE POULLIER, and LESLIE M. GREENWALD. 1991. "Health Care Systems in Twenty-Four Countries." *Health Affairs* Fall:22-38.

SHRESTHA, NANDA R., and JOHN PATTERSON. 1990. "Population and Poverty in Dependent States: Latin America Considered." *Antipode* 22:121-55.

SIVARD, RUTH L. 1989. *World Military and Social Expenditures.* Leesburg, VA: WMSE Publications.

SMITH, DAVID A., and DOUGLAS R. WHITE. 1992. "Structure and Dynamics of the Global Economy: Network Analysis of International Trade." *Social Forces* 70:857-93.

SO, ALVIN Y. 1990. *Social Change and Development: Modernization, Dependency, and World-System Theories.* Newbury Park, CA: Sage Publications.

STEVENSON, PAUL. 1972. "External Economic Variables Influencing the Economic Growth Rate of Seven Major Latin American Nations." *Canadian Review of Sociology and Anthropology* 9:347-56.

TSOKHAS, KOSMAS. 1980. "The Political Economy of Cuban Dependence on the Soviet Union." *Theory and Society: Renewal and Critique in Social Theory* 9:319-62.

TURSHEN, MEREDITH. 1989. *The Politics of Public Health.* New Brunswick, NJ: Rutgers University Press.

UBELL, ROBERT N. 1983 (December 8). "High-Tech Medicine in the Caribbean: Twenty-Five Years of Cuban Health Care." *The New England Journal of Medicine*:1468-72.

UGALDE, ANTONIO. 1984. "Where There Is a Doctor: Strategies to Increase Productivity at Lower Costs. The Economics of Rural Health Care in the Dominican Republic." *Social Science and Medicine* 19:441-50.

United Nations. 1992. *1990 Demographic Yearbook.* Forty-Second Issue. New York: United Nations.

UNESCO (United Nations Education, Scientific, and Cultural Organization). 1990. *Statistical Yearbook.* New York: UNESCO.

WAITZKIN, HOWARD. 1983. "Health Policy and Social Change: A Comparative History of Chile and Cuba." *Social Problems* 31:235-47.

WAITZKIN, HOWARD, and THERON BRITT. 1989. "Changing the Structure of Medical Discourse: Implications of Cross-National Comparisons." *Journal of Health and Social Behavior* 30:436-49.

WIARDA, HOWARD J., and MICHAEL J. KRYZANEK. 1982. *The Dominican Republic: A Caribbean Crucible.* Boulder, CO: Westview Press.

WILKIE, JAMES W. 1990. *Statistical Abstract of Latin America*, Volume 28.

World Almanac and Book of Facts. 1990. New York: Pharos Books.

World Bank. 1988. "World Development Indicators, 1988." *World Development Report.* New York: Oxford Press.

ZIMBALIST, ANDREW. 1987. "Cuban Industrial Growth, 1965-1984." *World Development* 15:83-93.

ZIMBALIST, ANDREW, and SUSAN ECKSTEIN. 1987. "Patterns of Cuban Development: The First Twenty-Five Years." *World Development* 15:5-22.

PART VI

GLOBAL THEMES

CHAPTER 20

Risk Evaluation
of Medical Technology
in Global Population Control

Ingar Palmlund

INTRODUCTION

Rapid global population growth is one of the major social and international problems where medical knowledge has been brought to bear in narrow, specific ways during recent decades. Control of population growth and the selection of population groups for growth or decline in numbers is at the core of the politics of families, clans, communities, and states. The imperative to survive and multiply is coded into our genes. Individuals, families, communities, and states grapple with, and strive to control, this imperative. At this time in history, global population growth is often denounced as a threat to the survival of humanity. The pressure on resources in certain parts of the world causes endemic famine, disease, and misery. Discontent causes people to migrate on a large scale to where they believe life is better. A wide array of political measures have been used for controlling population growth worldwide. In this century they range from the violent anti-semitism in Central Europe in the 1930s and 1940s and, presently, in the violent ethnic clashes in former Yugoslavia, to peaceful programs emphasizing sex education and distribution of contraceptives. Some types of population policies have been implemented by drawing on military knowledge and practices; others have drawn on medical knowledge and practices.

Discourses about risks and dangers seem to have a central function in the ordering of societies, not least in the struggle among social groups to elevate or to defend their place in the social order. These discourses are part of blaming and celebratory strategies, integral to the social competition. At a time when the discourse over the risks of population growth in some parts of the world heavily stresses the need for ethnic purification, it may be well to recall the close links between notions of purity versus pollution and notions of security versus danger (Douglas 1984). It may also be healthy to reflect on how societies promote growth and decline in population groups, within specific countries and globally. Governmental intervention in procreation-related behavior has a long historic precedent in pronatalist population policies, in the legal regulation of marriage as a social institution, and in laws designed to regulate sexual behavior.

The use of medical technology in dealing with global population growth during recent decades can be discussed against that background. The medical profession's attitude to population control has always been ambiguous. Its commitment to protect life was for a long time expressed by a reluctance to deal with contraception and abortion. These practices are by now, however, supported by a majority within the profession. Further, in many countries, groups within the medical profession have encompassed sociobiological ideas and acted against the risk of unlimited procreation by advocating and implementing forced sterilization of certain population groups.

Here, an overview will first be given of the current discourse concerning global population growth as a social problem in international politics. Then follows a description of social policy that defines this problem as one of fertility control and uses pharmaceutical technology as a solution. Finally, the evaluation of the benefits and risks of the use of pharmaceutical technology will be examined and some patterns in societal risk evaluation will be traced.

SOCIAL PROBLEM: THE CONTROL OF POPULATION GROWTH

The Problem

The 1990s are seeing a faster increase in global population than any decade in history. The fastest population growth takes place in the poorest countries. Although most people in the world have a higher standard of living than any of their forebears had, the number of poor, hungry, and illiterate people also is rising.

The pace of world population growth has accelerated steadily in the 20th century. Asia, Africa, Central America and tropical South America represent population increases two and three times greater than in the northern industrialized regions (Fox 1987). The number of human beings, currently 5.3 billion, is increasing by a quarter of a million every day. At the current growth rate, the global population should reach 11 billion by the end of next century, the year 2100. Stabilizing the world's population below 10 billion—just short of another doubling from today's level—is deemed possible, but would require a major increase of population control programs over the next decade (Sadik 1990). In international politics, one explicit goal is to reduce fertility in developing countries from 3.9 children per woman in 1990 to 3.2 in 2000–2005. The surest way to achieve sustained decline in fertility is to improve mother and child health, women's status and education, and to make family planning as widely available as possible to both women and men (Sadik 1990).

There is a worldwide trend toward lower rates of population growth, although regional variations around the general trend are marked. Population growth rates vary considerably among the regions of the world. The highest growth rate is presently found in East Africa (3.3 percent) and the lowest in Northern and Western Europe (0.1 percent) (Fox 1987). Globally, humanity is involved in a gigantic urbanization process. By the year 2000 there will be forty-eight metropolitan areas with five million or more inhabitants (Fox 1987). Sixty percent of the world's population will then live in urban areas (UNDP 1993, p. 206). A high proportion of the population is below the age of fifteen in many parts of the world, and in other parts the proportion of the aged is rapidly rising. In developing countries fertility has now declined by about one-third since the 1960s and about one-third of the married women in these countries use modern methods of family planning. Worldwide, voluntary female sterilization is the most used method of preventing unwanted births (Population Reports Dec. 1992, pp. 1–2).

The massive global population growth increases the stresses on the ecosystems, on water resources, and on the sensitive layer of air surrounding the globe. It adds to deforestation and soil degradation and makes sustainable development an even more difficult challenge for humanity than at present. People's discontent with living conditions induce them to move to urban areas and to richer countries. The large-scale, rapid urbanization adds problems of social organization with dimensions that are unprecedented in human history.

It has been part of international politics for several decades to regard the less developed regions of the world as the ones where population growth rates are to be suppressed. At the same time, groups and nations, where fertility is perceived as low, act to promote childbearing and childrearing. France, Japan, and Sweden are such countries, where reports on low natality raise fears that the domestic population might diminish in global importance (Herzlich 1990). Pronatalist movements grow in influence in certain countries. Poignant examples of the dualism in population politics are the social conflicts over women's rights to abortion in the U.S., a nation strongly committed to reducing population growth worldwide.

Technology, benefit, risk, and evaluation are key words in this essay on pharmaceutical technology used for global population control. The Greek word *techne* means art, craft, skill. The knowledge that humanity needs to manage its reproduction has grown tremendously during the past three decades. Thirty years ago the first industrially manufactured oral contraceptives were introduced on the market. That was the first time in history that a technological product based on advances in biochemistry was to be distributed as a drug to be consumed by millions of healthy individuals in many countries of the world. The introduction of this particular technological product on the global market took place at a time when the rate of global population growth was, in the industrialized countries, becoming an item on the agenda of problems in the world that ought to be attacked in order to ensure continued progress. Uncontrolled population growth was perhaps the first perceived ecological problem of global scope, calling for international support and collaboration.

One tenet of enlightened Western culture is to believe that global population growth is best kept in check by individual choices. To achieve sustained decline in global fertility, individuals must first be persuaded to adopt new ways of life. Improved education, especially for girls and women, has been shown to be one crucial factor in reducing birth rates, perhaps as crucial as women's and men's access to effective contraceptive technology.

Ideological Roots

Present concerns about global population developments are part of the continual human struggle to keep an appropriate balance between people and resources. Throughout history the growth of population has been associated with prosperity and strength. The advancement of the group is important for the individual members of it, in material terms, in spiritual terms, and in terms of growing larger and more powerful. To get hold of food for the group one perceives as one's own and to manage the fertility of the group have always been two of the most important functions of adulthood (Callahan 1972; Greer 1985). The group may be the family, the tribe, or the nation. Its members want it to survive and grow, if necessary at the expense of other groups—and fertility is highly valued.

Fertility is only partly defined by biology. Fertility is at the core of social behavior, tightly meshed with economy, social structure, and culture. Fertility behavior is powerfully molded by institutional and cultural settings. The social regulation of the fertility of individuals rests both on cultural constraints on the behavior of individuals, and on more conscious and goal-directed actions in society. Outside the family, ethnic and religious communities exert an influence on the present and future composition of their groups in terms of size, age, sex, and dominance; and social elites tend to attempt to control the fertility behavior of the masses in the society to which they belong (McNicoll 1987). The notion of human accountability to posterity seems to be at the core of the moral systems of many societies.

The management of fertility as both a personal and a social practice is rooted in the need to control existential conditions. It is firmly anchored in economic interests, the need to raise offspring, and the control and maintenance of property. It is partly a manifestation of patriarchal dominance: the fidelity required of wives and the chastity of unmarried girls have formed the two major building stones of the sexual morality in many societies. It is also a manifestation of the need for maintaining a workforce compatible with the prevailing economic conditions. Population control also draws on ideas about the superiority and the inferiority of specific groups. At times, eugenic objectives have dominated; other times population control measures have been motivated by wishes to alleviate suffering and to provide women and families with the means to regulate their own fertility.

Historically, social management always seems to have involved some kind of social control of fertility. Each society has its own rules about who may conceive children and under what circumstances, about how pregnant women should conduct themselves, about the proper process of birth, and about how children should be reared (Jaggar 1983). The extended family system ensured that knowledge and control of "family planning" could be transmitted through the generations. It asserted family interests against religious and secular power. In modern society, where the small nuclear family is the most common family unit, secular and religious institutional control over fertility management has gained in influence.

Population growth was attacked as a social problem in domestic politics, long before it emerged as a social problem in the context of international politics. In many countries, control of population growth has been at the core of legislation and governmental programs for different objectives: to prevent pregnancies and births in population groups where reproduction is considered contrary to national objectives; to provide sexual education and access to contraceptives and abortion assistance, so that couples and individuals themselves can control their fertility; and to provide incentives for people to have the number of children that the government considers appropriate for the nation.

During the early decades of this century, conflicts over women's and families' rights to control their fertility accompanied the rise to power of new social groups in many countries. Radical social welfare ideologies encompassed birth control, often in conflict with religious communities and with the social, including the medical, establishment. The birth control movement was allied to the eugenics movement but also to that of liberal and radical social reforms and had a strong flavor of utopian social engineering aiming at creating better societies. One of its concrete targets was to abolish prohibitions against the distribution and use of contraceptives.

After World War II, the scope of interest of the birth control movement within the industrialized countries expanded into the international realm. The goals were transformed into population politics, which were introduced as planned parenthood, family planning, and sexual education. National and international population politics during the twentieth century reveal how fertility control programs with the fecund poor as their target groups have been instituted both nationally and internationally. The initiators mostly belonged to the rich nations' dominating bourgeois strata, where fertility was low, voluntarily or involuntarily.

Institutionalization of Global Population Control

The notion of population growth as a global social problem emerged in the 1950s. Increasing attention was focused on the growth of population in the less developed areas of the world. Clean water, improved nutrition, better control of infectious diseases, and attention to mother and child health care had led to improved health and lower mortality. Better health increased the probability that a woman would conceive and retain a fetus to term. Lowered mortality raised the proportion of children who survived to the age of reproduction (Davis 1967). The increase in birth rates was perceived by some neo-Malthusian social scientists as a main destabilizing factor in the world economy—a factor that had to be brought under control. The high rate of population growth was seen as the result of alien technology, which had increased the effectiveness of health services independently of the production and consumption in the less developed countries (Fredriksen 1969). The neo-Malthusian model was employed both as a diagnosis of social problems and as a basis for prescribing solutions. Family planning and food production programs should be the political vehicles in the combat against population growth and in raising the quality of life in the less developed countries. The image of the mushroom cloud above the devastated Hiroshima, the emblem both of human progress and of ultimate threat to human survival during the 1950s, came to be translated into the exploding "population bomb." It shaped the imagery of the rising birth rates in the developing countries into a symbolic threat to humanity. The institutionalization of family planning on a global scale became a legitimate goal for international political action.

A World Population Emergency Campaign was launched on March 20, 1960—the year when the first pill for oral contraception was approved for sale on the U.S. market. Its message was that the high fertility of the lower classes, in this case the poor beyond the U.S. borders, is achieved at the cost of the sub-fertile hardworking middle class in the industrialized countries. Advertisements in *The New York Times* showed the U.S. taxpayer struggling under a huge burden labeled "Foreign Aid," and were signed by a number of influential and prestigious persons from the business community and academia (Greer 1985). By 1966 the U.S. President, Lyndon B. Johnson, announced that the U.S. government wanted to "act on the fact that less than five dollars invested in population control is worth a hundred dollars invested in economic growth" (Greer 1985).

Population growth was brought to public consciousness as multiplying the problems of both pollution and resource depletion. It was indicted as one of the leading culprits of environmental deterioration. Paul Ehrlich's book *The Population Bomb* propounded the gospel. An organization called Zero Population Growth, Inc. (ZPG) was created in 1968 in the U.S. Within a few years it had a membership of approximately 35,000, mostly white, middle-class, and well-educated young people, who actively campaigned for legislative bills consistent with reducing global population growth (Westoff 1974).

Fertility rates in the "underdeveloped" countries should be made to drop through adequate provision of contraceptives. The problem of the undesirable yields of human populations was attacked by the same methods as undesirable agricultural yields: research on technology—mostly in the field of reproductive endocrinology (Harkavy 1987)—distribution of products via a network of distribution centers and extension agents, targets quantified in terms of numbers of acceptors, and continuous measuring of how the targets were reached. Both the hardware—contraceptives and clinics through which to dispense them—and the software—training programs, schemes of incentives for workers and clients, statistical reporting systems, publicity campaigns—were made available, virtually free, to governments in Third World countries (McNicoll 1987).

In 1966, the Secretary-General of the United Nations U Thant received a statement by twelve heads of state on the need for family planning efforts under the auspices of the United Nations. In 1974, at the first intergovernmental political meeting on population in Bucharest, Romania, many leaders of the developing countries made their first clear statements in an international forum on their countries' population policies. The 1974 Conference led to the adoption of a **World Population Plan of Action**—a plan that came to serve as the guideline for the formulation and implementation of population policies and programs by many national governments. A special international body for population issues, the United Nations Fund for Population Activities (UNFPA), was also created (Salas 1984).

Almost all international agencies, in one way or another, now run activities with implicit population control objectives. Apart from the UNFPA, the major international bodies presently involved in contraceptive development are International Development Research Centre (IDCR), the International Organization for Chemical Synthesis in Development (IOCD), the World Bank, and the WHO Special Programme in Research, Development, and Research Training in Human Reproduction (HRP) (Mastroianni, Donaldson, and Kane 1990).

SOCIAL POLICY: CONTROL OF FERTILITY THROUGH PHARMACEUTICAL TECHNOLOGY

The Choice of Existing Technology

Fertility control was practiced and achieved by many means long before the invention of modern contraceptive technology. Social norms prescribing late marriages or long lactation of infants combined with abstention from coitus are known in many parts of the world as a means of regulating the pressure of population on available resources. Coitus interruptus, the use of contraceptives made from herbs or material from animal bodies, abortion, and infanticide have served to prevent and space pregnancies and to ensure the survival of families, tribes, and nations (Serlin 1981). When the methods of control of reproduction have allowed for a distinction between male and female offspring, many societies value males over females (Corea 1985).

Fertility management has involved not only interests in population control but also economic interests. A large contraceptive-producing industry grew up during the late nineteenth century, offering an array of more or less effective products, many based on the cheap rubber obtained from the Third World via the commercial channels of the British Empire. Early in this century the birth control movement gained momentum from a flood of literature on contraceptive methods, subsidized by the manufacturers of contraceptive hardware (Greer 1985).

The global contraceptive market opening up in the early 1960s had good prospects. In global reproduction politics, mirroring the conflicts of interest between West and East, and North and South in the world, modern medical and biochemical technology was to be employed. Family planning programs were organized, often outside the established channels for providing health services, as vertical programs designed to furnish one specific type of goods and services: those needed for fertility control. The product flow through these channels was significant. By 1968 the U.S. pharmaceutical companies' sales of oral contraceptives, for instance, were worth $108 million, and the production was about ten million pounds per year (Lawless 1977). Governments in some developed countries were major buyers.

The global family planning movement during the past three decades has clearly been devoted to the improvement and dissemination of modern medical and biomedical contraceptive technology—primarily oral contraceptives and intrauterine devices (IUDs)—produced by the pharmaceutical industry. Sterilization on a large scale also soon became part of family planning programs in many Third World countries. Early abortion, a principal factor in reducing fertility in many countries, has been rejected in many national and nearly all international population control programs.

Global population control was formulated as a medical or public health task—even though ordinary medical and public health considerations often were excluded. In spite of the lack of general public health services in the family planning programs, they were interpreted as necessary public health campaigns and acquired an assured popular support in industrialized countries, as well as among the elites in countries with high population growth. The programs for population control in Third World countries tended to be constructed with benchmarks and targets expressed in terms of numbers of family planning centers and clients, of pills and IUDs (Davis 1967). The family planning movement escaped official condemnation and censure by avoiding religiously tabooed but otherwise effective means of birth prevention. By concentrating on new, scientific contraceptives it respected the prohibitions attached to the old ones and introduced a new branch of medicine. To borrow the words of the sociologist Kingsley Davis, overpopulation had become a disease to be treated by a pill or a coil (1967).

The prime target groups for family planning programs have been women, often selected so that single women were excluded and women professing certain religious faiths were offered only selected methods. In many family planning programs the problem of women's and couples' motivation for family planning was reduced to a technological issue, namely the invention of a technical device that would be received by women. Women who did not quickly accept family planning were imputed with ignorance and with having cultural values that ought to be changed (Davis 1967).

By the end of 1968 it was estimated that eighteen million women in the world were taking oral contraceptives and that six million women were wearing IUDs. Because of adverse effects a high percentage of women in the former group discontinued after a brief period. Continuation-of-use rates for oral contraceptive users were lower than for those using IUD, when measured in comparable populations under similar circumstances (Notestein, Kirk, and Segal 1969). The market kept expanding. By 1973 the Office of Population of the U.S. Agency for International Development (AID) had $125 million to spend in a single year (Greer 1985). Part of this money was spent on buying government-subsidized IUD and chemical contraceptives, some of which were outdated stocks of oral contraceptives with high estrogen content from the big drug companies, to be distributed in the Third World in connection with programs for family planning education and sterilization (Greer 1985). By 1979, eight U.S. pharmaceutical companies were selling a total of thirty-six products under twelve brand names (Population Reports 1979). Approximately eighty million women in reproductive ages throughout the world were by 1979 using oral contraceptives (Hoover 1979).

Some industrialized nations, among them the U.S. and Sweden, have been particularly active in promoting family planning programs in Third World countries. The impact of the U.S. on global birth control policies can perhaps best be understood from the fact that, for long periods, the U.S. AID contributed half of the funds for the International Planned Parenthood Federation (IPPF) and the UNFPA, and gave significant contributions to the Pathfinder Fund, the Population Council, the Church World Service, the Association for Voluntary Sterilization and other international family planning programs (Greer 1985).

Three private foundations in the U.S.—Ford, Andrew W. Mellon, and Rockefeller—have been major sources of funds for reproductive science and contraceptive development, and initiatives to improve fertility control globally. In the 1980s, more than 80 percent of such research and development in the world was funded from the U.S. via the federal government, private foundations, and the pharmaceutical industry. The federal government, primarily through the National Institutes of Health and the U.S. AID, contributed nearly 60 percent of all funding worldwide. The development of new products was largely concentrated among companies in Europe, since within the U.S. the market—outside the profitable oral contraceptives market—had become uncertain because of increased litigation over industry's liability for the adverse effects of their products (Harkavy 1987). It should be added that the government under Presidents Reagan and Bush temporarily reduced its funding for international assistance involving the distribution of contraceptive drugs and devices via the IPPF and U.S. AID (Connell 1987).

The donations of contraceptive products to Third World countries have been large: in 1985-1988, alone, donor agencies provided on the average 74,267,000 monthly cycles of oral contraceptives per year to developing countries (see Table 1) (Population Reports 1988).

Future Technological Possibilities

The technologies used in family planning programs during the 1960s and 1970s were primarily condoms, oral contraceptives, injectable contraceptives, and IUDs. Estimates of the distribution and effectiveness of current contraceptive methods in terms of pregnancy avoidance are shown in Table 2.

New product development during the 1970s and 1980s included a variety of subcutaneous hormone implants, several models of intravaginal rings that would release steroid hormones, barrier contraceptives with improved spermicides, and menses inducers—that is, early abortifacients (Harkavy 1987). Dramatic changes in the range of available contraceptive technology are unlikely to

TABLE 1.   DONOR AGENCY DELIVERIES OF ORAL CONTRACEPTIVES, BY AGENCY, 1985–1988

DONOR AGENCIES	1985–88 THOUSAND CYCLES YEARLY AVERAGE
United States Agency for International Development (U.S. AID)	31,272
United Nations Population Fund (UNFPA)	15,150
International Planned Parenthood Federation (IPPF)	11,321
Family Planning International Assistance (FPIA)	8,614
Canadian International Development Agency (CIDA)	6,075
Pathfinder Fund	1,835
All donors	74,267

Source: *Population Reports*, Series A, No. 7, November, 1988:A-10.

occur in the 1990s (Maestroianni et al. 1990). Some contraceptive technologies that were being tested in 1990 are listed in Table 3.

Control of global population growth via women's bodies and women's fertility has been a major implicit objective in traditional family planning programs, as can be seen in Tables 3 and 4. With the advent of HIV/AIDS as a global pandemic, the nexus between disease control and family planning will probably have to be strengthened institutionally and by promoting contraceptive technologies that prevent both the spreading of sexually transmitted disease and the conception of unwanted children. Male sexual behavior and condom use will also have to be accorded much more attention in international population politics if these two objectives are to be met.

TABLE 2.   ESTIMATED CONTRACEPTIVE USE AMONG THE 45 PERCENT MARRIED COUPLES PRACTICING CONTRACEPTION, WORLDWIDE, 1980

CONTRACEPTIVE METHOD	ESTIMATED % USE AMONG CONTRACEPTORS		ACCIDENTAL PREGNANCY IN THE FIRST YEAR OF USE, %
	USA	WORLDWIDE	
Sterilization		32	0
Male	14		
Female	19		
Intrauterine device (IUD)	3	26	4
Pill and injectables	32	17	2*
Condom	17	17	10
Other	15	15	
Diaphragm			13
Foam/cream/jelly			15
Rhythm			19

*Oral contraceptives only

Sources: John Bongaarts, 1987, "The Proximate Determinants of Fertility," *Technology in Society*, Vol. 9, No. 3/4: 250-51 and Luigi Mastroianni, Jr., et al., eds. 1990, *Developing New Contraceptives: Obstacles and Opportunities* (Washington D.C.: National Academy Press), 16-19.

TABLE 3.   NEW CONTRACEPTIVE TECHNOLOGIES UNDERGOING EVALUATION, 1990

FEMALE METHODS

New ways of delivering contraceptive steroids (injections, implants, transdermal patches, vaginal suppositories and rings, and sublingual tablets).

New formulations of injectables using microspheres and microcapsules releasing two or more hormones.

Biodegradable pellets, the size of rice grains, inserted under the skin in the hip or upper arm, slowly releasing progestins. Pellet cannot be removed.

Vaginal ring, the size of a diaphragm, that continually releases steroids to suppress ovulation and thicken the vaginal mucus. Can be worn continuously for three months and then replaced, or for three weeks and then removed for one week to allow monthly bleeding.

Vaginal ring containing levonorgestrel, for continuous wear.

Transdermal patches providing slow, consistent release of contraceptive steroids to the bloodstream through the skin. Three patches, each effective for seven days, to be worn consecutively for three weeks, followed by a week without patch to allow menstrual bleeding to occur.

Osmotic pills for gradual release of contraceptive steroids, making lower and less frequent dosage possible.

Vaccine immunizing women against a placental hormone that is needed in early pregnancy, or against a hormone in the egg, or against the sperm.

Luteinizing hormone-releasing hormone (LHRH) analogs administered by injection, nasal spray, suppository, check insert, or oral capsule.

MALE METHODS

Developing a male vaccine does not seem feasible this century. Inhibin for sperm suppression and gossypol have been studied but seem not to meet requirements on safety and effectiveness.

MODIFICATIONS OF EXISTING METHODS

Modification of oral contraceptive formulations (desogestrel, gestodene, and norgestimate) to reduce dosage compared to the oral contraceptives currently on the market.

Devices for predicting ovulation in order to pinpoint the time for periodic abstinence (e.g., "personal rhythm clock" using a high precision thermometer and a calculator, or "ovutimer" analyzing changes in cervical mucus).

Biochemical methods for predicting ovulation (e.g., monoclonal antibodies for detecting hormones produced by the ovary; ovarian markers of follicular growth; or urinary estrogen assays).

New hormone-releasing IUDs and modifications to copper IUDs.

New spermicides, among others the beta blocking agent propanolol.

Disposable diaphragms containing spermicide.

Female condom, consisting of two flexible rings and a loose-fitting polyethylene sheath that lines the vagina so that sperm cannot enter the cervix.

New types of male condom that substitutes synthetic material for latex.

New female sterilization procedures, among them techniques for reversible sterilization and transcervical sterilization via chemicals placed at the opening of the oviduct.

New and reversible methods for male sterilization, including the insertion of various valves and plugs to block sperm transport and the injection into the vas deferens.

Source: Luigi Mastroianni, Jr., et al., eds., 1990, *Developing New Contraceptives: Obstacles and Opportunities* (Washington D.C.: National Academy Press), 31–39.

TABLE 4.   EXAMPLES OF CONTRACEPTIVE TECHNOLOGY APPROVED AND USED
OUTSIDE THE USA, 1990

- Depo-Provera taken by injection in women every three months by an estimated 14 million women worldwide. Approved in about 90 countries, including Canada, Sweden, and the United Kingdom.*
- Noristerat, a two-month injectable, approved in more than 40 countries, used by an estimated 800,000 women worldwide.
- NORPLANT®, a progestin-releasing contraceptive implant, approved in at least 12 countries.
- Multiload IUD, which is used by a large proportion of all IUD users in Europe.
- Chemicals that can be used to bring on a delayed menstrual period, among them the antiprogesterone RU-486, which is approved in France and China.
- The Filshie clip, made of titanium lined with silicone rubber and used to occlude the fallopian tubes during female sterilization. Approved for use in the United Kingdom and Canada.

*Now accepted for use in the USA.

Source: Luigi Mastroianni, Jr., et al., eds., *Developing New Contraceptives: Obstacles and Opportunities* (Washington DC.: National Academy Press), 37–39.

SOCIETAL EVALUATION OF BENEFITS AND RISKS OF TECHNOLOGIES USED IN GLOBAL POPULATION CONTROL

Benefits and Risks

The benefits of family planning programs and contraceptive technology have been *material*, providing societies with means to control population growth and individuals with means to control their own fertility. They have also been *economic*, providing revenue to the profitable pharmaceutical industry and to professionals active in the population control field. Further, they have been *symbolic*: assertions of influence over the human condition and power to control the fertility of others.

Fertility control technologies are highly publicized and forcefully promoted technologies. International development agencies, nongovernmental organizations supporting family planning, national family planning programs, industrial corporations producing the technology, and consultancy firms keep careful accounts of achievements.

In evaluations of the success of family planning programs, the risks that are most conspicuously addressed are the risks of unintended pregnancy. The perceived shortcomings seem sheerly the failure to reach planned implementation targets, or to deliver enough goods and services to the consumers, or to hold down birth rates. A less widely acknowledged shortcoming, however, has lain in the health risks of some forms of contraceptive technology. These risks are detected in the realm of medical practice, mapped by epidemiological surveys, and carefully analyzed in toxicological experiments and biopsies.

The full effects of pharmaceuticals and medical devices on the human body can be well known only when a large number of individuals have been exposed to the technology for many years. Contraceptive technologies such as oral contraceptives and IUDs are cases where the social benefits of new technologies initially were deemed so large that they were aggressively distributed without long-term testing for safety and efficacy—or without much regard for the adverse effects the technologies may have in exposed individuals. Part of the picture is also that when evidence of risks emerged, for instance in terms of women developing fatal thrombolic disease or cancer that was linked to their oral contraception consumption, the findings were initially rejected or met with strong resistance.

The importance accorded to the risks of contraceptives varies among societies, because of variations in the prevalence of the diseases involved, because of differences in knowledge, and because of the differences in social importance of the population groups exposed to risk. Most of the epidemiological and clinical studies of the health effects of contraceptives have been carried out in developed countries. Some scientists hesitate to generalize these results to the special health and cultural situations in the Third World. There are few studies of the effects of various contraceptive methods on the diseases in developing countries (Foege et al. 1989).

It should be kept in mind also that the health risks documented in industrialized countries have not been negligible. Oral contraceptives have been shown to increase the risks of cardiovascular disease, in particular, the risk of venous thromboembolism, myocardial infarction, and stroke (Inman and Vessey 1968; Vessey and Doll 1968; Mann et al. 1975; Mann and Inman 1975). They have also been linked to the development of certain types of cancer, among them breast cancer, cervical cancer, and endometrial cancer. These cancers are major causes of morbidity and mortality among women (IARC 1987). Their toll is rising in many countries. The rate of change in the dosage and composition of chemical substances used in oral contraceptives is one indicator of the hazards that earlier oral contraceptive consumers have created: the estrogen content, for instance, in oral contraceptives was 150 mcgs in 1960 and is now 35 mcgs or less. IUDs may cause more or less constant small bleedings. Major health risks that have been associated with IUD use are pelvic inflammatory disease (PID), tubal infertility, septic abortion, and uterine perforation (Foege et al. 1989). Barrier methods (condom, diaphragm, cervical cap, and sponge) provide less effective contraception than IUDs and oral contraceptives, but they protect against many sexually transmitted infections.

The hormones in oral contraceptives may have an impact on the human environment that goes beyond the adverse health effects on the consumer. Some reports point to ethinyl estradiol excreted from the bodies of oral contraceptive users as one of the sources of rising levels of environmental estrogens that disrupt the reproductive functions in wildlife and that also may be a contributing cause for the falling sperm counts among men (Sharpe and Skakkebaek 1993). Thus, nature may confront technology in ways that are both unexpected and undesired.

Social Interaction

The new contraceptive technologies have largely been interpreted as signs of scientific and technological progress. The development and marketing of these technologies have also contributed to the medicalizing and institutionalizing of fertility control. The power of the state has been brought to bear in the development and distribution of contraceptive technology: many governments have engaged in funding research, supporting product development, controlling safety and efficacy, purchasing products, and providing the institutional structures necessary to promote and distribute the products on a large scale to the public (Mastroianni et al. 1990).

The benefits and risks of contraceptives to human health are ultimately a concern for the individual. But they have also been addressed in social arenas: within the medical community, in the population control field, and in the politics of nations.

The medical community has lent legitimacy to family planning programs, although traditionally ambivalent with regard to fertility control. Some medical groups have been actively engaged in the testing and introduction of contraceptives, in performing sterilizations, and in setting up family planning programs; others have expressed serious concerns over the risks, in particular when inadequately tested products have been taken into use. The ambivalence in the Western medical community over the health risks of oral contraceptives, for instance, has been expressed in a dialogue with two peaks of intensity, one in the mid-1960s, when reports on deaths due to thromboembolic disease led to demands for caution in distributing the drugs, and the other in the 1970s when reports on different types of cancer linked to oral contraception consumption began to appear in the medical journals (Palmlund 1991). In both instances, the reports on risks were initially met by resistance and rejection—reactions contrary to the basic ethical principle in medicine "first, do no harm."

In the population control field, the necessity has been stressed to find means of preventing pregnancies that are effective, easy to use, and safe for most users. The discourse has concerned successes in terms of new, safer contraceptives and in measured numbers of acceptors, performed operations, inserted IUDs, and monthly cycles of oral contraceptives in different countries. The risks to human health of contraceptive use are acknowledged, sometimes accompanied by information on pregnancy and child-bearing as causes of increased morbidity and mortality.

In a classical, critical analysis of the international population politics and family planning programs of the 1960s, Kingsley Davis exposed some of the stakes (1967). He pointed out that the expressions "population control," "population planning," and "family planning" were used as euphemisms for pushing the new and efficient contraceptives through national mass programs under public health auspices. The long-range goals for the family planning movement were elusive, according to Davis. Population growth was seen as a self-evident problem. The population-policy movement was concerned only with the growth and the size of populations, and dealt only with the birth input. But the other two factors involved—mortality and migration—were left completely aside. The socioeconomic context of fertility was also neglected. Davis remarked that the entire question of goals instinctively was left vague, because thorough limitation of population growth would run counter to national and groups' hegemonic aspirations (1967).

In the politics of nations, the conflicts over risks of contraceptive technologies are a subset of the conflicts over social control. In India, the sterilizations of men as part of the family planning program in the 1970s caused violent riots, so serious that a change of government was necessary to appease the citizenry. In the U.S., also during the 1970s, educated, middle-class and upper-middle-class women organized to protect women against the risks of hormonal pharmaceuticals, oral contraceptives, and IUDs. Hearings in the U.S. Congress resulted in the introduction of restrictions in legislation and regulations. Many women and families sued for compensation for harm from the pharmaceutical industry and prescribing physicians. One outcome of these conflicts in the U.S. is that all but one of the large U.S. pharmaceutical companies withdrew from research on new contraceptives (Mastroianni et al. 1990). The strict rules for safety and effectiveness of pharmaceuticals marketed in the U.S. have served to keep out of the U.S. market many contraceptive technologies available elsewhere (see Table 4). Lately, the political pressure by pronatalist groups has made decisions to allow new types of contraceptives even more controversial than before. At the same time, women's issues have been accorded new importance by the U.S. government (U.S. National Institute of Health 1992) and some of the rules that prevented clinical trials of pharmaceuticals and medical devices in women have been lifted.

The benefits of family planning programs have been widely reported. Mostly, women and men have been aided in their pursuit of better control over their own fertility and over their life situation. However, their exposure to risks of adverse health effects also merits attention. It is obvious that women are more exposed than men to contraceptive technologies—perhaps a social choice embedded in choices of medical and biomedical development, perhaps a social choice reflecting how women's lives are valued. Populations in Third World countries have been exposed to health risks from contraceptive technologies, from which populations in some of the major industrialized countries were sheltered. Women in developed countries have been accorded more social protection against the risks of contraceptive technologies than women in the Third World.

The risk bearers' right to be informed about the health risks of contraceptive technologies is respected differently in different parts of the world. In a study of the marketing of pharmaceuticals in a number of less developed countries as compared to the U.S. and Great Britain, Milton Silverman, Philip R. Lee, and Mia Lydecker in 1982 provided evidence of how pharmaceutical companies tailored their information on the risks of commonly used pharmaceutical products differently in different countries—depending on the requirements or lack of requirements laid down in national laws and regulations. Oral contraceptives were among the pharmaceutical products on which they focused. Their survey showed that in the U.S. and United Kingdom identical indications and warnings were presented for all of the roughly forty oral contraceptive products listed and for thirty of thirty-two products listed for Africa. Oral contraceptives were promoted for contraception only in the U.S. and in Great Britain. In other countries' markets they were promoted also for other uses; the most common were regularization of the menstrual cycle, premenstrual tension, and menstruation. Some of the transnational manufacturing companies—among them the Dutch Organon, the West German Schering AG, and the US Wyeth—in some Third World national markets had omitted all warnings of risk (Silverman, Lee, and Lydecker 1982).

Silverman, Lee, and Lydecker documented what they called a blatant double-standard of drug promotion:

- In the industrialized nations, because of the existence and enforcement of appropriate laws and regulations, and perhaps due to the social responsibility of the drug companies, claims of drug efficacy are limited to those that can be supported by convincing scientific evidence, and hazards are openly disclosed.
- In the Third World, because of the nonexistence or nonenforcement of laws and regulations, and perhaps because of the social irresponsibility of the companies, claims of product efficacy are exaggerated to an almost ludicrous degree and hazards—some of them life-threatening—are minimized or not even mentioned (Silverman et al. 1982).

The authors emphasized that many products ousted from the markets in industrialized nations, or never approved for marketing, were readily available and widely promoted in the Third World. They also noted that with many important products, the risks of serious or lethal adverse effects were often minimized, glossed over, or totally ignored (Silverman et al. 1982). For Silverman, Lee, and Lydecker, the marketing of oral contraceptives is only one example of a common practice. It should be added that the access to information about toxicology and the effects of pharmaceutical technology is generally more limited in less developed countries than in industrialized countries (Silverman et al. 1982; Salinas 1988). Thus, most people in less developed countries are not enabled to make the informed choices about the benefits and risks of pharmaceutical products that they might want.

BENEFITS FOR WHOM? RISKS FOR WHOM?

Much social interaction revolves around the tools—the technology—we use for different purposes. The more "modern" the social setting of a group is, the more sophisticated the technology that is used for the group's survival and sustenance. The social control of technology, its production as well as its use, is a major theme in social interaction. The more powerful a group, the better it may be able to assert its interests in controlling technological development and technology use. And the corollary: the less powerful a group, the less it can assert control over the production and distribution of the technology it uses.

New technology is usually evaluated in a context of positive expectation. Benefits are the focus of attention. In the conventional economic discourse over benefits of technology, considerable attention has been given to how people make decisions in order to arrive at an optimal choice of technology. However, real people—as opposed to the theoretical economic man—do not optimize, they only search for satisfaction: people search out the solution to a problem that satisfies them first, rather than continuing the search until they find the absolutely best solution (Simon 1957). The benefits and risks of a technology are often distributed asymmetrically, with those bearing the risks not always also reaping the benefits of the technology use. Risk taking, in conventional economic discourse, is investing in an opportunity to reap benefits, usually larger than the investment. Also, in traditional economic discourse about the benefits and risks of technology, the fact that the social groups that reap benefits are often other than those that are exposed to the health risks and environmental hazards that the technology may lead to is often forgotten, or considered irrelevant, or simply repressed. It is assumed that if an economic transaction takes place—that is, if a technological product is moved from producer to consumer—there is a trade-off of benefits of different kinds, mediated via the price at which the transaction takes place. If, however, the risks of technologies are also taken into account, one finds obvious inequities.

Perhaps nonapparent risks of technology that fall far from those benefiting economically from the technology use have always been considered as externalities. Technological risks to human health or environment that nobody claims as important then fall outside the boundary of accounts. They are kept as externalities as long as the effects are sufficiently remote in time or space, or when the effects are borne by groups that are sufficiently distant from the situation of choice, or by groups that are sufficiently weak in terms of power not to have to be accorded attention. An investment in technology is not considered reasonable if the benefits from it are not high enough or do not accrue soon enough; the investment will be considered unreasonable if the costs are too high or if hazards accrue too early.

The word "risk" is a signal that people, or something that people value—life, health, or property—is being threatened. The social coping with risk can be approached as a completely rational behavior: risks are then identified, assessed numerically, and managed in the spirit of economic man. It is then assumed that guidelines for risk assessment will lead decision-makers to correct judgments.

However, the complex reality of social life reveals other patterns of social interaction concerning risks and hazards. Individuals differ in what they perceive as risk and how they perceive a risk. They have different attitudes toward risks of technology, depending on whether they are exposed to the risk voluntarily or involuntarily (Starr 1969). They differ in their evaluation of risks, depending on whether the risk seems to be catastrophic or "normal" (Slovic, Fischoff, and Lichtenstein 1979). Their attitude to a particular risk may be shaped by their economic resources and by the values they adhere to (Kasperson 1983).

Societies also demonstrate intriguing patterns in their attention to risk. Risks may be a matter of culture: countries and communities differ in what risks they select for the public attention and scrutiny (Douglas and Wildavsky 1983). Perceptions of risk and coping with risk are embedded in social culture and reflect the distribution of power between social groups. When damage becomes manifest or is perceived as imminent by groups with a voice in the public debate, the harm is usually not only physical or economic. There is also a breach of trust in the prevailing social structure and expressions of a loss of trust in those persons who are in positions where they are expected to protect the common weal. Fear and compassion for victims are driving forces that bring forth social demands for reform.

A power dimension is apparent in the evaluation of the risks of a technology. If powerful groups oppose an intended technology use, it does not take place. The selection of risk for the public agenda in society can be viewed as a manifestation of power, both economic and cultural. Certain effects of a particular technology tend to be publicly considered as risks of such character that social action is warranted; other effects of a technology may be just as negative according to an objective measure, but they do not arouse public anxiety and political concern. The role and standing of the elites associated with a technology are of importance in the handling of conflicts over benefits and risks. So is the attention that news media give to the issue and their construction of the controversy in presentations to the general public.

Hence, the perception of global population growth as a problem and a risk as well as the benefits or risks of the technologies to solve this problem must be examined as a process of cultural selection. As cultural products, they are molded by the power struggles in international and national politics. The discourse on one level appears as a genuine concern for the future of mankind and for the dismal conditions of life for poor and suffering people. On another level, it implies that inequity is inevitable, that some groups' interests and growth enjoy a self-evident right to protection, and that it is legitimate to limit the growth of other groups.

In the struggle between population groups, a wide range of measures are resorted to, from cruel violence at one end of a continuum to careful education to promote desirable contraceptive behavior, at the other end. The language of purity and danger draws metaphors from medicine and public health—hygiene versus degradation, normal growth versus runaway, diseased growth, and of the sprawling growth of megacities in poor countries, sometimes depicted as tumors on the global social body. The medical connotations of key concepts in the political discourse and the use of medical technology in implementing action lend legitimacy to the political enterprise. The medicalizing is emphasized in the forceful promotion of contraceptive products as part of modern scientific medicine. Concerns over how to deal effectively with population growth among the poor in the world also appear right in the middle of medical discourse over how to weigh human lives. A recent example is the controversy in *The Lancet* triggered in 1990 by Maurice King's article "Health Is a Sustainable State," where he argues that public health measures such as oral rehydration of infants should not be introduced on a public health scale in developing countries, since they ultimately increase the man years of human misery and add to the number of deaths by starvation (1990).

The benefits of the measures to curtail global population growth are often presented as having a self-evident utility. However, particular benefits accrue to particular groups in the global economy; not everyone benefits equally. Profits accrue to the manufacturers of pharmaceuticals and medical devices that donor agencies and governmental bureaucracies distribute through family planning programs. Salaries and grants accrue to those who work in the family planning movements and bureaucracies. Individually, the women and men who are better able to control their fertility reap the benefits of improved autonomy and enhanced influence over their own lives. The risks, if something goes wrong, also are borne by these "contraceptive acceptors."

What can we learn about culture, society, and medicine by reflection on the societal evaluation of the benefits and risks of technology in the management of global population growth?

First, social and cultural constructions are of great importance in shaping both individual lives and social life. We have seen how the notion of a social need—in this case the need to prevent further population growth—defined by social elites in the global society opens up a market, where social elites represented among producers of technology, professional groups, and governments collaborate to bring technological products to the consumers.

Second, human relationships are seldom symmetrical in terms of power. In the case of controlling global population growth, one specific interest has had to do with furthering the objectives of dominant groups in the world economy. The management of the risks of contraceptive technologies in global population control demonstrates that different values are attached to the health and life of different groups in the world as well as within a specific country.

Third, this analysis of technology used to control global population growth forces us to think of essential dimensions of social interaction: the asymmetry between male and female, between those with access to economic capital and education and those without, and between North and South in the world. Even where sophisticated scientific evidence about human health, survival, and environment seems to define the problems that need solving, it all boils down to what we as humans choose to do to each other.

REFERENCES

CALLAHAN, DANIEL. 1972. "Ethics and Population Limitation." *Science* 175 (February 4): 487–94. P. 3 in *Population: Dynamics, Ethics and Policy*, edited by Priscilla Reining and Irene Tinker, 1975. Washington, D.C.: American Association for the Advancement of Science.

CONNELL, ELISABETH B. 1987. "The Crisis in Contraception." *Technology Review* 90 (4):55.

COREA, GENA. 1985. *The Mother Machine*. London: The Women's Free Press.

DAVIS, KINGSLEY. 1967. "Population Policy: Will Current Programs Succeed?" *Science* 158:730–39. P. 31 in *Population: Dynamics, Ethics and Policy*, edited by Priscilla Reining and Irene Tinker, 1975. Washington, D.C.: American Association for the Advancement of Science.

DOUGLAS, MARY. 1984. *Purity and Danger*, London: Ark Paperbacks.

DOUGLAS, MARY, and AARON WILDAVSKY. 1983. *Risk and Culture: An Essay on the Selection of Technological and Environmental Dangers*. Berkeley: University of California Press.

FOEGE, WILLIAM et al. (eds.). 1989. *Contraception and Reproduction: Health Consequences for Women and Children in the Developing World*. Washington D.C.: National Academic Press.

FOX, ROBERT. 1987. *Population Images*. New York: United Nations Fund for Population Activities.

FREDRIKSEN, HARALD. 1969. "Feedback in Economic and Demographic Transition," *Science* 166 (November 14): 837–47. P. 125 in *Population: Dynamics, Ethics and Policy*, edited by Priscilla Reining and Irene Tinker, 1975. Washington, D.C.: American Association for the Advancement of Science.

GREER, GERMAINE. 1985. *Sex and Destiny: The Politics of Human Fertility*. London: Picador.

HARKAVY, OSCAR. 1987. "Funding Contraceptive Development." *Technology in Society* 9 (3/4):308.

HERZLICH, GUY. 1990 (May 17). "L'Obsession Démographique." *Le Monde*. Pp. 1, 22.

HOOVER, ROBERT. 1979. "Association of Exogenous Estrogens and Cancer in Humans." P. 354 in John A. McLachlan. (Ed.) *Estrogens in the Environment*. New York: Elsevier/North Holland.

INMAN, W. H. W., and M. P. VESSEY. 1968. "Investigations of Death from Pulmonary, Coronary and Cerebral Thrombosis and Embolism in Women of Child-Bearing Age." *British Medical Journal* 2 (April 27):193.

International Agency for Cancer Research. 1987. *IARC Monographs on the Evaluation of Carcinogenic Risks to Humans.* Supplement 7.

JAGGAR, ALISON M. 1983. *Feminist Politics and Human Nature.* Totowa, NJ: Rowman and Allanheld.

KASPERSON, ROGER E. 1983. "Acceptability of Human Risk." *Environmental Health Perspectives* 52:15–20.

KING, MAURICE. 1990. "Health is a Sustainable State." *The Lancet* 336 (September 15):664–667. With correspondence to the editor on October 13, 1990:936–37 and November 24, 1990:1312 and further comments by King, November 24, 1990:1312–13 and July 13, 1991:124.

LAWLESS, EDWARD W. 1977. *Technology and Social Shock.* New Brunswick, NJ: Rutgers University Press.

MANN, J. I., and W. H. W. INMAN. 1975. "Oral Contraceptives and Death from Myocardial Infarction." *British Medical Journal* 2 (May):245–48.

MANN, J. I. et al., 1975. "Myocardial Infarction in Young Women with Special Reference to Oral Contraceptive Practice." *British Medical Journal* 2 (May):241–45.

MASTROIANNI, LUIGI, JR., PETER DONALDSON, and THOMAS KANE (Eds.), 1990. *Developing New Contraceptives: Obstacles and Opportunities.* Washington D.C.: National Academy Press.

MCNICOLL, GEOFFREY. 1987. "Technology and the Social Regulation of Fertility." *Technology in Society* 9 (3/4):261–67.

NOTESTEIN, FRANK W., DUDLEY KIRK, and SHELDON SEGAL. 1969. "The Problem of Population Control." P. 153 in *The Population Dilemma,* edited by Philip M. Hauser. Englewood Cliffs, NJ: Prentice-Hall.

PALMLUND, INGAR. 1991. "Risk Evaluation and Estrogens." *International Journal of Risk and Safety in Medicine* 2:321–42.

"The Reproductive Revolution." *Population Reports.* Series M, No. 11 (December 1992):1–2.

SADIK, NAFIS. 1990. *The State of the World Population 1990.* New York: United Nations Fund for Population Activities.

SALAS, RAFAEL M. 1984. *Reflections on Population.* New York: Pergamon Press.

SALINAS, JULIO A. 1988. "Transfer of Regulatory Toxicology from Developed to Developing Countries." *Biomedical and Environmental Sciences* 1:392–405.

SERLIN, RENÉE. 1981. "Contraceptives: Back to the Barriers." *New Scientist* 91 (1264):281–84.

SHARPE, RICHARD M., and NIELS E. SKAKKEBAEK. 1993. "Are Oestrogens Involved in Falling Sperm Counts and Disorders of the Male Reproductive Tract?" *The Lancet* 341 (May 29):1392–95.

SILVERMAN, MILTON, PHILIP R. LEE, and MIA LYDECKER. 1982. *Prescriptions for Death: The Drugging of the Third World.* Berkeley: University of California Press.

SIMON, HERBERT. 1957. *Administrative Behavior: A Study of Decision-making Processes in Administrative Organizations.* New York: Macmillan.

SLOVIC, PAUL, BARUCH FISCHOFF, and SARA LICHTENSTEIN. 1979. "Rating the Risks." *Environment* 21: 14–39.

STARR, CHAUNCEY. 1969. "Social Benefits versus Technological Risk: What is Our Society Willing to Pay for Safety?" *Science* 165 (3899):1232–38.

United Nations Development Program. 1993. *Human Development Report 1993.* New York: UNDP.

U.S. Government, National Institutes of Health. 1992. "Women's Health Initiative Program Advisory Committee; Establishment." *Federal Register* 57, 164, 38312.

VESSEY, M. P., and W. R. S. DOLL. 1968. "Investigation of Relation between Use of Oral Contraceptives and Thromboembolic Disease." *British Medical Journal* 2 (April 27):199.

WESTOFF, CHARLES F. 1974. "United States" in *Population Policy in Developed Countries,* Bernard Berelson (ed.). New York: McGraw-Hill.

CHAPTER 21

Toward an Analysis of Medicalization in the Global Context

Eugene B. Gallagher

Joan Ferrante

INTRODUCTION*

Improving access to medical care involves issues of allocation: matching medical resources to clinical needs; setting priorities among treatments to be offered; and establishing criteria for the selection of patients. Inequities easily arise; special attention must be paid, and policies devised, to ensure fairness in meeting patients' needs and demands. Equity is easier to achieve when the platter of medical resources is full. However, when the supply is small and fixed (as with cadaver organs for transplantation), attention may focus narrowly on rationing the existing resources. However, any comprehensive analysis of equity in, and access to, medical care must encompass not only the short-run, existing supply but also the contextual forces in society—constituting the *preallocative* sphere—which shape the supply and use of medical care resources in the long run.

This chapter concerns events in the preallocative sphere. It describes *medicalization* as an emergent force that magnifies the importance of medical care

*This chapter is a revision of a manuscript that was published earlier: "Medicalization and Social Justice," by Eugene B. Gallagher and Joan Ferrante (1987), *Social Justice Research* 1(3): 377–92. The authors wish to thank the Plenum Publishing Corporation, publisher of *Social Justice Research*, for permission to publish this revision of that manuscript here.

for human welfare in contemporary society. By intensifying the relevance of medical care, the medicalization process creates the basis for high demand for it and for ensuing scarcity.

When resources are scarce, one looks more closely at their actual effectiveness and value. Is it possible that medical care is less effective than it is generally thought to be? If this is so, pressure on the supply and use of medical care resources might decline, or shift away from biomedicine toward so-called alternative medicine. Although the analysis presented here allows for these possibilities, its main thrust is to deal with powerful preallocative factors that intensify the call for greater abundance of (bio)medical care in society. One major factor is **social inclusion**; this ethical force brings economically deprived, socially marginal population groups into contact with the medical care system. We also discuss **biomedical transcendence** to show that biologically oriented but socially detached concepts of human function, disease, and health are working their way pervasively into contemporary culture. Biomedical transcendence creates a health- and medically oriented worldview that supplants earlier worldviews that exalted religious belief, economic productivity, or the nation-state. Biomedical transcendence reinforces political demands for access to medical care and for protection against health risks. It also champions social and environmental conditions that foster health in a collective sense above and beyond the clinical well-being of the individual. Biomedical transcendence also moves private and professional discussions of medical care into an issue-charged, public arena.

Finally, we discuss **health absolutism**, a highly articulated version of biomedical transcendence. Health absolutism places full, undivided responsibility upon individuals for preserving their health through personal actions that constitute scientifically justified means toward the ends of longevity, physical fitness, and healthy quality of life. Health absolutism assigns to health a supreme value in the Weberian sense of substantively rational action: it is a *summum bonum*, not a calculable entity to be weighed against other goals in life. It stresses the radical prevention—not mere postponement—of illness. As an ideology of prevention, health absolutism falls quickly into dogmatic rigidity. It holds individuals strictly accountable, ignores individual variations in susceptibility to illness (including genetic predispositions), blames victims (or holds that there are only agents, not victims), and dismisses arguments for broadened access to clinical medicine.

The medicalization process has been studied most intensively in the context of American society. It appears to be linked especially closely to a postmodern version of individualism in which earlier religious and utopian quests have been transformed into a socially decontextualized pursuit of health. This postmodern striving incorporates scientific methods and rationales with a systematic intensity reminiscent of earlier religiously motivated pursuits. Other factors also may stimulate the medicalization process in American society: (1) a strong biomedical research establishment, which, in its public outreach, proclaims the potential implications of basic research for the conquest of disease; (2) the extensive development of clinical medicine in a highly supportive economic and political milieu; and (3) an elaborated set of mass media, in both print and image, which respond to and further stimulate public concern with biomedicine, health, and disease.

Of course, none of the foregoing means that medicalization is an exclusively American phenomenon. Rather, it invites comparative studies of medicalization across societies. In regard to developing societies, which currently are fashioning their own institutions, resources, and policies for medical care, it also raises many questions of theoretical and practical interest—for example, does medicalization of necessity develop concurrently with modern medicine, or can biomedicine be introduced and widely distributed without the "overlay" of medicalization?

MEDICALIZATION

The term medicalization has come into frequent use within the past twenty years. It denotes the circumstance by which a biological explanation is offered, often with an accompanying medical remedy, for human difficulties that formerly were regarded as part of the natural order of things.[1] Medicalization includes the redefinition of deviant, socially undesirable behavior as having a medical basis. It embraces a vast array of behavioral aberrations, symptoms, complaints, illnesses, diseases, and disabilities for which biomedical accounts are available. It extends to life-cycle transitions and gender differences as well as to the effects of everyday excesses or deficits of sleep, food, sensory stimulation, medications, energy expenditure, interpersonal engagement, affective expression, stress, and other routine features of life.

Illustrations of medicalization include the following:

1. Medicalization has transformed obstetrics. Pregnancy now is medically supervised and childbirth is medically assisted.[2] In earlier times, childbirth was a domestic event in which expectant women were helped by female relatives and lay midwives (Newman 1981). As with other domains of medicalization, questions arise about the extent of medical technique applicable to normal pregnancy, and whether medical involvement in this area intrudes on women's own maternal competence.

2. The premenstrual syndrome ("PMS") is delineated as an endocrine-based stress process that affects some women. This paradigm is capable of explaining feelings of emotional tension and distress. PMS is an example of a human problem that in earlier times was either ignored or recognized but was not interpreted medically (Riessman 1983). According to a current hypothesis, violent behavior in females may be linked to the premenstrual syndrome. Whether confirmed objectively or not, this hypothesis expresses the logic of medicalization.

3. The male proclivity to violence, especially in its extreme forms, is associated with another line of explanation in medicalization, namely genetic aberrations such as the XXY syndrome.

4. Obesity is explained medically. It is treated with medically supervised diets and as a last resort, with surgery (Raymond 1986).

5. The process of dying has become highly medicalized through intensive efforts to prolong life, particularly the pressure in hospitals to "do everything."

6. The current attempt to seat the cause of depression in pathological brain biochemistry is a medicalizing mode of explanation.

A semantic cue to medicalization can be found in terminology that refers to depression as depressive *illness* and to schizophrenia as schizophrenic *illness*. (Sometimes the word *disease* is used instead.) The addition of the word illness conveys the notion that, as with any bodily illness, schizophrenia and depression have etiologic sources that are objectively measurable; although the symptomatology (confused thinking or depressive affect) is psychological, the cause is somatic. In contrast, when both cause and symptomatology are "in the mind," suspicion arises concerning the intentionality or voluntariness of the problem. By shifting the locus of the patient's difficulty to his brain, medicalization provides a firm shield against such suspicion. Thus, instead of being regarded as weak-willed, attention-seeking, or malingering, the emotionally troubled patient is regarded as medically ill and is entitled both to treatment and respect.

Medicalization frequently provides a rationale for a specific medical treatment and thus becomes a preallocative factor affecting the demand for, and supply of, medical resources. The veridicality of medical procedures—whether in fact they are effective and whether they are scientifically based—is a recurrent issue that represents an important dimension of medicalization and also affects the validity of demand for medical services in society.

The history of medicine is an extended account of the correction of fallacious information, often stubbornly entrenched, and of the replacement of useless or harmful techniques by others that are more solidly grounded and more effective. With all the advantage of hindsight, one can look back on bloodletting, blistering, trephining, and moxibustion as examples of ancient errors overcome by enlightenment.

Another instructive example can be found in uroscopy, the long since outmoded system of interpreting the appearance of a patient's urine (Entralgo 1969; Reiser 1978). Medieval physicians obviously were on the right track in inspecting urine, but their system of interpretation was so faulty that one can ask whether they were really any closer to the diagnostic truth than were other experts who examined the patient's horoscope. Further biomedical progress no doubt will invalidate some procedures used widely today. Contemporary medicine must still acknowledge uncertainty—about a particular practitioner's skill in providing a service or technique, and about the effectiveness of a treatment for a given patient with a given disease (Fox 1976).

We also cite two additional variable components of the medicalization process:

1. The extent to which it performs the function of social control in society— that is, when socially undesirable behavior is labeled or regarded as biologically caused and therefore amenable to treatment by medical experts. Though such treatment is given ostensibly to cure or ameliorate illness, at times it may be tantamount to the punishment or ostracism of an offender rather than to medical treatment of a sick person. For example, alarm AIDS has sometimes led to proposals to isolate identified about AIDS

patients in a restrictive way that has less relation to helping the patient than to alleviating public concern.

2. The extent to which medicalization attaches a social label which, in the present state of biomedical knowledge, can be grounded firmly in scientific fact. Medicalized labels sometimes are used not because they have much scientific justification, but because of a desire to induce a person to accept the sick role or to arouse others' sympathy toward him. This can be done, for example, by attributing a person's frequent drunkenness to a deficiency in an alcohol-metabolizing enzyme, or by characterizing erratic moods as the effect of the premenstrual syndrome.

For treating the patient, it makes a difference whether the truth claims implicit in medicalization labels are correct. In the present argument, however, this point is secondary to understanding the dynamics of medicalization. Medicalization is a preallocative process by which society comes to interpret and assimilate scientific discovery and its application in medicine. The mass media, catering to strong popular interest in medical news, present scientific information in compelling, dramatic language. In the process of medicalization, the esoteric knowledge of researchers and the technique-oriented knowledge of practitioners feed into the everyday concerns of laymen. The political and economic interests of organized professionals also figure into the process. As a social process, medicalization contains its own complex logic, which it is the task of the social scientist to unravel.

Variations between societies in value structures and in levels of political control affect the impact of these components of medicalization. In a liberal democratic ethos, the labeling of deviant behavior as biologically based can lead to the more humane and more individualized treatment of afflicted persons. In the lexicon of Conrad and Schneider's *Deviance and Medicalization* this process constitutes a paradigm shift from "bad" to "sick" (Conrad and Schneider 1992). In both traditional and modern autocratic societies, however, medicalization and medical labeling can justify the restrictive treatment of afflicted persons. Theories of deviant or problematic behavior linked to genetics, and eugenic policies arising from such theories, tend especially to become ideological masks for repression.

SOCIAL INCLUSION

This exposition has shown that medicalization is an expansive process, bringing many aspects of problematic human experience and behavior into its purview. Medicalization also moves in another direction: social inclusion. This mode of expansion follows a different dynamic: the application of medical care not only benefits persons but it also confirms them more fully in their human personhood. Medical care gives stronger legitimacy and texture to their membership in society.

For comparison, the history of public education provides an illustration of social inclusion outside of medicine. The United States and the countries of western Europe adopted the practice of free compulsory education during the nineteenth century. Sociohistorical analyses of this phenomenon emphasize the role of mass education in promoting the solidarity of the modern nation-state. Strang and Soysal (1986) observe: "In the West, the rise of the nation state as the sovereign power replaced other sources of authority in the society (family, estates, communal and religious authorities)."

Free public education was extended to members of previously marginal or excluded social strata. It also restructured existing educational programs by reducing the importance of sectarian religious content and of subnational languages; at the same time it promoted skills relevant to citizenship and vocation. The product of the new educational system—a population educated into a basic literacy and a national culture—was believed to be of benefit to the entire society, over and above the ways in which persons as individuals were equipped to participate in it.

Despite the many differences in the social roles, institutional patterns, and technologies employed in medical care and in education, the two institutions are similar in that both affect persons as individuals, whether penetrating the patient's biological or mental apparatus. Both have significant public aspects; yet they also have private meanings and implications for the individual. Education is a vehicle for contributing to collective welfare; receiving it also paves the way for later ties between the individual and inclusive social groups such as labor unions, professional societies, and civic associations. By the same token, medical care enables individuals to participate in social life by restoring function and relieving distress.

Medicalization as discussed above provides a rationale for expanding the use of medical care as a fundamental tool in improving human life. Yet medicalization as a multitiered process contains another ingredient that is essential to account for the increasing valuation of medical care and medical thinking in society. This additional ingredient is what we referred to above as the cultural ideal of "biomedical transcendence." In the following section, we conceptualize biomedical transcendence as an emergent societal pressure that moves public consciousness toward a greater reliance on medical knowledge for defining the worth of human life and for furthering human well-being.

BIOMEDICAL TRANSCENDENCE

Contemporary societies show a strong tendency to finance and organize medical care on the basis of community or public facilitation, removing it from the realm of market goods that are purchased from the recipient's current income.[3] Various mechanisms have been established or proposed to accomplish this purpose: private insurance, tax-exempt savings accounts, employment-based insurance or direct provision of care, public insurance, or public service by professionals who are the functionaries of the ministry of health. A second trend, contained within the first, is that a greater proportion of medical care costs tends to be paid from funds collected by public levy, whether from general tax revenues or from designated medical social security funds. Nations vary greatly in the extent of public involvement. The United States stands at one extreme in its reliance on private, out-of-pocket payment for medical services and in the correspondingly small proportion of public payment; socialist societies with extensive public provision and the abolition or severe curtailment of privately provided services stand at the other.

What causes the trend toward public involvement in medical care?

One answer to this question is that governments have the authority and responsibility to protect the public health. This responsibility has been centered largely around communicable diseases—measures for isolating afflicted persons, and environmental safeguards against infections and pollutants. Even before biomedical science discovered the mechanisms of infection, such measures were implemented on the basis of prescientific intuitions about disease propagation—for example, quarantine regulations, the employment of rat guards on ships at anchor, and the siting of hospitals in relatively "clean" areas of cities. The germ theory of disease and the subsequent identification of specific pathogens led to vaccines and other countermeasures, which greatly reduced the threat of infectious disease.

Do all members and categories of the public benefit equally from public health protection? Historical inequities have existed because of socioeconomic divisions in society and the marginal position of groups such as immigrants. The bourgeois stratum of society has used public health measures to protect itself from contamination—formerly understood in a moral sense ("sin") as well as a medical sense ("germs")—by the lower classes. Such inequities probably have become less important, though lower-class persons, through their occupational and other daily exposures, still face significantly greater health risks than persons in higher social classes (Graham and Reeder 1979).

Although the major infectious killers such as cholera, smallpox, and tuberculosis have receded in importance, we now witness a new widespread concern about the potential of the physical environment to damage health. Reports in the media intermittently raise anxiety about insidious effects that biomedical research uncovers and for which prevention will come in the future, "too late for us now." Microbiology has been joined by biochemistry as the scientific source for discerning the long-term effects of radiation and noxious substances in air, food, and water.

The physical environment is a medium of social inclusion; when it contains threats, it arouses collective fear and action. Universal health risks that are environmentally based and susceptible to biomedical assessment—even with a large degree of tentativeness by scientists—make everyone a potential patient. They create acute political and economic dilemmas in which the value of health is weighed against other values such as economic growth, entrepreneurial opportunity, and national sovereignty.

The concept of externality in social economics is useful in explaining how medical and public health matters have assumed great importance in contemporary life. In the words of economist Victor Fuchs:

> Many observers . . . believe that urbanization and the growth of population and income have increased the importance of *externalities* . . . an externality in health exists if Brown's consumption or other actions have favorable (or unfavorable) effects on Smith's health, but these effects are not reflected in the prices that

Brown faces and there is no feasible way for Brown and Smith to make a private arrangement that would cause Brown to take these effects into account (1979, p. 168).

Cigarette smoking is a timely example of negative externality. If Brown smokes in Smith's presence, he compels Smith to become a passive smoker of his (Brown's) exhalations. Smith's health may be damaged as a result; further, he is exposed to odors he may prefer not to smell. Conceivably Brown could pay Smith an agreed-upon penalty charge for smoking in the latter's presence. A full accounting of the damage that Brown's behavior does to Smith also should include the possibility that because Brown smokes, he himself will become ill, and then his treatment might draw upon tax dollars paid by Smith. Brown could also compensate Smith in appropriate measure for this prospective economic damage. In the absence of such private arrangements, a negative externality has been created, which may be dealt with in a public or collective mode. The decision may be made that it is Brown's right to smoke, which Smith must accept; or that Brown cannot smoke at all or only in restricted areas; or still other regulatory, nonmarket solutions to the problem may be achieved.

For an individual who smokes cigarettes, we may substitute instead a newsprint or smelting plant that pollutes the air, and we may proceed to analyze Smith's (i.e., the general public's) reactions and claims. Now, however, the situation is complicated by the fact that the "smoker" is not engaged in a personal habit but is a productive employer whose technology happens to degrade the environment.

These instances concern externalities that manifest themselves in an interdependent physical environment. In addition, however, certain nonenvironmental, psychological externalities also comport with the idea of biomedical transcendence. Fuchs (1979, p. 168) writes, "A special kind of externality . . . concerns society's unwillingness to 'see' some of its members (typically the very poor) take unusual risks or pursue degrading activities. An example is the inhibition to the sale of kidneys or other organs by living donors." Fuchs also states that "an unrelenting pressure for a more egalitarian society is one of the most important explanations for the growth of government in health and other areas." This pressure reflects a psychological or value externality which, through public legislation and policy, aims at promoting access to medical care. Fuchs believes that such efforts actually do little to improve health but that the very fact that they are debated and undertaken reveals the basic societal value placed on medical care. Thus he writes: "In my view, national health insurance and other government interventions in health are best viewed as political acts undertaken for political and social objectives relatively unrelated to the health of the population."

Such acts and programs do not always concern the public health in a collective sense; they may also pertain to the medical care of individuals. In other words, the public finds a negative externality in lack of access to medical care by individuals even in the absence of contagion or other direct risk to the public health. General social concern about the availability of clinical medicine is, thus, a second aspect of the paradigm of biomedical transcendence, beyond the public health aspect.

Mark Field, a sociologist, is more explicit than Fuchs in analyzing the social forces that foster public concern about the medical care of individuals. Field (1980) writes:

> I believe that a secular trend can be detected in the evolution of health systems . . . to either a national health insurance scheme or some form of a national health service or socialized medicine. Two major factors, in my opinion, are the prime-movers in that evolution: one is the ideological one of equity that sees inequality before morbidity and death as unfair and undemocratic: society there-fore must see to it that access to care is freed of the constraints of income, class, social origins, and so on. Closely related to this, though often left unsaid, is the idea that society as a *whole* benefits from a reduction in morbidity and a length-ening of life expectancy, if only for economic reasons of productivity. . . . The "collective" benefits then derived from a healthy citizenship serve to justify "com-pulsory" levies since health is seen as benefiting all, and not only those who specifically receive health services (1980, p. 401).

The valuing of health as a collective good, and of access to medical care even beyond any proven benefit, confirms the strength of biomedical transcend-ence as a cultural pressure in contemporary society. That is, the broad availabil-ity of medical care cannot be ascribed only to its functional role in promoting a healthy workforce or in reducing threats to the public health. Entirely apart from these considerations, a great deal of medical care is invested in economically nonproductive citizens, such as children, the elderly, and the disabled, in the name of human dignity and equity. Such investment reveals the evolving logic of social inclusion and a correlative tendency to make medical care a talisman of human dignity.

HEALTH ABSOLUTISM

Cultural trends encourage extremist impulses, political offshoots, and social movements that seek to translate general models into literal reality. As a vigorous cultural emergent, biomedical transcendence has produced an intense ideology that assigns a supreme value to health. The concept of *health absolutism*, first suggested by Talcott Parsons and subsequently elaborated by Searle (1984), cap-tures the essence of this ideology. Health absolutism focuses with special inten-sity on the fact that many people place their health at risk by the way they live—through alcohol, drugs, smoking, casual sex, poor diet, sedentary habits, and exposure to stress.

The closely related health promotion/disease prevention (HP/DP) move-ment has promulgated notions of healthy lifestyle, based on statistical analysis of disease risk factors, as a tool for mass education (Coreil et al. 1985). Government involvement in financing and organizing health care has coincided with the growth of the HP/DP movement in the United States. In the face of mounting public apprehension about health care costs, the goals and methods of a sociomedical movement that promises to prevent illness have great appeal for reducing costs as well. Some of the more enthusiastic themes of the HP/DP movement smack of health absolutism.

For example, despite ample medical evidence supporting the assertion that many people would be healthier if they modified their lifestyle, they can only postpone disease; they cannot prevent it forever. Moreover, much disease has an uncontrollable, contingent aspect; in a group of persons who share a health-risking lifestyle, one may be stricken by disease while the rest go untouched. Further, the role of one's involuntarily acquired genetic inheritance may be far more important than one's voluntarily assumed lifestyle. Exaggerated emphasis on health-promoting behavior also may lead to a disparagement of already sick and handicapped persons and to a societal retreat from involvement in financing of medical care—on the simplistic grounds that the sick have only themselves to blame.

For everyone—not only those who are sick—the new order of medical membership in society entails responsibilities to maintain health as well as rights of access to medical care. The pattern of biomedical transcendence implies this idea. In the paradigm of health absolutism, however, the responsibilities overwhelm the rights. Though the individual's health usually supports his accomplishment of other goals, at times it may conflict with various personally enjoyable activities, with making a living, or with achieving other significant goals in life. The absolutist extreme consistently rejects goals and activities that put health at risk.

With its focus on the radical prevention of illness, the concept of health absolutism moves entirely within the preallocative sphere of medical care. Rather than analyzing the criteria and resources for allocating medical care, it preempts such analysis. At the limit, health absolutism would lead to Samuel Butler's utopia of Erewhon, where it was a crime to be sick (1927). In that society, those who broke the law by being sick were punished, not treated.

CRITIQUES OF MEDICALIZATION

In the above discussion, we set forth the main features of medicalization and explicated the related concepts of social inclusion, biomedical transcendence, and health absolutism. It is generally agreed that medicalization is a theoretically cogent, empirically supportable concept for explaining the expansion of medical care in modern society. Less agreement is found, however, on the actual social merit of the medicalization process. Is it a benign trend that promotes individual and social well-being, or an unwholesome trend that exaggerates the need for, and benefit of, medical care? Here we present briefly the views of four social scientists who have looked closely at this phenomenon.

Irving Zola and Ivan Illich, who have played leading roles in originating the concept of medicalization, take a negative view. Zola (1986) believes that medicalization creates injustice. He argues that the exaltation of health as an ideal and the perfection of medical technique may weaken individuals in making autonomous choices about their lives, free of dependence on experts. Zola also fears the potential creation, through medical labeling, of biological underclasses—for example, groups of persons whose participation in society is thwarted not by traditional categories such as race or religion but by biological categories such as obesity or genetic defect. He recognizes that the medical redefinition of conditions such as mental illness and alcoholism confers social respect on their bearers, but he fears that this respect is purchased through the sacrifice of their personal autonomy on an altar of medical expertise. Further, he believes that the medicalization of problems amounts to a case-by-case individualization that dissipates the concerted energy needed to defeat social injustice.

Illich's (1975, 1994) critique of the medicalization process is even more severe than Zola's. Like Zola, he is concerned with the power issue inherent in elevating medical experts into arbiters of human welfare. In addition, he also believes that the exaltation of biomedicine diminishes the dignity of human beings, by sapping their capacity to deal with anxiety, suffering, and death. Illich dismisses as misguided all attempts to secure a fairer distribution of health care resources and to ensure the quality of health care. Measures to promote patients' understanding of medical procedures he dismisses as "consumer protection for addicts" (1975). In regard to inequality in the distribution of medical care, he writes:

> Health care is now costly and unevenly distributed, but multiplying health professionals would only increase symptoms, therapies and demands. The control by doctors over the production of medical goods renders them scarce. Increased budgets, more rational production, more public controls over distribution, the reduction of medical privileges, and a return from scientific to clinical medicine could decrease costs, render access more equitable, and treatment more effective. But there is also a great advantage to the present limitations. Limited medical benefits also mean limited iatrogenic byproducts. If outputs were to be increased, goals more rationally controlled, and distribution of access more equitable, the present system could deepen its sickening effect and decrease the coverage for self-care (1975, p. 80).

Two other scholars of medical care, Renee Fox and Richard Titmuss, present a more optimistic critique of medicalization, though they are also aware of its negative potentials.

Fox and Titmuss imply that medicalization can perform a socially integrative function in modern society. They are less concerned than Zola about the aggrandizements of the medical profession. Unlike Illich, who fears that modern medical care diverts people from a morally dignifying confrontation with life and death, Fox and Titmuss see it in an appropriate, if limited, modern equivalent to communal and lay care of the sick, disabled, and frail carried out in earlier epochs.

Fox believes that medical care is becoming a central sphere of activity in which modern society explores and negotiates new meanings of the human condition. Fox writes that "health, illness, and medicine . . . involve and affect every major institution of a society, and its basic cultural grounding" (1977) and that "the health-illness-medicine complex has become a metaphorical language and a symbolic medium through which American society has been grappling with fundamental questions of value and belief, basic to our cultural tradition and collective conscience, that ramify far beyond medicine" (1985).

Similar implications can be found in Titmuss's (1971) sociological analysis of blood transfusion. He regards blood transfusion as a modern, scientifically based analogue to the compassion of the biblical Good Samaritan, who went out of his way to help the stranger who lay robbed and beaten on the roadside. By implication, the Samaritan's active kindness to the stranger affirms the common humanity of both the helped and the helper, just as blood transfusion affirms the biological unity of the human species. Though Titmuss deplores pecuniary motivation and commercial practice in the selling of blood, he is optimistic about the prospects for community blood banking and the principle of altruistic donation. Blood transfusion is only a small part of the modern medical enterprise, but it and the associated forms of organ transplantation demonstrate that formerly useless biological materials can closely link human beings. Although biomedical knowledge has demystified the human body and has stripped it of mythic properties that were strong sinews in the pattern of earlier cultures (e.g., prescientific beliefs in sorcery, witchcraft, and the evil eye; causes of infertility; the doctrine of maternal impressions), scientific knowledge affords a medium by which new collective beliefs and hopes are kindled.

CONCLUSION

Zola, Illich, Fox, and Titmuss have extensively analyzed contemporary medical care and have offered interpretations that evaluate, for better or for worse, the directions in which the process of medicalization is moving. Of these four writers, Titmuss is most concerned about the equity and quality of specific health services; the growth of private entrepreneurship in blood banking might lead to lower-quality services (e.g., contaminated blood), which would fall most heavily on poor people in a private market. Titmuss's conception of the medicalization process as a cultural phenomenon is less acutely developed; he seems to argue that biomedicine will continue to advance and will find application in society, but that in broad outline this trend is benign. In other words, technology such as blood banking takes care of itself unless, in exceptional circumstances, public policy formulation or intervention is necessary to ensure the application of science for community benefit. Titmuss's implicit model of the penetration of society by biomedical science is passive; in contrast, Zola, Illich, and Fox present a more differentiated picture of the active internal dynamics and societal implications of the medicalization process.

Given the social inequities already present in the distribution of medical care, students of medical care must carefully explore the medicalization trend. Will it exacerbate or alleviate existing inequities? We have not answered that question here, but we have identified factors that must be taken into account in dealing with it. We have depicted the forces of medicalization as operating in a preallocative arena, where quantities of supply and demand for medical service have not yet been fixed—where, in other words, the adjudication of claims and of conflicts over resources has not yet become an issue. Once resources become fixed, social policy will face the more difficult task of allocation in a field of scarcity.

According to our preallcoative analysis, the medicalization process is broadly responsible for the increasing importance of medical care in society and for the increasing share of material, organizational, and financial resources devoted to it. This increasing "bulk" probably has been accompanied by a somewhat more egalitarian distribution of medical care, especially through government programs such as (in the United States) Medicaid for the poor and Medicare for the disabled and elderly (who tend also to be poor). Future prospects for greater equity are uncertain however. Political conservatism, in the name of self-responsibility for health, might diminish the medical resources available through taxation and social security; as a result, the system would be skewed against the disadvantaged strata in society. Other trends, however, such as the strain toward social inclusion and the ideal of biomedical transcendence, tend in the opposite direction—that is, toward stipulating as essential to one's civil status in society a core of human-biological integrity. This core includes access to healthful environments and to medical care (De Craemer 1983; Susser 1993). This conception of civil "personhood" would guarantee a minimum "decent" level of medical care to the poor, which might well be much less than better-off persons could purchase in a private market. The notions that ill health is something that one "does to oneself" and that medical care is only marginally effective cannot be applied *only* to the poor as a rationale for excluding them completely from medical care.

The interplay of the trends described here remains to be further delineated. What we have presented is intended as a prolegomenon to further analysis of medicalization, particularly in its comparative cross-national and cross-cultural manifestations. Medicalization is itself a complex, heterogeneous process but it should be examined in relation to two other trends: (a) toward equity, including medical equity, in societies, and (b) toward the increasing bulk of, the differentiation in, and the economic outlay for the medical care sector of modern societies.

As a general orienting hypothesis we propose that medicalization, health equity, and medical care advance together. We are well aware of exceptions, however; in geographically remote societies or peasant societies with low literacy, for example, medical care can be "inserted" almost as a foreign body via medical outpost dispensaries or helicopter services that are innocent of medicalization implications and that do very little to promote basic social equity. Also, equity in access advances by increments, not steadily; it does not keep in step with new powers of medical care. Yet in a program of theoretically informed research, exceptions such as these, no less than confirmations, can enrich our knowledge.

NOTES

[1] Conrad (1975) maintains that medicalization is "defining behavior as a medical problem or illness and mandating or licensing the medical profession to provide some type of treatment for it." Abercrombie et al. (1984, p. 133) define medicalization as "the increasing attachment of medical labels to behavior regarded as socially or morally undesirable. The implication is that modern medicine can cure all problems (including vandalism, alcoholism, homosexuality, dangerous driving, or political deviance) once these are recognized as 'diseases.' The term is used by critics of modern medicine who argue that doctors have too much political influence in issues where they are not in fact professionally competent to make judgments."

[2] This transformation is one of the farthest-reaching within the process of medicalization because it deals with a life-cycle stage rather than with ill health. The juncture in a society's medical evolution at which 50 percent of births occur in hospital can be compared to better-known economic turning points—for example, when 50 percent of the labor force becomes nonagricultural (that is, industrial) or when the industrial force becomes predominantly white-collar rather than blue-collar.

[3] In current debate on health care reform in the United States, most discussion centers on the financing of medical care. Angell (1994) recently captured the key issue succinctly in these words: "It is

no longer possible to structure a health care system without a third-party payer, because medical care is so expensive and the need for it is so unpredictable. The only question is who should be the third party."

REFERENCES

ABERCROMBIE, NICHOLAS, STEPHEN HILL, and BRYAN S. TURNER. 1984. *The Penguin Dictionary of Sociology*. New York: Viking Penguin.

ANGELL, MARCIA. 1994 (April 7). Letter to the editor (Editor's reply). *New England Journal of Medicine*. 330(14): 1012.

BUTLER, SAMUEL. 1927. *Erewhon and Erewhon Revisited* New York: Modern Library.

CONRAD, PETER. 1975. The Discovery of Hyperkinesis: Notes on the Medicalization of Deviant Behavior. *Social Problems*. 23 (Oct.): 12–21.

CONRAD, PETER, and JOSEPH W. SCHNEIDER 1992. *Deviance and Medicalization* (2nd ed.) Philadelphia: Temple University Press.

COREIL, JEANNINE, J. S. LEVIN, and E. GARTLY JACO. 1985. Life Style—An Emergent Concept in the Sociomedical Sciences. *Culture, Medicine, and Psychiatry*. 9: 423–37.

DE CRAEMER, WILLY. 1983. A Cross-cultural Perspective on Personhood. *Milbank Memorial Fund Quarterly/Health and Society* 61(1): 19–34.

ENTRALGO, P. LAIN 1969. *Doctor and Patient*. New York: McGraw-Hill.

FIELD, MARK G 1980. The Health System and the Polity: A Contemporary American Dialectic. *Soc. Sci. Med.* 14A: 397–413.

FOX, RENEE C 1976. Medical evolution. In J.J. Loubser, R.C. Baum, E. Effrat, and V.M. Lidz, (eds.), *Explorations in General Theory in Social Science*. New York: Free Press. Pp. 773–87.

————. 1977. The Medicalization and Demedicalization of American Society. *Daedalus* 106(1): 9–22.

————. 1985. Reflections and Opportunities in the Sociology of Medicine. *J. Health Soc. Behav.* 26(1): 6–14.

FUCHS, VICTOR R. 1979. Economics, Health, and Post-industrial Society. *Milbank Mem. Fund Quart.* 57: 153–82.

GRAHAM, SAXON, and LEO G. REEDER. 1979. Social Epidemiology of Chronic Diseases. In: Freeman, Howard E., Sol Levine, and Leo G. Reeder (eds.), *Handbook of Medical Sociology*, 3rd ed. Englewood Cliffs, NJ: Prentice-Hall. Pp. 71–96.

ILLICH, IVAN. 1975. *Medical Nemesis*. London: Calder and Boyars.

————. 1994. Brave new biocracy: Health Care from Womb to Tomb. *New Perspectives Quarterly*, 11(1):4–12.

NEWMAN, L.F. 1981. Midwives and Modernization. *Med. Anthropol.* 5: 1–12.

RAYMOND, C.A. 1986. Experts Hold Hope for Obesity Treatments Targeted to Specific Regulatory Miscues. *J. Am. Med. Assoc.* 256: 2302–03; 2306–07.

REISER, STANLEY J. 1978. *Medicine and the Reign of Technology*. New York: Cambridge University Press.

RIESSMAN, CATHERINE K. 1983. Women and Medicalization: A New Perspective. *Soc. Pol.* 14(Summer): 3–18.

SEARLE, C. MAUREEN. 1984. *Health Tyranny, Health Absolutism*. University of Kentucky, Lexington. Unpublished.

STRANG, D., and Y. SOYSAL. 1986. The Timing of National Education: Nineteenth-Century Europe. Paper presented at meeting of the American Sociological Association, New York City. Unpublished.

SUSSER, MERVYN. 1993. Health as a Human Right: An Epidemiologist's Perspective on the Public Health. *American Journal of Public Health* 83(3):418–26.

TITMUSS, RICHARD M. 1971. *The Gift Relationship—From Human Blood to Social Policy*. New York: Pantheon Books.

ZOLA, IRVING K. 1986. Medicine as an Institution of Social Control. In: Conrad, Peter, and Rachel Kern (eds.), *The Sociology of Health and Illness—Critical Perspectives*, 2nd ed. New York: St. Martin's Press. Pp. 379–90.

Index